ANTONY
AND CLEOPATRA

EDITED BY

RICHARD MADELAINE

Senior Lecturer in English, University of New South Wales

✝

CAMBRIDGE
UNIVERSITY PRESS

PUBLISHED BY THE PRESS SYNDICATE OF THE UNIVERSITY OF CAMBRIDGE
The Pitt Building, Trumpington Street, Cambridge CB2 1RP, United Kingdom

CAMBRIDGE UNIVERSITY PRESS
The Edinburgh Building, Cambridge CB2 2RU, United Kingdom
40 West 20th Street, New York, NY 10011–4211, USA
10 Stamford Road, Oakleigh, Melbourne 3166, Australia

First published 1998

Printed in the United Kingdom at the University Press, Cambridge

Typeset in Monotype Ehrhardt 10/12.5pt, in QuarkXPress™ [SE]

A catalogue record for this book is available from the British Library

Library of Congress cataloguing in publication data

Shakespeare, William, 1564–1616.
Antony and Cleopatra / edited by Richard Madelaine.
p.   cm. – (Shakespeare in production)
Includes bibliographical references and index.
ISBN 0 521 44306 7 (hardback) – ISBN 0 521 62904 7 (paperback)
1. Shakespeare, William, 1564–1616.   Antony and Cleopatra.
2. Shakespeare, William, 1564–1616 – Stage history.   3. Shakespeare,
William, 1564–1616 – Dramatic production.   4. Shakespeare, William,
1564–1616 – Film and video adaptations.   5. Cleopatra, Queen of
Egypt, d. 30 BC – In literature.   6. Antonius, Marcus, 83?–30 BC –
In literature.   7. Egypt – In literature.   8. Rome – In literature.
9. Tragedy.   I. Madelaine, Richard.   II. Title.   III. Series.
PR2802.A2M28   1998
822.3'3–dc21   97–18013   CIP

ISBN 0 521 44306 7 hardback
ISBN 0 521 62904 7 paperback

SHAKESPEARE IN PRODUCTION

ANTONY AND CLEOPATRA

SHAKESPEARE IN PRODUCTION

SERIES EDITORS: J. S. BRATTON AND JULIE HANKEY

This series offers students and researchers the fullest possible stage histories of individual Shakespearean texts.

In each volume a substantial introduction presents a conceptual overview of the play, marking out the major stages of its representation and reception. In this context, no single approach to the play can be described as more 'authentic' than any other. The extrapolations of Tate, the interpretations of Dryden, the upholstering of Charles Kean and the strippings-down of Marowitz are all treated as ways of reading and rewriting Shakespeare's text and understood in terms of contemporary audiences, tastes and sensibilities.

The commentary, presented alongside the New Cambridge edition of the text itself, offers detailed, line-by-line evidence for the overview presented in the introduction, making the volume a flexible tool for further research. The editors have selected interesting and vivid evocations of settings, acting and stage presentation and range widely in time and space.

The plays of Shakespeare are a particularly rich field for such treatment, having formed a central part of British theatrical culture for four hundred years. Major stage productions outside Britain are also included, as are adaptations, film and video versions.

ALREADY PUBLISHED
Much Ado About Nothing, edited by John F. Cox
A Midsummer Night's Dream, edited by Trevor R. Griffiths

FORTHCOMING VOLUMES
Hamlet, edited by Robert Hapgood
Macbeth, edited by John Wilders
Much Ado About Nothing, edited by John Cox
The Tempest, edited by Christine Dymkowski
Julius Caesar, edited by James Rigney
King Henry V, edited by Emma Smith

CONTENTS

List of illustrations	*page* vi
Series editors' preface	ix
Acknowledgements	xi
List of productions	xii
Introduction	1
List of characters	139
Antony and Cleopatra	141
Bibliography	326
Index	338

ILLUSTRATIONS

1 Mrs Faucit as Cleopatra (mocking at Antony in 1.3.83–5) in Kemble's 1813 Covent Garden production. Engraving of 1814. *page 37*

2 Isabella Glyn's hand kissed by Thidias (Henry Loraine as Antony in the background) in Vining's production at the Princess's Theatre in 1867. Engraving from *Illustrated London News* (25 May 1867). *page 53*

3 The galley scene in Tree's production at His Majesty's Theatre in 1906: Lyn Harding (Enobarbus), Beerbohm Tree (Antony), Norman Forbes (Lepidus), Basil Gill (Octavius), Julian L'Estrange (Pompey), Herbert Grimwood (Menas). Photograph: Rotary. *page 62*

4 The monument, with Vivien Leigh as Cleopatra, just before the lifting of Antony (Laurence Olivier) in Benthall's 1951 production at St James's Theatre. Photograph: Angus McBean. *page 91*

5 Peggy Ashcroft with her court (in 1.5) in Byam Shaw's Stratford production of 1953. Photograph: Angus McBean. *page 94*

6 Margaret Whiting as the dead Cleopatra, subject to multiple male gaze, in Helpmann's Old Vic production of 1957. Old Vic Archives, University of Bristol Theatre Collection. Photograph: Angus McBean. *page 98*

7 Richard Johnson as Antony laying hands on Janet Suzman as Cleopatra in 3.13 of Nunn's RSC production of 1972. Photograph: Reg Wilson. *page 105*

8 Helen Mirren as Cleopatra and Michael Gambon as Antony with a dangerous scarf in Noble's 1982 RSC production. Josette Simon as Iras, M. Fitzgerald as Mardian and Sorcha Cusack as Charmian. Photograph: Mark Williamson. *page 118*

9 Judi Dench as Cleopatra, Miranda Foster as Charmian and asps in Hall's 1987 National Theatre production. Photograph: John Haynes. *page 123*

10 Clare Higgins being restrained from stabbing the messenger in Caird's 1992 RSC production. Photograph: Clive Barda. *page 126*

11 The hauling of Antony in Harrison and Parsons's 1992 Sydney Theatre Company production, with John Stanton as Antony, Sandy Gore as Cleopatra and Fiona Press and Laura Keneally as Charmian and Iras. Photograph: Robert McFarlane. *page 133*

12   Eva Mattes as Cleopatra, dead, in Zadek's 1994 Edinburgh
      production. Photograph: D. Sillitoe.   *page 134*

The illustrations are reproduced by courtesy of the Shakespeare Centre Library, Stratford-upon-Avon (1, 3), the executor of the estate of Angus McBean (4, 5, 6), the respective photographers (7, 8, 9, 10, 11) and *The Guardian* (12). Illustration 2 is from the author's collection.

SERIES EDITORS' PREFACE

It is no longer necessary to stress that the text of a play is only its starting-point, and that only in production is its potential realised and capable of being appreciated fully. Since the coming-of-age of Theatre Studies as an academic discipline, we now understand that even Shakespeare is only one collaborator in the creation and infinite recreation of his play upon the stage. And just as we now agree that no play is complete until it is produced, so we have become interested in the way in which plays often produced – and pre-eminently the plays of the national Bard, William Shakespeare – acquire a life history of their own, after they leave the hands of their first maker.

Since the eighteenth century Shakespeare has become a cultural construct: sometimes the guarantor of nationhood, heritage and the status quo, sometimes seized and transformed to be its critic and antidote. This latter role has been particularly evident in countries where Shakespeare has to be translated. The irony is that while his status as national icon grows in the English-speaking world, his language is both lost and renewed, so that for good or ill, Shakespeare can be made to seem more urgently 'relevant' than in England or America, and may become the one dissenting voice that the censors mistake as harmless.

'Shakespeare in Production' gives the reader, the student and the scholar a comprehensive dossier of materials – eye-witness accounts, contemporary criticism, promptbook marginalia, stage business, cuts, additions and rewrit-ings – from which to construct an understanding of the many meanings that the plays have carried down the ages and across the world. These materials are organised alongside the New Cambridge Shakespeare text of the play, line by line and scene by scene, while a substantial introduction in each volume offers a guide to their interpretation. One may trace an argument about, for example, the many ways of playing Queen Gertrude, or the political transmutations of the text of *Henry V*; or take a scene, an act or a whole play, and work out how it has succeeded or failed in presentation over four hundred years.

For, despite our insistence that the plays are endlessly made and remade by history, Shakespeare is not a blank, scribbled upon by the age. Theatre history charts changes, but also registers something in spite of those changes. Some productions work and others do not. Two interpretations may be entirely different, and yet both will bring the play to life. Why? Without setting out to give absolute answers, the history of a play in the theatre can often show where the energy and shape of it lie, what has made it tick, through many permutations. In this way theatre history can find common ground with literary criticism. Both will find suggestive directions in the introductions to these volumes, while the commentaries provide raw material for readers to recreate the living experience of theatre, and become their own eye-witnesses.

J. S. Bratton
Julie Hankey

This series was originated by Jeremy Treglown and published by Junction Books, and later by Bristol Classical Press, as 'Plays in Performance'. Four titles were published; all are now out of print.

ACKNOWLEDGEMENTS

I am grateful to the many generous people who helped me in the writing of this book. Foremost among them are Jacky Bratton and Julie Hankey, who offered practical advice and encouragement in the best tradition of general editorship, Kate Flint, who lent me her notes on productions of the play, and two colleagues at the University of New South Wales who were always beforehand with help and understanding, John Golder and my wife Louise Miller.

I am also indebted to Tim Mares, for exchanging information with me about Australian and other productions, to Malcolm Edwards, director of the Actors Touring Company's *Cleopatra and Antony*, for talking to me about the production, and to Joanna Reid, the company's general manager, for supplying me with material. Among numerous librarians and archivists who have assisted me, I would especially like to thank Sylvia Morris of the Shakespeare Centre Library, Janet Birkett of the Theatre Museum, Nicola Scadding of the Royal National Theatre and Wesley Slattery of the Sydney Theatre Company. I am grateful to Sarah Stanton at Cambridge University Press for both scholarly and technical help, and to Audrey Cotterell for her meticulous copy-editing.

I have, of course, benefited from the published work of other scholars concerned with the stage history of this play, notably Margaret Lamb, to whose book, *'Antony and Cleopatra' on the English Stage*, I refer frequently, and two recent editors of the play, Michael Neill and David Bevington. I am delighted to be able to use David Bevington's New Cambridge Shakespeare text in this volume.

The errors in the book are all my own work. I have 'normalised' quotations from nineteenth-century and later sources, as far as spelling, use of italics, minor punctuation and capitalisation are concerned.

PRODUCTIONS

A select chronology of English-language productions; unless otherwise stated, their location is London.

date	director	actors	theatre
December 1606?	William Shakespeare?	Richard Burbage? John Edmans? or William Ostler?	Globe or/and Blackfriars
3 January 1759	David Garrick	David Garrick, Mary Ann Yates	Drury Lane
15 November 1813	J. P. Kemble	Charles M. Young, Harriet Faucit	Covent Garden
21 November 1833	William Charles Macready (Alfred Bunn)	William Charles Macready, Louisa Anne Phillips	Drury Lane
1838		William Hield, Ellen Tree	New Orleans
27 April 1846	Edmund Simpson	George Vandenhoff, Harriet Bland	Park, NY
22 October 1849	Samuel Phelps	Samuel Phelps, Isabella Glyn	Sadler's Wells
3 March 1855	John Douglass	Henry Marston, Isabella Glyn	Standard
7 March 1859	Edward Eddy	Edward Eddy, Elizabeth Ponisi	Broadway, NY
10 September 1866 (later toured with Walter Montgomery, Mattie Reinhardt)	Charles Calvert	Charles Calvert, Adelaide Calvert	Prince's, Manchester
15 May 1867	George Vining	Henry Loraine, Isabella Glyn	Princess's
8 October 1867 (later with Rosa Cooper at the Prince of Wales, Sydney from 10 May 1869)	Walter Montgomery	Walter Montgomery, Louisa Cleveland	Theatre Royal, Melbourne
20 September 1873 (later toured with Frank Clements)	Frederick Chatterton	James Anderson, Ellen Wallis	Drury Lane
2 April 1877	Benson Sherwood	Joseph Wheelock Sr, Agnes Booth	Niblo's Garden, NY
26 November 1877 (earlier with Thomas Keene in San Francisco and on tour)	Rose Eytinge	Frederick Warde, Rose Eytinge	Broadway, NY

date	director	actors	theatre
25 February 1882	Louise Pomeroy	J. B. Steele, Louise Pomeroy	Theatre Royal, Sydney
8 January 1889	Henry Abbey	Kyrle Bellew, Cora Brown-Potter	Palmer's, NY
2 November 1889	George C. Miln	George C. Miln, Louise Jordan	Her Majesty's Opera House, Melbourne
18 November 1890 (and on tour in America)	Lewis Wingfield (Lillie Langtry)	Charles Coghlan, Lillie Langtry	Princess's
March 1897 (24 May 1897 at Olympic, London)	Louis Calvert	Louis Calvert, Janet Achurch	Queen's, Manchester
14 April 1898	Frank Benson	Frank Benson, Constance Benson	Memorial, Stratford
29 March 1900	Frank Benson	Frank Benson, Constance Benson	Lyceum
27 December 1906 (and on tour in Berlin)	Herbert Beerbohm Tree	Herbert Beerbohm Tree, Constance Collier	His Majesty's
8 November 1909	Louis Calvert	E. H. Sothern, Julia Marlowe	New, NY
23 April 1912	Frank Benson	Frank Benson, Dorothy Green	Memorial, Stratford
26 December 1912 (on tour in 1913 in Australia, then to Durban)	Oscar Asche	Oscar Asche, Lily Brayton	Theatre Royal, Melbourne
23 April 1921	William Bridges-Adams	Edmund Willard, Dorothy Green	Memorial, Stratford
4 December 1922	Robert Atkins	Wilfrid Walter, Esther Waterhouse	Old Vic
19 February 1924	Frank Reicher	Rollo Peters, Jane Cowl	Lyceum, NY
15 July 1924 (preceded by a brief season at the King's, Hammersmith)	William Bridges-Adams	Baliol Holloway, Dorothy Green	Memorial, Stratford
30 November 1925	Andrew Leigh	Baliol Holloway, Edith Evans	Old Vic
3 February 1927 (Australian tour; Lorna Forbes played Cleopatra for the first few performances)	Allan Wilkie	Allan Wilkie, Frediswyde Hunter-Watts	Theatre Royal, Hobart
11 July 1927	William Bridges-Adams	Wilfrid Walter, Dorothy Green	Cinema, Stratford

24 November 1930	Harcourt Williams	John Gielgud, Dorothy Green	Old Vic
17 April 1931 (at Prince of Wales, Birmingham, 6 June 1931; also Stratford Summer Festival, 29 June 1931)	William Bridges-Adams	Gyles Isham, Dorothy Massingham	Cinema, Stratford
17 September 1934	Henry Cass	Wilfrid Lawson, Mary Newcombe	Old Vic
15 April 1935	Ben Iden Payne	Roy Emerton, Catherine Lacey	Memorial, Stratford
15 October 1936	Theodore Komisarjevsky	Donald Wolfit, Eugenie Leontovich	New
10 November 1937	Reginald Bach	Conway Tearle, Tallulah Bankhead	Mansfield, NY
23 April 1945	Robert Atkins	Anthony Eustrel, Claire Luce	Memorial, Stratford
20 December 1946	Glen Byam Shaw	Godfrey Tearle, Edith Evans	Piccadilly
26 November 1947 (and on tour)	Guthrie McClintic	Godfrey Tearle, Katharine Cornell	Martin Beck, NY
11 May 1951 (in tandem with *Caesar and Cleopatra*; later at Ziegfield, NY)	Michael Benthall	Laurence Olivier, Vivien Leigh	St James's,
28 April 1953 (later Prince's, in Autumn 1953 and on continental tour)	Glen Byam Shaw	Michael Redgrave, Peggy Ashcroft	Memorial, Stratford
6 March 1957	Robert Helpmann	Keith Michell, Margaret Whiting	Old Vic
31 July 1960	Jack Landau	Robert Ryan, Katharine Hepburn	Festival, Stratford, Conn.
31 July 1967	Michael Langham	Christopher Plummer, Zoe Caldwell	Festival, Stratford, Ont.
23 July 1969	Peter Dews	John Clements, Margaret Leighton	Festival, Chichester
15 August 1972 (part of Roman season, with *Julius Caesar*, *Coriolanus*, *Titus Andronicus*; revived 7 July 1973, Aldwych)	Trevor Nunn	Richard Johnson, Janet Suzman	Memorial, Stratford

Also a television version, produced by Jon Scoffield, broadcast 28 July 1974 (ATV, UK) and 1 January 1975 (ABC, USA)

date	director	actors	theatre
9 August 1973	Tony Richardson	Julian Glover, Vanessa Redgrave	Bankside Globe
9 June 1976	Robin Phillips	Keith Baxter, Maggie Smith	Festival, Stratford, Ont.
24 August 1977	Toby Robertson, for Prospect Theatre	Alec McCowen, Dorothy Tutin	Old Vic
('in contrast with' *All for Love*; previously at Edinburgh Festival, later on tour; revised version, February 1978)			
10 October 1978 (revived 6 July 1979, Aldwych)	Peter Brook	Alan Howard, Glenda Jackson	Memorial, Stratford
19 April 1979	Estelle Parsons	Francisco Prado, Kathleen Gaffney	Interart, NY
20 April 1981 (PBS, USA) 8 May 1981 (BBC2, UK)	*Jonathan Miller*	*Colin Blakely, Jane Lapotaire*	*BBC/Time– Life TV*
13 October 1982 (revived 21 February, Gulbenkian Studio, Newcastle and 12 April 1983, The Pit, Barbican)	Adrian Noble	Michael Gambon, Helen Mirren	The Other Place, Stratford
22 April 1983	Keith Hack	Keith Baxter, Judy Parfitt	Young Vic
27 July 1983	Rex Cramphorn	Frank Gallacher, Lindy Davies	Playbox, Melbourne
15 May 1985	Robin Phillips	Denis Quilley, Diana Rigg	Festival, Chichester
26 May 1986 (previously Theatr Clwyd, Mold)	Toby Robertson, Christopher Selbie	Timothy Dalton, Vanessa Redgrave	Theatre Royal, Haymarket
9 April 1987	Peter Hall	Anthony Hopkins, Judi Dench	Olivier
1988	Michael Kahn	Kenneth Haigh, Franchelle Dorn	Shakespeare, Washington
2 February 1989 (touring, 'updated' *Cleopatra and Antony*)	Malcolm Edwards, for Actors Touring Company	Patrick Wilde, Pauline Black	Lyric Studio, Hammersmith
9 April 1991 (on tour 29 May –8 June 1991)	Tony Hegarty, for Commonweal Theatre Company	Andrew McDonald, Susan Curnow	Shaw
16 May 1991 (previously at the Everyman, Liverpool)	Yvonne Brewster, for Talawa Theatre	Jeffery Kissoon, Dona Croll	Bloomsbury

date	director	actors	theatre
27 April 1992	Wayne Harrison, Philip Parsons	John Stanton, Sandy Gore	Wharf, Sydney
5 November 1992 (revived Barbican 26 May 1993)	John Caird	Richard Johnson, Clare Higgins	Memorial, Stratford
1993	Charles Towers	Henry Woronicz, Megan Cole	Oregon
1 June 1995	Vanessa Redgrave	Paul Butler Vanessa Redgrave	Riverside Studio 1
29 September 1995 (touring production)	Barrie Rutter	Barrie Rutter, Ishia Bennison	Viaduct, Halifax

INTRODUCTION

The peculiarities of the play's stage history

In view of the gradual narrowing of the Shakespeare repertoire, the frequency of performance of *Antony and Cleopatra* in the last twenty-five years is a remarkable phenomenon in a strange stage history. Despite the fascination of the play's subject matter (the fatal liaison of a famous Egyptian queen and a powerful Roman general), nothing certain is known about performances in Shakespeare's lifetime and the play failed to gain a secure hold on the stage until the middle of the nineteenth century. To attempt to explain such facts is to grapple with sociological and cultural factors and with ways of reading stage history as well as this particular play.

Some of the reasons for such a stage history, though not the most important or interesting, are practical theatrical ones. At the most basic level, the large cast and the length of the play are inhibiting, but not prohibiting, factors. Doubling can be resorted to, as was usual in the Jacobean theatre; cutting usually has been. It may be that the First Folio, the sole textual authority for this play, prints 'diverse things . . . that the length of the Play would not beare in the Presentment',[1] but in Shakespeare's day continuous staging gave the action an uninterrupted pace that was sadly lacking in the sole eighteenth-century and the many nineteenth-century productions, when the curtain fell at the end of each scene, with maximum noise and delay. Nicholas Rowe and later editors between them imposed forty-two scene divisions on Shakespeare's text, so that a performance of the whole play seemed a practical impossibility as long as curtain-dropping was practised. But cuts were not always imposed simply to save performance time; the Drury Lane production of 1873 cut about half the text but provided extraneous spectacle, song and dance, according to the taste of the period. Cutting is one of the easiest means of encouraging both actors and audience to interpret the play in accordance with the director's point of view, which is usually closely related to contemporary theatrical conditions and perceived audience expectations. Bowdlerisation has been normal from David Garrick until recent times, and more extensive cuts have commonly been made to reduce the geographical and thematic scope of the play and the

---

1 Title page of the 1623 Quarto of Webster's *The Duchess of Malfi*; this was another
  King's Men's play, and one that the title page says was performed at both the
  Blackfriars and the Globe.

number of characters, and, less obviously but more importantly, to assist the construction of the protagonists according to the desired emphasis.

Doubtless the chronicle-style plotting of the play made it less appealing to those eras that put a premium on complex plots or on economical ones, although Samuel Johnson asserted, in just such a generation, that the play's 'power of delighting is derived principally from the frequent changes of the scene'.[2] Nineteenth-century critics responded to directors' scenic embellishment without liking the play's frequent scene-changing or its chronicling, and some modern reviewers complain of the play's 'geographical restlessness'[3] despite its comparatively painless nature under modern performance conditions.

The cost of production has also been a factor, especially in the nineteenth century, with its pictorial approach to costumes, scenery and properties: the expense of the 1873 production is said to have made Frederick Chatterton coin the much-quoted dictum, 'Shakespeare spells Ruin, and Byron Bankruptcy';[4] and a reviewer of Frank Benson's production of 1898 wrote 'the play is one upon which an unlimited expenditure might be incurred' (*Stratford-upon-Avon Herald*, 8 April 1898).

The major problem of staging *Antony and Cleopatra* has perhaps been that it is more theatrically complex than Shakespeare's other major tragedies: its strong satirical element modifies the nature of the tragedy and allows widely different responses to the two protagonists. Directors in ages which stressed the heroic qualities in Antony's struggle have had to tamper with (or, in the Restoration, abandon entirely) a text which resolves its satirical attack on both protagonists' failings by celebrating their nobility and unity in death.

Actors and reviewers alike tacitly acknowledge the play's complexity in emphasising the extremely taxing nature of the protagonists' roles. Even touchstone performances like those of 1953 have made reviewers lament the difficulties of both leading parts. Peter Fleming wrote of Peggy Ashcroft's, 'although we hear a great deal about [Cleopatra's] infinite variety, we get only brief glimpses of most of its facets: so that however brilliantly an actress plays the part she is always liable to be accused of leaving something out' (*Spectator*, 8 May 1953). Of Michael Redgrave's performance Ivor

2 *Shakespeare's Works*, Notes on *Antony and Cleopatra*, in *Prose and Poetry*, p. 606.
3 Michael Billington's phrase in the *Guardian*, 7 November 1992.
4 The saying is variously attributed, but in 1889 Joseph Knight (Introduction *to Antony and Cleopatra*, Henry Irving Edition, p. 119) gave it to Chatterton, as did the *Birmingham Daily Post* reviewer (15 April 1898); so does William Winter (*Shakespeare*, pp. 450–1), who points out that Chatterton had produced Byron's *Manfred* in the previous month.

Brown remarked, 'None, I think, will ever be a complete Antony, poet, pillar of the world, and strumpet's fool. Shakespeare made the task impossible' (*Observer*, 3 May 1953). When J.C. Trewin, reviewing Trevor Nunn's production, said of the play 'its demands are exorbitant. We do ask for a Double First' (*Birmingham Post*, 16 August 1972), his implication was that the play requires not two separate first-class performances but mutually responsive ones that are entirely convincing in their relationship.

Whilst *Antony and Cleopatra*, of all Shakespeare's plays, seems to offer the star actress most opportunities, it might be argued that this play, paradoxically, suffered most from the introduction of actresses to the English stage. Apart from the issues of age, range and the ability to both sound and look sexually alluring and responsive, the role demands physical violence from the actor in the first messenger scene. It may be that the combination of these requirements was more readily managed by a boy actor, who could happily put on a tawny front and work comparatively uninhibitedly within the performance conventions and audience expectations of the Jacobean theatre.[5] For a theatre manager or director, the task of finding the right actress for the role of Cleopatra has always been exceptionally difficult, and the reasons for this lie in cultural conditioning. Mrs Siddons is said to have refused the role in 1813 on the grounds that she could not have respected herself had she acted the part 'as it ought to be played' (Genest, *English Stage*, vol. VIII, p. 419), and one of the most tenacious notions among reviewers from at least 1825[6] until recent times is that an Englishwoman's temperament is incompatible with Cleopatra's nature. Whilst many English Antonys have been seen as lacking the requisite ardour, they have caused less critical concern, largely because the broader cultural anxieties are centred on the woman: as both the exotic erotic protagonist and as the actress portraying her.

If it is crucial for audiences to see the lovers as passionate, the appearance of Cleopatra herself is for most onlookers the starting-point of the theatrical illusion. Given the moral connotations of 'fair' in Shakespeare's day, 'upon a tawny front' (1.1.6) is at least semi-abusive in Philo's mouth, and likely to have encouraged a tendency in the play's first audiences to interpret Cleopatra at face value. But such a reading might well have been more charitable than Philo's; Shakespeare's contemporaries distinguished between 'tawny moors' and 'blackamoors', and Aaron, who 'will have his soul black

---

5 Juliet Dusinberre ('Squeaking Cleopatras', p. 57) writes of the boy actor's 'male body' being 'subjugated to the energy released by the fiction of gender transference'.

6 This is surely the implication of 'were Madame Calatani an English actress she alone, I think, might realize the idea formed of Cleopatra by Shakespeare' (James Boaden, *Kemble*, vol. I, p. 396), and perhaps also of Mrs Siddons's famous remark.

like his face' (*Titus Andronicus*, 3.1.204),[7] is, unlike Cleopatra, at an extreme end of the moral spectrum. Cleopatra's 'tawny' skin is 'olive-coloured', like that of the 'tawny' gypsies in a favourite masque of James I's, *The Gypsies Metamorphosed*. When Cleopatra says she is 'with Phoebus' amorous pinches black' she is speaking of amorous experience, and perhaps 'sun exposure'[8] rather than of literal skin colour. Antony, of course, often doubts Cleopatra's nobility of character, and on one occasion (using the etymological connection between 'gipsy' and 'Egyptian') he applies the term 'gipsy' to the 'false Egyptian' that 'at fast and loose / Beguiled' him (4.12.28-9), and says she is acting true to racial type. The notion of Cleopatra as changeable and opportunist is often voiced by the Romans, but, just as Antony's attitude to the connection between her nature and her skin colour is constantly changing, so for Jacobean audiences Cleopatra's complexion was metaphorically variable: exotically and dangerously located between 'fairness' and blackness, suggestive of eastern sexual promise and moral ambivalence.

The set of conventions within which the Jacobean boy actor created an illusion of morally ambivalent sex appeal was distinct from those obtaining in various cultures and theatres after the introduction of actresses. With the employment of actresses came new assumptions about representation, and different audience expectations of it: whilst in 1610 Henry Jackson saw the boy actor playing Desdemona as 'she',[9] by 1661 the transvestite convention had become a 'curiosity' and some official cognisance was being given to the old Puritan objection that such representations were unnatural.[10] Of course, the 'natural' performances of actresses, on and off the stage, were conditioned by social constructions of their profession and of the feminine. From 1660 they were vilified in misogynistic attacks that likened them to prostitutes because they displayed themselves for others' gratification as a means of gaining financial independence. Initially in England the connection between the two professions was not merely theoretical: of the first generation of English actresses, only a quarter were able to lead 'respectable' lives; on stage all of them were sexually exploited.[11] Working conditions for, and social attitudes to, actresses have gradually been modified, but the relationship between the performance of actresses and the cultural construction of femininity has continued to dominate the realisation of the part of Cleopatra, and it is in precisely these terms that the part is uniquely provocative among Shakespeare's major female roles.

7 All references to this play are to Alan Hughes's New Cambridge Shakespeare edition.
8 See Anthony G. Barthelemy, *Black Face Maligned Race*, pp. 33–4, 147n1.
9 Julie Hankey, in the Introduction to her Plays in Performance edition of *Othello*, p. 18, draws attention to Jackson's pronoun.
10 See Elizabeth Howe, *The First English Actresses*, pp. 25–6.   11 *Ibid.*, pp. 33–7.

Its provocativeness was acutely felt in Victorian times, when notions of the feminine and of respectability were at a premium, and actresses were under suspicion for abandoning privacy and woman's ordained role as guardian of the home,[12] a suspicion fuelled by their high divorce rates in both Britain and America. Julie Hankey has shown ('Helen Faucit and Shakespeare', pp. 51, 55) how Helen Faucit attempted to reconcile the paradox of feminine privacy in public performance, and how her writing about Shakespeare's heroines reflected a Victorian urge to canonise Shakespeare's women, with the aid of bowdlerisation and other means of decorporealisation. It is not surprising that Faucit neither played nor wrote about Cleopatra. Neither is it surprising that, in order to maintain her image, she needed to isolate herself theatrically, for Cleopatra *was* being staged: her mother, Harriet Faucit, had played the part for Kemble in 1813 and her sister, Harriet (Mrs Bland), was the first New York Cleopatra in 1846.

If Helen Faucit was outnumbered by Harriet Faucits, so Victorian unease with Cleopatra was outweighed by other considerations, and *Antony and Cleopatra* was (re)established as a stage play. In post-Coleridgean critical judgement it was a great work, whose poetry had the power to ennoble, whose imperial theme could also be seen as edifying, and whose mixture of the erotic and the edifying was heady. Yet, whilst Helen Faucit's husband, Theodore Martin, idealised the actress as poetess or instructress (Hankey, 'Helen Faucit and Shakespeare', p. 57), any actress's attempt to poeticise sexual passion on the Victorian stage was fraught with difficulties. For the actress, a sense of the aesthetic responsibilities of playing Shakespeare compounded the problem of reconciling the conflict between the social requirement of respectability and the theatrical requirement of displayed sexuality. Indeed, the requirements of this play seem to cut across generic boundaries: *Antony and Cleopatra* is a tragedy, but its female protagonist is a sexual enchantress. In the Restoration, Shakespeare's play had been displaced by Charles Sedley's and John Dryden's largely because of the belief that sexually assertive women had their place in comedy but not in tragedy. Dryden's Cleopatra is far more 'virtuous' than Shakespeare's, and offered some encouragement to succeeding generations who wanted to transmute Shakespeare's Cleopatra into something closer to the conventional female tragic protagonist: textual modification was the result, but not a happy one, because to modify Cleopatra's variety is to diminish her power to enchant.

Reviewers' tendency to wish for a foreign Cleopatra, in the face of disappointment in an English one, highlights the cultural nature of the problem of sexual demonstrativeness. The attempt to circumvent it has

12 See Hankey, 'Body Language', p. 227.

been mainly a matter of wishful thinking, but the theory is that only an actress foreign enough to be free from English inhibitions about sex and violence, but capable of doing justice to the verse on the poetic route to nobility, can successfully play a 'bad' woman flouting the conventions of her society.[13] But reviewers, like managers and directors (and like them, almost exclusively male until recently), have made simplistic assumptions about the conventions of naturalism and the casting of Cleopatra. In particular, critics have often been crass about actresses' potential 'sexiness': one hailed Janet Suzman's 'foreignness' because she was born in South Africa, whilst others regarded the likes of Peggy Ashcroft, Glenda Jackson or Judi Dench as miscast, even if they gave them credit for acting against expectation and thereby acknowledged the importance of acting ability. Whilst recognising the difficulty of the part, reviewers have been quick to blame actresses for failure in it, and have seldom been sensitive to the problems caused by cultural conditioning. John Genest, quoting Mrs Siddons's famous remark, called it 'a very foolish reason' (*English Stage*, vol. VIII, p. 419), though a reviewer of Miss Phillips's rendition in 1833 did feel guilty about wishing the actress to live up to the character.[14] The 'Englishness' debate of the 1950s concentrated on the actresses' side of the cultural problem in performance, without really acknowledging the other side: male attitudes to actresses and to Cleopatra herself. Throughout the play's stage history, reviewers, responding to the various acting and casting strategies used to try and satisfy the perceived expectations of audiences, reveal their own cultural assumptions in ways that underline the difficulty of the actresses' and managers' tasks. In writing about the actresses in particular, many reviewers, modern as well as Victorian, expose misogynistic assumptions about the character of Cleopatra, as 'the worst woman in history', as a *femme fatale* with a nasty turn of mind, or as a brainless, or at least a shameless, manipulator.[15]

---

13 Henry James explores this issue in the person of Miriam Rooth in *The Tragic Muse*; Peter Sheringham speaks of her living without 'moral privacy', in 'a high wind of exhibition' (Harmondsworth, Penguin, 1982, p. 130): see Hankey, 'Body Language', p. 234. Hankey, p. 237, also quotes Bernard Shaw's remarks about (English) ladies being educated to conceal their feelings and 'the essence of acting' being 'expressiveness' (in Preface to *Ellen Terry and Bernard Shaw: a Correspondence*, ed. Christopher St John, New York, Fountain Press, 1931, p.x).

14 His ideal Cleopatra 'would almost amount to weakness to pray for' (*Athenaeum*, 23 November 1833).

15 For 'the worst woman in history', see *Illustrated Sporting and Dramatic News*, 12 January 1907; for the notion of her spitefulness and cruelty, see *Spectator*, 27 October 1849; for the suggestion that Cleopatra is not intellectually endowed, see *Era*, 26 November 1930.

Their view of Cleopatra, and of Antony's 'dotage' on her, is as resistant as the stalwart Romans of the play to any attempt to poeticise the protagonists' passion. Some such critics deride the discrepancy between the heroic nature of the lovers' language and the non-heroic nature of their actions (though many recent productions have made ironic capital out of it). The pervasively influential A.C. Bradley called the play 'the most faultily constructed' of all Shakespeare's tragedies,[16] and some reviewers have seen the 'problem' of the protagonists' verbal heroism in terms of what Anthony Cookman dubbed the play's 'underlying flaw':

> He is a great soldier broken down by debauchery, she is a wanton; and the heroism of words they use about each other cannot quite conceal the facts . . . at the shock of Fulvia's death the instinct of domination suddenly asserts itself against the instinct of sex . . . It is important that we should be given a memorable glimpse in these scenes of the old Antony with his energy, his judgment and the joy of action still strong in him. Once Cleopatra has nodded him to her again, there is little in the broken soldier to justify her wonderful panegyrics through which the tragedy is meant to close on a note of awe.
> (*Tatler*, 20 March 1957)

Of course not all critics or members of audiences will read the play in this way, and most modern responses to the glorification of sexual obsession are likely to be unhealthier than Bernard Shaw's in his reading of the play as 'vaguely distressing to the ordinary healthy citizen' (*Three Plays for Puritans*, pp. xxvii–xxviii). With or without one eye on commercial appeal, the protagonists' sexual obsession in *Antony and Cleopatra* can certainly be presented as a kind of psycho-spiritual quest, and the play's geographical restlessness as epic struggle.

If it has, at some times and in some places, been 'customary to cast over-ripe actors with beautiful voices in the roles of the lovers' (*Sunday Telegraph*, 20 August 1972), that is because it is possible, and often necessary, in the theatre to rely on the poetic projection of passion. Productions of Shakespeare and the expectations of their audiences have been influenced by the many non-naturalistic movements in modern drama since the late nineteenth century, and the modern theatre is not governed (though it is influenced) by notions of naturalistic representation. The main casting problem with the protagonists now is not so much one of age or appearance as of sexual chemistry, though of course the two issues are linked, as is usefully recognised in the recent tendency to align the lovers' sexuality with middle-aged neuroses and fantasies. The key to success, which has seldom been sighted in the play's stage history, lies in the right combination of

16 Quoted by Emrys Jones in his Introduction to the Penguin edition, p. 23.

acting ability, exploitation of theatrical conventions and sexuality in the protagonists' interaction.

The play's current popularity in the theatre (with actresses as much as with actors, directors and audiences) cannot wholly be explained without some reference to the marked changes in western cultural values and aesthetic attitudes which are reflected in, and have to some extent been influenced by, recent social and critical theories. One legacy of reader response theories is a more general awareness of the multiplicity of 'viable' readings of any work of art or performance (theatrical practice has usually taken this for granted); a legacy of feminist and postcolonial theories is a sharper awareness of the relationship between sexual politics and the operation of patriarchal political power, and in the current literary and performance climate, supposed liabilities have been re-inflected. The distinctive nature of the play's tragic form (with its strong satirical element and its absence of villains) focusses an audience's attention on the protagonists' responsibility for their own destinies. The debate-inducing absence of 'internal direction' is now a selling point. A key feature in this respect is the lack of soliloquies: we can never be sure that Cleopatra is not simply performing for the stage audience, and Roman soldiers and politicians keep voicing their view that she, as the quintessence of Egypt and the feminine, is merely an exotic courtesan posing as a queen. That adds to her fascination for modern audience members, who may wish to read both protagonists' behaviour in terms of the instability of human personalities. Above all, what is now recognised as the potential source of good and 'relevant' theatre is the challenge of representing the attractions of an uncontainable woman who so memorably subverts the assumptions of colonising patriarchy. Cleopatra contradicts Charmian's passive model of female behaviour ('Cross him in nothing'), has worn Antony's sword (albeit offstage) and embodies the attractions of intermingled desire and power.

Egyptomania and *Antony and Cleopatra*

It is more than a coincidence that a major international 'Egyptomania' exhibition[17] should have been mounted at a time when *Antony and Cleopatra* is enjoying unprecedented popularity on the stage. The exhibition displayed western artefacts that offer the exotic contained, whilst acknowledging its appeal in varying degrees. Jean-Marcel Humbert defines 'Egyptomania' in the exhibition catalogue in terms of appropriation: 'it is

17 At the Louvre, Paris, 20 January–18 April 1994, the National Gallery of Canada, Ottawa, 17 June–18 September 1994, and the Kunsthistorisches Museum, Vienna, 16 October 1994–29 January 1995.

not enough to copy Egyptian forms – artists must "re-create" them in the cauldron of their own sensibility and in the context of their times, or must give them an appearance of renewed vitality, a function other than the purpose for which they were originally intended'.[18] Thus Egyptomania will 'diverge from current archaeological knowledge', as did the nineteenth-century pictorial productions of *Antony and Cleopatra*, which made the queen a symbol of oriental exoticism,[19] despite knowledge of her Greek origin and despite the directors' concern with archaeologising *details* (a commercial selling-point in the climate of interest, and not a sign of an archaeological spirit).

Christiane Ziegler points out[20] that the passion for Egyptian things in the West dates from Roman culture, and that a politicised Roman vision of Egypt became the model for western Egyptomania in the Renaissance and has largely remained so, despite direct contact with ancient Egyptian civilisation from the time of Napoleon's Egyptian campaign. The Roman attitude to Egyptian things was, predictably, ambivalent and ultimately appropriating. Even the cult of Isis had its Roman followers, and the myth of Osiris's resurrection through the agency of his wife Isis (to which Shakespeare's Cleopatra alludes in 'Husband, I come') was supplanted only when Rome embraced the Christian promise of resurrection. In *Antony and Cleopatra* the allusions to Egyptian mysteries tend to be qualified by Roman cultural self-preoccupation. Cleopatra's monument has perhaps some mysterious, as well as merely exotic, otherness; Antony does call the queen an enchantress, but that description becomes embittered by his and other Romans' cynicism; and the most important applications of the supernatural in the play are to Antony's fate and his desertion by the Roman god, Hercules.

Thanks partly to the vocal predominance of Romans until the last long scene of *Antony and Cleopatra*, the keynote in the construction of Egypt in the play is hedonism. Cleopatra, surrounded by women and eunuchs in an extravagant court supposedly given over to feasting and sexual indulgence, is the 'Egyptian dish', the very personification of exotic Alexandria and its eastern pleasures. Antony, gone native, is the 'strumpet's fool', following Cleopatra in love games that lead to her retreat to the monument. His

---

18 'Egyptomania: a Current Concept from the Renaissance to Postmodernism', in Jean-Marcel Humbert et al., *Egyptomania*, pp. 21–6, 21.

19 Christiane Ziegler makes this point generally about nineteenth-century depictions of Cleopatra in 'Cleopatra, or the Seductions of the East', in Humbert et al., *Egyptomania*, pp. 554–61, esp. p. 558.

20 'From One Egyptomania to Another: the Legacy of Roman Antiquity', in Humbert et al., *Egyptomania*, pp. 15–20.

Roman conditioning, which deplores the waste of time and political occasion, allows Antony the magnanimous to cope better with feasting than with the flaunting of sexual indulgence. The play itself exhibits the exhibitionists, but it also shows their deep-seated concern not to be exhibited by the imperialist who is colonising the earth. If Cleopatra is transported to Rome, it can only be in chains. In Rome itself, Octavias are the desired norm and the only glimpse ordinary Romans can expect of Cleopatra is the sight of a squeaking boy playing her as a whore. The squeaking boy is a significant puppet of the urge to control by appropriation which is inherent in the concept of Egyptomania. Egypt is the erotic exotic that is the polar opposite of Rome's writing of political duty in stone, but Rome's desire to subdue the exotic politically is also one kind of response to exoticism's perennial appeal. Caesar's response to Egypt's otherness is to wish to demonstrate his power over it without close involvement, an exercise of control that doubtless gives him pleasure. Antony struggles with his Romanness, and in the end must kill himself like a Roman, because the urgency of his attraction to the exotic means it cannot be subdued to his sense of duty and honour. Both ways are Roman forms of 'conquest' or containment, but they exhibit very different degrees of awareness and acknowledgement. Ziegler[21] claims that Cleopatra was 'as much part of the Roman and Hellenistic civilisations as she was of the Egyptian'; though a Greek, she was the best known Egyptian ruler until the deciphering of the hieroglyphs in 1822. This was largely because 'Rome saw Cleopatra as the embodiment of Egypt at a critical moment when it could have gained dominion over the entire Mediterranean world'; her historical character was coloured by her vanquisher Octavius's propaganda: she was seen as the enemy of Rome, a dissolute foreigner, a woman with (inappropriate) absolute power.

Productions of *Antony and Cleopatra* will always be coloured by Egyptomania in more than one sense. At the basic level, they enact Shakespeare's complex treatment of the Cleopatra story in the context of Renaissance sexual and power politics and of his age's privileging of Roman cultural values. As a theatrical phenomenon, a production of this Shakespeare play (as opposed to others) may sometimes indicate a response to a surge of interest in Egyptian issues. When Egypt is news, that is one cultural factor in the complex decision-making process that brings about theatrical productions, a process that must be increasingly commercial if Shakespeare is not to spell Ruin. Yet any revival of the play is, to at least some small degree, a testament to the enduring nature of Egyptomania,

---

21 'Cleopatra, or the Seductions of the East', in Humbert et al., *Egyptomania*, pp. 554–61, esp. p. 554.

which is self-referential,[22] and much influenced by the attitudes of patrons, scholars, travellers, museum curators and artists. At the level of interpretation, all productions offer an approach to the play's Egyptomania, whether exploitative or reductive of its pictorial aspects, whether or not they emphasise its Jacobean mode (by using 'Veronese' costumes, for example), whether celebratory or satirical of Roman imperial appropriation. The stage history of the play illustrates the range of possible permutations.

Exotics and politics

The drive to contain exoticism in western culture helps explain the story's appeal to Shakespeare and his contemporaries, and the appeal to later generations both of the story itself and of Shakespeare's complex dramatisation of it. For Europeans, the mainstream nature of Roman civilisation was established by the Roman colonisation of Europe and the use of Latin as universal language. To most classically educated people of Shakespeare's and later generations, the monuments of Rome and its colonising politics were central and accessible (and the main medium of knowledge of ancient Greek culture); exotic cultures like the Egyptian were mysterious but marginal, and mainly accessible through Rome, in Alexandrian form.[23] To that extent, the attitude of scholars and archaeologists was inherently politicised: Rome had supplanted Egypt, at least in terms of power politics. Generally speaking (though dramatists were not regarded as potential subversives for nothing), the English of Shakespeare's age not only tended to identify with the Romans culturally; they shared, in deed as well as thought, most of their patriarchal principles, including the identification of colonisation with the spread of civilisation – and the marginalisation, and forceful containment, of women with 'whorish' tendencies. Until recent times, much the same might be said of succeeding generations: from a late twentieth-century standpoint, this seems particularly true of the Victorian age. It is in this context that we should read reviewers' observations about the unsuitability of English actresses for the role of Cleopatra and the peculiarities of the play's stage history: it is not so much a question of casting as of the cultural implications of the protagonists' tragic status.

In Jacobean performances of the play, the Egyptian and Roman settings were established verbally and by means of costumes, tawny fronts and

22 See Humbert, 'Egyptomania: a Current Concept from the Renaissance to Postmodernism', in Humbert et al., *Egyptomania*, pp. 21–6, esp. p. 21.
23 See Ziegler, 'From One Egyptomania to Another: the Legacy of Roman Antiquity', in Humbert et al., *Egyptomania*, pp. 15–20, esp. pp. 18–19.

exotic attendants such as eunuchs and soothsayer; it might be argued that since only the men wore historical costume, dress in this play confirmed not only the cultural centrality of men but also that of the Romans.[24] It is probably true that for audiences and directors a historically impressionistic attitude to the Egyptian and Roman cultures has remained more significant than representation of the Egyptian and Roman settings as such; and this may have had an inhibiting effect on the use of modern costumes in this play.[25] After all, modern dress has generally been used to point up thematic connections[26] as much as to insist on Shakespeare's 'relevance', and in *Antony and Cleopatra*, whose thematic concerns cannot easily be separated from issues of cultural identity, modern dress (being less distinctive) tends to obscure the thematic contrast between Rome and Egypt, though simple colour-coding can work well.

Shakespeare's indebtedness, often closely verbal, to his main source, Sir Thomas North's translation of Jacques Amyot's French version of Plutarch's *Lives of the Noble Grecians and Romans*, is indisputable, but Shakespeare's presentation of that part of the story he dramatises is significantly different, even if many of North's politico-moral value-judgements are reflected in the remarks by Caesar and lesser Roman commentators about the protagonists' political irresponsibility. Shakespeare dramatises the complexities of the sexual and power politics, and satirises the manipulative 'certainties' of the Roman political stance as surely as he represents the hedonism of the Egyptian court. In terms of its structural use of satire and debate to complicate audience response, the play has some affinities with *Coriolanus*; it might be said that Shakespeare's use of structure and of theatrical dynamics subverts the politico-moral narrative of his source, though of course sexual and power politics remain central issues in the drama.

Shakespeare may also be making contemporary political references in the play. Cleopatra's assault on the messenger is a possible allusion to Queen

24 The possible exceptions are politically unpowerful: the 'Egyptian' who enters at 5.1.48 SD and who presumably wore orientalising costume, and the eunuchs, whose costumes were perhaps more occupational than national (as may have been the case for Roman soothsayers).

25 Rather than what Margaret Lamb, *Antony and Cleopatra*, p. 172, dismisses as conservatism bred from 'the difficulties of the piece'. Only Komisarjevsky's production of 1936 (where the costumes were more fantastical than strictly modern), McClintic's of 1947, Richardson's of 1973, and four other notable productions since (Brook's, Noble's, Zadek's and Rutter's), have used modern dress.

26 Encouraged by the use of literary criticism as an aid to theme-hunting (Wilson Knight's books were useful in that respect and widely cited from the forties to the sixties), it coincided with the rise of the director as interpreter.

Elizabeth's treatment of attendants.[27] Her line about innocents and thunderbolts may well have had resonances for Jacobeans who knew anything of court life in Elizabeth's last years, of which Sir John Harington wrote, 'When she smiled, it was a pure sunshine that everyone did choose to bask in if they could; but anon came a storm from a sudden gathering of clouds, and the thunder fell in wondrous manner on all alike.' (quoted in Neale, *Queen Elizabeth*, p. 219) But broader parallels between Cleopatra and Elizabeth as powerful and self-dramatisingly wilful queens may also have been registered – how consciously is another matter – by the play's first audiences. Their closeness to the succession crisis may have prompted recognition of the political fact that, like Elizabeth, Cleopatra preserved her power as Prince despite her gender, by remaining unmarried,[28] though she was no Virgin Queen (her lovers were, of course, top Romans, politically powerful); if her anger at Antony's marriage to Octavia indicates more than sexual jealousy, she only allows herself to articulate marital thoughts when dying. There is some Elizabethan evidence for the currency of the parallel between Elizabeth and Cleopatra as *femmes fatales* to ambitious men: Fulke Greville explained his destruction of his own closet drama in terms of the political dangers of a parallel being perceived between Antony and Cleopatra and Elizabeth and Essex.[29] F. H. Mares, noting that a Jesuit referred to Raleigh as the 'darling of the English Cleopatra',[30] hints that the Elizabeth–Cleopatra parallel may have been a source of possible political suppression of Shakespeare's play; but whether a perceived parallel was as politically dangerous in the early years of James's reign is less certain. We can only speculate about if and how such a connection was suggested in Jacobean productions, though Cleopatra's 'tawny front' meant any allusions were likely to be expressed in terms of costume or manner. The supposed

27 Though, as Michel Foucault says in *Discipline and Punish*, the theory of the day was that treatment of offenders should reflect the prince's power over subjects' bodies, and his/her determination to make the punishment fit the crime. The messenger is guilty of no crime and is merely doing his duty, but he endangers his body because his message offends majesty's person: the tyrannical Saturninus goes a step further and hangs the Clown because he is upset by the message in *Titus Andronicus*, 4.4.

28 In the play her formal marriages to two younger brothers in succession are not taken seriously; even Caesar's 'tumble on the bed of Ptolemy', 1.4.17, is merely a rhetorical arrow in the quiver of his moral indignation against Antony.

29 '*Antonie and Cleopatra*, according to their irregular passions in foresaking Empire to follow sensuality, were sacrificed in the fire; the executioner, the author himselfe . . . in the practice of the world, seeing the like instance not poetically, but really, fashioned in the Earl of Essex then falling . . . this sudden descent of such greatness . . . stirred up the author's second thoughts' (*Prose Works*, p. 93).

30 'Shifting Perspectives', p. 73, citing Neville Williams (*Elizabeth I*, p. 166).

parallel may have had a slight influence on modern productions. Beginning with Harcourt Williams's of 1930, a number of productions with Veronese-style costumes, some featuring red-haired Cleopatras, offered audiences a chance to make the association, though their directors almost certainly intended nothing beyond a Renaissance atmosphere. A more modern English royal connection with an American Cleopatra crossed the minds of American reviewers in 1937 when Tallulah Bankhead set about getting a suntan for the part; she was rumoured to have been inspired by the role of Wallis Simpson in the 'Windsor romance' (*Bridgeport, Connecticut Post*, 29 August 1937), and it was noted that Bankhead herself was a former friend of the Prince of Wales (*Syracuse, New York Post-Standard*, 1 September 1937).

It has also been speculated[31] that the play carries a Roman political message for James I, who liked to be known as the Second Augustus and saw himself as bringing about a new peaceful age: the first Augustus's time of peace was seen in Shakespeare's day as a precondition for the birth of Christ. Such a reading makes much of Caesar's 'The time of universal peace is near' (4.6.5) and tends to ignore those elements of the satire directed against the 'boy' Octavius's manipulations and the emphasis at the end of the play on the protagonists' suicides as 'mock[ing] / The luck of Caesar' (5.2.279–80). Shakespeare's drama deals with Octavius rising rather than with the august statesman, but it is possible that in early performances the actor of Octavius played down the young man's political ambitions and played up his role as peacemaker; his imperialism is doubtless more in tune with Shakespeare's age than our own. Modern directors who have recognised the difference between Jacobean and modern attitudes to political rule have not necessarily succeeded in making Caesar attractive to modern audiences: Trevor Nunn was reported as saying 'Octavius Caesar was the Elizabethan ideal of the monarch, the good governor. He was the Bobby Fischer, always five moves ahead' (*Evening Press*, Dublin, 30 August 1972), but Ian Christie found Corin Redgrave in the part 'a cold teetotal politician who makes the prospect of universal peace seem a threat' (*Daily Express*, 16 August 1972).

The Jacobean *Antony and Cleopatra*

We have no definite evidence of performances of the play in Shakespeare's lifetime, and can therefore perhaps assume that it was not performed frequently, though it is probably as safe to assume that it *was* performed. Roslyn Knutson, in *The Repertory of Shakespeare's Company*, concludes

31 Emrys Jones, e.g., mentions both the Elizabethan and quasi-Augustan connections in the Introduction to his Penguin edition, p. 47; for the James connection see H. Neville Davies, 'Jacobean *Antony and Cleopatra*', pp. 123–58.

that Roman history plays were generally popular, and makes the salutary observation that a play's popularity cannot accurately be gauged by whether it was published or alluded to. She also comments on the uncertainties of performance history in the few years after the plague of 1606.

Many scholars have assumed that *Antony and Cleopatra* was first acted at the first Globe, but it remains a matter for speculation. The Lord Chamberlain's records of 1669 list *Antony and Cleopatra* as 'formerly acted at the Blackfriars', and that seems likely, but is by no means certain. Emrys Jones thought 'Shakespeare himself may have conceived it as primarily a Blackfriars play – as written for an indoor theatre, with a fairly small, intimately placed audience' (Introduction, Penguin edition, p. 7). The smaller private theatre offered the theatrical advantages of a more 'claustrophobic' atmosphere, appropriate to this play's often satirically framed wars-indoors and also suitable for a stylised presentation of its battle scenes. On the other hand it may be instructive to contemplate modern productions of the play that have been small-scale: some reviewers of Adrian Noble's thought that 'as an epic of passion on the empire-spanning scale, *Antony and Cleopatra* does not exactly lend itself to reduced theatrical circumstances or any form of physical confinement' (Keith Nurse, *Daily Telegraph*, 14 April 1983).

The Blackfriars' artificial lighting may have been advantageous in a production of *Antony and Cleopatra*, as it clearly was to John Webster's *The Duchess of Malfi*, with its wax figures and shadow-chasing, though it is worth remembering that Webster's play was also performed at the Globe. A modern naturalistic view of theatrical conventions would hold that night scenes (such as the 'supernatural' scene, 4.3) are likely to work better in an indoor theatre, but Globe audiences readily suspended disbelief when torches on the daylit stage indicated that it was night; and in any case it seems that the auditoriums of private theatres remained lit during the performance. What the Blackfriars may have offered in the 'supernatural' scene was better acoustics, in association with greater intimacy, when the '*Music of the hautboys is under the stage*'. The Blackfriars may just possibly have been a more practical venue for such notorious scenes as the hauling of Antony, but the question of the height of the stage balcony at the Globe remains contentious,[32] and there may have been little difference in hauling height at Globe and Blackfriars. When Shakespeare wrote the play (before the King's Men had permanent use of a private theatre), he must, in considering the feasibility of the hauling business, have envisaged the

---

32 Scholars generally agree on somewhere between nine and thirteen feet (from stage to balcony floor), but practical staging considerations (pertaining to this scene, among others) have had the height of the upper stage balcony in the International Shakespeare Globe Centre architects' plan modified to 9ft 6in: see Paul Nelsen, 'Sizing Up the Globe', p. 11.

likelihood of its being performed at the Globe, even if he preferred the Blackfriars. The scenes now generally regarded as problematic in staging terms (the 'supernatural' scene, the monument scene, the death-scene) may also have caused headaches for the King's Men, but they are likely to have been equally difficult at both theatres.

Consideration of the Blackfriars venue also raises the question of the play's date. The King's Men appear to have used the Blackfriars on occasions before their official takeover in 1609, but when they first did so is uncertain.[33] The availability of the Blackfriars for an early performance of the play is likelier if one favours a first production date close to the Stationers' Register entry of the play on 20 May 1608. Although it is true that entry of a play often seems to be close to its first performance, this is by no means an infallible guide. A more compelling reason for a later date is the supposition that the King's Men acquired in about 1608 a number of experienced boy actors capable at least of the three supporting female roles in *Antony and Cleopatra*.[34] But recent scholarly opinion, following J. Leeds Barroll's influential article ('The Chronology of Shakespeare's Jacobean Plays'), tends to favour late 1606 as the likely first production date, and the few contemporary indications of the play's performance tend to support this earlier date.

Even at face value, the statement in the Lord Chamberlain's records that the play was 'formerly acted at the Blackfriars' does not necessarily imply that it was performed there whilst Shakespeare was still alive. Of possible indirect evidence that it was in fact performed somewhere in Shakespeare's lifetime, the most interesting is in Samuel Daniel's 1607 revision of his play *The Tragedy of Cleopatra*, where the description of Antony, suspended halfway as he is hauled up to Cleopatra, may derive from Daniel's having seen a performance of Shakespeare's play, presumably at the Globe.[35] There are possible recollections of other moments in the play in Daniel's revision, and

---

33 They were presumably using it shortly after taking the lease in August 1608, but their first full season there may not have been until 1610. See Keith Sturgess, *Jacobean Private Theatre*, pp. 2–3.

34 See W. Robertson Davies, *Shakespeare's Boy Actors*, p. 132, and Cecile de Banke, *Shakespearean Stage Production*, p. 108; following Baldwin, Banke claims that the company altered radically in 1608, with the death of Sly and Fletcher, the taking in of boys from the Children of the Queen's Revels, the use of the Blackfriars in winter and the possible retirement of Shakespeare.

35 R. H. Case noticed the passage in his 1906 Introduction (in M. R. Ridley's Arden edition, xxvi), but Joan Rees ('An Elizabethan Eyewitness', pp. 92–3) emphasised its probable reflection of performance practice. However, John Wilders (in his New Arden edition, p. 73) suggests that Daniel, in his capacity as licenser of court plays, may have seen Shakespeare's manuscript.

some parallels in other contemporary works;[36] and in Barnabe Barnes's *The Devil's Charter*, performed by the King's Men at court on 2 February 1607, two young princes are murdered by the application of 'aspics', called 'Cleopatra's birds', to their breasts. Margaret Lamb (*Antony and Cleopatra*, p. 33) suggests that the King's Men may have used the same property asps in both plays.[37]

The King's Men, the company in which Shakespeare was a major shareholder and for which he wrote *Antony and Cleopatra*, was undoubtedly the most prestigious and stable theatre company of the period. Their success can be gauged by three interrelated facts: they were in the enviable position of owning their theatre, the Globe, which was purpose-built; they played with increasing frequency at court from the late 1590s; the royal patent, changing their name from the Lord Chamberlain's Men to the King's, was, in keeping with Queen Elizabeth's moneysaving tradition of having suitable commercial plays performed at court, a prestigious but essentially pragmatic form of recognition of their continuing commercial success. Whilst the King's Men had the incomparable advantage of having Shakespeare as one of their main dramatists and also brought into being many of the other major plays of their age, their repertoire was extensive and catholic, and doubtless ruled by a sound sense of what made good popular theatre. The company operated in many respects as a collective, with shareholders such as Shakespeare writing, acting and being involved in other aspects of production, and there is evidence that dramatists were sometimes obliged to make or 'consent' to cuts or modifications to their texts, on commercial rather than aesthetic grounds.[38] *Antony and Cleopatra* is a long play[39] and

---

36 See Case, Introduction to Ridley's Arden edition, pp. xxv–xxviii. He also records some less convincing verbal parallels in *Nobody and Somebody* (revised 1606?) and *Bussy D'Ambois* (1605?). E. K. Chambers, *Elizabethan Stage*, vol. III, p. 220, citing Charles Gayley, notes one in *The Woman Hater* (1606/7?). The Menas–Pompey exchange in 2.7.68–71 seems to have been remembered by the anonymous author of *A Horrible Creuel and Bloody Murther* (1614): see Martin Wiggins, 'An Early Misinterpretation of *Antony and Cleopatra*', pp. 483–4.

37 There is also a reference to 'Cleopatres crimes' in 'our lustfull Theaters' in Robert Anton's *Philosophers Satyrs* (1616), p. 46, but of course this may not be a specific reference to Shakespeare's play (see Michael Steppat, *Critical Reception*, pp. 1–2).

38 I borrow 'consent', which may not imply authorial enthusiasm, from the publisher's preface to the Beaumont and Fletcher First Folio; see also the 1623 title page of *The Duchess of Malfi*, quoted earlier.

39 3,050 lines in this edition, as compared to an average of 2,520 in the period between 1603 and 1616, and 2,803 in the thirteen Shakespeare plays first produced in this period: these are the averages (based on the old Cambridge edition for Shakespeare) calculated by A. Hart, 'The Length of Elizabethan and Jacobean Plays', pp. 139–54.

would almost certainly have been cut in performance, not necessarily more radically for performance at the Blackfriars than at the Globe.[40] We can only guess at which passages might have been omitted. Those that least affect the narrative are always vulnerable, and the cutting practice of later periods may be something of a guide, period prejudices (of the bowdlerising and anti-supernatural kind) aside. In the substantially different versions of the text of such plays as *Hamlet* and *King Lear* there is evidence that Shakespeare sometimes made authorial revisions with an eye to the play in performance. Whilst we have only a Folio text for *Antony and Cleopatra*, some scholars consider that there are signs in 4.15 of authorial revision.[41]

Whether or not *Antony and Cleopatra* was cut in early productions, the pace of performance is likely to have been fast. Continuous staging, without pauses between scenes or acts (in the public theatre at least), with portable properties carried in or out by actors involved in the scene, meant that neither actors nor audiences were hindered by the conception of forty-two scene divisions familiar to readers of modern texts of the play.[42] Such divisions were a literary rather than a theatrical convention in Shakespeare's day, though act divisions did provide intervals, with musical entertainment, in the private theatres, and this custom probably continued at the Blackfriars after the King's Men's occupation, since intervals allowed the candles to be trimmed. The flexible and imaginative use of stage space in the Jacobean theatre allowed a mode of representation, with rapid spatial and temporal transitions, that has something in common with that of the modern cinema. The same areas and the same major properties could be used for both Rome and Egypt; costume and racially identifiable or exotic attendants, such as the '*eunuchs fanning her*' of 1.1, helped indicate geographical place. Costume was not historically or geographically 'accurate', but another stimulus to the imagination. Judging by the scant evidence we have – graphically only Henry Peacham's sketch of a misremembered or

40 Sturgess, *Jacobean Private Theatre*, assumes that the all-boy companies' practice of performing inter-act music was continued when the King's Men took over the Blackfriars and implies (p. 103) that King's Men's plays performed there were shorter than those performed at the Globe, but these assumptions may not be correct. When all-boy companies played at the private theatres and provided concerts as part of the entertainment, their plays were not radically shorter; Hart's average for plays performed by the Children of the Chapel and of the Queen's Revels between 1600 and 1614 is 2,417.

41 Though David Bevington, in his New Cambridge Shakespeare edition, p. 263, believes Dover Wilson's suggestion that Shakespeare intended to cut 'some seventeen lines' has been 'convincingly refuted' by David Galloway.

42 But imposed on it, between them, by Rowe, Pope, Hanmer, Capell and Dyce in their editions; for this play, the First Folio marks only 'Actus Primus. Scena Prima'.

composite scene from *Titus Andronicus* – characters in Roman plays seem to have worn a mixture of historically approximate costume and contemporary dress. It looks as though the 'historical' costumes were mainly worn by the male characters and the contemporary ones by the female characters, a situation that obtained after the introduction of actresses and until comparatively recent times, probably because of a desire to display female attractiveness in the most obvious way and to ensure that expensive garments were redeployable in other plays and (in the case of actresses) possibly also on the stage of life. The relatively permanent interior decoration of the theatres almost certainly reflected Renaissance and public generalities rather than English and domestic particularities: the tiring-house facade in public theatres such as the Globe was probably decorated with neo-classical ornamentation and some of the woodwork painted to look like stone or marble, and it is likely that the decoration of the private theatres was similar. Given the nature of the lighting, such decoration must have impinged on the audience's consciousness.[43] In performances of *Antony and Cleopatra* the style of decoration may well have suggested, as background to the subversion and destruction in the action of the play, not the Egypt–Rome dichotomy of later productions, but a common denominator in those centres of power: the manifestation of social hierarchy and control in signs of order and display.[44] The use of the thrust stage – surrounded on three sides by members of the audience – in relation to rear stage and upper stage areas, encouraged the development of conventions of interpretative perspective, often in association with older interpretative devices. *Antony and Cleopatra* uses the presenter-figure in the same mode as other satirically inclined contemporary plays: that is, presentation is only an occasional function of the characters involved and it is always given a pretext,[45] either conversation with another observer (as with Philo's opening remarks, probably delivered from in front of a stage pillar) or that of the reactive aside (as with many of Enobarbus's comments). Both, like the device of the soliloquy, presumably capitalised on the presenter's proximity to (part of) the audience, in a manner comparable with the filmic close-up. The size of the

43 This is clearly true of the daylit public theatre; in the private theatre the windows had shutters and it seems probable that stage and auditorium were continuously candlelit, though the auditorium may have been relatively darker: see Sturgess, *Jacobean Private Theatre*, pp. 44–7.

44 J. S. Bratton makes a similar point about performances of *King Lear* at the Globe in the Introduction to her Plays in Performance edition of the play, p. 5.

45 The presenter-figure can be traced back at least to the Tudor moral interlude, but the Elizabethan–Jacobean presenter is only a part-time commentator, whose function is more satirical or ironic than straightforwardly moral.

theatre and its acoustic nature must have had some bearing on the overall style of delivery. William Armstrong ('Actors and Theatres', p. 198) cites evidence that the adult companies developed a quieter style for performance in the smaller indoor private theatres, and presumably they had formerly adjusted their style when performing in public theatres of different sizes (for example, the Rose as opposed to the Globe), though the acoustic differences may have been less marked.

Elizabethan and Jacobean actors prepared for their roles in ways significantly different from their successors. They were provided only with their own part and appropriate cues, and because of the size of companies' repertoire and the brief run of individual plays, rehearsal time was likely to have been very limited and may have been given only to large ensemble scenes. Star actors, both comic and tragic (who were major attractions for public theatre audiences) played a large number of roles in repertory, and for them, as for all the other members of the company (for whom doubling was usual), memorising was a major component of their work. These facts of repertory life, as well as earlier theatrical traditions, help to account for the acceptance of improvisation in comic acting and, to a much smaller extent, in more serious roles.[46] Even in comic acting the riskiness of improvisation must have been lamented in some quarters, particularly the dramatists': in his advice to the players, Hamlet says 'let those that play your clowns speak no more than is set down for them' (*Hamlet*, 3.2.31–2).[47] In *Antony and Cleopatra*, the Clown's part is limited to one brief appearance with asp and figs, but it is at a crucial moment in the play. Whether the first Clown (presumably Robert Armin, whose style is generally regarded as more sophisticated than that of his predecessor, Will Kempe) improvised can only be a matter for speculation, but in the part 'set down' for him, his reluctance to leave despite the queen's repeated farewells may be Shakespeare's allusion to, or parody of, the uncontained nature of theatrical clowning.

Antony's part was almost certainly written with Richard Burbage in mind. Burbage, a second-generation actor brought up to the Elizabethan public stage, was the most famous actor of his time, and chiefly celebrated for his tragic roles, including Hamlet, Lear and Othello. It is difficult, and perhaps dangerous, to try and separate fashions in dramatic style from fashions in acting style, and inevitably when modern scholars try to trace 'develop-

---

46 In Marston and Barkstead's *The Insatiate Countess*, for example, 'Isabella *falls in love with* Massino' and Massino is directed to '*Tell him all the plot*' (John Marston, *Works*, vol. III, 2.1.109 SD, 4.5.43 SD). This play seems to have been performed by the Queen's Revels at the Whitefriars, *c*.1610, but such improvisatory practice was probably common to all the companies.

47 All references to this play are to Philip Edwards's New Cambridge Shakespeare edition.

ments' in Elizabethan and Jacobean acting style they oversimplify. To say that Burbage's style reflected better than Edward Alleyn's heroic vein the demands of the new generation of dramatists and audiences is probably to say no more than that both were men of their time. In their respective heydays Alleyn and Burbage were praised for the same qualities,[48] though of course the implied definition of such qualities, which we would term 'naturalism' and 'consistency of characterisation', may have been different. Burbage was celebrated for total immersion in his roles,[49] and it may be that, when *Antony and Cleopatra* was ready for performance, his own style, and indeed acting style generally, had changed since Titus lamented the lack of a hand to 'grace [his] talk' and 'give it action' (*Titus Andronicus*, 5.2.17–18), but we can be certain that gesture remained a vital and integral part of the actor's expression.[50] Actors who have been formally taught a system of rhetorical gesture can manage to translate their study into a seemingly 'natural' means of actorly communication.[51] Richard Flecknoe noted Burbage's use of facial and manual gesture to maintain characterisation, 'never falling in his Part when he had done speaking; but with his looks and gesture, maintaining it still unto the heighth'.[52] The convincing nature of Burbage's performances doubtless owed a good deal to his professional restraint and discretion, the artifice of the 'natural' style of a great actor, who can 'hold as 'twere the mirror up to nature' whilst delivering his lines 'trippingly on the tongue'.

The recognition that 'naturalism' is a form of artifice which, at its most

48 See William A. Armstrong, 'Shakespeare and the Acting of Edward Alleyn', pp. 82–9.
49 'A Funerall Elegye' praised his Hamlet thus – 'Oft haue I seene him, leap into the Graue/ Suiting the person, which he seem'd to haue/ Of a sadd Louer, with so true an Eye/ That theer I would haue sworne, he meant to dye' (quoted in Edwin Nungezer, *Dictionary of Actors*, p. 74) – and Richard Flecknoe in 1664 called him 'a delightful Proteus, so wholly transforming himself into his Part, and putting off himself with his Cloathes, as he never (not so much as in the Tyring-house) assum'd himself again until the Play was done' (*A Short Discourse of the English Stage*, quoted in Chambers, *Elizabethan Stage*, vol. iv, p. 370).
50 It is important to distinguish between Titus's consciousness (as a noble Roman played by an Elizabethan actor) of the proper rhetorical role of manual gesture and an awkward self-consciousness about, or over-literalness in, gesturing, of the sort denounced in 1601 by Philip Rossiter ('The old exploded action in comedies when if they did pronounce Memini, they would point to the hinder part of their heads, if Video, put their finger in their eye'; quoted by Alan S. Downer, 'Prolegomenon', pp. 625–36) and implicitly by Hamlet in his much vaunted advice (*Hamlet*, 3.2.1–36).
51 As B. L. Joseph's 1952 production of *Macbeth* demonstrated to reviewers; see Alexander Leggatt, 'The Companies and Actors', in Barroll, Leggatt, Hosley and Kernan, *Revels History*, vol. iii, p. 115.
52 *A Short Discourse of the English Stage*, quoted in Chambers, *Elizabethan Stage*, vol. iv, p. 370.

satisfactory, conveys messages 'trippingly' is a good basis for understanding the relationship between literal and extra-literal meaning in theatre of the period. Dramatists often used blatantly sensational action and images for the simultaneous titillation and edification of their audiences. Shakespeare's own work prior to *Antony and Cleopatra* – from *Titus Andronicus* to *King Lear*– is witness to the fact that violence, as much as sexual excess (and often in association with it), can be given emblematic significance without limiting the range of an audience's potential responses to the sensational images. Whilst we can take it for granted that a readiness to read pictures emblematically was a culturally determined characteristic of audiences of Shakespeare's time, we should not underestimate the complexity of dramatists' use of emblematic material or of audiences' response to it.[53] Complex drama thrives on ambiguity, and the dynamics of *Antony and Cleopatra* are in no way confined by emblematic indicators. It is likely that, as R. Mac G. Dawson suggests ('But Why Enobarbus?'), Enobarbus wore a red beard in early productions, in keeping with his name; but an audience's response to Enobarbus is enriched rather than circumscribed by an awareness of the depiction in morality plays of Judas as a red-haired betrayer. In the same way, an audience's response to Cleopatra registers, but is not restricted by, Philo's way of reading her 'tawny front'. Many of the play's more memorable and important stage images have emblematic overtones, but their dramatic meaning is extended and intensified by conflicting emotional, as well as conflicting moral, connotations. The manner of Cleopatra's death is the prime example of complex presentation in an emblematic context. When the queen speaks of the asp as a baby at her breast, she may well be imaging herself as the goddess Isis with her child Horus, but the audience see her 'child' in the form of a snake. The iconography of a woman holding a serpent is fraught with ambiguity, and in emblematic terms Cleopatra's breast may be viewed from several perspectives.[54] Members of an audience are 'free' to read the asp as a tragic instrument of apotheosis: changeable lust (the serpent) becomes committed love (the baby), through the agency of an ennobling death (the worm).

---

53 In emblems of the period the pictorial element is often ambiguous, since the picture is intended to be read in conjunction with its 'word' or motto, or in the light of its interpreting text. Because plates or even woodcuts were expensive, the same picture was often re-used in emblem books with a different moral meaning, and Webster comically illustrates the potential ambiguity of emblems when he brings one on to the stage in *The White Devil*, 2.1.

54 It is a breast of affliction, nibbled at by conscience and fatally bitten by the worm of mortality (see Chastity, Sin and Affliction in Cesare Ripa's *Iconologia* (pp. 66–7, 383, 90–1); Cleopatra's suicide redeems her honour, but is the outcome of her giving suck to the serpent of concupiscence which lurks in the genitally allusive basket of figs.

Yet the freedom of an audience to read is impinged upon by directorial interpretation (which may resort to cutting or rearranging lines, as well as pointing up, or imposing, visual images), and of course all productions are interpretative. We know nothing for certain about the Jacobean equivalent of directorial intervention, though most modern scholars tend to assume it was less extensive; equally, many think that dramatists at least attended rehearsals of their own plays in Shakespeare's time.[55] Whether boy actors in major female roles were more carefully instructed than the adult actors is another issue; it may be that their apprentice status meant their instruction was left to their master in the public theatres; in the private ones, where they were nominally apprenticed to the manager of the company, the dramatist may well have been expected to take responsibility.[56] Whatever the convention, it does seem likely that Shakespeare would have thought it useful to give advice personally to the first actor of Cleopatra.

Whether Shakespeare wrote Cleopatra's part with a specific boy in mind is less certain because of the implications of the status of boy actors as apprentices,[57] but such a large and daring role, with its three supporting female roles, certainly suggests that Shakespeare was confident that a virtuoso boy and three other highly competent ones would be available. We know little about the training of boy actors, but, since in the public theatres it took the form of an apprenticeship intended to produce a competent adult actor, we should perhaps assume that it did not only involve the performing of female roles. Boy actors with unbroken voices[58] were presumably given unimportant roles, female and male. That of the eunuch Mardian was probably one of the latter; it has some affinities, in its self-conscious badinage about sexual desire and performance, with the roles

55 Some Restoration actors liked to trace the provenance of their interpretation back to Shakespeare (see John Downes on Thomas Betterton in *Roscius Anglicanus*, p. 24), and in 1613 Johannes Rhenamus wrote that English actors 'are daily instructed, as it were in a school, so that even the most eminent actors have to allow themselves to be taught their places by the dramatists' (Preface to *Speculum Aestheticum*, translated by David Klein, in 'Did Shakespeare Produce His Own Plays?', p. 556).

56 This point is made by Leggatt, *Revels History*, vol. III, p. 113.

57 Carol Rutter thinks that major female roles such as Cleopatra may have been played by adult rather than apprentice actors (Rutter (ed.), *Documents of the Rose Playhouse*, pp. 124–5), but she is extrapolating from one costume payment of doubtful significance. The convention in contemporary lists of *dramatis personae* of placing the female characters last, whatever their dramatic or social position, seems to reflect the apprentice status of their actors.

58 In *Hamlet*, 2.2.390–1, Hamlet jocularly hopes the boy player's 'voice like a piece of uncurrent gold be not cracked within the ring', but of course the boy is still in employment, and Hamlet is alluding to a temporary disablement in which the breaking voice is neither reliable nor resonant.

apparently given to younger boys in the satirical plays written at the turn of the century for all-boy companies by dramatists such as Marston. It is highly likely that the maturer boy actors were trained to speak major female roles in a voice 'ever soft, / Gentle, and low, an excellent thing in woman' (*King Lear*, 5.3.246–7); just as modern female Cleopatras ideally have a good contralto voice, so the ideal boy for the part would have had both maturity and a naturally rich voice. Whether boy actors were less culturally inhibited than modern female actors in such a role as Cleopatra is worth fleeting speculation. Their experience as apprentices may have given them some sense of the prejudice or subjugation women habitually suffered under patriarchy, but they were adolescents looking forward to playing a man's part in a male world.[59] Cleopatra's role was, of course, a special case, in that she was a monarch in her own right, and it is doubtless true that the first actor of the part was more conscious of the Renaissance princely model provided by Elizabeth I, who had the 'heart and stomach of a king' and (she might have added) the violent temper too. As late as 1924 a reviewer of Dorothy Green's performance in the first messenger scene wrote 'the Elizabethan Cleopatra was no doubt much more hysterical than any modern actress would care to be or dare to be' (R.C.R., *Birmingham Post*, 17 July 1924).

The first actor of Cleopatra, then, was almost certainly a youth rather than a boy in the modern sense.[60] If he had formerly been a member of an all-boy company,[61] he may well have had some ten years' experience as an actor, and may equally have felt at home in the Blackfriars theatre, if the play was ever performed there. We are on safer ground with speculation about the first Cleopatra's likely age and experience than with attempts to name him. Thomas W. Baldwin simply asserts that it was 'probably' John Edmans; P. Levi has the edge in suggesting William Ostler, since Ostler is at least listed as one of the 'Principall Actors' in the first Folio, but he may not have joined the King's Men until 1609, and then as an adult actor.[62]

59 Dusinberre ('Squeaking Cleopatras', p. 55), writing interestingly about the competitiveness built into the protagonists' roles, sees the boy actor as 'playing the part of an Empress, possibly to his own master, Burbage himself, whom he is allowed, in theatrical terms, to supersede'.

60 Michael Hattaway, *Elizabethan Popular Theatre*, pp. 83–4, thinks that the boys joined adult companies between 10 and 13 and 'played boys' parts until they were about twenty'.

61 In *Hamlet*, 2.2.322–3, Hamlet speaks of such as 'grow[ing] themselves to common players – as is most like if their means are no better'.

62 Thomas W. Baldwin, *Shakespearean Company*, pp. 277–8, P. Levi, *William Shakespeare*, p. 279; see also G. E. Bentley, *Jacobean and Caroline Stage*, vol. II, p. 610. Ostler's possible adult status may not matter should Rutter be right (see above).

We have some evidence in the play for the contemporary costuming of the boy Cleopatra. We know he wore a bodice and farthingale from 'Cut my lace, Charmian' (1.3.71), but he probably also wore his bodice low-cut. The most dramatic part of the stage picture of Cleopatra's death, her putting an asp to her breast, is a detail Shakespeare did not find in Plutarch;[63] for all the emblematic implications of the 'suckling', Shakespeare's initial interest in Cleopatra's breast may have been fired by the fashion for *décolletage*.[64] The Puritan I.H. may have been specifically thinking of boy actors when he denounced players 'who by their wantonizing stage-gestures can ingle and seduce men to heave up their hearts and affections . . . by how much more exact these are in their venerean action, by so much more highly are they seated in the monster-headed multitude's estimation'.[65] The boy actor's sexiness as Cleopatra was conveyed by means of language (verbal and non-verbal) and convention, including costume and staging, sometimes exotically erotic: the eunuchs fanning Cleopatra on her first entry are of considerable extra-literal assistance. Shakespeare emphasises the sexual games Cleopatra plays to keep Antony on the hook (see 1.3), and allusions and descriptions make up for lack of body contact. There was *some* contact, all allowable within the convention; mainly kisses, whose impact is increased by the verbal boosting in the text: after his crushing defeat, in 3.11, Antony says to Cleopatra, 'Give me a kiss. / Even this repays me' (lines 69–70) and of course Jacobean audiences took his word for it, as their successors have done. Commenting on the King's Men's performance of *Othello* in Oxford in 1610, Henry Jackson described the actors as moving the audience 'to tears' as much by gesture or action as speech, and singled out for praise the boy actor playing Desdemona, who 'pleaded her case very effectively throughout, yet moved [us] more after she was dead, when, lying on her bed, she entreated the pity of the spectators by her very countenance'.[66] In the first performances of *Antony and Cleopatra* the boy speaking the lines 'I shall see / Some squeaking Cleopatra boy my greatness' (5.2.218–19) must have been a good enough actor, and a mature enough one, not to come across as a boy squeaking them; if Shakespeare had not thought

63 He probably got it from Nashe or from contemporary paintings of Cleopatra: see G. Watson, 'The Death of Cleopatra', pp. 409–14.
64 See C. W. and P. Cunnington, *Handbook of English Costume in the Seventeenth Century*, p. 82. Cordelia's references to her false sisters' 'professèd bosoms' and Lear's to his expectation of Cordelia's 'kind nursery' may well glance at such dresses in *King Lear*, 1.1.118, 266 (all references to this play are to Jay L. Halio's New Cambridge Shakespeare edition).
65 *This World's Folly* (London, 1615); quoted in David Wiles, *Shakespeare's Clown*, 50.
66 Excerpts in the Fulman Papers (Library of Corpus Christi College), vol. x, 83v,84r, translated in *The Riverside Shakespeare*, p. 1852.

he could rely upon that he would hardly have written such a play, let alone such lines.[67]

Theatrical interpretations of the play depend as much on an emotional response to Cleopatra's nature as Antony's 'dotage' does, and the playing of Cleopatra has been as much a sociological index as an acting feat. Given that Shakespeare was a sharer in the most successful theatrical company of his day, his conception of the role of Cleopatra could hardly have been independent of his awareness of the conditions and conventions of Jacobean staging. The role of Cleopatra is written for a boy actor operating within specific conditions, and when theatrical circumstances changed, interpretation of the role was directly affected. The death of Burbage in 1619 and the retirement of Shakespeare (possibly in 1608) may have contributed to the apparent neglect of the play thereafter, and were probably more palpable at that stage of James's reign than any perceived political dangers in the play's subject, situations or characters.

The Restoration and *All for Love*

The introduction of actresses at the Restoration had a less immediate effect on the role of Cleopatra than on the roles of Shakespeare's other important female characters, because of the predilection of the age for heroic conceptions and modes: Dryden's attitude to the lovers prevailed even when *All for Love* did not. The King's Company seems never to have played *Antony and Cleopatra*, as they were licensed to do, and it appears to be one of only three Shakespeare plays not performed in some version in this period.[68]

It is not surprising, in an age which produced a version of *King Lear* with a happy ending (in the interests of poetic justice), that *Antony and Cleopatra* lacked appeal. What is most significant is that there were alternative versions of the story to hand, in the form most palatable to critics and audiences of the time: Sedley's *Antony and Cleopatra*, first performed at Dorset Garden in February 1677, and Dryden's *All for Love*, probably first produced in December of the same year at the Theatre Royal, Drury Lane. *All for Love* had fourteen London productions in the period to 1818 (the busiest decade being the 1720s, when there were thirty-three performances) and the part of Cleopatra was taken by the leading eighteenth-century actresses, including Anne Oldfield, Peg Woffington, Mrs Yates (who was both Shakespeare's Cleopatra in 1759 and Dryden's in 1766), and Mrs

---

67 Hattaway, *Elizabethan Popular Theatre*, p. 84, makes a similar point about a non-squeaking Cleopatra.

68 The other two being *Love's Labour's Lost* and *Two Gentlemen of Verona*. See Charles B. Hogan, *Shakespeare in the Theatre*, vol. 1, p. 461.

Siddons, who famously refused to play Shakespeare's but performed Dryden's on one occasion in 1788, when James Boaden felt her acting 'showed the daring atrocity of crime' but 'virtually banished' 'the notion of frailty' (quoted by Winter, *Shakespeare*, p. 437).

Sedley and Dryden used the strict neo-classical form then considered appropriate to serious subjects, and observed the 'unities' of time, place and action, Sedley beginning his action after Actium and Dryden setting his in Alexandria on the last day of his protagonists' lives and taking Octavia to Cleopatra. Sedley's play lacks Dryden's range: Genest thought he 'made a mountain out of a molehill' in so enlarging upon the Thidias episode (*English Stage*, vol. I, p. 208), which Dryden deftly incorporates, by way of report, into Cleopatra's half-hearted flirtation with Dolabella. In terms that reveal the formal preoccupations of his age, Dryden boasted that his play observed the unities 'more exactly' than 'the *English* Theater requires', with 'every Scene in the Tragedy conducing to the main design, and every Act concluding with a turn of it' (Preface, page 10, lines 23–4, 26–7, in *Works*, vol. XIII, ed. Novak).

Both Sedley's and Dryden's plays have far fewer speaking parts than Shakespeare's, with strong thematic emphasis on the heroic love–honour conflict. Dryden's dozen characters exclude Octavius but include Antony's two daughters by Octavia. His Prologue lightheartedly assures the audience that Antony 'bates of his mettle; and scarce rants at all' (line 11) and Antony's heroic conflict, signalled at his first entrance by his '*disturb'd Motion, before he speaks*' (1.1.202 SD), is extended and displayed by means of the role Dryden gives to Antony's 'general', Ventidius, who supplants, outranks and outclasses Shakespeare's rough-hewn Enobarbus. This 'good old Man' (1.1.266) is, in his altruistic way, as much a manipulator of Antony's emotions as the self-interested Alexas is of Cleopatra's; it is Ventidius who produces Dolabella and then 'Octavia, *leading* Antony's *two little Daughters*' (3.1.238a SD), as a means of persuading Antony to leave Cleopatra. Dryden's debate-style emphasis is on thematically functional parallel or contrasting pairs of subsidiary characters rather than on the protagonists themselves, whose interaction is minimal and regularly under close observation by their manipulators. Not only is their dialogue continually placed in such a context, but what action there is in the play never seems to occur for its own sake, but for extra-literal purposes.

The play is much more about Antony's dilemma – he loves Cleopatra beyond 'all, but Honor' (1.1.423) – than about Cleopatra, who does not appear until the beginning of the second act and fails to live up to her self-description as one whose 'Love's a noble madness' (2.1.17), who disdains Antony's 'Respect' because that belongs to wives (2.1.82), and who fears she will 'do some wild extravagance / Of Love, in publick' (2.1.449–50). She is never intense enough in her passion nor comfortable enough with her sexuality to embody such promise or to sound convincing when she taunts Octavia for lacking 'those black endearments / That make sin pleasing' (3.1.442–3); but she is single-minded in her devotion to Antony and manages to stand up to those who oppose it: Octavia and, in his last phase, Alexas. Dryden makes his Cleopatra virtuously faithful, at the expense of her variety, by transferring her guile to Alexas, a villainous eunuch whose power-play is a function of his envious impotence and who invents the story of Cleopatra's suicide simply to save his own skin. Even when Cleopatra attempts, at Alexas's suggestion, to arouse Antony's jealousy by playing up to the young man Dolabella, she merely goes through the motions, and blames the Fortune that makes her 'bear the branded Name of Mistress' (3.1.464) for this rare instance of misbehaviour; by temperament, she says, 'Nature meant me / A Wife, a silly harmless houshold Dove' (4.1.91–2). By comparison Octavia seems less harmless; if she forces herself to play the wife in duty, she also reveals the resentment of the scorned and neglected wife who knows the power of her brother. This impression must have been reinforced in the first production by the casting of Elizabeth Boutell as Cleopatra – Edmund Curll said she was small and 'Childish' in appearance; 'her Voice was weak, tho' very mellow; she generally acted the young Innocent Lady whom all the Heroes are mad in Love with'[69] – and Katherine Corey as Octavia: she was a large woman who often played shrewish wives. Dryden, in the cause of the generic requirements of Restoration tragedy, turns Cleopatra into a wife *manquée*, despite his Octavia's describing her as a 'bad Woman' (3.1.355) and a 'faithless Prostitute' (4.1.389), and she is certainly very self-conscious about her status as a mistress, even when kissing the dead Antony's lips (5.1.447–8). This self-consciousness, and her good breeding, determine the manner of her suicide: she gets her women to bare not her breast but her arm, and the audience do not see the asp bite it: she '*Turns aside, and then shows her Arm bloody*' (5.1.488 SD).

Dryden's attitude to the story of Antony and Cleopatra, and to appropriate ways of dramatising it, is set out clearly in his Preface to *All for Love*, which might reasonably be taken to represent an 'educated' view of the period,[70] of the kind likely to influence the selection of plays for performance. He applauds the 'excellency of the Moral: for the chief persons

---

69 Quoted in John Dryden, *Works*, vol. XIII, ed. Novak, Commentary, p. 377.

70 Whilst the Preface presses the case of the 'poet' as isolated from (and superior to) wits, critics and other elements of potential audiences, Dryden is hardly suggesting his own eccentricity in matters of taste.

represented, were famous patterns of unlawful love; and their end accordingly was unfortunate' (Preface, p. 10, lines 7–10). His own treatment of the protagonists was a result of his steering a 'middle course' through the ancient historical accounts, but Dryden considered their wilful 'crimes of love' inhibited the working up of pity 'to a greater heighth'. He also felt that, in transporting Octavia to Alexandria, he had underestimated the extent to which the 'compassion she mov'd to herself and children, was destructive to that which [he] reserv'd for *Antony* and *Cleopatra*; whose mutual love being founded upon vice, must lessen the favour of the Audience to them, when Virtue and Inocence were oppress'd by it' (Preface, p. 10, lines 14, 17–18, 30–1; p. 11, lines 1–3). His reservations about the moral (though not dramatic) soundness of *Antony and Cleopatra* are tempered by admiration for Shakespeare's 'style' (the quality of his language and his blank versification), which seemed to him all the more astonishing because Shakespeare did not live in a 'polite' age. Whilst admitting that some modern French writers have demonstrated that insipidity can be the corollary of politeness, Dryden asserts that the language of *All for Love* is necessarily more restrained and decorous than that of Shakespeare's play because 'some actions, though natural, are not fit to be represented; and broad obscenities in words, ought in good manners to be avoided' (Preface, p. 11, lines 26–8). Dryden's tribute to Shakespeare in remaking one of his stories in blank verse (albeit in entirely different mode) is perhaps as much as a Shakespeare supporter ought to expect in Restoration circumstances.

The stage history of *All for Love* reflects a shift in the eighteenth and early nineteenth centuries in moral attitudes to Cleopatra. As E. Novak points out (Commentary in *Works*, vol. XIII, p. 378), the casting of the notorious Elizabeth Barry as Cleopatra and the chaste Anne Bracegirdle as Octavia in 1704 indicates a very different approach to production, one made plainer still in the excision of passages sympathetic to Cleopatra in later printed versions and prompt copies.[71] Once the giving of wifely virtues to the archetypal seductress seemed morally offensive, the way was open for such a rehabilitation of Shakespeare's Cleopatra as Garrick attempted in the mid eighteenth century. But Dryden's attitude to the supposed excesses of *Antony and Cleopatra* proved surprisingly durable, and the more logical solution appeared to be the conflation of Dryden and Shakespeare in the early nineteenth century: Dryden's stripped-down Cleopatra was implausible in her own right and pointed to Shakespeare's, but Shakespeare's needed 'dignifying' in the Dryden manner, by the use of excision and bowdlerisation to reduce her variety. Thus in 1813 and 1833 Shakespeare's

71 See Commentary in *Works*, vol. XIII, pp. 377–8, n.63. Novak cites the 1776 printed version and the 1811 Folger prompt copy.

play was performed in versions that conflated it with *All for Love*, and was not performed in a 'pure' (though heavily cut) form in England until 1849; ten years later, Edward Eddy's production in New York used a generous measure of Dryden.

Beyond that, Dryden's influence continued to be felt in elements of nineteenth-century staging: the occasional omission of the first messenger scene, Pompey's galley, and the asp-bringing Clown were sanctioned by Dryden's text, as was the transfer of the barge speech (though only Kemble gave it, as in Dryden, to Antony himself); other borrowings were the ceremonial crowning of Antony by Cleopatra, with an Egyptian dance, the avoidance of the hauling of Antony, the short lapse of time between the lovers' deaths, and sometimes the presence of Antony's corpse at Cleopatra's suicide. Possibly Miss Glyn's famous smile on taking the asp owed something to 'Th' impression of a smile left in her face' (5.1.510) by Dryden's dead Cleopatra. Lamb suggests that *All for Love* influenced the staging of Shakespeare's play in another respect: 'Cleopatra still dies in the hierarchical seated pose of Egyptian funerary sculpture instead of on her Jacobean daybed' (*Antony and Cleopatra*, p. 39). This notion, borrowed from W. M. Merchant (*Shakespeare and the Artist*, p. 49), is, when stated in such bald terms, an oversimplification. Garrick's production may in fact have been the first to use a '*Bed, or Sopha*', for Cleopatra's death (printed edition); the productions of 1813, 1833 (both admixtures with Dryden) and 1849 all followed suit, and it is curious that these productions were not influenced by Dryden's staging if its influence in this respect was so pervasive.

Garrick's important failure

David Garrick's production of *Antony and Cleopatra* at Drury Lane in 1759 is the first properly documented production of the play and the first to use actresses and changeable scenery on what was essentially a 'picture stage' (four feet had been removed from the forestage at Drury Lane in 1696).[72] It ran for only six performances, but it was an 'important failure',[73] in that it was a careful attempt (preparations took at least five months) to revive Shakespeare's play, by the leading actor and theatrical entrepreneur of the age.

Garrick and the Shakespearean editor and scholar Edward Capell produced an abridged text for the occasion. This was the first of many on which directors have consulted scholars on the staging of this play, but

72 See George W. Stone, *London Stage*, Pt 4, p. xxxviii.
73 In Auden's phrase in 'Musée des Beaux Arts'.

Garrick's own reputation as actor, writer and theatrical entrepreneur also contributed to a prevailing belief in theatrical circles that good actors themselves are the best interpreters of plays.[74] The Garrick–Capell text reduced the number of minor characters and scenes (to twenty-seven, though generally the retained scenes were kept whole), condensed locations (to streamline shifting of the painted scenery) and made some transpositions. The famous 'barge speech' was given to Thyreus (Thidias renamed, following the editor Lewis Theobald) as a set piece,[75] and in the printed text it appears early in the first scene, after the protagonists' exit, though in the Folger promptbook it is in its rightful place. Enobarbus was played by a comic actor, Edward Berry, and Thomas Davies (who played Eros) said that 'on one occasion Mossop acted Enobarbus and "wanted humour" – which is likely enough, since he was one of the most tragical of tragedians' (Winter, *Shakespeare*, p. 435). The expectation of humour in the playing bolsters speculation that Enobarbus's part was doubled with the Clown's in Shakespeare's time.[76] But for reasons that Dryden would have approved, bawdy lines were cut and characters like Enobarbus polished by the removal of rough patches. Predictably enough, the scene with Pacorus's body (3.1) was cut, as was the 'supernatural' scene (4.3), and in general the political scenes were cropped. Lamb is a little misleading in claiming that, 'like the theater itself since Shakespeare's time, the stage events seem to have moved inside; the Capell–Garrick text sets Antony indoors between battle scenes ("*A room in the palace*") and wherever else possible' (*Antony and Cleopatra*, p. 46). The Folio text is, of course, location-unspecific, in keeping with the staging conventions of the time, and in most cases Capell's indicated 'locations' for scenes correspond to the ones invented by those modern editors who still feel obliged to provide them; but Capell's indications of location point to one effect of the introduction of moveable painted scenery. Garrick's battle scenes were spectacularly swelled with supernumeraries recruited 'in the streets and alleys about Drury Lane',[77] and perhaps wearing their street clothes on stage. Their numbers represented the extent of the political stakes; their presence must have countered any sense of domestication deriving from the curtailment of the political scenes.

74 See the quotations in Stone, 'Garrick's Presentation', p. 33. In more recent times Harley Granville-Barker claimed in the *Preface* to *Antony and Cleopatra* that actors are 'the sole interpreters Shakespeare has licensed'.

75 John Genest (*English Stage*, vol. IV, p. 544) claims the reduction of characters 'was done without any regard to propriety' and complains about the number of lines given to Thyreus; this may have been due to the influence of Sedley, in making much of the Thidias episode in his play.

76 See Martin Holmes, *Shakespeare and Burbage*, pp. 191–2.

77 Kalman Burnim, *David Garrick, Director*, p. 32.

Garrick had apparently been attracted to *Antony and Cleopatra* as a vehicle for 'spectacle and pageantry (currently much in vogue at Drury Lane and Covent Garden)'[78] and because it had novelty value as an unrevived Shakespeare play. The production played to packed houses, and the Prince of Wales attended twice, but, according to the prompter Richard Cross, the play 'tho' all new dress'd & had fine scenes did not seem to give ye audience any great Pleasure, or draw any applause' (*Diary*, 3 January 1759). Garrick had had 'new Roman Shapes' made up especially for the play (*Letters*, p. 284), and William Winter comments that he 'presented it with rich scenic embellishment and gave more than the usual attention to correctness of costume . . . he dressed the players in Roman garments, except that the necks of his Romans were clothed with black stocks, according to long-established stage custom' (*Shakespeare*, p. 435). The actors wearing Roman costumes were probably, as on the Jacobean stage, those playing principal male characters; what contemporary illustrative evidence there is suggests that Cleopatra (and presumably Octavia) wore modified contemporary dress, as did attendants.[79] In Garrick's pageant for the Shakespeare Jubilee of 1769, the male Egyptian attendants, including the eunuchs (who wear long 'oriental' robes with their fans, and two of whom hold honorific umbrellas over the protagonists), are blacked up and turbanned.

Garrick hinted at his own miscasting as Antony when he wrote to George Steevens, the Shakespearean editor, that the play 'gain'd ground Every time it was play'd, but I grew tir'd & gave it up – the part was laborious'.[80] Garrick's tiredness probably corresponded with his illness during the latter part of the run (Cross, *Diary*, 18 January 1759), but his efforts as Antony were not widely appreciated. His 'easy and familiar, yet forcible' delivery (Davies, *Garrick*, vol. I, p. 40) might, by modern audiences, be thought appropriate to the role. It was opposed stylistically to the older declamatory style and traded upon volatility, especially the rapid transition from one emotion to another. But contemporaries seem to have regarded Garrick's small stature as a drawback in this particular part, and he 'disliked' Roman costume because it did not flatter his 'slight' figure (Winter, *Shakespeare*, p. 435). Thomas Davies said Garrick was not 'sufficiently important and commanding' for a play with so much action: 'the actor who is obliged continu-

---

78 David Bevington, Introduction to his edition, p. 48.
79 See, e.g., Mrs Yates in *All for Love*, 1768, illustrated in Bevington's edition, p. 49 and the 1770 engraving of the Jubilee pageant, illustrated in Lamb, *Antony and Cleopatra*, p. 48.
80 Undated letter, *c*.1770, in the Folger Library, quoted in Lamb, *Antony and Cleopatra*, p. 45.

ally to traverse the stage, should from person attract respect as well as from the power of speech'. What Davies implies is that the role was unsuitable for Garrick to the extent that it had 'more dignity of action than variety of passion' (*Dramatic Miscellanies*, vol. II, p. 240).

One constant in the stage history of *Antony and Cleopatra* from this point onwards is the exceptional difficulty for a theatre manager or director of the task of finding the right actress for the role of Cleopatra. Mary Ann Yates had been paid to retire by Thomas Sheridan seven years earlier, after an unsuccessful debut in *Henry VIII*, but by the beginning of 1759 (when she was 30) she had come on well at Drury Lane. Boaden said she 'courted a likeness to the statues of antiquity in the solemn composure of her attitudes' (*Kemble*, vol. I, p. 353); her grave demeanour was undoubtedly an asset in the final scene, but Davies thought her 'fine figure and pleasing manner of speaking' were also 'well adapted to the enchanting Cleopatra' (*Dramatic Miscellanies*, vol. II, p. 240). John Hill, the (presumed) author of *A letter to the Hon. Author of the New Farce, called The Rout*, judged her 'an inferior CLEOPATRA to Mrs. Woffington' in *All for Love*, but conceded she had 'sufficient powers to procure her applause' (*A letter*, p. 39). Mrs Yates may have been more imposing than her Antony: John Taylor, speaking generally of her stage presence, told John Campbell she was 'the most commanding person he had ever looked upon before he saw Mrs Siddons' (*Dictionary of National Biography*). As Cleopatra in *All for Love* seven years later, 'her haughty features and powerful voice carried her well through rage and disdain' (quoted in Winter, *Shakespeare*, p. 436); since the Garrick–Capell text retained the Folio's striking, haling and dagger-drawing, it is likely that her playing in the messenger scene was one of the highlights in 1759. The text allowed her to capitalise on it, not only by including the follow-up scene with the messenger, but also by letting her launch herself at Seleucus.

Garrick's revival failed chiefly because of persistent, though more subdued, antagonism to the play's idiom. Hill, for example, commended the production values of 'scenery, dresses, and parade' because they not only rescued *Antony and Cleopatra* 'from the closet' but also diverted 'attention from the poet' (*A letter*, p. 39). The Garrick–Capell text punctuates the lines in accordance with the notion of rhetorical balance prevalent in the age, and occasionally it adds or reorders words to make up a pentameter or regularise the metre.[81] But, in choosing to revive *All for Love*, with Mrs Yates as Cleopatra (and William Powell as Antony), in 1766 and again in

---

81 E.g, at 5.1.15 'A greater crack' becomes 'A greater crack in nature' and at 5.2.297 'Come, thou mortal wretch' becomes 'Come, mortal wretch'.

1772 (with Spranger and Ann Barry in the leading roles), Garrick apparently submitted to Hill's verdict that Dryden's 'soft flowing numbers' were 'more sympathetic to the tender passion'.

'A salad of Shakespeare and Dryden': Kemble and Macready

The next two productions of *Antony and Cleopatra* used texts that combined Shakespeare's with Dryden's. The first of these hybrids was John Philip Kemble's at Covent Garden in 1813, with Charles M. Young and Harriet Faucit in the title roles. Its text is generally thought to have been arranged by Kemble himself;[82] it was what Lord Byron called 'A salad of Shakespeare and Dryden'.[83] The 'Advertisement' prefacing the printed edition dresses the salad in these terms:

> Shakespeare's Play has been, already, altered, abridged, &c. &c. – but it has stood the test of modern times less than many of our great Bard's revived dramas, which are, now, kept before the Spectators, from year to year: – Something has been wanting to render it what is termed a *Stock* Play: – *Dryden's* Play has been long upon the shelf; nor does it appear suited to the present taste, without much departure from the original; but there is much to be admired in both the Plays.

Whether Kemble, in his desire to rehabilitate *Antony and Cleopatra*, had originally intended to do it with Dryden's help is another matter. A manuscript[84] which appears to have been prepared by him but never performed, abridges Shakespeare's text with fewer characters and some transpositions, in the manner of Garrick's version. Herschel Baker claims that '*Antony and Cleopatra* had always been one of [Kemble's] favourites, and only Mrs Siddons' refusing to play in it had deterred him from bringing it forward long before' (*Kemble*, p. 323). Her refusal is presumably also the reason why Kemble did not take the part of Antony himself, despite having been a famous Coriolanus.

The 1813 text, as well as adding many whole passages from *All for Love*, follows Dryden's precedent in omitting the characters of Pompey (so losing the galley scene, usually a theatrical highlight), the Soothsayer and the Clown (Charmion, as she is spelt, is sent to fetch the basket of figs); the

---

82 Though H. Neville Davies (in his Introduction to the facsimile edition of the printed edition of 1813) suggests that it may have been prepared by George Colman; Kemble wrote some minor alterations and additional stage business in a copy of the printed text now in the Shakespeare Centre Library.

83 Letter to John Murray, 16 November 1813 (*'Alas! the Love of Women!'*, vol. III, p. 207).   84 Dated about 1800, in the Folger Library.

'supernatural' scene is omitted, and so is Enobarbus's desertion; the suiciding Eros is replaced by Ventidius, the hauling of Antony is avoided, and Cleopatra never meets Caesar. Cleopatra's lack of security-consciousness at her monument, which removes a major staging difficulty, is one of many 'dignifying' modifications which simplify her character: in the messenger scene she uses one phrase of the original verbal violence but none of the physical. Her death-scene is much abbreviated, and almost subsumed by a spectacle with choral backing, the 'grand funeral procession' whose prime focus is on the corpse of Antony (1813 printed edition, pp. 82–4). Liberties are also taken with Shakespeare's language, including the bowdlerisation already practised by Garrick; in Kemble's 4.3, which turns into Dryden's 3.1, some of Shakespeare's 'barge' speech is recycled, in a manner that amazed George Odell: 'Antony (O these star actors!) delivers to Dolabella, Enobarbus's splendid description of Cleopatra on the barge; or, to be perfectly fair, he delivers the first half of Shakespeare's and the second (and worse) half of Dryden's. Could anything be more equitable?' (*Shakespeare*, vol. II, p. 68)

Mrs Siddons may not have been entirely absent from the 1813 production, in the sense that Kemble was probably drawing on his experience at Drury Lane in 1788, when he and his sister starred in *All for Love*, a production 'noteworthy for its attention to historical accuracy in its depiction of ancient Rome and Egypt' (Bevington, Introduction to his New Cambridge edition, p. 50). Kemble had antiquarian interests, but his emphasis on Egyptian scene-setting in 1813 doubtless owed much to the outbreak of Egyptomania sparked by Napoleon's Egyptian campaigns and their accompanying archaeological discoveries, disseminated by Dominique-Vivant Denon's *Voyages dans la Basse et Haute Egypte*, published in 1802. Politically, Egypt was implanted in the British consciousness by the Battle of the Nile; culturally, by Thomas Hope's influence on interior decoration and (for a broader cross-section of society) by the opening of the Egyptian Hall. Built in 1811–12 in Piccadilly by the antiquarian William Bullock, the Hall was the first London building in 'Egyptian' style and offered some 15,000 objects to view.

There was in any case, as Lamb suggests (*Antony and Cleopatra*, pp. 52–3), a pressing reason for Kemble to emphasise spectacle at the expense of poet, as Garrick did: the vast size of the rebuilt theatres at Covent Garden and Drury Lane, and the increased competition after 1807. The size of the new Covent Garden not only created problems for the actors, in terms of projection difficulties and the need for larger gestures and coarser acting styles; it also caused (as Baker points out in *Kemble*, pp. 295–305) resentment among many of the patrons, which culminated in the 'Old

Prices' riots of 1809 that forced Kemble to restore the shilling gallery.
Particular sources of complaint were the higher admission charges and the
increased number of private boxes, which were seen as encouraging the
presence of more prostitutes and kept women. Some malcontents may have
seen a production of *Antony and Cleopatra*, however Drydenised, as a challenge to public morality and order: after all, in the Prologue to *All for Love*
(*Works*, vol. xiii, ed. Novak, pp. 14–15) Antony is described, perhaps not
entirely ironically, as 'a Pattern, and Companion fit, / For all the keeping
Tonyes of the Pit'.

For those members of the audience interested in what was happening on
stage, the quality of the acting in *Antony and Cleopatra* seems not to have
been the main attraction. The *Examiner*'s critic found Harriet Faucit
'pretty and genteel'; with 'her monotonous voice and uniform manner', she
lacked majesty and variety (5 December 1813). Genest thought the play
'ought not to have been brought forward without a first rate actress in
Cleopatra – Mrs Siddons would have made a glorious part of Cleopatra
(supposing the part not to have been mutilated) and perhaps have fixed the
play in the favour of the public' (*English Stage*, vol. viii, p. 419). Given the
cultural problem acknowledged in Mrs Siddons's refusal to play the part,
the part's mutilation and the fact that Faucit was not a 'first rate' actress, it
is hardly surprising that her performance was 'genteel', in keeping with the
nature of the text and of the production. William Hazlitt, however, saw in
Faucit's performance something he thought should not have been there,
'the affected levity of a modern fine lady' (*Morning Chronicle*, 16 November
1813). It probably sprang as much from the hybrid nature of the text as
from Faucit's inadequacy: 'levity' suggests that she had not caught the
Drydenising spirit of tragic dignity, despite the simplification of her part;
its 'affectation' indicates the strained nature of her attempt at
Shakespearean variety, however finite the text had rendered it.

Hazlitt's estimation of Young's 'just and impressive' Antony was shared
by the *Examiner*'s reviewer, who singled out the 'equable beauty' of Young's
acting, although it lacked Kemble's 'faculty of sometimes electrifying the
audience with enthusiasm'. The same reviewer airily dismissed the rest of
the company as 'hardly worth a line', but went on to give dishonourable
mentions to William Abbot as Octavius, who 'converted the deliberate hyp-
ocrite into a noisy blusterer', and Crumpton and Creswell for playing
Maecenas and Agrippa 'in so ludicrous a style of burlesque', apparently
designed to caricature the government's 'great managers'. The satirical
allusions, according to Hazlitt, were 'eagerly seized by the audience'.

Members of the audience who had taken the play-bills at face value may
have been less disappointed. The bills promised 'entirely new' Egyptian

1 Mrs Faucit as Cleopatra (mocking at Antony in 1.3.83–5) in Kemble's 1813 Covent Garden production. Engraving of 1814.

decor and costume and gave prominence to 'the sea fight at Actium' and 'the grand funeral of Antony and Cleopatra with an epicedium'. The Folger manuscript of the uninterpolated and unstaged *Antony and Cleopatra* has wishful descriptions of scenery that presumably indicate what Kemble had in mind at the time, though the scenery used in the production of 1813 may have been as different as the text (the printed text gives no details of decor). In the manuscript the intended decoration of Cleopatra's palace is eclectic in a manner suggestive of the Ptolemaic period; the stage is to be 'open as far back as possible', allowing a perspectival view of ships, monuments including 'Cleopatra's obelisk' and three statues. Kemble notes what were apparently his intended sources for the palace's decoration: 'Norden's Antiquities of Egypt, Montfaucon, Mr Knight's Antiques'. The first two were books,[85] but the latter was presumably Richard Payne Knight's museum room in his Soho Square house, many of whose ancient bronzes, coins and gems are now in the British Museum. The manuscript stipulates that 'the house of Caesar' should be 'as modest as possible', its three statues contrasting with those in Cleopatra's palace; by contrast with both the other dwellings, 'the house of Lepidus' is 'gawdy, superfluously gilded, &c'. In 1813 Kemble's novel attention to Egyptian costume, to which the Jameson prints attest, may have been influenced by the publication in the previous year of an enlarged edition of Hope's *Costumes of the Ancients*.[86] Kemble's Egyptian costumes were no token affair like Garrick's Egyptian attendants' outfits, but once again male costume seems to have been more elaborately 'authentic' than female, Cleopatra's and Charmian's costumes resembling the neo-classical dresses then fashionable, with the addition of Egyptianising accessories.

The sea fight and the grand funeral received their harshest notice from the *Times* critic, who saw 'unwieldy and unpicturesque confusion' in the former, and found Bishop's epicedium 'feeble', despite the eight-part choir with forty-five listed singers.[87] He did like the staging of the funeral, but objected to the 'narrow, gaudy' biers provided for the lovers (16 November 1813). Otherwise these two expensive interpolations seemed to have been accepted as the highlights by both the satisfied and the severe critics: that is, on their own terms by those who found the production 'such an object of attraction' and as representatives of 'the magnificent raree-show so usual at this Theatre' by those who did not (*Examiner*). Given that the text was a 'miserable and inconsistent . . . piece of patchwork', the success of the production was 'rather due to the scenery than to the merits of the piece as it is now performed' (*Scourge*, 1 December 1813). This could be read as a comment either on the times – 'spectacle is the order of the day: the intel-

---

85 Bernard de Montfaucon's *L'Antiquité expliquée et représentée en figures*, 10 vols., Paris, 1719–24 and Frederick L. Norden's *Travels in Egypt and Nubia*, London, 1741, 1757, 1795.

86 As Holmes suggests in 'A Regency Cleopatra', pp. 46–7. One of the Jameson prints is illustrated in Lamb, *Antony and Cleopatra*, p. 55.

87 Other new music – overture, marches, act symphonies – had been provided by William Henry Ware.

lect yields precedence to the eye, and to painting, and the contrivances of machinery; truth and taste, and sentiment, are the melancholy sacrifice' (*Theatrical Inquisitor*, December 1813) – or on the theatre's managers, who 'regale us now and then . . . with a fragment of Shakespeare; they strip it indeed of many of its chief beauties, but then to make amends, they supply its mutilations by gorgeous ornament and pompous shews . . . *Antony and Cleopatra* is acted for the sake of the sea-fight and the funeral procession' (*Examiner*, 19 December 1813). A single critic blamed Shakespeare, in terms that recall Davies's comment on the unsuitability of the play for Garrick's talents: 'This Drama possesses a continued hurry of action, and engages attention by a succession of incidents and scenes, in which there is more bustle than business, and more pomp than nature' (*Bell's Weekly Messenger*, 21 November 1813). Like Garrick's production, Kemble's seems to have begun to capture the audience's interest and appreciation and then to have lost momentum, perhaps partly because the acting was less impressive than the spectacle and, in this case, perhaps partly because a number of reviewers forcibly expressed their opinion that a Shakespeare production should offer more than spectacle. Kemble's production ran for half as long again as Garrick's, and still amounted to only nine performances.

William Charles Macready's production at Drury Lane in 1833, which featured Macready and Louisa Anne Phillips in the main roles, was hastily thrown together (unlike Garrick's and Kemble's) and seems to have run for only half as long as Garrick's. At the time of this production, Macready was under contract to Alfred Bunn, who was managing both Covent Garden and Drury Lane in difficult financial circumstances, operating both theatres with a single company. In the run-up to the production, Macready was concerned about his salary,[88] and in staging *Antony and Cleopatra* Bunn took cost-cutting measures, including recycling costumes and properties: 'nothing was allowed to be new but a cloak' (Macready, *Diaries*, vol. I, p. 79). The reviewers could hardly fail to notice; the *Athenaeum* critic commented on old friends among the costumes and said 'nearly all' 'the better properties' were '"neat as imported" from Covent Garden' (23 November 1833). Relations were strained between Macready and Bunn, who believed the British public liked only the 'extraneous excitement' of theatre; the *Theatrical Times* (I (1846), p. 51) called him 'the presiding genius of dramatic humbug, the great incarnation of managerial quackery'.[89] Macready wrote of 'the incompetency of Mr Bunn from his ignorance of the art he has to deal with' (*Diaries*, vol. I, p. 69) and may have been less surprised than

88 See Downer, *The Eminent Tragedian*, p. 131.   89 *Ibid.*, p. 129.

dismayed when he arrived at the theatre on 19 November: 'Went to rehearsal of *Antony*, which was in a very backward state, and mounted with very inappropriate scenery, though beautifully painted by Stanfield' (*Diaries*, vol. 1, p. 79).

The text in the manuscript promptbook[90] contains seventeen scenes, with a particularly heavy admixture of Dryden in the fourth and fifth acts, a good deal of rewriting and transposition throughout (Enobarbus delivers the barge speech early in the first scene, shortly before the first entrance of the lovers), and the expected bowdlerising ('the grossnesses are all excluded' (*Atlas*, 24 November 1833)). By contrast with Kemble's, this version keeps Eros (giving Ventidius's lines to him in Dryden passages), Enobarbus and Pompey (though it cuts 2.1 and, whilst keeping a galley scene, cuts all the revelry!). Like Kemble's production, it curtails the violence in the messenger scene, and like Kemble and following Dryden, it omits the Soothsayer, the Clown, the 'supernatural' scene and the meeting of Caesar and Cleopatra, and avoids the hauling of Antony (following Dryden more closely than Kemble does). At the end, Iras brings in the basket, and, as in Kemble, Cleopatra loses lines along with her life, though she is not upstaged in the same way by the funeral: when Caesar orders 'great solemnity', the play merely ends with '*Dead march*', as Shakespeare might have expected. Reviewers were not disturbed by the changes to the text, and the *Athenaeum*'s verdict typifies contemporary opinion: 'in these times [the play] could not be represented in the state in which it is handed down to us; and, indeed, many times it would require, previously to representation, an experienced and judicious hand to reject its undramatic parts and not mar the most dramatic'. The critics' responses to the acting were less accommodating.

The production was manifestly under-rehearsed and 'the general effect was that which we suppose would be produced if a company of performers, strange to each other, were suddenly brought together without rehearsal', hissed the *Atlas*. Octavius seemed for once to be at a loss for words: King carried a copy of the play, and had 'to apply to it often to be able to repeat the text' (*Morning Post*, 22 November 1833). As Enobarbus, Cooper was 'too swaggering', conveying not 'roughness' but 'the bluntness of the bully' (*Morning Chronicle*, 22 November 1833). Macready had been compelled by Bunn to appear as Antony, despite his resistance and his feeling unwell

---

90 Cumberland's Acting Edition of about 1833, which claims to be 'printed from the acting copy', contains no Dryden and omits scenes mentioned by reviewers; it seems safe to conclude that the manuscript prompt copy more nearly represents the text of the production.

before the opening night. He had given serious attention to the play earlier that year,[91] and had performed the part of Antony once at Newcastle;[92] he conned his lines more conscientiously than King, but his *Diaries* suggest that, like Garrick, he found the role 'laborious' and ineffective. He judged his own performance as below par: 'I . . . was raw, efforty, and uncertain in the scenes of passion, but had just taken precaution enough to make my pauses, although not to make use of them' (21 November 1833; *Diaries*, vol. I, p. 80). Macready's pausing to suggest mental or emotional process was not universally admired, and the *Athenaeum* reviewer blessed the curtailing of his habit: 'his whole soul seemed to be in the part, and there was a total absence of stage trick'. The *Morning Post*, declaring that a plausible Antony must be 'in face and figure the *beau idéal* of manly beauty', considered him badly cast in physical terms: 'it was not that Mr Macready did not appreciate the character, or that he lacked any perception of its beauties, but he had not the power to execute the conception'.

The *Morning Chronicle* reviewer lamented the inability of even a good-looking Cleopatra to compensate for the perceived staging problems of the play, which 'drags terribly in the representation, and the shifting of scene so often in the course of a single act, without the explanations that used to accompany such rapid changes, make[s] the whole story hardly intelligible'. The critic from the *Athenaeum* fancied that a ravishing Cleopatra such 'as it would almost amount to weakness to pray for' might alleviate the play's intrinsic heaviness, but none of the reviewers found inspiration, except perhaps to prayer, in Miss Phillips. Her action was 'angular', but she 'played Cleopatra considerably better than she looked it': despite applying an 'artificial brown to her complexion', she 'was still much too fair, especially when contrasted with her mulatto attendants' (*Morning Chronicle*). She was perhaps the first female Cleopatra to wear brown make-up; in keeping with the nineteenth-century antiquarian pictorial mode, her complexion was on the Mediterranean (perhaps the Ptolemaic) side, if not exactly Shakespeare's 'tawny'. Phillips's Cleopatra was slated by the *Atlas* as

> flurried and nervous, and consequently boisterous and oppressive . . . The unbridled passions turned mere termagant on her hands – the changeling

91 The promptbook manuscript, in Macready's hand, is dated 13 July 1833.
92 A little earlier than Kemble's production (9 April 1813), though 'with little effect, for Antony, the voluptuary and doting spoilt child of Fortune, was not within the compass of a tyro, as I then was' (quoted in Winter, *Shakespeare*, p. 448); his Cleopatra was Miss Sulivan, whom, in an anonymous note pinned to the box-entrance door, he was accused of kicking (see J. C. Trewin, *Mr Macready*, pp. 32–3).

moods were ducks of the head, and whimpers of the eyes – the prodigal love and luxurious tastes were mere fondlings and a blaze of rouge. She carried passion to an extremity that rendered it ludicrous, and tossed and flaunted until Egypt's Queen – the haughty, the loving, the beautiful – was quite sunk in an actress who had literally got out of her depth.

Given the limits of her acting ability, it is not surprising that Phillips lacked buoyancy in waters as culturally dangerous as they are theatrically deep. Like Faucit, she responded nervously to the Shakespearean requirement of variety, despite its modification in the acting text. The 'boisterous' nature of her response was at the opposite extreme from Faucit's, and it is tempting to think that this was partly a reaction to the failure of Faucit's gentility, but this is unlikely after a twenty-year gap.[93] Like many of her successors', Phillips's performance improved at its close, and 'her last scene, after the death of Antony, was extremely beautiful. She was here impassioned, lofty, dignified.' Macready was also praised for his dying fall: 'The bitter feelings which assail Antony after his disgraceful flight were vividly portrayed. His last scene, where the news of Cleopatra's death wholly disgusts him with existence, was pathetic in a very high degree' (*Times*, 22 November 1833). The high points of Macready's and Phillips's acting were at least in passages that were largely Shakespeare.

What was well received was the only element of the production wholly prepared for the occasion, the scenes painted by Clarkson Stanfield,[94] marine artist and prominent scene-painter in the new style, notable for 'the bold broad effects it introduced and the impact these had under the new gaslight, which from 1817 concentrated unprecedented brilliance and public interest on the scenes'.[95] Public enthusiasm for Stanfield's Egyptian scenery was presumably fired by the fashion for Egypt, which may, in turn, have influenced Bunn's determination to stage the play. Egypt had certainly remained in the public eye since Kemble's production. The colourful explorer Giovanni Battista Belzoni's excavations of ancient tombs and sites from 1816 to 1819, funded by the British Consul-General, Henry Salt,

---

93 When Glyn played the part sixteen years after Phillips, she seems to have been unhampered by any sense of precedent, and to have faced the challenge boldly, unlike the less gifted Faucit, whose only actress-predecessor was Mrs Yates in 1759. Glyn, of course, was performing a different kind of text from her predecessor, as was Faucit.

94 The *Atlas* reviewer commented on the 'grandeur' of 'the magnificent palace of Cleopatra, the vast and sublime scenery of Egypt, with its solemn pyramids and temples, its idols and sleepy sphynxes, the promontory of Actium gliding into the sea, and the drowsy atmosphere that falls upon the whole' (24 November 1833).

95 Pieter van der Merwe, 'Roberts and the Theatre', p. 32.

resulted in the shipping of memorable objects to the British Museum, including the colossal granite bust of Rameses II from Thebes and the alabaster sarcophagus from the grotto-sepulchre of Seti I. The latter was rejected by the Museum as too expensive[96] and bought by Sir John Soane in 1824 for his private museum, which he gave to the nation in 1833.[97] Belzoni, on his return to England in 1820, exhibited many of his discoveries at the Egyptian Hall, and in the same year published his *Narrative of the Operations and Recent Discoveries*, together with his wife Sara's *Trifling Account of the Women of Egypt, Nubia and Syria*. Enthusiasm for Egypt was also stimulated by the excitement surrounding the deciphering of the hieroglyphs in 1822, to which the British explorer Sir John Gardner Wilkinson made a contribution.

Yet, as reviewers noted, 'the pleasure of scenic correctness' was 'curtailed by the carelessness of the stage appointments'. Cleopatra's robe was 'tarnished', her attendants were 'commonplace', the properties failed to suggest Egyptian extravagance, and the opposing armies were not properly distinguished (*Atlas*). Nor could the grandly composed processions counter the impression of a makeshift production. In these circumstances it is not surprising that it was 'indifferently received by an indifferent house' (*Morning Chronicle*). Like Garrick's and Kemble's failures, Macready's had some importance in the sparse early stage history of the play. Odell's view was that after Kemble's departure public taste was 'ever more and more desirous of novelty, of show, spectacle, dancing and clowning' (*Shakespeare*, vol. II, p. 117) and that in the fifteen years before Macready's production 'Shakespeare's plays . . . were relegated more and more to the background in public and managerial esteem' (p. 124). The significance of the 1833 production of a Shakespeare play that was never 'stock' lies partly in its having happened at all under such conditions; but it can also be seen as paving the way, if only in terms of a tradition of spectacular (and cut-and-pasted) productions beginning with Garrick. It is largely a question of hinted potential, which, particularly in spectacle-loving times, can have a 'snowballing' effect that proceeds from habituation of audiences to both theatrical effects and the more memorable passages of the play itself. Stanfield's scenery

96 Salt had trouble getting the Museum to buy the antiquities found and shipped by Belzoni because the trustees and other influential men did not consider Egyptian antiquities 'fine art' like those of Greece and Rome: see Edward Miller, *That Noble Cabinet*, p. 199.

97 Soane started to collect antiquities soon after becoming professor of architecture at the RA in 1806, the collection being partly for the benefit of his own and other students; it was catalogued in 1827 and (by Soane himself) in 1830.

contributed to an appreciation of the potential of Egyptian spectacle, if in a broader and more decorative manner than Kemble's archaeologically based costumes and (presumably) scenery.

Victorian undulation and education: Miss Glyn and her audiences

A curious feature of Victorian stage history is the incidence of burlesques, farces and travesties of Shakespeare.[98] These versions represent one extreme in the general effort to locate Shakespeare's drama-as-entertainment amid prevailing notions of 'high' and 'low' culture, and to profit by it in more than one sense. At the other extreme, Miss Glyn had a major role to play, as will be seen. But even at the travesty end of the market *Antony and Cleopatra* is an interesting case. A farcical version of the story did not appear in London until nine years after Macready's production, and in both New York and Sydney, burlesque versions preceded the first production of Shakespeare's play.[99] Whilst these 'low' versions may glance at the fancy for toga plays in 'high' circles, they clearly have little to do with Shakespeare as such – but they are oblique expressions of period attitudes to the story in relation to the norms of repressed sexuality and expressed imperialism. Victorian productions of Shakespeare's play negotiated these attitudes largely by resort to spectacle, and the respectability of its ostensible historical interest and educational value, though Isabella Glyn is so important because the power and intensity of her performances derived from an attempt to cover the full range of the role, including the sexual implications of the 'undulations of the Eastern form'.

The first *Antony and Cleopatra* of the period was also the first American

98 There were, of course, precedents for the mode of such entertainments in Elizabethan jigs and in eighteenth-century afterpieces.

99 In London Charles Selby's farce was performed in 1842, and followed later by a sequel; Francis Burnand's two burlesques were produced in 1866 and 1873, and a travesty by W. Sapte Jr was performed in 1891 (see William Davenport Adams, '*Antony and Cleopatra*', p. 271 and *A Book of Burlesque*, p. 145). A burlesque by J. M. Field was performed in New York and Philadelphia for at least fifty years from its first performance in New York in 1843 (see C. B. Young's stage history in John Dover Wilson's New Shakespeare edition). Farcical or burlesque versions were also performed in New York in 1846, 1859 and 1889, years when Shakespeare's play was produced there (see T. Allston Brown, *New York Stage*, vol. I, p. 174, vol. II, p. 136 and George Odell, *New York Stage*, vol. XIV, p. 362). Selby's farce was performed at the Royal Olympic Theatre, Launceston, for the first time 'in the colony' on 24 May 1847 (playbill); at the Royal Victoria Theatre, Sydney, in 1855 and 1856 the notorious Lola Montez was Cleopatra to F. Folland's Antony in what is called a 'farce' and later a 'comedietta' (*Sydney Morning Herald*, 29 August 1855 and 7 January 1856).

production of the play, in New Orleans in 1838, with William Hield and English actress Ellen Tree in the title roles. Tree was enjoying great popularity in America at the time, but she is unlikely to have been convincing in the part.[100] New Yorkers did not see the play until 1846, when Edmund Simpson offered it at the Park Theatre. His Cleopatra was Harriet Bland, *née* Faucit, a daughter of Kemble's Cleopatra; the Antony, George Vandenhoff, was also English-born, and the Enobarbus was Humphrey Bland. Like Garrick's production, it ran for only six performances despite expensive scenery and costumes and competent acting. Vandenhoff 'warm[ed] up into a naturally impassioned style' and Mrs Bland 'rose to a high degree of impassioned excellence' (*Albion*, 2 May 1846, quoted in Odell, *New York Stage*, vol. v, p. 182).

Samuel Phelps opened his production – equally expensive, well dressed and competently acted – at Sadler's Wells in 1849. He himself played Antony, and Macready may partly have had this production (widely regarded as Phelps's best) in mind when, on his retirement in 1851, he endorsed Phelps's efforts to continue serious Shakespearean production.[101] Phelps's *Antony and Cleopatra* set a new record of twenty-two performances, running to crowded houses long enough to recover expenses. The production was important not only because it starred Isabella Glyn, the first actress to become famous for the role (it remained her best), but also because it demonstrated the actability (and financial viability) of an all-Shakespeare text (albeit cut, in ways not dissimilar to Garrick's) in the nineteenth-century theatre, in a way that ensured that the play was never again Drydenised as a matter of course.

The text used by Phelps[102] reduced the number of scenes, to lessen the demands on the scene-shifters on the small, under-equipped Sadlers Wells stage.[103] The production used wings that could be changed in front of the audience, but scene-changing was in any case a noisy business: 'when the shrill whistle of the prompter rang through the house as the signal for the shifting of each pair of flats, frequent changes of scene were much more

---

100 Charles H. Shattuck describes her style as 'impeccably pure and decorous in the proper Victorian manner' (*Shakespeare on the American Stage*, vol. 1, p. 105), though she did sometimes play male roles, including Romeo.

101 See Downer, *The Eminent Tragedian*, pp. 4 and 339. Phelps had alternated Othello and Iago with Macready, among other shared acting experiences.

102 The promptbook is in the Folger Library.

103 See Odell, *Shakespeare*, vol. 11, p. 275. Odell also notes that the texts in *The Complete Works of Shakespeare*, supposedly edited by Phelps and published in 1854, are not acting versions, and reports Coleman's claim that the editing was in fact done by E. L. Blanchard.

likely to be distracting than delighting'.[104] A number of whole scenes were cut, including the first three in Act 3 – 'the historical vicissitudes being here too rapidly and closely followed' (*Examiner*, 27 October 1849) – and the first three in Act 4. Many passages were bowdlerised, and some speeches reassigned (to reduce the number of characters); the Seleucus episode was omitted and, like Kemble and Macready, Phelps used scene changes to avoid the difficulties of lifting Antony and scaling the monument.[105] As in Macready's production, the play ended with a '*Solemn March*', but before '*gradually sink[ing] on Couch and d[ying]*', Isabella Glyn went to the front of the stage, smiling rapturously at the thought of reuniting with Antony, to apply the asp to her bosom and foreground her royal death. The lovers' first entrance was preceded by eighteen dancers (dancers accompanied the protagonists in Macready's production), and their entry was swelled by many extras, including '*8 Egyptian guards with idols*'. The revelry in the galley scene was played up and the *Times* reviewer thought it 'one of the most striking scenes of the play' (24 October 1849); although in Garrick's production the song to Bacchus was expanded 'in Rehearsal' (printed edition), this was probably the first time critics (as opposed to audiences) regarded the galley scene as one of the play's more memorable episodes.

In the promptbook many of Cleopatra's 'oriental' and amorous fascinations are choreographed in a style that might be called modern: 1.3 opens with '*Cleopatra making a Salaam as she Enters*' and when she says 'I am sick and sullen', she '*affects to fall into the arms of Charmian*'; in the following dialogue with Antony, the directions are: '*holding him off*', '*going to him*', '*throws herself into his arms*', '*gets from him to RC*'. Glyn had been a pupil of Charles Kemble, Sarah Siddons's youngest brother, and John Coleman said of her Cleopatra in a production 'on a scale of great splendour' at Newcastle about 1854, in which he played Antony: 'Accurately parroted in the archaistic methods of Mrs Siddons, many of Isabella's performances were intelligent, picturesque, and even striking. I have not seen . . . so good a Cleopatra' (quoted in Winter, *Shakespeare*, p. 449). It may be that the detailed directions in the Phelps promptbook (most of them are for Cleopatra) helped Glyn to become 'animated by a new fire . . . The formality of gesture is not quite subdued, but it resolves itself into some very effective *poses* in the scenes of queenly distress' (*Times*). Her animation may have been nurtured as much by the absence of intimidating antecedent as by guidance; neither Glyn nor her reviewers were burdened by notable past success, let alone a

104 *Daily Telegraph*, 22 September 1873, referring to earlier productions of about this period.
105 At Sadler's Wells, where the majority of the audience sat in the pit, their sight-lines had to be taken into account. See Shirley S. Allen, *Samuel Phelps*, p. 241.

tradition of Cleopatras.[106] The reviewer for the *Illustrated London News* thought the nature of both protagonists' parts helped free their acting styles (something similar had been implied of Macready's Antony, though circumstances also dictated his approach):

> Such characters as these break up a performer's mannerisms, and do him accordingly infinite good. A similar effect was produced on Miss Glyn. In this almost impossible character of Cleopatra she put forth new energies, and exhibited a versatility of power which surprised those most acquainted with her style and the scope of her genius. She dared at once at that 'infinite variety' . . . She combined grace and dignity . . . Georgeous in person, in costume, and in her style of action, she moved . . . according to the situation and sentiment to be rendered. Withal she was classical, and her *poses* severely statuesque. Altogether, Miss Glyn's performance . . . is the most superb thing ever witnessed on the modern stage.   (27 October 1849)

Glyn had met the challenges, as much cultural as aesthetic, of the part. Though she acted under her mother's maiden name and was known to the divorce court, she made Cleopatra acceptable on the Victorian stage: she poeticised passion by articulating it in delivery and gracefully emotive gesture or small-scale action; as in the case of Mrs Yates, her 'statuesque' 'poses' lent classical authority, and thereby assurances of nobility, to the part.

Glyn's success was in some measure due to mastery of the displacement of passion into more oblique forms: her most admired scenes were those with the messenger and the asp. The physical violence of the first messenger scene was perceived (especially by managers and reviewers) to be problematical for actresses. Mrs Yates had been allowed the violence of the Folio's stage directions in 1759, but nineteenth-century inhibitions ensured their deletion in this production, as in Kemble's and Macready's, and restricted Cleopatra to one blow and a drawn dagger in 1866 and 1867. Despite this censorship of physical action, Glyn made the scene memorably passionate (though some took her to be practising 'oriental cruelty'),[107] and set the pattern for later Victorian productions – in which the Folio violence was reinstated, and the drubbing of the messenger became an outlet for sexual frustration – and for modern renditions, which tend to be more comfortable with female violence and its contemporary manifestations, invocation of the mid-life crisis notwithstanding. Despite the suppression of Cleopatra's physical violence in the messenger scene, the *Times* critic thought Glyn's rage 'bordered perhaps on extravagance'; the *Spectator*'s

---

106 This is explicitly stated in a *Times* review of Chatterton's production (22 September 1873), quoted later in the text.   107 See *Spectator*, 27 October 1849.

went as far as to see it as a revelation of Cleopatra's wickedness, 'the stronger manifestation of the lurking devil which peeps out in her blander moments' (27 October 1849). Not since the boy actors, or possibly Mrs Yates, had there been such a memorable display of 'vehemence and power corresponding to the language she had to deliver. But it was in the fifth act, when preparing for her death, that the better phases of the character and the more refined parts of the action tested the fitness of the actress for this assumption' (*Athenaeum*, 27 October 1849). Miss Phillips had in the end made a good death, but here at last was a Cleopatra who had lived up to her death, 'who portrayed the changing moods of Cleopatra . . . with delightful spontaneousness' and 'abandoned herself' to death 'with a smiling and eager majesty that converted it into a triumph' (Marston, *Our Recent Actors*, p. 215). The *Atlas* reviewer thought she made Antony's departure more affecting too: 'her scene over the dead body of Antony . . . made tears irrepressible in the most obdurate eyes' (3 November 1849).

Phelps's Antony was not admired as much as his adaptation and stage management of the play. It was 'less delicately shaded' than Glyn's Cleopatra, but he was spirited and 'most successful in giving the notion of the half conscious recklessness with which the infatuated man rushes to his destruction' (*Times*). He 'wanted grace and the romantic ardour of passion' (Marston, *Our Recent Actors*, p. 202), though the critic from the *Examiner* saw 'masterly bursts of passion'; the *Era*'s reviewer thought that, 'though his declamation was at times formal', his scene with Eros was 'the best in the play' (28 October 1849). Shirley Allen's conclusion is that Phelps was 'unconvincing in the Egyptian scenes', good at abandoning himself in the galley scene and best at struggling to free himself from Cleopatra (*Samuel Phelps*, p. 180). It might also be assumed that, as has happened so often, the two protagonists performed well independently but failed to convince the audience that there was sexual chemistry between them. The curmudgeonly critic from the *Literary Review and Stage-Manager* (22 November 1849) opined 'decidedly the best played characters in the piece are Mr Bennett's Enobarbus, and Mr Graham's Eros'. George Bennett had played Eros in Macready's production, and acted Enobarbus with a 'rugged honesty of manner'; G.K. Dickinson, 'though he occasionally allowed too much energy to carry himself and voice away, was a very satisfactory Octavius Caesar' (Phelps and Robertson, *Samuel Phelps*, p. 109).

The *Illustrated London News* praised the 'management' for staging the play 'in the spirit in which it was composed. They have done their best to realise the past, and to bring the historic into actual presence. The Egyptian scenes are exceedingly *vraisemblable*; that on board of Pompey's galley . . . is exceedingly life-like.' Though the *Times* critic described the Egyptian views as 'decorated with all those formal fantasies with which we have been familiarised through modern research', the emphasis seems to have been on gas-lit realism rather than anything like Kemble's antiquarianism: 'Mr Phelps has judiciously thrown himself with full vigour into the work of decoration, resolved that when the interest flags the pictorial illustration shall attract' (*Spectator*). The scenery was painted by F. Fenton, many of whose 'Egyptian scenes, indeed, were admirable' (Phelps and Robertson, *Samuel Phelps*, p. 109). The engraving published with the *Illustrated London News* review shows the Roman men wearing simple Roman costumes and Cleopatra and her attendants wearing essentially Victorian dresses (and hairstyles); the print of Glyn as Cleopatra gives her 'Egyptian' jewellery and decoration; and hints at her naturally 'dark' complexion (she may have further darkened it with the kind of make-up Phillips wore, but reviewers do not say so). The *Atlas* critic described the costumes as 'splendid and appropriate, more especially the Roman and that of Cleopatra. The coloured contrasts of the Roman mantles is also finely and picturesquely arranged; the Egyptian robe-dresses are deficient in this respect.'

Reviewers generally thought Phelps's production 'surpasses all his previous efforts' (*Times*) and testified to 'the loud plaudits which marked its progress, and the deafening approbation which attended the fall of the curtain' (*Literary Review and Stage-Manager*, 25 October 1849). *Antony and Cleopatra* enticed to the unfashionable and inconvenient venue of Sadler's Wells 'the tide of play-goers, which has hitherto been so slow to "set in" from the West-end of town towards this theatre' (*Atlas*). Phelps's production also seems to have encouraged reviewers to take a more enthusiastic view of the play itself. Of course old objections were voiced, against its alleged longwindedness and Shakespeare's disrespect for the 'unity of time and place', which 'requir[es] a keen and attentive listener to follow through the mazes of the story . . . Hence this play is not known as an acting one, nor will it, we should imagine, ever regain its position as a stock piece' (*Era*). But the new enthusiasm was expressed forcefully in the *Illustrated London News*, at the expense of Dryden and the unities – 'This magnificent play is a masterpiece of dramatic construction with the most difficult of subjects. Our admiration of it will increase if we compare it with Dryden's *All for Love*' – and the *Athenaeum* critic emphasised the play's challenge to its audiences: 'the interest of this magnificent play is decidedly of an epic character. It requires an audience specially educated to appreciate its sublimity and beauty.'

Phelps's production assisted the education of audiences in the abstract and in the long term, especially by introducing Isabella Glyn, as the first major actress-Cleopatra and the century's most successful one. Her success in the part undoubtedly assisted the establishment (or re-establishment) of the play's reputation in the theatre. But productions do not always influence their successors as much, or in the same ways, as theatre historians tend to think: despite Bennett's presence in the cast, the *Times* critic wrote of the lack of precedent for Phelps's production of *Antony and Cleopatra*. Given the centrality of the sense of familial, national and imperial responsibility to the moral sensibility of the age, later Victorian audiences were offered undemanding, much abbreviated versions of the play by Charles Calvert and by Frederick Chatterton. There was a tendency not to educate audiences for the play, but rather to try and make it conform to the prevailing theatrical taste for melodrama with expensive spectacle.

But when Glyn next played Cleopatra in 1855 in John Douglass's East End production at the Standard Theatre, Shoreditch (capable of holding 5,000), with Henry Marston as Antony, reviewers again raised the issue of education and Shakespeare. This time the houses were crowded with a different class of person, 'for the most part respectably attired, and deeply attentive to the business of the scene': 'That the star system should have this tendency to the East, and that the legitimate – the Shakespearean – drama should be so readily planted among the masses, is a sign of the times not to be disregarded, and partly to be accounted for by the improved education of the people' (*Illustrated London News*, 10 March 1855). The *Athenaeum* critic was optimistic (and condescending) in the opposite way; for him the 'poetic drama' could educate through the imagination of the ill-educated:

> To such a throng of the working and shop-keeping people was a high poem presented last Saturday; and so little was there to fear that the appeal would not be answered, that the different compartments of the theatre, each devoted to its especial class of spectators, were crowded to excess . . . there were no signs of impatience; the applause which occurred at wide intervals was generally judicious, and that at the fall of each act-drop enthusiastic. The poetic drama rejected by the frivolous and the fashionable has yet a home in the heart of the working class; and can operate as an influence, even when not understood, on the imagination of the masses.
>
> (*Athenaeum*, 10 March 1855)

The actors had their parts to play in the educative process; two years later, writing about various Glyn performances at the Standard, the *Athenaeum* reviewer (22 August 1857) praised her for 'retain[ing] the classical, dignified style of her later performances, making no effort to obtain applause, but commanding the deepest attention . . . Its continued appreciation by the audience of this neighbourhood is perhaps the most noteworthy fact in the current history of the stage.' Glyn's public readings of the play – for which she had a particular precedent in Mrs Siddons's reading of *Antony and Cleopatra*, and a general one in Charles Kemble's Shakespearean readings – had, in the same terms, an educative as well as a commercial purpose, and they were given abroad as well as at home.[108] It is presumably to these that the *Athenaeum* critic refers in claiming that 'frequent readings have given a rapidity and finish to her style, which enabled her to deliver the text with a succession of glancing lights and minute shades that keep the watchful spectator in perpetual surprise' (10 March 1855). Charles Dickens was less impressed by this technique; as amateur actor and performer of public readings, he may be guilty of a little professional jealousy in complaining that, in Douglass's production, she '"read" her part like a Patter song – several lines on end with the rapidity of Charles Mathews, and then one very long word'. Dickens was also condescending, but pessimistically, about the audience at the Standard, claiming they were 'confounded' and 'wondering, towards the end of the Fourth Act, when the play was going to begin' (letter to Wilkie Collins, 4 March 1855, *Letters*, vol. II, p. 638). Dickens seems to have been in the minority; the *Illustrated London News* asserted that, with its 'dash, rapidity, force, dazzling effect', Glyn's performance 'must now be accepted as one of the most perfect impersonations on the stage of Europe'.

Marston had played Pompey in Phelps's production; 'his style is of the classical kind' and 'for tenderness and amorous pathos [he] is not to be excelled' (*Illustrated London News*). It may be that, emerging like Glyn from the Kemble school and demonstrative in the tender passion, he made a more credible stage lover to Glyn than Phelps. At any rate, he 'looked the part well, and acted it with his usual intelligence' (*Athenaeum*). The same critic liked Dale's Pompey, but hurled 'decided condemnation' at John Bradshaw 'for his singular and bizarre manner of pronouncing the part' of Octavius; Dickens complained about his looking heavier and twenty years older than Antony. To this date the Caesars appear to have been emphatically unimperial, but there is no hint in Victorian productions of a satirical attitude towards Caesar or his followers of the sort that two reviewers detected in Kemble's. In terms of topical and educational value, the imperialism of Caesar's 'peacemaking' annexations doubtless supplemented the

---

108 Kemble's were given in 1844 and Glyn's first reading in 1851 (*DNB*); Winter, in *Shakespeare*, p. 460, praises a Glyn reading he attended in New York in 1870. At the Stuyvesant Institute, *Antony and Cleopatra* had been included in Fanny Kemble's readings in 1848 and in George Vandenhoff's (wearing Shakespearean dress) in the following year (Odell, *New York Stage*, vol. V, pp. 498, 595).

Egyptian archaeological interest of the play for directors and audiences in
an England mindful of its 'responsibilities' towards an empire upon which
the sun never set. Even Dickens found the decor 'very brightly and creditably got up'; the *Athenaeum* said 'the scenery was well painted, appropriate, and new; the dresses rich and picturesque, – constituting a spectacle
but little inferior to the "standard" specimens of the kind so frequently wit-
nessed in Oxford Street'. Its appeal, as with the 'standard' specimens, was
not unconnected with Egyptomania, which was being offered as a stimulant
to the imagination of the masses as surely as Shakespeare. Its latest form
was the Egyptian Court at the Crystal Palace, which Joseph Bonomi the
younger helped Owen Jones arrange in 1853; Bonami had been on expedi-
tions with Wilkinson[109] and Karl Richard Lepsius,[110] returning after the
latter to execute a series of drawings from which Henry Warren and Joseph
Fahey painted a panorama of the Nile exhibited in London and the large
towns.

The building of the Suez Canal (from 1859 to 1869), the beginning of
Egyptian tourism and the growing Orientalist movement in painting, architecture and interior decoration may help explain a comparative spate of
English productions in 1866, 1867 and 1873; but, equally, in the right commercial and cultural climate, one production begets others. New York also
saw a relative flurry: a production in 1859, a reading of the play by Glyn at
Steinway Hall in 1870 and two productions in 1877. When George Vining's
production opened in 1867 at the Princess's Theatre, London, with Henry
Loraine as Antony, 'the triumph of the evening', as might have been
expected, was Glyn's Cleopatra (*Athenaeum*, 18 May 1867). The same
reviewer states that the reputation gained by Glyn from her public readings
of the play had encouraged the management to try it on at a West End
theatre. The Princess's was an appropriate venue in one sense: it had been
the site of Charles Kean's spectacularly historical Shakespearean revivals –
which did not, however, include *Antony and Cleopatra* – before his retirement in 1859. But, if the *Illustrated London News* critic (25 May 1867)
observed aright, the Princess's audiences had grown used to less demanding

---

109 In 1824; in 1857 Sir John Gardner Wilkinson wrote a companion to the Crystal
Palace Egyptian collections called *Egypt at the Time of the Pharaohs*; his most
important work was *The Manners and Customs of the Ancient Egyptians* (3 vols.,
London, 1837, with 2 later vols.), a scholarly compilation, but intended also for
travellers. Wilkinson left his collection to Harrow in 1864 and other antiquities to
the British Museum.

110 The Prussian government expedition of 1842–44; Bonami was an important
Egyptological illustrator and hieroglyphic draughtsman, and curator of the Soane
Museum from 1861 until his death in 1878.

2 Isabella Glyn's hand kissed by Thidias (Henry Loraine as Antony in the background) in Vining's production at the Princess's Theatre in 1867. Engraving from *Illustrated London News* (25 May 1867).

fare and did not hang upon Miss Glyn's lips like the very different audiences at the Standard twelve years earlier: 'She loves every word of the dialogue she has to utter; and it is not her fault if the audience do not love it too.'

The audiences at the Princess's were not shortchanged on spectacle in 1867. The designers, Thomas Grieve and Frederick Lloyds, had worked on Kean's revivals; most of the scenic effects for this production were recycled from Charles Calvert's of the previous year, augmented by Lloyds, who was responsible for the much-appreciated galley scene, 'beautifully adorned with moonlight effects'. Grieve was admired for his ability 'to realise on the stage the most magnificent of buildings and the most extensive landscapes, with minute attention to details' (*Athenaeum*) and it was noted that the banks of the Nile were painted after David Roberts's *Sketches in Egypt and Nubia*[111] and that the costumes were 'bright and appropriate' (*Era*, 19 May 1867). However, one observer with a sharp eye for archaeological detail later recalled nostalgically Kemble's decor and objected to Vining's scenes depicting the Colosseum '60 years before a

111 Published in 1846–50; Roberts had formerly painted theatrical scenery and was renowned for his architectural and topographical work.

stone of it was laid' and generally representing Rome 'in the faded hues of 1855, not the brilliancy of 2,000 years ago'; to him, the Roman costumes were barely adequate and the Egyptian costumes 'utterly beneath contempt' (note at the end of *Lacy's Acting Edition*, p. 80).

Lamb (*Antony and Cleopatra*, p. 77) thinks the existence of Grieve's scenery 'was perhaps a motive' for Vining's production: the management may well have considered the combination of such scenery and such an actress as Glyn irresistible. The *Athenaeum* critic commented, 'all this scenic ornamentation is, in this instance, not a substitute for good acting, the drama being exceedingly well cast'. The text used was the one prepared by Calvert for his own production and later touring. It has the usual bowdlerising and other cuts; it omits the Antony and Octavia scenes and Enobarbus's desertion (until 4.6), and makes provision for the play to end either with Cleopatra's death or after Caesar's speech. The galley scene, like Phelps's, emphasises revelry, and two of the more spectacular moments also recall Phelps's production: an Egyptian ballet at the entrance of the lovers, and a lavishly attended triumph of Antony and Cleopatra as the finale of Act 3 (4.8). The text allows some physical violence in the messenger scene, but avoids the long haul for Antony; he is simply carried in to a '*couch*' in the monument.

Loraine, 'a fine classic figure', was not much noticed by reviewers, who concentrated on Glyn, then properly middle-aged at 44 and playing for the third time a part she had made her own. She was 'able to satisfy the eye as thoroughly as the judgment. The consciousness of her power over the heart of Antony is expressed in every look and gesture' (*Athenaeum*). Either her performance had become more frankly erotic or her reviewers had become franker, or both: the *Examiner* critic (8 June 1867) wrote, 'the luxury of sensual enjoyment is in her tone of voice', her death is 'one of self-indulgence, not self-sacrifice'; whilst the reviewer from the *Athenaeum* was overwhelmed:

> The witchery of the blandishments, the Asiatic undulations of the form, the variety of the enchantments, the changes of mood, the impetuous passion, and in the end the noble resignation:– all these points are brought out with an accuracy of elocution and with a force of genius which leave no doubt in the mind that Miss Glyn is as great an actress as ever adorned the English stage.

Charles Calvert in Cottonopolis: archaeology and atmospherics

Between Glyn's second and third appearances in the play, two other significant productions were mounted, neither in London. Edward Eddy's in 1859 ran for three weeks and was the last production at the old Broadway

Theatre, New York. The text contained a good deal of Dryden and the production relied on elaborate costumes and scenery, including a moving panorama of the Nile. Eddy was an energetic Antony, whilst Elizabeth Ponisi, English-born, was 'not quite fascinating enough to make one throw away an empire' (*Herald*, 8 March 1859, quoted in Odell, *New York Stage*, vol. VII, p. 112).[112]

Charles Calvert's production of *Antony and Cleopatra* opened at the Prince's Theatre, Manchester in 1866, with Calvert and his wife Adelaide in the title roles. It later toured, with Walter Montgomery and Mattie Reinhardt as the protagonists, and in 1867, Montgomery, American-born and English-trained, offered (as actor-manager) the first Australian production of the play at the Theatre Royal, Melbourne, with Louisa Cleveland as Cleopatra; according to a play-bill advertising its last performances in 1869, it was an 'immense success', only removed from the boards 'to make room for fresh novelties'.[113] As one of Calvert's Shakespearean revivals in Manchester in the decade from 1864,[114] his *Antony and Cleopatra* was a fresh novelty to local audiences: 'not even the oldest playgoer in Manchester had ever seen it. It was a revelation' (Adelaide Calvert, *Sixty-Eight Years on the Stage*, p. 81). If revelatory, it seems not to have changed local critics' view of the play in the way that Phelps's affected at least two London reviewers'. One critic, explaining why *Antony and Cleopatra* was so rarely staged, claims – amid the usual remarks about density of historical incident and unmemorable speeches – that 'the play analyses or exhibits no profound human passion' and that 'Egypt, in her glory, and classic Rome, have no points of contact with modern, other than student and antiquarian, thought' (unidentified review, pasted into George Beck's copy of the play, New York Public Library). The decor of Calvert's production, by Thomas Grieve and Frederick Holding, manifested an interest in archaeological details on somebody's part. Cleopatra's palace was, the same reviewer says,

---

112 Eddy revived his production with other Cleopatras: Julia Dean Hayne and Alice Grey (see Odell, *New York Stage*, vol. VII, p. 112). Brown lists other American performances in this period, but they were presumably of selected scenes or severely cut, since they were performed with another play, often Shakespearean. Of interest is a production with James Anderson at the Broadway in 1853, twenty years before his appearance in Chatterton's production (*New York Stage*, vol. I, p. 396).

113 It opened on 8 October 1867 and had ten initial performances: see Eric Irvin, *Dictionary of Australian Theatre*, pp. 29 and 198. The play-bill, which is dated 19 August 1869, is reproduced in Paul McGuire et al., *The Australian Theatre*, p. 118. Montgomery also played Antony in Sydney, to Rosa Cooper's Cleopatra, in at least three performances at the Prince of Wales Theatre, opening on 10 May 1869 (*Sydney Morning Herald*).

114 See Alfred Darbyshire, *The Art of the Victorian Stage*, p. 36.

'designed from the palace of Edfou' and the interior of the monument 'from the temple of Ezueb'; the former was 'decorated in colour with the figures and hieroglyphs which explorers and the British Museum have made familiar' – but familiar to whom? The interests of designers and reviewers may be broader (or deeper) than those of average theatre-goers, and it may have been the novelty, workmanship or decorative appeal that brought 'cheer after cheer from the pleased spectators' as 'scene after scene is displayed'. Some of the sets were scenic views (the promontory of Actium and the banks of the Nile) and, for contrast, there was the 'classic elegance' of Caesar's house. The costumes were rich and 'have been prepared from the best authorities, so as to make them historically accurate' (*ibid.*); the managers of the theatre had 'sanctioned the expenditure of quite a large sum of money. My husband went over to Paris to purchase the armour and regalia, &c., from the celebrated firm of Le Blanc Grainger' (Calvert, *Sixty-Eight Years on the Stage*, p. 81).

The 'accuracy' of such sets and costumes partly stems from actor-managers' concern with historical verisimilitude. Victorian notions of theatrical verisimilitude may have embraced the idea of educating audiences in the customs of ancient cultures, but those notions were neither rigid nor extensive: the accompaniments to the spectacle, the musical arrangements and the ballets, were not conceived in the same vein, and it is difficult not to conclude that verisimilitude had more to do with atmospherics than accuracy as such. Kemble's attention to archaeological detail, and what Cary Mazer calls the 'pedantry' of Charles Kean's Shakespearean revivals in the 1850s (*Shakespeare Refashioned*, p. 9), may have been an attempt, not entirely conscious, at validating their addition of spectacle to the work of the 'poet'. Kean's revivals probably also made archaeologising Shakespeare *de rigueur*, and there is a useful sense in which the approach may be termed a fashion. Like most fashions, it tried to balance the familiar with the novel, owing something to precedent, something to current attitudes to what was appropriate as well as what was appealing, and something to commercial oneupmanship. It would be naive to expect theatrical sets to be archaeological reconstructions: their realism was, particularly under the gaslighting introduced after Kemble's production, broadly conceived out of necessity, and tended to rely upon what the tourist, rather than the archaeologist, would take for genuine.

Calvert's production also drew upon precedent and prevailing ideas of theatrical style in using music (not at all archaeological) to supplement the scene-setting: there was a chorus, a singing Charmian (Miss Markham) and music by Giacomo Meyerbeer, Felix Mendelssohn and Henry Bishop (his song to Bacchus and drinking chorus were both encored). As usual, the 'poet' was sacrificed to make all this possible: 'more scenery and less Shakespeare' was 'held forth as a temptation to the lieges of Cottonopolis; but even this bait failed to justify the outlay incurred' ('Remarks' prefaced to *Lacy's Acting Edition*). Calvert made the accustomed changes (cuts, transfers, transpositions) but no additions: defensible, in Victorian eyes, 'on the ground that it prevents a tedious amount of scene-shifting, and that it introduces by-play to fill up time while the most elaborate scenes and groups are being prepared' (unidentified review, Beck's copy). In a return to Macready's arrangement, Antony 'dies in the monument, and his body remains there to the end' (*ibid.*). For the same reviewer, the acting was the least impressive element in the production. Like most other English actresses of the period, Adelaide Calvert avoided the 'voluptuous aspect' and then managed to die well; from the Clown's entry to the end, she 'played with a fervour for which the earlier scenes had not prepared us'. Her husband, as Antony, showed (like Phelps) 'a recklessness in love and death – that makes an audience thrill with its magic power' (unidentified reviewer, quoted in Winter, *Shakespeare*, p. 452). He, too, was best in his last phase, presenting 'a picture which, displaying his settled despair, his deep humiliation, and yet his love for Cleopatra, strong even in death, is beautiful and most poetic in conception and execution. The chill and silence which creep over the audience are the best testimony to its power' (*ibid.*).

'Gaud, and glitter': from Chatterton to Tree

The kinds of audiences who, in the age of the diorama and the panorama, found elaborate scenery more fascinating than Shakespeare's text or Miss Glyn's undulations, seemed to justify those managers from Chatterton to Tree whose approach to Shakespeare was almost wholly pictorial. They did not always provide commercial vindication: Frederick Chatterton's production in 1873 at Drury Lane was his, and the play's, most lavishly spectacular to date, and its financial failure is said to have made him equate Shakespeare with Ruin. On the other hand, Henry Abbey's production in New York in 1889 ran for fifty-seven consecutive performances and briefly in other cities, and Herbert Beerbohm Tree's had ninety performances at His Majesty's Theatre, London, before being shipped in its entirety to Berlin.

Chatterton believed 'that a play to be acceptable to all classes in a large theatre must appeal to the eye and the senses as well as to the understanding; that the action must be accompanied by spectacle, and the play itself must be adapted to the dramatic fashion of the time in which we live' (quoted in Dutton Cook, *Nights at the Play*, vol. I, p. 293). His Antony, James Anderson, who was in his mid-fifties and had been a member of

Macready's company, was shocked by the truncated nature of the acting version, and seems to have been equally disturbed by the large audience's living up to Chatterton's expectations: 'The spectacle (it could not be called a tragedy, being all made up of scenery, processions, ballet, gaud, and glitter) was accepted with maddening demonstrations of approval by the pit and galleries; but the "judicious few" looked coldly on' (Anderson, *An Actor's Life*, pp. 316–17).

Some reviewers were among the cold onlookers,[115] but many wished power to the pruner's elbow; the *Times* critic (22 September 1873) approved of Andrew Halliday's cuts in the acting edition, out of 'respect for unity of place', and was relaxed about the instability of the text: 'the play . . . has become widely different from that which years ago Mr Phelps produced at Sadler's Wells, and in which Miss Glyn, by her admirable performance of Cleopatra, may be said to have created a new character, so completely had the Egyptian Queen faded from the memory of the playgoing public'. Halliday's version reduced the play to twelve scenes, about half the length of the original, with all the Roman scenes in the second act; when Ellen Wallis later toured in the provinces, with Frank Clements as Antony, they played a still further abbreviated version, which she herself arranged (see Winter, *Shakespeare*, p. 450). Halliday justified himself by reference to German criticism of Shakespeare, and, in the Preface to his acting version, wrote 'if half a loaf be better than no bread, surely it is better to have a little of Shakespeare than none at all' (p. v) and 'Shakespeare in his own time was regarded, not as legitimate, but as a sensational dramatist' (pp. vi-vii), who, by implication, would have used more pictorial sensations if he had lived in Victorian times; thus his text is updated 'by realizing the famous Barge Scene, transferring it from the Cydnus to the coast of Egypt' (p. vi). Other sensational insertions were the substitution of the marriage of Antony and Octavia – with processions, boys' choir and ballet – for the galley scene (since all Pompey scenes were omitted) and a memorable battle of Actium, in which '"Greek fire" is hurled among the combatants, and every second sees some twenty or thirty warriors tumbling helplessly about in the waters' (*Daily Telegraph*, 22 September 1873). Notable changes were Enobarbus's exit after his 'O thou blessed moon' speech (to reduce the number of deaths) and the use of a temple of Isis setting (taking inspiration from Dryden) for the last scene, in which Cleopatra falls on the altar and her actual asp-taking is not shown. In other respects, Halliday simply followed precedent, with an Egyptian ballet in the first scene, Mardian as the mes-

---

115 The *Saturday Review* critic (27 September 1873), for example, saw the production as a rehearsal for the Christmas pantomime.

senger, struck only once by Cleopatra, and avoidance of the hauling and of the meeting between Cleopatra and Caesar. Most reviewers liked Halliday's compression and tidying, though there were specific objections, to the 'squeamishness' of the bowdlerising of the 'salad days' and cross-dressing speeches and the omission of Enobarbus's death (*Athenaeum*, 27 September 1873), or to the omission of Pompey and the substitution of the marriage of Antony and Octavia (*Illustrated London News*, 27 September 1873).

But, for reviewers, the exciting spectacle in the first three acts meant that 'the longer speeches and the gloomier close of the fourth act, unaided by any excelling scenic display, thus came as a kind of anti-climax' (*Era*, 28 September 1873); despite 'filling up the stage at the end with flambeau-bearing mourners, the eye . . . refuses to be comforted' (*Daily Telegraph*) and 'the general impression was . . . that the great effects of the modernised tragedy had been brought forth too early' (*Era*). In the process, Shakespeare was made to look inferior to scenery:

> During the first three acts, in which there is 'one halfpenny worth' of Shakespearean 'bread' to 'an intolerable deal of' scenic 'sack', the delight of the audience with everything set before it was unbounded. In the concluding act, which was wholly Shakespearean, there was a gradual cooling, and the verdict at the end, though favourable, was far less enthusiastic than it would have been could the play have ended with the fight at Actium . . . the most dramatic scenes, and the most sublime poetry that the stage has known, proved not only ineffective but wearisome.
>
> (*Athenaeum*)

The play's political topicality may have been one reason for the spate of American and British, and the two Australian, productions which followed Chatterton's. Egypt's bankruptcy in 1876 led to the joint control of Egyptian finances by Britain and France, and British military intervention from 1882 resulted in Gordon's famous death at Khartoum in 1885 and the Anglo-Egyptian expedition to the Sudan in 1896. One of 'Cleopatra's Needles' was erected in London in 1878, the other in New York in 1881. Whatever thread connects them with Shakespearean performance, they are a prime example of Egyptomaniacal appropriation, since the ancient Egyptian obelisks from Heliopolis (predating Cleopatra by over 1,000 years, their naming nicely revealing the namers' preconceptions) had been moved by Octavius to Alexandria in 12 BC.

The five non-British productions between Chatterton's and Lillie Langtry's were all mounted in the same extravagantly pictorial mode and cut the text to emphasise costume and scenery. Benson Sherwood's nineteen-scene production at Niblo's Garden, New York in 1877 was heavily lopped and transposed; later in the same year, Rose Eytinge produced the play at the Broadway Theatre, and as Cleopatra wore, with her dark complexion, costumes she claimed were historically correct and jewellery copied from archaeological sources.[116] In 1882, an expensive production at the Theatre Royal, Sydney, included in a 'Grand Shakespeare Festival', paid 'minute attention to archaeological detail' (*Sydney Morning Herald*, 27 February 1882) and George C. Miln's production at Her Majesty's Opera House, Melbourne in 1889 featured wrestling as well as dancing and singing, and a rocking stage for the galley scene.[117] This was the year of Henry Abbey's lavish production, with fourteen scenes in six acts arranged by Kyrle Bellew, at Palmer's Theatre, New York, which omitted Octavia and much else. 'Pruning' did not necessarily result in a playing time of less than four hours. In some productions, spectacular effects occupied more time than predicted, and the remedy was further cutting at the beginning of the run. In the Langtry–Wingfield production at the Princess's Theatre, London in 1890, the text was pruned harder after the first night, and in Louis Calvert's disastrous 1909 production[118] for the opening of the New Theatre, New York, the text, divided into thirteen scenes in five acts, was further shortened after the 'general rehearsal', chiefly by the omission of the galley scene. In the latter case, spectacle was also sacrificed, since an elaborate galley set had been created, but the period principle was preserved of excising scenes superfluous to the main action.

Louis Calvert's earlier production of 1897, opening at the Queen's Theatre, Manchester for eight weeks, then transferring to the Olympic, London, used a four-act text, with 'many transpositions and running on of scenes, the two scenes of Cleopatra with the Messenger being put together' (*Stage*, 3 January 1907); this version was partly based on his father's, but with more cuts in the later scenes (the temporary triumph of Antony was omitted); Antony killed himself outdoors, perhaps for the first time in the century, and, with Antony at her feet, Cleopatra died upright on her throne – as Mrs Langtry had done, perhaps under the influence of Sarah Bernhardt's death-scene in Victorien Sardou and Emile Moreau's *Cléopâtre*, which had opened in Paris less than a month before,[119] though Ellen Wallis's falling on the altar in 1873 may have been the necessary break with the couch-deaths of the previous sixty-year period.

116 See Gerald Bordman, *American Theatre*, p. 114 and William C. Young, *Famous Actors and Actresses*, vol. I, p. 347.

117 Programme note by Agnes Dobson for her production in Adelaide in 1938.

118 Perhaps this production should not be described as his: disputes with Marlowe and Sothern, who had been expecting to co-direct the production, caused him to withdraw from it (see Shattuck, *Shakespeare on the American Stage*, vol. II, p. 279).

119 Bernhardt played the Sardou role in London two years later.

Frank Benson, who was first to produce the play at the Stratford Festival (in 1898;[120] then at the Lyceum, London in 1900 and again in Stratford in 1912), used the Memorial acting edition 'with a few necessary transpositions of scenes, which number eighteen in all, comprised in the five acts' (*Birmingham Daily Post*, 15 April 1898); for the first time on the English stage since Garrick's production, Antony was hoisted up to Cleopatra. Her death was also staged on top of the monument (Lamb, *Antony and Cleopatra*, p. 89), presumably to save scene-changing time, but one unimpressed critic found the death-scenes too long and urged their condensation (*Stratford-upon-Avon Herald*, 22 April 1898).

Herbert Beerbohm Tree, in 1906, approached the text less gingerly; he spoke of 'the scrappy nature of the printed version' of the play (*Scotsman*, 28 December 1906). One reviewer, opining that in Shakespeare's text 'the development of the plot is downright sluggish in the earlier scenes; the action is perplexingly jerky, and dramatic incidents are exceedingly scarce', was glad that Tree had 'cut something like two hours out' (*Sporting Life*, 28 December 1906). Even so, the period complaint was heard about the length of the death-scenes, extended by a simulation of the hoisting with a quick scene-change. Tree's version began (like Langtry's) with 1.4 followed by the arrival of the lovers in Cleopatra's barge, but the opening image was Tree's own, a projected dissolving Sphinx, and he ended the play with the same image, to the confusion of some of the audience[121] and the annoyance of some critics: 'upon this assumption – that Shakespeare was an inarticulate genius, unable to explain what he imagined! – Mr. Tree founds his entire treatment of the play' (H. Hamilton Fyfe, *Pall Mall Gazette*, 2 January 1907). A surprising (and prophetic) degree of hostility was expressed in some quarters towards the 'prince among showmen' and his 'using the pruning knife upon the sacred text', giving 'the go-by to the merely historical portions' and 'disengaging its essential essence' (*Western Morning News*, 29 December 1906) to produce 'a raree show, tagged with Shakespearean phrases' (*Speaker*, 2 January 1907). There were specific complaints about 'the sacrifice of some of the varying moods of Cleopatra' (*Observer*, 30 December 1906). Whilst the beauty of Tree's spectacle was

120 Later in the same year Helena Modjeska, at the age of 58, played Shakespeare's Cleopatra at the Baldwin Theatre, San Francisco, and elsewhere in the country, though not in New York; unsuited to the part, she sought 'to make Cleopatra a very proper person' and was 'light, fanciful, almost elf-like' (reviews quoted in Shattuck, *Shakespeare on the American Stage*, vol. II, p. 135).

121 The *Telegraph* reviewer wrote, 'the audience seemed undecided whether to go or to stay when the stage was darkened at the end of the play preliminary to the second exhibition of the Sphinx' (28 December 1906).

3 The galley scene in Tree's production at His Majesty's Theatre in 1906: Lyn Harding (Enobarbus), Beerbohm Tree (Antony), Norman Forbes (Lepidus), Basil Gill (Octavius), Julian L'Estrange (Pompey), Herbert Grimwood (Menas). Photograph: Rotary.

generally given its due, the note of hostility proceeded from aesthetic assumptions very different from the actor-managers' of the previous thirty years, and was prophetic of changes in audience expectation and staging practice. The critic from the *Leeds Mercury* consoled himself with 'the knowledge that the incoherence of the dramatic representation', which he took to be 'the common fault of most of Shakespeare's plays nowadays', 'must needs drive many to the book itself' (28 December 1906), and another reviewer squarely blamed the staging practice of the day:

> Shakespeare cannot be played as he ought to be played until we return to that simple alternation of front scenes with set-scenes which reproduces in some measure the common practice of the Elizabethan stage . . . The practice of making even front scenes so elaborate that a curtain must be dropped, and a musical interlude played, while they are being set, not only wastes time, but fritters away the interest of the audience. Moreover, it tempts the manager to compress as many episodes as he possibly can into a single 'set', and so perverts that chronological sequence of events which Shakespeare must be held to have carefully thought out, and which can scarcely ever be tampered with except to his serious disadvantage.　　(*Tribune*, 28 December 1906)

The fashion for archaeological detail continued throughout the period, but spectacle as such, usually including the scenic views of imaginative tourism, was always primary, and – aided by the increasing use of electric lighting in the 1880s – there was a growing interest in the relationship between colour and lighting, demonstrated most clearly in the Tree production. The costumes for Chatterton's production were 'designed by Mr E. C. Barnes in accordance with the authorities supplied by the Roman and Egyptian antiquities in the British Museum' (*Era*, 28 September 1873) and Langtry's production, which attracted a complaint about 'pseudo-archaeological detail' (*Times*, 19 November 1890), used a set for the monument, with a grand staircase and a pair of enormous statues, that was possibly inspired by the more massive examples of Egyptian statuary in the British Museum. Tree's scenery was admired for its 'massive effects' as well as its 'effects of perspective' (*Referee*, 30 December 1906), but in the 1909 New Theatre production, with scenery painted by Ernest Albert after drawings by Jules Guérin, the 'spacious and handsome' sets with 'vast, massive pillars and huge curtains' tended to dwarf the actors (Winter, *Shakespeare*, pp. 464–7). The actors were not the prime consideration in such productions – the *Punch* reviewer of Tree's claimed that Shakespeare 'was constantly being sacrificed to the picture' and that the actors were 'regarded as a mobile section of the scenery' (O.S., 2 January 1907) – but the spectacle itself could be regarded as a source of information and edification.

In their approach to the play, late nineteenth-century directors were inevitably more indebted to archaeologists and historians than to literary scholars.[122] Benson got Lyall Swete, who played Enobarbus, to make 'a careful study of the standard authorities upon Egyptology' (*Stratford-upon-Avon Herald*, 8 April 1898);[123] as a result of these efforts, the interior of the monument was furnished with 'furniture chiefly of ebony and silver, the walls adorned with hieroglyphics and processions of Egyptian gods' (*Birmingham Daily Post*, 15 April 1898). One reviewer found the Roman scenes bracing; it was 'like seeing Plutarch acted. The conventions and usage of Roman society are faithfully copied. We get an idea of the luxury of patrician life and the discipline of camp' (*Birmingham Daily Gazette*, 15 April 1898). Tree spared no expense of trouble or money over such details as the Romans' armour; the showing of 'antiquity so accurately restored' 'was a personal triumph for Messrs. Harker and Ryan; for Mr. Macquoid and the British Museum assistance' (O.S., *Punch*, 2 January 1907). Sir Lawrence Alma-Tadema, that 'marbellous' artist (as *Punch* called him), had designed some sets for Benson's *Antony and Cleopatra* and Tree's *Julius Caesar* in 1898, and two reviewers of Tree's *Antony and Cleopatra* detected the influence of his pictures on some of those sets.[124] His paintings of scenes from ancient history (mainly Greek and Roman, but sometimes Egyptian), with their fastidious archaeological detail, contributed directly to the popularity of the Egypto-Roman subject in this period, but were also regarded as educational; and Benson and Tree took advice from Alma-Tadema on 'manners, carriage, and deportment' (Mazer, *Shakespeare Refashioned*, p. 19). Lillie Langtry also took advice, but in a more casual manner: 'During the rehearsals I sat next to Lord Hartington at a dinner-party one evening, and he helped me very much with suggestions, being brimful of Egyptian and Greek lore' (Langtry, *The Days I Knew*, p. 233).

Archaeologising aside, the spectacle was generally atmospheric, ingenious and diverting, often literally picturing famous descriptions in the text. Chatterton's decor was the responsibility of William Beverley, widely regarded as the best atmospheric scene-painter after Stanfield; his 'pictorial illustration of the words of Enobarbus . . . could scarcely be surpassed'

---

122 Tree was mainly interested in 'that elaboration of scenery which the pedantic students of Shakespeare affect to dislike' (*East Anglian Times*, 28 December 1906).

123 The reviewer cites 'the English classic "The Manners and Customs of Ancient Egypt", which, by the way, has recently been added to the Memorial Library, and the German scholar Lepsius's standard work on the same subject, and the French authority, Prisse d'Avennes'.

124 *Daily Chronicle*, 28 December 1906 and J.J.N., *Manchester Guardian*, 2 January 1907.

(*Times*, 22 September 1873); it and the battle of Actium were 'marvels of ingenuity and taste' (*Athenaeum*, 27 September 1873). A 'tableau' of Cleopatra's barge also featured in Rose Eytinge's production, and the lovers made their first entry in the barge in Langtry's and Tree's. Benson Sherwood's production showed the coronation of Antony by Cleopatra, while Langtry's celebrated Antony's triumphal reception by Cleopatra. The battle of Actium was also enthusiastically staged at Niblo's Garden and in Benson's production (with tableaux of 'a sea fight between the Roman and Egyptian fleets' and 'After the Battle, evening coming on, and the Egyptian galleys in flames'). The revelry on Pompey's galley featured in Sherwood's production (with a panorama by George Heister showing the galley's moonlit voyage up the Nile), and in Benson's and Tree's. Benson's 1898 production added new costumes to his 'celebrated wardrobe' and had elaborate scenery, variously painted by M. Le Maistre, Hugh Freemantle, W. J. Helmsley and W. Hall, and properties weighing twenty and a half tons crammed on to a small stage, including the sets for the palace 'with magnificent golden throne', and both the exterior and interior of the monument (*Birmingham Daily Post*, 15 April 1898).

Ballets were standard in pictorial productions, but in Mrs Langtry's, the *Times* reviewer (19 November 1890), timing the performance at four and a half hours, complained about the 'oriental pantomimes'.[125] Oscar Asche's Australian production featured an 'Egyptian cymbal ballet' with 'Zara's fantastic pas seul' (*Sydney Morning Herald*, 21 April 1913). Like the ballets, incidental music contributed to the entertainment and atmosphere and, towards the end of the pictorial movement, there was an attempt to make the music more 'oriental' along with the 'pantomimes'. In Benson's production Michael Balling's setting of the drinking song in the galley scene was 'vociferously applauded' (*Birmingham Daily Post*, 15 April 1898); Balling, who wrote all the incidental music (incorporating 'oriental strains' from Bedouin music), had been involved in the Wagner Festival at Bayreuth, which led some reviewers to lament the absence of comparable facilities at the Shakespeare Festival: one claimed that the 'pitiful smallness of the stage' in Stratford meant that 'several of the tableaux . . . could not be put on, and the effect of the rest was marred by crowding' (*Birmingham Daily Gazette*, 16 April 1898). Tree's production used 'appropriately Oriental music, composed specially by Mr. Raymond Roze' (*Stage*, 3 January 1907).

The extravagant productions of the late Victorian period reached their

125 And about the 'bewildering effect' of too much scene-shifting and too many extras, as did a reviewer of Louis Calvert's London production: 'our only complaint was with the tableau-curtains, whose fall on each scene made a play of seventeen acts' (*Illustrated London News*, 12 June 1897).

apogee in Herbert Beerbohm Tree's Edwardian production, 'on that scale of lavish splendour which is inseparable from His Majesty's Theatre, and has from time to time enraged critics and students who prefer their Shakespeare "neat"' (*Daily Mail*, 28 December 1906). Joseph Harker's scenes showed 'his unrivalled sense as a colourist' and 'the tableau to which Mr. Ryan has given the setting is of a magnificence in colouring, grouping of figures, and Eastern display beyond what has ever been approached at His Majesty's' (*Telegraph*, 28 December 1906). The costumes and movements of the supernumeraries under careful lighting made memorable pictorial effects: in the galley scene the dancers' 'mouse-grey and silver garments take mysterious purple and blue colours under the limelight as they whirl about silently in a weird dance' and the attendants in the 'tableau scene' of the Return of Antony to Alexandria had 'enormous pink and brown wings that they hold wide when standing at attention, and fold forwards when they make their obeisance to their queen' (*Queen*, 12 January 1907). The atmosphere of 'the languorous, luscious East' was established by the set of Cleopatra's 'rich apartment, glowing with golden decoration, and with its beautiful women in graceful attitudes on the cushioned floor' (*Leeds Mercury*, 28 December 1906); Constance Collier's six costumes served not only as 'an excellent model for fancy dress at the balls of this season' (*Glasgow Herald*, 31 December 1906) but also made a major contribution to the mood of Egyptian sensuality: 'Gold tissue and kindred materials look exquisite while she is in repose, but in her moments of fury and agitation seem scant and unsatisfactory' (*Daily Graphic*, 28 December 1906). The male attire was less scant but no less becoming. 'Mark Antony, Caesar, Pompeius, Lepidus, and the other Roman warriors seem to be wearing golden armour, while their cloaks are obviously of the rarest silks, and their helmets have the appearance of graven metal' (*Manchester Evening Chronicle*, 28 December 1906); one reviewer admired Caesar's silver helmet, 'glinting through the play like the crescent moon'. Reassuringly for imperialists, 'this helmet is the last thing upon which the eyes rest as the Emperor of the world looks upon the greatest of the world's lovers lying dead before him' (*Truth*, 2 January 1907).

Though literal limelight, and even the role of the actor-manager, were by then becoming obsolescent, Langtry and Tree showed in their productions their fondness for the metaphorical limelight (in a way that Louis Calvert and Benson did not). In the Langtry–Wingfield production, the dying Antony was taken away by his guard and left to expire offstage, his body being brought back to join the monument furnishings for Cleopatra's death; this was one solution to the period complaint about the extended nature of the lovers' deaths, but (given that Enobarbus's death was also omitted and that the play ended with Cleopatra's 'O Antony!') it certainly ensured that Mrs Langtry's death was unupstageable. Tree's staging of his own death not only prolonged it with a scene-shifting *faux*-hauling, but it gave him an unmissable expiry, whereby Cleopatra's kiss seemed to 'quicken' him, and he rolled over her on to the floor. Whilst he was still on his feet, Tree's outfit foregrounded his role as producer of colourful specta-cle rather than as lover: 'he loved the clangor of swords and the gold and purple of his mantle. Amidst the shifting harmonies of the scene, he trod as one on air, conscious always that he alone was the Master of the Show' (*Star*, 28 December 1906). The same reviewer heard the fanfares accompa-nying his entrances and exits as Tree's blowing his own trumpet: 'if poor Antony really lived in such a strepitous atmosphere, his flight into Egypt should evoke our sympathy'.

Egotism aside, an obvious cause of the actor-managers' limelight-seeking was the tendency of pictorial productions to cramp the style of their actors, who were highly conscious not only of the prominence given to the specta-cle and its lighting, but also of the noise associated with scene-shifting. On the opening night of Chatterton's production, the veteran Anderson was 'stunned and cowed by the furious noise of preparation for "heavy sets" behind the scenes that destroyed all power of acting in front' (Anderson, *An Actor's Life*, p. 317). Reviewers of such productions tend to pay scant atten-tion to acting skills, one declaring, 'in giving precedence to the spectacular portion of the entertainment, we are following the example of the public as well as that of the management' (*Athenaeum*, 27 September 1873).

Managers of the time tended, in casting Cleopatras, to make superficial naturalistic assumptions about the 'equipment'[126] needed for the role and seemed unable to distinguish actresses' professional skills from their attrib-utes as women. Pictorial Cleopatras were generally distinguished by their being decorative (good-looking and often young), by their dying well (profiting, perhaps, from a natural restraint and a natural sense of relief), and by their tendency to find culturally tolerable physical correlatives for passion in messenger-beating or form-revealing dresses, or both. In the integrity of her conception of the role of Cleopatra, Miss Glyn was very much the exception rather than the nineteenth-century rule. Ellen Wallis, at the age of 17, seemed by comparison 'a mere girl, under the influence of her first passion' (*Era*, 28 September 1873); 'her voice was exhausted . . . before the end of the second act, and the pathos of the later scenes seemed as much a result of sore throat as of inspiration' (*Athenaeum*, 27 September

---

126 The *Sportsman* critic wrote of Constance Collier's 'imposing and attractive equipment' (28 December 1906).

1873). She was a prime example of the actress cast on the basis of prettiness and youth rather than character and maturity, presumably on the naturalistic (if historically inaccurate) assumption that the former attributes are more generally irresistible, to audiences as well as Antonys.[127] Whilst such actresses had youth in common with the boy actor who presumably first played the part and in whose mouth the famous lines about her 'salad days' (1.5.76f.) would have had the kind of theatrical irony familiar on Elizabethan and Jacobean stages, that irony proceeds from acceptance of the convention of boy actors. Under a naturalistic regime there is a perceived need for equivalence in the ages of the actors and of the characters they play, whether the middle-aged protagonists or their 'boy' antagonist Caesar (Dickens mocked Octavius's looking older than Antony in Douglass's production of 1855).[128]

Other Cleopatras of the period were more mature in appearance. At Niblo's Garden, the Sydney-born Agnes Booth was 'stately, authoritative', and later that year Rose Eytinge 'pleased the eye and satisfied the sense of voluptuousness and luxury, without either profoundly stirring the imagination or touching the heart' (Winter, *Shakespeare*, pp. 459–60). In Sydney, Louise Pomeroy gave her best performance to date by rising above her 'stiff and artificial style of acting' (*Sydney Morning Herald*, 27 February 1882), but in Melbourne, Louise Jordan was 'wanting in physique' for the part (*The Theatre*, Sydney, 1 December 1889) and, like Pomeroy, had an American accent, which reviewers regarded as a defect. For Cora Brown-Potter,[129] who was playing on her home ground, accent was not the problem. Winter thought the 1889 production at Palmer's Theatre, New York, had been mounted 'chiefly for the purpose of exploiting the beauty of a pretty woman, who possessed social prominence' (*Shakespeare*, p. 464). But social prominence, professional acting and the role of a 'bad woman' did not sit easily together in the period. Mrs Brown-Potter's social set attended her performances, but were apparently as scandalised (and fascinated) by her self-display in gauzy costumes and flesh-coloured tights as

---

127 More modern examples are Margaret Whiting, who, at 24, looked too young in 1957, and Catherine Lacey, whose acting in 1935 was more persuasive.

128 Similar complaints were made about modern productions: Octavius looked older than Antony in the Robertson/Selbie production, and Iden Payne's production and Byam Shaw's in 1953 suffered from insufficient contrast between Antony and Caesar.

129 *Née* Urquhart, she was 'known variously as Mrs Potter, Mrs Brown-Potter, or Mrs Potter-Brown', because her brother-in-law, a minister, 'sued to prevent her from besmirching the family name when she went on the stage' (Bordman, *American Theatre*, pp. 262, 277).

the establishment theatre critics. On the opening night, when she bared her breast to the fangs of the asp and the gaze of the audience, 'it is said that her husband watched this performance from the back of the house, fled horrified, and never laid eyes on her again' (Shattuck, *Shakespeare on the American Stage*, vol. II, p. 123). Charles Shattuck (p. 124) notes that, amid general disapproval of her onstage behaviour, a couple of reviewers did praise Brown-Potter's 'passionate' acting; this fact, and acknowledgement of some professional resentment of her amateur origin, need balancing against Winter's contemptuous dismissal of her performance. The casting of Brown-Potter may have been commercially cynical, but it probably reflected crude naturalistic thinking, of the class-conscious sort, about Cleopatra's queenliness.

On such a basis Lillie Langtry played the role the following year in London. Langtry, a famous beauty and one of the better-known mistresses of the Prince of Wales (Brown-Potter was also one of his favourites), had the commercial advantage of established sexual notoriety outside the theatre, and apparent qualifications for the part in her familiarity with both royalty and passion. If Mrs Brown-Potter was the 'belle of the modern ball-room' (Winter, *Shakespeare*, p. 462) who got carried away, Mrs Langtry, who did not, 'was evidently a Cleopatra who had gone the round of the best country houses' and was 'doubtless an adept with the cue' (Walkley, *Playhouse Impressions*, p. 46).[130] Critics tended to agree with Langtry that her death was the best part of her performance.[131] She complained of the brevity of the love scenes and, less plausibly, that their 'bickering' made 'the moods of the Egyptian Queen . . . so foreign to my nature that I found them very difficult to portray'; it is of her attempt that the elderly lady is supposed to have remarked, 'How very different from the home life of our own dear Queen!'[132] Whilst Langtry as actress played upon her social notoriety, she was too self-conscious to be able to act it out on stage, unlike Lola Montez, the 'bad woman' in public,[133] who was eminently suited to the role of Cleopatra in Victorian farce, as she demonstrated to Sydney's delight in 1855–6.

130 Despite the bowdlerising in her text of the lines about billiards.
131 Tree, who was performing elsewhere, 'arrived in time for Cleopatra's death, and was very enthusiastic, but I am sure that was the scene I played and stage-managed the best' (Lillie Langtry, *The Days I Knew*, p. 233).
132 See, e.g., *Morning Post*, 26 April 1921.
133 Her liaison with King Ludwig I of Bavaria got him deposed and endangered her life in 1848, and her idea of damage control was to horsewhip newspaper editors; she was happy to play herself in *Lola Montez in Bavaria* or to repeat her 'spider dance' for goldminers (see Young, *Famous Actors and Actresses*, vol. II, pp. 811–14).

Doubtless a desire to stabilise her social position had something to do with Langtry's failure, but it demonstrated that the verisimilitude of the protagonists' passion is what matters in tragedy, and the blurring of life and art is not necessarily helpful. Langtry was no more convincing than Eleanora Duse, the subject of scandal from the beginning of her relationship with Giuseppe Verdi's librettist, Arrigo Boito,[134] and promisingly foreign, but whose stage embraces were 'chilly' (Archer, *1893*, p. 176). A good-looking Cleopatra may have social and sexual, and therefore box-office, allure offstage, without being able to demonstrate on the stage how and why she has tied Antony to her rudder.

Janet Achurch made a greater impact in 1897. The first of many red-haired English Cleopatras, she had 'Rossettian hair and beauty to match' (Shaw, *Plays and Players*, p. 244), reflecting specifically Anglo-Saxon assumptions about appearance and sexual behaviour. Her appearance may have reinforced the cultural assumptions of the reviewer ten years later who called Cleopatra 'the worst woman in history' and asked of Collier 'why has she not red hair?' (*Illustrated Sporting and Dramatic News*, 12 January 1907). About Achurch's acting there was strong disagreement. Unlike Julia Marlowe in Calvert's later New York production, she was easy, though not necessarily delightful, to hear;[135] whether she also lacked majesty and 'poetry' is a moot point. James Agate saw 'majesty' and 'physical passion' (*Brief Chronicles*, p. 175), but the *Illustrated London News* reviewer said she 'disappointed us by an artificial and monotonous elocution and by strange vocal tricks which never carried conviction' (12 June 1897); her performance was apparently more stylised in London (Archer, *1897*, p. 157). Shaw liked her 'energy' but not her 'modern republican' 'contempt for ceremony and artificiality': 'When Miss Achurch comes on one of the weak, treacherous, affected streaks in Cleopatra, she suddenly drops from an Egyptian warrior queen into a naughty English *petite bourgeoise*, who carries off a little greediness and a little voluptuousness by a very unheroic sort of prettiness' (*Plays and Players*, p. 191). Whilst this accusation of undignified modernity has something in common with Hazlitt's against Faucit, in that it derives from a perceived lack of majesty, it is less directly concerned with

134 He translated *Antony and Cleopatra* for her, cutting it to emphasise Cleopatra's part. His version was first performed in Milan in 1888, but was better received on tour on the continent than in Italy (see John Stokes, Michael R. Booth and Susan Bassnett, *Bernhardt, Terry, Duse*, p. 147).

135 Marlowe was 'fair to see and delightful to hear', acoustics permitting: the production was marred by the New Theatre's bad design, but both protagonists were miscast, Marlowe having a 'flowery air of sweet ingenuousness' (Bordman, *American Theatre*, p. 660).

tragic seriousness and more to do with class and style. It also relates issues of dignity and class to the 'problem' of Englishness. In the following year, Constance Benson was praised for trying to make sense of the part. Her Cleopatra was 'a little beyond her physical capacity, and . . . lacks the broad humanity which Shakespeare has imparted to it' (*Stratford-upon-Avon Herald*, 15 April 1898), but 'she coaxes, she wheedles, she upbraids, she cajoles, with the self-abandonment of a woman touched with the fire of a consuming love. In a word, she makes a most difficult character, and one most foreign to English ideas – comprehensible, pathetic, fascinating' (*Birmingham Daily Gazette*, 15 April 1898). In his Introduction to the Langtry acting edition (p. viii), Arthur Symons looked for foreign salvation, wishing that Sarah Bernhardt would assay Shakespeare's Cleopatra; after seeing Constance Collier, the *Observer* critic asked, 'unless in Madame Sarah Bernhardt, is there a possible Cleopatra on the stage of to-day?' (30 December 1906). English actresses looked uncomfortable in the role, and even in Benson's third production in 1912, which 'marked a considerable advance' (*Birmingham Mail*, 24 April 1912) and in which the young Dorothy Green was well received, she was considered 'a shade too excitable, a shade too restless' (*Birmingham Daily Post*, 24 April 1912). In such a part, 'want of repose' is probably more a fault in the eyes of Victorian and Edwardian than modern reviewers, though 'restlessness' and 'repose' regained currency in late 1980s reviewing;[136] whilst the term relates most obviously to desired majesty, it is perhaps a touchstone for English feelings of discomfort about 'infinite variety', in both Cleopatras and reviewers.

Some reviewers found Constance Collier's Cleopatra too 'modern' (*Daily Mail*, 28 December 1906). Made up with 'dusky brown skin' (Collier, *Harlequinade*, p. 186), she 'gleamed an Eastern queen, raven as the night, with teeth glistening like moonlight between the red passion of her lips' (*Liverpool Courier*, 28 December 1906), but for all her archaeologising make-up, she gave out more modern signals, 'dress[ing] herself in clinging robes which half conceal and half reveal her form' (*Morning Post*, 28 December 1906); she had been slimming for the part (Collier, *Harlequinade*, p. 184). As in the cases of Achurch and Marlowe, she reduced Cleopatra's grand and foreign 'passion and design' to the unpoetic, *déclassée* local version, and 'appeared to be only playfully flirting – as a Brixton shop girl might flirt' (*Sporting Life*, 28 December 1906). Her most memorable scenes

---

136 Phillips had lacked repose, as had the young Wallis (*Illustrated London News*, 27 September 1873), and even the mature Glyn's acting had 'too much motion' (*Illustrated London News*, 25 May 1867). Barbara Everett thought Judi Dench just missed 'the repose' of Cleopatra's 'effortless sense of power' (*Times Literary Supplement*, 24 April 1987).

were 'when she performs a species of jiu-jitsu on an unoffending and obsequious messenger' (*Pelican*, 2 January 1907), her lamentation over the dead Antony and her death-scene; but her voice was said to be 'too restricted in range' (*Evening News*, 28 December 1906) and her enunciation unclear; she also revealed an 'involuntary indifference when she is a listener' (*Ladies' Field*, 5 January 1907).

Pictorial Antonys usually managed to look the part, and often to appear 'manly' or 'energetic' – though at Palmer's Theatre the clean-shaven 34-year-old English actor Kyrle Bellew 'appeared in the person of an effeminate stripling' (Winter, *Shakespeare*, p. 462) – but not to be convincing as lovers; they were good at self-recrimination, convincing in the scene with Eros, and, like their Cleopatras, good at dying. In 1873 Anderson 'was endowed with lofty stature and a fine voice' (Towse, *Sixty Years of the Theater*, p. 65), and came with his own outfits, 'some splendid Roman armour made by M. Granger, of Paris, and a classical toga copied from that of Talma' (Anderson, *An Actor's Life*, p. 315). Reviewers found him 'ultra-declamatory in style' (*Athenaeum*, 27 September 1873), but energetic. In the Langtry–Wingfield production, Charles Coghlan was too loud and too long for Arthur Walkley, who complained that he 'shouts all his lines *fff*' and 'is perpetually counting twenty-six between his sentences' (*Playhouse Impressions*, pp. 45–6). Louis Calvert, in his production of 1897, 'was, physically speaking, a perfect Antony, and his performance was marked throughout by strength and intensity, yet missed erotic passion and tragic power' (*Illustrated London News*, 12 June 1897); Shaw thought him overweight. In Calvert's New York production, E. H. Sothern was 'earnest' but 'unsuited to the part, physically, temperamentally, and in artistic style' (Winter, *Shakespeare*, pp. 464–7). Frank Benson suggested 'the moodiness' of Antony', but was best in 'the stern rather than in the melting mood' (*Birmingham Daily Gazette*, 15 April 1898). In Tree's performance, 'when lines slipped from his memory, he waved his hand deprecatingly towards his splendid scenery, as though to an alleviation or an excuse' (*Academy*, 5 January 1907); some reviewers did excuse him on the grounds that he was 'burdened with the cares of production and with the responsibility of management' (*Northern Advertiser*, 29 December 1906). Whilst the credibility of English Antonys has received less attention than that of their Cleopatras, they have equally tended to lack the necessary ardour. The *Times* reviewer said of Tree's, 'An Italian writer recently complained of our Englishmen's *fredezza sensuale* . . . it would be odd if an Antony were to show himself Anglicised in that particular direction. But no doubt Mr. Tree will become more demonstratively amorous by and by . . . he is used to "magnoperating"' (28 December 1906). Others saw his Antony as not having 'the strength of his vices' (*Manchester Dispatch*, 28 December 1906) and, like

Benson's, as 'more convincing when despairing or hating than when love-making' (*Sporting Life*, 28 December 1906). Some found fault with Tree's appearance (thinking he looked too young) or delivery: 'he spoke almost all his emotional passages on one rather hoarse, high note' (*Daily Mirror*, 28 December 1906) and used 'mechanical alternations of fortissimo and diminuendo' (*Tribune*, 28 December 1906).

Some trends are discernible in the playing of supporting roles in pictorial productions. As might be expected in an imperialist age, the part of Octavius became more prominent. Perhaps for the first time, Frank Kemble Cooper 'made a "hit" in it' in the Langtry–Wingfield production (Winter, *Shakespeare*, p. 453). In 1897, G.F. Black was praised for speaking his verse well (Archer, *1897*, p. 72) and in Tree's production Basil Gill's Caesar was 'a noble and an imposing figure' (*Truth*, 2 January 1907), if 'inclined to bark' (O.S., *Punch*, 2 January 1907), and 'a far more robustious personality than Antony himself. It would be difficult to say how much point is lost in the play by this topsy-turvy arrangement' (*Times*, 28 December 1906). Enobarbus was appreciated, for his self-recrimination as much as for his cynicism, and his celebrated speech enjoyed as a set-piece, despite the spectacle of the real thing in many productions. In Chatterton's, 'Mr Ryder made Enobarbus a more prominent personage than he perhaps ever has been before' (*Era*, 28 September 1873), Lyall Swete's Enobarbus was praised in 1898 and in Tree's production, J. C. Trewin was not alone in thinking that, as far as acting was concerned, 'Lyn Harding's gruff Enobarbus ruled the night' (*Shakespeare on the English Stage*, p. 41); he was vigorously applauded for his barge speech and praised for 'his fine presence, resonant voice, and robust style' (*Manchester Evening News*, 28 December 1906).

Attention was also given to the smaller parts. In Benson's 1898 production, Oscar Asche was praised for his Pompey. The Australian-born Asche was, in 1912–13, to tour Australia in a very expensive production whose scenic splendour (the scenery was by Joseph Harker) surpassed *Kismet*'s;[137] he was the Antony to his wife Lily Brayton's 'brilliant effort' as a red-haired Cleopatra.[138] As Lamb says (*Antony and Cleopatra*, p. 90), Benson's main legacy was the experience in repertory Shakespeare that he gave both actors (who also included Randle Ayrton and Baliol Holloway) and future

137 'At the Theatre Royal, Melbourne . . . owing to the great depth of the stage, we were able to produce on a scale which only one other English-speaking theatre, Drury Lane, would permit of' (Asche, *Oscar Asche*, p. 142). Asche took *Kismet*, which he had rewritten and first successfully produced in London, with him to Australia as well.

138 The *Sydney Mail*, quoted in Katharine Brisbane (ed.), *Entertaining Australia*, p. 167. It is an index of the lamentable neglect of the stage history of Shakespeare in Australia that Bevington, in the Introduction to his New Cambridge edition, p. 59, should list Brayton as one of the actors who 'stayed away' from the role of Cleopatra.

directors (including Robert Atkins and Harcourt Williams). In Louis Calvert's English production, Agate approved of the way in which Cleopatra's maids were used to establish 'the atmosphere of the East' and particularly noticed Iras (*Brief Chronicles*, p. 179); in 1906 Alice Crawford was commended for her 'repose' in the last scene (B.L., *Evening Standard*, 28 December 1906), not the only time in the play's stage history that Charmian looked like upstaging her queen.

'Released in action': Stratford and the Old Vic, 1921–45

The beginning of the modern stage history of *Antony and Cleopatra* is marked by decisive breaks with the Victorian tradition of staging, freeing the play from that identification with spectacle which dated back to Garrick but was particularly strong in the late Victorian period. The staging revolution was largely brought about by a rejection (already voiced by some reviewers of Tree's production) of Victorian preconceptions, and was abetted by financial and theatrical conditions in the twenties. The economic situation militated against expensive productions as economic recession deepened into the Great Depression: in Australia it was the death in 1930 of the touring Allan Wilkie Shakespearean Company, which included *Antony and Cleopatra* in its repertoire.[139] Eric Bentley's contention that 'the simplicity of the "new" Shakespeare' had 'social as well as merely formal significance. It was less expensive; and it was designed for a less wealthy public' is supported by the fact that the Stratford and Old Vic productions in this period were not taken very seriously by some of the influential (and snobbish) newspaper critics. But Bentley overstates his case in claiming that Lilian Baylis, founder of the Old Vic, was 'more important in this connection than Granville-Barker' because 'her aim was nothing less than to make Shakespeare popular' (*In Search of Theater*, p. 114). As far as *Antony and Cleopatra* is concerned, it is vital not to underestimate the role of William Bridges-Adams in Stratford and the influence on him (and on Harcourt Williams at the Old Vic) of Granville-Barker's notions of how Shakespeare's text should be staged for maximum dramatic impact. Harley Granville-Barker has almost certainly been the single greatest influence on twentieth-century directors. An actor-producer turned writer, his *Prefaces*, grounded in his practical work in the theatre, have been accorded the status of academic authority (and recently reprinted), though initially his credibil-

---

139 In the twenties the company had performed twenty-seven of Shakespeare's plays (see Brisbane (ed.), *Entertaining Australia*, p. 214); *Antony and Cleopatra* opened in Hobart in 1927 with Allan Wilkie and his wife Frediswyde Hunter-Watts (initially Lorna Forbes) in the leading roles. Wilkie used curtains and backdrops; his designer, Arthur Goodsall, had worked with Poel's Elizabethan Stage Society.

ity and influence were straightforwardly theatrical. According to Bridges-Adams, Granville-Barker owed much to William Poel, who, at the turn of the century, had pioneered the production of the plays of Shakespeare and his contemporaries in conditions approximating Elizabethan ones. In turn he directly influenced Harcourt Williams.[140] *Antony and Cleopatra* was one of Granville-Barker's favourite plays,[141] though his planned production of it was prevented by the outbreak of the First World War. Bridges-Adams, Robert Atkins and Williams presented the play comparatively uncut, with a new pace that demonstrated its stageability to the satisfaction of most critics, directors and actors, and it enjoyed a burst of popularity that has not been surpassed until recently: in the twenty-year period between the two world wars there were as many professional productions of *Antony and Cleopatra* in England as in the whole of the nineteenth century.

Bridges-Adams and Atkins were keen to return to the rapidity and simplicity of the staging of Shakespeare's day. Their approach to the task was influenced by the opinions of contemporary scholars about Elizabethan practice, and the use of traverse curtains reflected the now-discredited notion that there was a permanent 'inner stage' in Elizabethan and Jacobean theatres, as well as the very unElizabethan assumption (derived from scenic theatre tradition) that 'locations' could not change without curtain-closing; the use of comparatively uncut texts by 'unaBridges-Adams' and Atkins reflected Elizabethan practice, though their texts were probably compiled more in the anti-pictorial spirit of 'whole Shakespeare' than in the spirit of Elizabethan pragmatism.

In his Stratford Festival production of 1921, Bridges-Adams's twenty-nine scenes, 'all of them adequate and artistic, and some of a rare beauty, succeeded one another swiftly and without a hitch' (*Morning Post*, 25 April 1921); most reviewers found the three-hour production, with only minor cuts, remarkably brisk. Bridges-Adams had installed a cyclorama at Stratford and used traverse curtains,[142] as he had done at Oxford two months earlier;[143] the scenery 'suggested space, colour and empire' whilst

---

140 See John Gielgud, *Early Stages*, p. 189, Harcourt Williams, *Four Years at the Old Vic*, p. 94 and Speaight, *Shakespeare on the Stage*, p. 150.

141 See *Prefaces* and Trewin, *Shakespeare on the English Stage*, pp. 203–4.

142 See Sybil Rosenfeld, *A Short History of Scene Design*, p. 178.

143 In February Bridges-Adams had produced the play, with twenty-nine scenes and two intervals, for the Oxford University Dramatic Society, with scenery of his own design, the Egyptian scenes being based on a Greco-Roman temple to Hathor and Cleopatra (Cathleen Nesbitt) wearing ostrich feathers like the goddess; 'two permanent pillars of this temple remained during the entire action, the traverse-curtain being drawn between them in the Elizabethan manner' (*Birmingham Post*, 10 February 1921).

being 'easily manoeuvrable' (Ellis, *Shakespeare Memorial Theatre*, p. 44). Bridges-Adams used two intervals, since he believed the play fell naturally into three parts, but, in a curtsey to the act-drop tradition, 'lower[ed] the curtain for a moment to indicate the orthodox division into five acts' (*Morning Post*, 26 April 1921). W. A. Darlington thought this production Bridges-Adams's best to date, partly because his 'methods' suited the play's 'swift changes of time and place'. But the sheer pace of his production style made the remnants of pictorialism more intrusive: 'the backcloth of a closing scene may be observed rolling up before the front curtains have had time to screen it from view' and 'the voices of the actors at the front of the stage are almost drowned in the noise caused by the stage hands getting the next set ready' (*Through the Fourth Wall*, pp. 73, 46).[144]

Bridges-Adams directed the play three more times in Stratford, twice more with the same Cleopatra, Dorothy Green (in 1924 and 1927), and twice (in 1927 and 1931) in the Cinema in Greenhill Street, which was used as a makeshift after the old theatre had burnt down, and whose acoustics distorted the louder scenes. Many reviewers disliked his lighting in 1921: 'half tones and half lights make pretty stage pictures, but are too great a strain on the audience and a severe handicap to the actor' (*Stratford-upon-Avon Herald*, 29 April 1921). Complaints about lighting abound in reviews of this period, and whilst there is little doubt that it was often unsatisfactory, especially at Stratford (and particularly in the Cinema), its inadequacy probably resulted from attempts to use lighting in a 'modern', flexible fashion rather than as a mere adjunct to scenery. Technical skills, in the days prior to the rise of the lighting director, appear not to have been matched to aesthetic considerations. In 1925 at the Old Vic, Andrew Leigh's lighting had a 'peculiarly cold quality', in which, said Agate, 'the Egyptian temperature seemed to be a good ten degrees below freezing point' (*Brief Chronicles*, p. 176); the large new stage at Stratford caused lighting problems for Ben Iden Payne, whereby 'certain make-ups and wigs which looked effective up stage failed to stand the test of different lighting down stage, and vice versa' (M.F.K.F., *Birmingham Mail*, 16 April 1935); whilst in Theodore Komisarjevsky's production, 'the stage pales and darkens, smiles and gleams, glows and flashes so often and so restlessly that the whole emphasis is on the electrician' (*Times*, 15 October 1936).

Bridges-Adams's importance to the stage historian is compounded by his casting of Dorothy Green. In 1921 reviewers found her Cleopatra 'more mature' than in 1912; her appearance was 'striking', with a peacock head-dress 'contrasting in colour with the braided hair of bright red, and set above

---

144 In 1927 one critic also complained of the superfluous 'playing of martial music in the orchestra' at the fall of the curtains between scenes (*Morning Post*, 13 July 1927).

a countenance which in its scornful beauty might have been copied from an Eastern gem' (R.C.R., *Birmingham Daily Post*, 25 April 1921). Her impact was reduced by the defective lighting, but, like Glyn in 1855, 'there were times when [she] held the audience breathless' (*Stratford-upon-Avon Herald*, 29 April 1921). Like Glyn, too, Green had 'the majesty of style without which Cleopatra sinks to a petulant, spoiled child' and 'a fine voice which she uses to bring out the music of the verse' (Darlington, *Through the Fourth Wall*, p. 74). Her best scenes were also ones in which Glyn had excelled, the messenger scene and her preparation for death; 'her acting was a triumph of understanding both in the round and in detail, of swift April changes, of right co-ordination of tone and gesture and expression' (F.A.C., *Birmingham Gazette*, 25 April 1921). Glyn's and Green's best scenes were the very ones that even average English Cleopatras could manage creditably, and one of Green's less enthusiastic reviewers raised the problem of Englishness: 'Miss Green's is a personality too English, and, if I may say so, too correct, for the exotic languors of the East' (*Truth*, 25 June 1924). Most critics, however, were satisfied with a superb example of the English product.

Green's Antony in 1921, Edmund Willard, was, like many English predecessors and contemporaries, 'a good, honest, manly piece of work' (W. A. Darlington, *Daily Telegraph*, 28 July 1921), but performed unevenly, partly because he stole his own thunder by being too passionate at the beginning. Her next Antony, in Bridges-Adams's production for the Stratford Summer Festival in 1924,[145] was Baliol Holloway, formerly an Enobarbus and equally rugged, but with a tendency to 'break all his lines half-way through and to deliver them in a sharp monotonous staccato' (*Queen*, 25 June 1924). He played the part again, this time for Andrew Leigh at the Old Vic, in the following year, looking perhaps too noble but his delivery still irritating. Green's third Antony, Wilfrid Walter, had already played the part for Atkins in 1922, when he was 'a living and fighting man of action', but sometimes sacrificed 'his verse to his vigour' (*Times*, 8 December 1922). In 1927 his vigorous appearance was read variously: at face value, as ironically emphasising Antony's weaknesses, or as a mere decorative front.[146]

It is not surprising that in a period between wars there should be some production emphasis on Enobarbus as an instrument of cynical satire and on the sinister potential of some of the play's lesser figures. Whilst the starting-point in each of these productions was an inherited 'bluff' and soldierly Enobarbus, the part was given sharper delineation by Baliol Holloway, who had been Lepidus and the Clown in 1912; he was widely praised for playing

145 Preceded by a brief season at the King's Theatre, Hammersmith.
146 For the latter two readings, see *Daily Telegraph*, 12 July 1927 and *Morning Post*, 13 July 1927 respectively.

Enobarbus with 'an almost rancid quality in his biting humour' and acting 'the final scenes of remorse with a deep and moving emotion' (*Morning Post*, 26 April 1921). Randle Ayrton was a 'splendidly whimsical' as well as a deeply repentant Enobarbus (*Birmingham Mail*, 8 June 1931), and when he played the part again again he gave 'a dryly cynical yet richly humorous and human rendering' (*Stage*, 16 April 1935). Other lesser roles were also given a new dimension in productions of this period. John Maclean was commended for his 'delightful portrayal of the rustic clown' (*Stratford-upon-Avon Herald*, 29 April 1921) and in 1927 Charmian (Lydia Sherwood) and Iras (Edith Johnson) made the most of their comparatively passive roles by 'play[ing] up to the caprices of Cleopatra with ironical understanding' (K.M.C., *Birmingham Gazette*, 18 July 1927). Kenneth Wicksteed also took his opportunity and made Alexas 'a sinister, awe inspiring figure' (*Stage*, 14 July 1927); the Alexas in Bridges-Adams's previous production, Alfred Harris, had given 'an unusual, and unusually good, performance' (*Times*, 19 June 1924). In 1931 Roy Byford added Mardian to the minor characters who could be played as 'sinister' (Kemp and Trewin, *The Stratford Festival*, p. 152), and was 'unctuously amusing' in the part again in 1935 (*Stage*, 16 April 1935). The Caesars of the period were notable for being sinister in appropriately dominant fashion, in the world of *realpolitik*. Percy Rhodes's Octavius was 'commanding, cool, and calculating' (F.A.C., *Birmingham Gazette*, 25 April 1921). Eric Maxon, who in 1924 had been 'a rough, soldierly Enobarbus' (*Times*, 19 June 1924), was, in 1927, commended for his 'scornful righteousness' as Caesar, which 'emphasised the contrast between himself and Antony' (K.M.C., *Birmingham Gazette*, 18 July 1927); similarly, his stage sister, played by Esme Biddle, with her 'cold, regal, statuesque handsomeness', was 'a perfect contrast to Cleopatra' (R.C.R., *Birmingham Post*, 18 July 1927). Maxon was a commanding Caesar again in 1931 .

Robert Atkins, who had been Tree's Ventidius but had also acted with Benson's company and was a disciple of Poel, is usually credited with bringing the new Shakespearean staging practices of Granville-Barker and Poel to *Antony and Cleopatra* at the Old Vic in 1922, despite Bridges-Adams's production at Stratford in the previous year. The reason for this – aside from the influence of earlier stage historians – probably lies in the Old Vic's position as a popularising venue for Shakespeare (Atkins directed all the Folio plays there between 1920 and 1925) and in Atkins's more determinedly neo-Elizabethan break with naturalistic scenery and use of an add-on forestage. Atkins used a cyclorama and traverse curtains (like Bridges-Adams), and a 'quick black-out' between scenes.[147] He added to the pro-

---

147 Letter from John Laurie to Margaret Lamb, quoted in Lamb, *Antony and Cleopatra*, p. 107.

scenium stage a forestage which 'gets rid of the orchestra and brings the actors now and then into a more intimate relationship with the audience', but whose lower level and abrupt tapering made the audience 'conscious of the invasion' of a separate space by the actor (*Daily Herald*, 18 September 1922). The forestage was unpopular with actors and critics, and seems to have been put to less practical use than the traverse curtains. Like Bridges-Adams, Atkins used a largely-uncut text (his had thirty-one scenes) and a minimum of intervals (Atkins had only one); at the fast pace, this usually went down well and drew large audiences, for whom the play 'was released in action and made almost unbearably clear' (*Westminster Gazette*, 9 December 1922). The *Graphic* reviewer, however, sniffed at 'the holus-bolus school which produces Shakespeare without a cut' (16 December 1922), as Agate was to do in considering Leigh's production of 1925: 'one almost fears the management of the Old Vic has succumbed to the fetish of performing these plays as they were written. One or two small scenes might certainly have gone, and so long an interval between the dying of the two protagonists is certain to make for anti-climax' (*Brief Chronicles*, p. 174). Neither Atkins nor Leigh could offer Dorothy Green in that long interval. Atkins's Cleopatra, Esther Waterhouse, 'misse[d] something of the passion that raises Antony's love for her clear of the Romans' contempt for it' (*Times*, 8 December 1922).

If there were economic reasons, as well as ideological motivation (partly theatrical, partly social), for the neo-Elizabethan movement of the twenties, its celebration of uncluttered simplicity and pace was also in keeping with the aesthetic spirit of the age. In that respect, the tendency towards abstraction in sets was a direct expression of the culture of the period, and in keeping with interpretative tendencies. The Egyptian scenes in *Antony and Cleopatra* must have had a particular appeal in an age preoccupied with Egyptian motifs in the plastic arts, with seductress figures, of whom Cleopatra is the archetype, and with lithe women in archaic dress who look unmistakably modern, as reviewers said of several Cleopatras of the period. Egyptian motifs were modish because of Howard Carter's search for Tutankhamun's tomb and eventual discovery of it in 1922 – which may also have been a minor stimulant for the four productions whose makeshift nature provided such ironic contrast with Tutankhamun's splendours: Atkins's a little later that year, Bridges-Adams's of 1924 and 1927 and Leigh's of 1925, in which 'Alexandria and Rome only possessed two pieces of furniture between them' (Agate, *Brief Chronicles*, p. 176).

When Andrew Leigh succeeded Atkins at the Old Vic in 1925, he mounted an *Antony and Cleopatra* 'full of interesting experiments' (*Morning Post*, 2 December 1925), all of which drew some critical fire. Aside from casting Edith Evans as Cleopatra and getting her to die on a sofa (a return to the pre-Langtry nineteenth-century tradition, though Leigh may have seen it as a return to the Folio), the most interesting experiment was the decor, designed by John Garside in twenties mode, with settings 'most effective and decorative in their simplicity' (*Era*, 2 December 1925), but which made Agate long for 'Tadema-like excesses in bathroom marble' (*Brief Chronicles*, p. 176). Edith Evans, who had played Cleopatra in *All for Love* in 1922, was admired for her intelligence and art, but generally considered miscast: she 'seemed to lack not passion, but animal fire' (*Times*, 3 December 1925), though 'her beautiful voice' was 'so full of every variety of light and shade' (*Era*). Ivor Brown thought her 'unequalled' in the passages usually done well by English Cleopatras, 'the tempests of her rage' and 'the calm splendour of her going hence' (*Saturday Review*, 12 December 1925), but she was not majestic in the manner of Green, or even of Waterhouse.

Green played her final Cleopatra, for Harcourt Williams at the Old Vic, as unabashedly middle-aged, in a production 'remarkable for its thought-fulness rather than its broad sweeps of passion' (*Era*, 26 November 1930); previously, Green's 'method' had been welcomed by the *Times* reviewer as 'by contrast with the methods of other Cleopatras, deliberately austere' (16 July 1924). Her 'austerity' presumably dominated as she aged and matured, and her art was often remembered nostalgically later, as Glyn's had been. Her last Cleopatra graced the first production of the play in Renaissance dress since the Jacobean period. Both Bridges-Adams and Atkins favoured stage Roman and Egyptian costume, but in 1930, under the influence of Granville-Barker's view that the play's costumes should be based on those in Veronese's paintings,[148] and to designs by Paul Smyth, Williams used 'Veronese' costumes to provide 'the peacock-strut of a Renaissance Orient with all the archaeology left out and all the romance left in' (Ivor Brown, *Weekend Review*, 29 November 1930). A padded Renaissance doublet and grizzled beard helped John Gielgud to look Elizabethan, though at 26 he seemed both too young and too thin for the part (Gielgud, *Early Stages*, p. 189); his speeches were lustrous, but he strutted too much. He was, however, 'wonderfully deflated' by Ralph Richardson as Enobarbus (Speaight, *Shakespeare on the Stage*, p. 150), who, wearing the 'eponymous brazen beard',[149] and, after his desertion, 'civil-ian, almost penitential, garb', was 'extraordinarily effective and affecting' (Crosse, *Shakespearean Playgoing*, p. 67). Williams himself doubled Messenger and Clown and 'paradoxically he got a good deal of fun out of

148 See Speaight, *Shakespeare on the Stage*, p. 149, Trewin, *Shakespeare on the English Stage*, pp. 136, 138, and Bridges-Adams quoted in *Daily Herald* (3 April 1931).
149 Neil Porter had also done so in 1925.

the former and made the latter eerie and sinister', as Horace Sequeira had done in 1925 (Crosse, *Shakespearean Playgoing*, p. 68). One critic saw the costumes as de-emphasising the 'conflict between Roman pride and Eastern magnificence' (*Era*, 26 November 1930), but Ivor Brown endorsed Williams's view[150] in describing 'the picture' as 'not only lovely in itself but composed and unified in its courtly riches' (*Observer*, 30 November 1930). The production did record business and was allowed an extra week's run, and Williams had taken another neo-Elizabethan step away from Victorian and Edwardian pictorialism.

In the following year, Bridges-Adams produced his final *Antony and Cleopatra*,[151] this time with Renaissance costumes, presumably influenced by Williams, and perhaps directly by Granville-Barker, whose *Preface* had been published the previous year.[152] Some reviewers had not read it, and were puzzled and irritated by Bridges-Adams's costumes: one said of Cleopatra and her women, 'it says much for their acting that at times we almost forgot their incongruous raiment' (*Stratford-upon-Avon Herald*, 8 May 1931). Gyles Isham looked dignified, though like Gielgud, he seemed too young for Antony; unlike Gielgud, he failed to project 'the conquering hero beneath the romantic dallier'. Dorothy Massingham managed to be both 'tempestuous' and regal in her outfits (*Birmingham Mail*, 8 June 1931), but T. C. Kemp and J. C. Trewin, who judged her 'a good average Cleopatra', considered her 'hampered by her costumes' and thought Kenneth Wicksteed's Alexas the only character whose dress 'suggested Imperial Egypt'. Nevertheless they acknowledged Bridges-Adams's defence: 'It is the only way of saving a line like "Cut my lace, Charmian" from absurdity, and it is one way out of Wardour Street, from which this play has suffered much' (*Stratford Festival*, pp. 151, 152).

If 'Veronese' costumes displayed the colours of anti-Victorian 'authenticity', the cinema-screens of Wardour Street provided more contemporary frames of reference for the staging of Cleopatra as a 'vamp'. Revealing dresses and 'braided hair of bright red' (R.C.R., *Birmingham Daily Post*, 28 April 1921) contributed to Green's 'alluring' appearance (*Referee*, 22 June 1924) on her second and third appearances as Cleopatra, and set the standard for twentieth-century English actresses, who, with surprisingly few

---

150 See Williams, *Old Vic Saga*, p. 97.

151 At the Cinema in Stratford, and later at the Prince of Wales Theatre, Birmingham.

152 Granville-Barker's influence continues in this respect. In 1946 Byam Shaw used modified Renaissance dress, and recent productions have tended to use Veronese-style costumes, if less consciously under Granville-Barker's aegis: Robertson's of 1977, Hack's of 1983, Miller's BBC TV version, Hall's 1987 production and Caird's of 1993.

exceptions, have represented Cleopatra in terms of highly Anglicised notions of wantonness: pale-skinned, frequently red-haired and often clingingly or scantily clad.[153] It may be that such depictions 'play up', as Ralph Berry says, 'the straightforward psychological aspects of the relationship between Antony and Cleopatra',[154] but the ultimate origin of such representations is the theatrical instinct to make Cleopatra's allure as immediate (and hence 'modern') as possible. There was a decidedly cinematic flicker in Edith Evans's (and Baliol Holloway's) appearance, she in the fringed costume, cobra circlet and braided hair[155] of a flapper turned squaw and he in a leopardskin borrowed from Tarzan. In New York in the previous year,[156] Jane Cowl was a twenties Egyptian Queen, 'pert and saucy' (Heywood Broun, quoted in Leiter and Hill (eds.), *Encyclopedia, 1920–1930*, vol. I, p. 31), whilst in 1934, in an up-to-the-minute setting at the Old Vic,[157] Mary Newcombe looked and played Cleopatra as 'a brilliantly clever, highly complex, neurotic lady of our own times' (Agate, *Brief Chronicles*, p. 179). Leslie Rees, who found her 'beautiful and glamorous', thought 'her long leg-stride reminds you of Garbo' (*Era*, 19 September 1934);[158] to Ivor Brown, 'the ladies of the camp and court were oddly

153 Agnes Dobson consciously decided not to play Cleopatra as a vamp in her adaptation for the Independent Theatre in Adelaide in 1938, explaining that the lovers were middle-aged and that the historical Cleopatra 'dressed modestly in Greek robes which didn't show any more than her hands and her head' (quoted in Brisbane (ed.), *Entertaining Australia*, p. 235).

154 'The Imperial Theme', in Richard Foulkes (ed.), *Shakespeare and the Victorian Stage*, pp. 153–60, 159–60.

155 See the familiar photograph of the lovers, reproduced, e.g., in Bevington's edition, plate 10 and Lamb, *Antony and Cleopatra*, plate 15. Braided hair had been associated with Cleopatra at least since Collier's time, but it is the combination of elements that is striking here; the costumes 'gave more than occasion for prosaic distraction' (H.H., *Observer*, 6 December 1925).

156 Frank Reicher's production at the Lyceum Theatre curiously used Tree's version and was 'heavy with carpentry' and 'entr'acte pauses', but still managed to be 'ultramodern and colloquial' (John Corbin, *New York Times*, 24 February 1924) and to use a traverse curtain in the Actium scene and tapestries in the monument.

157 On the 'new permanent stage with apron equivalent and stairways leading up from the orchestra', Cass's decor used strong, modern colours: 'the settings and costumes of David Ffolkes flame brilliantly – orange columns, purple and green surrounds' (Leslie Rees, *Era*, 19 September 1934); the traverse curtains were decorated with 'black and red streaks of lightning (or were they bayonets?)' (*Punch*, 26 September 1934).

158 Michael Sayers saw her as 'an Egypto-Hellenic red-haired first-cousin to Lady Macbeth . . . a prostitute past her prime' (*New English Weekly*, 4 October 1934), but to the *Punch* reviewer she was 'an emphatic blonde' (26 September 1934).

modern . . . It was a new idea to present Charmian as a Garbo part' (*Observer*, 23 September 1934). The lovers' relationship also seemed modern, with more rage than passion in it. Herbert Farjeon said of Wilfrid Lawson, 'I have never seen an Antony who appeared to be less in love with Cleopatra. I have never heard an Antony who made more noise' (*Shakespearean Scene*, p. 174).

Newcombe's clever Cleopatra, in combining a contemporary appearance with intellectual complexity, invited dismissal as too modern; but, in finding her 'neurotic', Agate seems to imply that intellectual sophistication is incompatible with sensuality in any woman. 'Neurotic' may also imply 'undignified', but Agate is not primarily calling Newcombe that (as Faucit and the *fin de siècle* actresses were called undignified): the ground seems to have shifted in the accusation of modernity, as dominant stereotypes of the modern woman have changed (though dignity and sexiness remain incompatible in the stereotypes); now the charge is lack of sensual appeal. Nine years earlier, reviewers had accused Evans of over-intellectualising the part; she, too, dressed in ways that reflected the vampish modes of the period without restricting her acting to vamping. But when Green played her final Cleopatra, not looking modern because she was wearing Veronese costume, the *Era* critic directed his accusation at Cleopatra herself. Doubtless more familiar with the childishly wicked vamp image of his own era than with the historical Cleopatra,[159] he thought Green 'suggested qualities of brain which Antony's mistress certainly never possessed' (26 November 1930), and may have been the first reviewer, though certainly not the last, to object explicitly to the portrayal of Cleopatra as an intelligent woman.

Three years after Newcombe, in a New York production that only ran to five performances,[160] Tallulah Bankhead wore lavender organdy and sequins (*Pittsburgh Sunday Telegraph*, 19 October 1937); in her 'restless modernism', she exhibited 'the garishness of a night-club queen' (Brooks Atkinson, *New York Times*, 11 November 1937) and John Anderson took her Egyptian gestures for 'hootchy-kootchy posturings' (*New York Evening Journal*, 11 November 1937). She surprisingly 'deprived [Cleopatra] of overt sexuality and allure' (Leiter, *Encyclopedia, 1930–1940*, p. 38), possibly because she was acting under her husband John Emery's gaze as

---

159 See Lucy Hughes-Hallett, *Cleopatra*, especially ch. 10.
160 Reginald Bach's production at the Mansfield Theatre was overdesigned and cost $100,000; William Strunk Jr's text rearranged and reduced the text to two acts and fourteen scenes, with 'most emphasis upon the political and battlefield aspects'; the production was 'slowly paced, incompetently spoken, badly edited' (Brooks Atkinson, *New York Times*, 11 November 1937).

Octavius.[161] Her Antony, Conway Tearle, 'roared throughout the performance like a bull of Bashan' (Sidney B. Whipple, *World Telegram*, 11 November 1937), but this was more likely a response to Lawson's precedent than to Bankhead's vamping. Between Newcombe and Bankhead, two English productions offered Cleopatras whose vamping abilities were less foregrounded, for either spatial or linguistic reasons. In Iden Payne's production the Egyptian costumes were 'somewhat attenuated and range from a loin cloth to a bodice and skirt which strive vainly to get together' (W.H.B., *Western Daily Mail*, 16 April 1935) and Cleopatra, the red-haired Catherine Lacey, 'looked most alluring, moved with slender grace, and played with an abundance of spirit' (M.F.K.F., *Birmingham Mail*, 16 April 1935). Yet Ivor Brown

> felt a touch of frost on the Nile, as one often does on English versions of this piece . . . He presented no strumpet's fool, and she no lustful gipsy. And without the hot-house air stirred by this bellows and this fan the play is pointless. It is not easy, I know, for the English theatre to capture this ecstasy; our blood is not so nimble. (*Observer*, 21 April 1935)

Brown contrasted Iden Payne's opening with that of the 1923 production at the Burgtheater in Vienna, when 'two Austrians . . . somehow filled the air with Eastern dalliance and the luxury of sensual devotees'.[162] Brown implicitly recognises that the cultural problem of Englishness is compounded by the theatrical need for an Interactive Double First. But the comparative chill of the atmosphere also had something to do with problems of scale. Whilst the period's emphasis on simplicity tended to diminish difficulties like those caused by the Egyptian sets at the end of the nineteenth century, the dimensions of the new Memorial Theatre stage encouraged upsizing. Lacey was 'a beautiful miniature' (Trewin, *Shakespeare on the English Stage*, p. 168) and in danger of being dwarfed by the heavy architecture of Aubrey Hammond's set and by her monotonous but massive Antony, Roy Emerton: 'when she kissed him she had almost to

---

161 If this is so, she makes an interesting contrast with Brown-Potter (though her husband was not an actor, and she may not have known he was in the audience), and with Michael Redgrave, who seems to have over-compensated for consciousness of spousal observation in 1953. Stage actors seldom manage, as did Burton and Taylor in their film, to live up to the protagonists' ease with public demonstrativeness.

162 Whilst Brown said the production was 'otherwise not to be compared with our English pomps and splendours', the acting, costumes and stagecraft were excellent and the pace was fast: 'The system of curtains renders very swift changes possible, the intervals often lasting less than a minute while the stage is darkened. Only one long interval is made after the third act' (*Shakespearean Quarterly*, 2 (October 1923), p. 39).

climb into his arms' (E. A. Baughan, *News Chronicle*, 17 April 1935). There was an art deco flavour to the Egyptian court scenes, 'with the principal characters silhouetted against a deep blue sky, and the subsidiaries arranged in bas-relief style on steps or against towering pillars' (*Stage*, 16 April 1935), but Iden Payne had a penchant for representational scenery, which he did not see as incompatible with continuous action,[163] and the actors had sometimes to compete with the decor. The galley scene, played against the competition of a garishly painted backcloth, was unintoxicating: 'Mr Iden Payne's handling of this party might be taken as evidence of a well-spent life' (Brown). Such inhibition was not unusual in the period, curiously enough in a partying age,[164] but it is the more surprising in this production, given the enthusiastic carousals of the pictorial tradition.

Komisarjevsky's notorious production at the New Theatre, London,[165] gave 'interesting experiments' a new meaning and several reviewers apoplexy, though not W. A. Darlington, who wrote 'some of his groupings and colourings were wonderfully fine, and his two conventionalised perma-nent settings lent themselves to every possible purpose' (*Daily Telegraph*, 15 October 1936). Komisarjevsky designed his own scenery and costumes. In their idiosyncracy, the costumes might be called ahead of their time or, indeed, Veronese gone modern: Donald Wolfit recalled Eugenie Leontovich 'clad in the scantiest draperies and surmounted by a fireman's helmet, adorned with large white plumes' (*First Interval*, p. 171), Wolfit himself wore 'a voluminous night-shirt, road-mender's boots, and a Greco-Roman breastplate with razor-strops dangling from it' (M.R., *Era*, 21 October 1936) and Menas had a 'uniform made chiefly of seaweed' (Darlington). Hubert Harben, living up to his predecessors and to his outfit as Alexas, 'behaved like an offended bishop in an Elizabethan ruff' (Darlington), whilst Leon Quartermaine as Enobarbus was inappropriately 'the silky diplomat' (Agate, *Brief Chronicles*, p. 184). But the Antony of the less than solidly built Wolfit – who, like Gielgud before him, felt he was too young for the part (*First Interval*, p. 170) – was 'solid and unimaginative' in conception (Farjeon, *Shakespearean Scene*, p. 175). Komisarjevsky made textual changes that, particularly in the light of Stratford and Old Vic prac-tice for the past fifteen years, seemed worse than nineteenth-century cuts,

163 See T. C. Kemp and J. C. Trewin, *The Stratford Festival*, pp. 174–5.
164 In Bridges-Adams's production of 1921, the galley scene was regarded, with the monument scene, as the best (F.A.C., *Birmingham Gazette*, 25 April 1921), but in 1924 his revels were 'rather self-consciously hilarious' (*Times*, 16 July 1924); Atkins's in 1922 was 'curiously ragged' (*Times*, 8 December 1922) and in Leigh's 'Pompey's supper-party needs enlivening' (*Times*, 3 December 1925). Perhaps the reviewers' unenthusiasm can be put down to superior party-experience.
165 After a trial week in Glasgow.

though they were not; his transpositions were resented because they 'were not needed to save scene-shifting' (Crosse, *Shakespearean Playgoing*, p. 98). The rearrangement gave some prominence to the Soothsayer, opening with his predictions about Iras and Charmian, replacing the soldiers with him in the 'supernatural' scene and doubling the part with the Clown's; such thematic emphasis has become standard directorial practice in more recent times: the Soothsayer–Clown combination was a feature of John Caird's 1992–3 production. But most critics were quick to dismiss Komisarjevsky's production (which ran for only four nights) on the grounds of Leontovich's skimpy English. Disapproval of a Russian actor's performing in English was not in itself the issue:[166] Agate's and Charles Morgan's (*Times*, 16 October 1936) attacks on Leontovich were on her temperamental inadequacy for the role of Cleopatra. Darlington said she could not have acted the part in any language, and her performance undermined hopes of foreign salvation from the problem of Englishness. Agate found some consolation in Margaret Rawlings's Charmian, who, with English reticence, 'refrained from wiping Cleopatra off the stage till after she was dead'. The reviewers' real quarrel was with the foreign director's perceived arrogance in rearranging Shakespeare's text and allowing his tragic language to sound grotesque.

Near the end of the war, Atkins produced the play again, this time for the Stratford Festival and without forestage. His style of production had changed little in twenty-three years: with colourful costumes and scenery by J. Gower Parks, he differentiated clearly between Egypt and Rome and 'in a triumphant ordering of the stage, always suggests magnificence, and the verse does the rest'. David Read played Caesar with 'precise frigidity and reserve' (J.C. Trewin, *Observer*, 29 April 1945), but the lovers just missed the poetry of their roles. Claire Luce, an American former dancer (in art deco terms, ideal training for a seductress), almost caught the critics in her 'feminine coils', but they demanded more of 'the majesty on which Shakespeare insists' (*Times*, 25 April 1945) and speech 'as rich in sound as in subtlety' (Trewin). Anthony Eustrel failed to realise that 'Antony's tragedy is the tragedy of middle age', so his 'magnanimities and heroisms and follies and humiliations' were 'at a remove from poetry' (*Times*). Trewin noted that Atkins had wisely cut the Seleucus scene, but regretted his omission of the 'supernatural' one. The point to which Atkins had helped bring English productions of the play is perhaps best illustrated by comparison with the other wartime production, Jean-Louis Barrault's at

---

166 James Agate had approved of the playing of Aspatia in *The Maid's Tragedy* by a
   Chinese actress, Rose Quong, at the Renaissance in 1925 (*Brief Chronicles*, p. 141) as
   'a daring and vocally successful experiment', and the more exacting English critics
   had always taken actors to task over their pronunciation of Shakespeare.

the Comédie-Française, which, with its sea fight and spectacular galley scene, was much more in the Victorian pictorial tradition.[167]

'A few bright particular stars': post-war West End productions

The first of the post-war commercial productions of the play in the West End of London, Glen Byam Shaw's at the Piccadilly Theatre in 1946, starring Godfrey Tearle and Edith Evans, was post-war and transitional in a fairly literal way. The austerities (worse than pre-war ones) and the tentativeness of the search for new forms in the aftermath of the war are apparent in many of the features of the production. The most obvious of these was perhaps the set. Trewin emphasised the set's controversial nature, which, he said, 'ranked in boldness with the *Hamlet* and the *Romeo and Juliet* of the mid-thirties' (*Shakespeare on the English Stage*, p. 203). It was, in a sense, a development of pre-war neo-Elizabethan preconceptions, as were other aspects of the production: its continuous action, with full text and only one interval, its modified Veronese-style costumes and its occasional use of traverse curtains; even its lighting, of which Agate complained that there was 'no suggestion that we are in Egypt or Rome or anywhere except the colder parts of Iceland' (*Sunday Times*, 29 December 1946). A permanent set was a novelty in productions of this play – though ten years earlier Komisarjevsky had used two, one either side of the interval – and in many respects it was modern, being multifunctional, severe and rather obtrusive, not only because it was placed far forward to accommodate sightlines, but also because architecturally it was post-fascist,[168] with its column–tower–monument and the recess beneath it that suggested 'an airraid shelter or an elevator with sliding doors' (Rylands, 'Elizabethan Drama in the West End', p. 105). It was also modern in being designed (like the costumes) by Motley, a group of three English women who had been producing stage designs for Shakespearean and other productions since the early thirties. Although the set was conceived of as incorporating the main features of the Elizabethan public theatre, it looked very unElizabethan, not only in style but in obtrusiveness (largely a function of its being a set rather

---

167 The production, in André Gide's translation and starring A. Clarimond and Marie Bell, opened a few days after Atkins's. With decor and costume by Jean Hugo and music by Jacques Ibert, it was 'a magnificent show, perhaps too magnificent. It seems as if the producer's aim is to redeem the cold classicality of Gide's style by a rich display of colours and shapes and movement' (Henri Fluchère, 'Shakespeare in France', p. 123).

168 By this I mean that, with its tower standing centrally on a platform, it seems to belong to the 'architecture of coercion' that celebrates the centralisation of power and looks back to the monumental forms of the fascist architecture of the thirties.

than an integral part of the theatre's architecture), and in its leaving insufficient room for processions (a consequence of its forward positioning and there being no forestage). George Rylands, who had himself directed the play for the Marlowe Society in Cambridge in 1934 and 1946, deplored the 'permanent solids', as obliterating 'the essential contrast' between Rome and Egypt, but the *Times* reviewer, seeing the play as 'the hardest to confine within the limits of the modern localised picture-frame stage', thought the set allowed Shaw to 'impose' on the action 'a genuine continuity' (21 December 1946).

This production was also post-war and transitional in the sense that it featured 'stars' of the pre-war period. Like the Oliviers of the next West End production and Michael Redgrave of Shaw's second production, Tearle was a film star, but in 1946 he had come out of retirement to play Antony; Edith Evans was 58, and probably felt the need of the red wig she wore.[169] They both performed memorably. For Darlington, Evans came closest to fusing Green's queenliness with Luce's seductiveness in a way that makes Cleopatra 'a living and breathing woman' (*Daily Telegraph*, 21 December 1946) and Crosse especially liked 'her luxury of grief in Antony's absence' (*Shakespearean Playgoing*, p. 65). Tearle used his mature 'rich, resonant voice and noble presence' to advantage, so that 'for once we have an Antony who is really an old lion dying and not a martial Romeo' (*Times*). Less than a year later, he was starring with leading American actor-manager Katharine Cornell in a production, directed by her husband Guthrie McClintic at the Martin Beck Theatre, New York, that was decidedly post-war in its treatment of imperial expansionism: 'Shakespeare's soldiers are Nazis, Pompey a Göring, Caesar a Baldur von Schirach, the rank and file a squad of heiling stormtroopers' (Bentley, *In Search of Theater*, p. 28). Bentley was not impressed by the novelty of this politicisation by updating and commented, 'so poetry dwindles into journalism'. The production, however, set a record by running for 127 performances before touring as far west as Chicago, for another 73 performances.[170] The extent to which its veteran stars (he was 63, she was 49) were responsible for this success can be gauged by a contemporary radio quiz competitor's respond-

169 Kathleen Lea 'was struck by the actress's likeness to portraits of Queen Elizabeth' (F. H. Mares, 'Shifting Perspectives', p. 72), but Lionel Hale thought she resembled Queen Victoria (*Daily Mail*, 21 December 1946).

170 This 'expensive and weighty' production used a fairly full text and made 'ingenious use of permanent stairs and acting platforms combined with painted back-drops'; Tearle, 'robust and rollicking', played an Antony who had deteriorated because of 'self-indulgence and self-conceit', whilst Cornell lacked sensuality but 'rose to truly noble heights' at the end (Rosamond Gilder, 'Shakespeare in New York', pp. 130–1).

ing 'Antony and Cleopatra' when asked to 'Name two ancient sports' (Hobson, *Theatre 2*, p. 138).[171]

In Byam Shaw's production there seems to have been some disjuncture between the contemporary design and the acting styles of the principals. Tearle and Evans most impressed the veteran critics Darlington and Crosse, and Stephen Potter noted that Tearle's gestures were not 'newly observed from life, in the modern manner: but reality is suggested as vividly in the exact and graceful execution of the gestures of stage convention' (*New Statesman*, 4 January 1947). Much the same was said of Evans. They were decidedly star actors, in both positive and negative ways: thoroughly professional, however miscast. Evans played the part very much in her own style, even dying on a sofa, as she had in 1925; outside the famous set pieces, Tearle delivered his lines 'a shade too casually or impatiently' (Alan Dent, *News Chronicle*, 21 December 1946). He and Evans played in disparate styles, Evans being 'best in the raillery and mischief' and both being 'at their best when they are apart' (Ivor Brown, *Observer*, 22 December 1946). George Rylands, reviewing post-war Shakespeare productions in 1948, lamented the loss during the war of the ensemble ideals of Baylis and the Old Vic, 'the orchestral rather than the virtuoso performance'; in the new 'showy' productions, the eyes of the public and the critics were 'blinded by the glamour of a few bright particular stars' ('Elizabethan Drama in the West End' p. 103). To the very different commercial basis of West End productions, such criticisms could probably always be applied, and, in any case, Stephen Potter commended the production's generally high standard and liked its eschewing of the inanities of ensemble-togetherness, with 'all that excessive friendliness and shoulder clapping'. The major supporting roles were played well – Crosse thought Michael Goodliffe, who played Caesar as a tight-lipped politician, the best he had seen (*Shakespearean Playgoing*, p. 151) and the unimpressed Rylands considered that Anthony Quayle 'did something to steady the play, although he played Enobarbus as a Brigade Major rather than a Sergeant Major' ('Elizabethan Drama in the West End', p. 105).

---

171 Not all veterans have the requisite charisma and staying-power: Isabella Glyn successfully played Cleopatra at the age of 60 in public readings, but many considered Edith Evans in the theatre at 58 implausible. Recently, Richard Johnson, returning to the part of Antony after twenty years, was generally considered too autumnal, whilst Vanessa Redgrave was a 'youthful 58-year-old' as Cleopatra but her Antony, Paul Butler, seemed 'elderly' (Nicholas de Jongh, *Evening Standard*, 2 June 1995). As a last resort, directors might justify the casting of veterans in terms of historical consciousness and the notion that Antony's and Cleopatra's ages of about 56 and 38 might be adjusted upwards to compensate for longer modern life-spans.

Michael Benthall's 1951 production for the Festival of Britain, played alternately with Bernard Shaw's *Caesar and Cleopatra* in St James's Theatre, also featured a novel setting: this was the first time a revolving stage had been used in a production of *Antony and Cleopatra*. The sets, designed by Roger Furse, were 'adaptable' for the Shaw play and allowed a 'swift glowing effect' (Trewin, *Shakespeare on the English Stage*, p. 219); the arrangement was less obtrusive than that in 1946, and, though the design also featured columns, they were more naturalistically conceived, and the setting, nicely lit, was appealing and spacious. There were four acting areas on the revolving stage: the action in Rome materialised before a row of open, plain columns; that in Egypt before a curtained, Corinthian-columned structure, with the open columns seen in the background; and unlocalised playing areas between these variously represented shipboard or battlefield scenes. The stationary forestage was also used. A sphinx-monument structure was used for Antony's death and its other side was the backdrop to Cleopatra's. T. C. Worsley liked the way in which the setting allowed rapid transition from Egypt to Rome, and the built-in contrasts of location were schematically reinforced by costumes, with the Romans in cobalt cloaks and Antony and the Egyptians in scarlet (*New Statesman*, 19 May 1951).[172] Benthall's production made 'an often successful use of sub-sidiaries and crowds' (*ibid.*), but Alice Venezky thought that, 'while such a stage permits a greater flow of action than in the recent American produc-tion with Katharine Cornell, the latter production better achieved the sense of grandeur and magnificence' ('Current Shakespearian Productions', p. 336).

The Oliviers' status as a star couple (Vivien Leigh had also played Cleopatra in Gabriel Pascal's film *Caesar and Cleopatra* of 1945) may have partly determined the 'ruthless' cuts and 'expert' 'soldering-up' of Benthall's text, which allowed *Antony and Cleopatra* to be played as if it were *All for Love*, with the 'domestic' love story accented and Cleopatra's waverings censored (Rylands, 'Festival Shakespeare in the West End', pp. 140–2). As was implied of the Calverts in 1866 and the Bensons in 1898 and 1900,[173] the playing of passion by theatrical couples has not been conspicu-

---

172 In its structural use of such simple contrasts, the production had something in common with the one in 1947 at the Dublin Gate Theatre, starring Micheál MacLiammóir and Meriel Moore, in which the Romans were in scarlet and gold and the Egyptians in white, turquoise and lapis lazuli, with litters, lotus flowers and serpents. See MacLiammóir, 'Three Shakespearian Productions', p. 91.

173 Couples on the American and Australian stages, such as Marlowe and Sothern in 1909, Asche and Brayton in 1912–13, Wilkie and Hunter-Watts in 1927–8 and Dewhurst and Scott in 1959, have been equally unforthcoming.

4 The monument, with Vivien Leigh as Cleopatra, just before the lifting of Antony (Laurence Olivier) in Benthall's 1951 production at St James's Theatre. Photograph: Angus McBean.

ous for its conviction. By 1951 Olivier and Leigh had outlived their scandalous reputation[174] and behaved too much like the married couple they were, though Rylands thought the 'popular success' of their production was partly explained by 'the fact that the two amorous protagonists were played by a married pair, twin stars of stage and screen, as famous in their day as

174 See Hughes-Hallett, *Cleopatra*, pp. 340–1.

Marcus Antonius and the Egyptian Queen in theirs' (p. 140). As in 1946, many reviewers saw the stars as miscast but as turning in inspiringly professional and subtle performances, especially in the final two acts. A relieved Trewin wrote that neither 'acted in the grand-operatic manner: they let the play carry them upward' (*Shakespeare on the English Stage*, p. 219).

The experiment of cross-casting the play with Shaw's presented some problems, and Harold Hobson thought Olivier's Antony was 'more showy and less impressive than his Caesar' (*Sunday Times*, 13 May 1951). Olivier was a 'clever Antony', who missed the 'rich folly of the unlimited sensualist' but was 'infinitely tragic' when he came to his end with Eros (Ivor Brown, *Observer*, 13 May 1951). Just as scanty dresses do not necessarily reveal Cleopatra's eroticism, so short hemlines on Roman kilts cannot be relied upon to exhibit Antony's amorousness. A rising kilt-line and falling sandal-line, particularly in this production and in Robert Helpmann's of 1957, put forward many a shapely military Roman leg, but the outfits helped neither Olivier nor Keith Michell with their sensuality. According to Darlington, Olivier's interpretation had the only quality which Tearle's lacked, an essential 'streak of cruelty and imperiousness' (*Daily Telegraph*, 12 May 1951). Olivier took advice on interpretation, asking John Dover Wilson, in a car after a performance, about Antony's nobility; and receiving his considered opinion in writing a month later.[175] It is a nice image of the theatre consulting the academy. Olivier also gave advice: to his wife, on delivery. Leigh had vocal range, technical sophistication and emotional power, and in the later scenes, when her husband/'husband' had departed, she was 'faultless' (*Times*, 12 May 1951). Wearing 'a flowing off-ginger wig' (Harold Conway, *Evening Standard*, 12 May 1951), heavy red lipstick and nail polish (Scott, *Antony and Cleopatra*, p. 43), Leigh was the archetypal English Cleopatra, 'cold, smooth, pale, and dazzlingly beautiful' in contradiction to the text; but the 'intelligence in her performance' proved an 'adequate substitute for heat, duskiness, and even wrinkles' (Hobson). The Oliviers were well supported by a star from another galaxy, Robert Helpmann, whom some critics thought better cast in the Shaw play, but whose wintry and sinister Octavius was 'a very good shot indeed for a great ballet dancer to make at a man whose joints were of iron' (Hobson). Norman Wooland's Enobarbus was regarded as insufficient both in his barge-speech and his remorse, and Venezky declared him 'not nearly as good as Kent Smith's in the Cornell production' ('Current Shakespearian Productions', p. 336). When Benthall's production moved to New York for its sell-out season,

---

175 See Felix Barker, *The Oliviers*, p. 302.

Wooland was replaced by Harry Andrews, who was also to play the part in 1953. The London production was studied by Renzo Ricci, and to an extent imitated in his 1953 production at the Teatro Eliseo, Rome, with Eva Magni and Nando Gazzolo.

Glen Byam Shaw's second, and more significant, production of *Antony and Cleopatra* also travelled; it opened at the Stratford Festival in 1953, then went to the Prince's Theatre, London in the autumn (by which time it had improved, according to the critics), and finally on tour to Paris, Brussels and Amsterdam. Lighting was vital to its style, and in London 100 new lighting points and four extra switchboards were installed in the theatre, as well as a new cyclorama. The backcloth was lit with varying shades of blue to represent Rome, and with red limes to create the sultry climate, physical and emotional, of Egypt. The result was that the transformation from Rome to Egypt was achieved with 'cinematic celerity' (*Birmingham Sunday Mercury*, 3 May 1953). This is probably the first time the term 'cinematic' was used of a production of this play, and though it is here used only of rapid scene-change (in a very full text), the illuminated-cyclorama technique struck T.C. Worsley as particularly illusionistic, with a bareness that made for 'a most effective isolation of the characters, silhouetted against the coloured background, alone with their words' (*New Statesman*, 9 May 1953). There was critical consensus, too, that the production's 'magnificence consists in avoiding magnificence' for the sake of 'rapid sequence' (*Times*, 29 April 1953).

As in Byam Shaw's 1946 production, Antony Hopkins's music, 'reedy and sensuous for the love scenes, clashing and clangorous for the frenzied' battle scenes, combined with the Motley costume design (strident tones for the Alexandrian court and cold greys and off-whites for Rome) to create an atmosphere 'heavy with love and war' (E.R.A., *Nottingham Guardian*, 30 April 1953). The set design, also by Motley, was open and minimally equipped with a shallow flight of stairs and 'a couple of slender pillars', so that 'a sail let down from above' and 'some sparse ship's furniture' could suggest Pompey's galley, and the set for Cleopatra's monument was 'a simple piece of arched masonry with gigantic Egyptian wall figures', 'released hydraulically from below' (*Scotsman*, 30 April 1953).

This production was outstanding for the general quality of its acting as well as of its production style, and the lovers' performances were still being used as a touchstone by reviewers forty years later. At the time, critics preferred it to Benthall's production: Michael Redgrave and Peggy Ashcroft were a more convincing couple than the Oliviers and the supporting and ensemble acting was better. Tall and burly, Redgrave looked exactly right

5 Peggy Ashcroft with her court (in 1.5) in Byam Shaw's Stratford production of 1953. Photograph: Angus McBean.

and was a more fervent soldier and sexual warrior than Olivier. Kenneth Tynan thought Redgrave approached Ashcroft too voraciously, 'clawing at her clothes like a berserk pickpocket' (*Evening Standard*, 1 May 1953); his being married to the production's Octavia, Rachel Kempson, may have accounted for the self-conscious exaggeration of his passion. In Stratford, his delivery was 'full of deliberate gutterals and sibilants, of carefully extravagant laughs and plotted suspirations', but, as predicted, his 'astonishing bravura' did (by the time he played in London) 'eventually subdue and absorb those artificialities of style' (Brian Harvey, *Birmingham Gazette*, 29 April 1953); this might be attributed to his meeting the challenge of the difficult but liberating part, as was said of both Phelps and Glyn in 1849. Redgrave was modern in emphasising the middle-aged nature of his crisis, revealing 'the inner ravages made by his dissoluteness, vanity and over-worked charm' (*Times*), but also convincing in his gradual ennoblement. The interpretation was 'superbly maintained, passion and guilt fighting it out desperately till the last' (Worsley).

The production was also modern in its vivid depiction of the struggle for domination, and Lamb (*Antony and Cleopatra*, p. 152) has commented on the way in which the stairs of the set and the stage were used to show political or sexual dominance. Despite Redgrave's fervour, Ashcroft was dominant on the sexual-political battleground. With her 'golden voice' and 'rare feeling for the tragic poetry' (Worsley), her equally memorable performance was on a different scale. Like Lacey in 1935, she was small, pale, red-haired and playing to a large Antony, but 'her miniature of Cleopatra depicts with wonderfully vivid touches of colour so many of the qualities which belong to the ideal Cleopatra that we willingly concede the rest' (*Times*). Some reviewers called Ashcroft 'miscast' (like Evans and Leigh before her), on the grounds that she lacked both tempestuousness and 'voluptuousness' (Cecil Wilson, *Daily Mail*, 29 April 1953). Most critics found her, if not voluptuous, sexually demonstrative, suggesting a 'physical passion which is without fastidiousness' (*Times*); her London Cleopatra was 'more frankly sensual' (*Punch*, 11 November 1953). But her performance sparked a heated 'Englishness' debate.

Tynan claimed that the role in the play 'which English actressses are naturally equipped to play is Octavia', that 'the great sluts of world drama, from Clytemnestra to Anna Christie, have always puzzled our girls; and an English Cleopatra is a contradiction in terms'.[176] The *Picture Post* reviewer disagreed, and explained the problem in terms of actresses in general: 'the

---

176 Dusinberre ('Squeaking Cleopatras', pp. 58–60) discusses Tynan's attitude in terms of modern reviewers' confusion of role and actress.

part was written for a boy and Shakespeare, who knew exactly how far he could tax the credulity of his spectators, refrained from exposing two *actors* to an appropriately torrid love-scene. Cleopatra's allure . . . lies not in the action of the play, but in the poetry of its speech alone' (7 November 1953). This is, in cultural terms, to the point, though it does the boy actors little justice in suggesting that they were not actors at all. Richard Findlater addressed himself to both difficulties, temperament and verse-speaking, and saw Cleopatra as permanently impaled on the horns of a dilemma: 'no English player, it seems, can act Cleopatra, and no actress of any other nation can speak it' (*Tribune*, 20 November 1953). Findlater's assessment of Ashcroft was coloured by a patriarchal prejudice he shared with the critics of Evans, Green and Newcombe; he considered her 'too intelligent for such exotically feminine stupidity' as Cleopatra's. In addition to the handicap of intelligence and the usual one of cultural conditioning, Ashcroft had, he thought, inadequate actorly equipment for the poeticisation of passion: 'too English for so violent and public a lovelife; too limited in voice for such a range of poetic richness. Her Cleopatra is queenly, but there is no gipsy in her; she has appetite, but no joy in the game.'

In appearance Ashcroft was 'whitely wanton' (Ivor Brown, *Observer*, 3 May 1953); wearing 'a flaming wig of red hair'[177] and Hellenic costumes, she played the part not as a wily oriental but as a Ptolemaic queen, with a mental calibre that rivalled Antony's and, as she said, 'gave her the power to destroy him' (*Picture Post*). It is a sign of changing cultural attitudes that her intellectual equality with Antony was not resented as Green's had been in 1930; reviewers liked her ability to use words both to subjugate Antony and to express her love for him, to be 'a queen and a lover in spirit rather than body' (C.L.W., *Birmingham Mail*, April 29, 1953). Trewin, making the term 'intellectual' sound more like a compliment than it did when applied to Evans, Green or Newcombe, wrote 'Acting against herself, Peggy Ashcroft secures an intellectual conquest'; her success in the role had the 'additional spice of being a triumph over the general expectation' (Worsley).

Redgrave had a worthy opponent in the political struggle also: Marius Goring's Octavius was hailed by Trewin as the best he had seen, though he looked too mature for the part.[178] Goring, well known to the public for his

---

177 John Barber associated her red hair with Cleopatra's reputation as 'history's most cordial courtesan' (*Daily Express*, 5 November 1953), which seems to be the standard carried by the succession of red-haired Cleopatras since Achurch.

178 Richard Buckle thought he looked the same age as Redgrave (*Plays and Players*, December 1953); there had been a similar problem in Iden Payne's production (P.D.H., *Leamington Chronicle*, 19 April 1935).

role as Hitler in the BBC series *The Shadow of the Swastika*, asserted 'the relentless authority of Rome with a cool, lofty, but never insensitive implacability' (Brian Harvey, *Birmingham Gazette*, 1 May 1953). His 'pale face', 'incisive speech', and 'tight lips' were indices of a 'cold calculating mind' (T.C.K., *Birmingham Post*, 29 April 1953); 'ice-eyed', he identified Rome's authority with his own goals, 'his face turned toward some horizon of personal destiny'. The supporting roles were played with distinction: Harry Andrews provided a suitable contrast to both Redgrave and Goring with his unusually forthright Enobarbus, playing him as 'a rough, bluff captain who avoids the pitfalls in over-quoted lines and presents a good round figure of the man' (G.R.A., *Coventry Evening Telegraph*, 29 April 1953). Donald Pleasence was also praised for throwing 'a great deal of light on the character of Lepidus' and Tony Britton showed 'the liveliness and boldness of Pompey' (*Morning Advertiser*, 6 May 1953).

Cinematics and politics: from Helpmann to Langham

The previous year's political crisis over Suez added piquancy to Robert Helpmann's 1957 *Antony and Cleopatra* at the Old Vic, which radically departed from the recent practice of 'star'-casting. Helpmann, who had been Benthall's Octavius, chanced his arm with two young actors, fellow Australian Keith Michell, who was 30, and Margaret Whiting, who was 24,[179] but backed them with a strong ensemble. In the two major supporting roles, Derek Godfrey played Enobarbus 'in the sergeants' mess style', and drew considerable sympathy for 'the mixed-up veteran' (*Times*, 29 March 1957), and Leon Gluckman's Octavius, though a suitably chilly contrast, tempered political calculation with fraternal love for Octavia, temporary tolerance of Antony and wry amusement at the antics of his fellow triumvirs.

Like his predecessors, Helpmann used a skilfully lit flexible single set (by Australian designer Loudon Sainthill) in a production described both as 'pictorial' and 'cinematic'. The decor's 'accent on size' and the production's 'bombastic fanfares' (*Scotsman*, 11 March 1957) could be read as symptomatic of Cecil B. de Mille's pervasive influence on the staging,[180] and Margaret Whiting's shapeliness prompted the claim that Shakespeare could be 'as revealing as Hollywood' (*Indicator*, 1 June 1957). But others

179 Helpmann had originally intended Australian actress Coral Browne for the part.
180 De Mille had made *Cleopatra* in 1934, starring Claudette Colbert, though this is probably not what the critic had in mind.

6 Margaret Whiting as the dead Cleopatra, subject to multiple male gaze, in Helpmann's Old Vic production of 1957. Old Vic Archives, University of Bristol Theatre Collection. Photograph: Angus McBean.

saw Helpmann's cinematic borrowings as more imaginative, especially his 'fading' scenes in and out by the subtle use of groupings and back-cloth changes. The set, dominated by obelisks ('Cleopatra's Needles'), which clever lighting turned into Roman pillars, not only accommodated the play's geographical restlessness, but assisted 'cinematic' juxtapostion, allowing Helpmann 'to bring the Cleopatra who is present to Antony's mind's eye in Rome advancing from the other side of the stage to begin her scene in Alexandria' (*Times*, 6 March 1957). Sainthill's costumes and lighting combined to contrast the coolness of Rome with the earthiness of Egypt, and the staging's spectacular climax was the monument scene with Cleopatra (in jet black) and her ladies silhouetted against a blue sky.

The production, which ran for fifty-three performances, was hailed for its coherence and clarity; Trewin resented the two intervals because they interrupted the swift flow and 'simple majesty' of the fairly full text (*Illustrated London News*, 16 March 1957). Helpmann's style supported the strengths of Michell, whom Trewin saw as 'in the centre of this production', by emphasising the council and galley scenes, where Michell excelled as the world conqueror, temporarily free of Cleopatra. The production tended to highlight the contrast between such 'masculine' scenes and the 'feminine' ones involving Cleopatra and her women. Unlike Whiting, and unlike Gielgud in 1930, Michell was not generally thought too young for the part, though Frank Jackson said he 'behaved with as much bouncing energy as a teenage rock'n'roller' (*Reynolds*, 10 March 1957). Whilst 'not so colossal a wreck as Redgrave's, nor as commanding as Olivier's', Michell's Antony bestrid the stage (*Times*, 29 March 1957). More politico-military leader than lover, he tried to be ardent in his love-making, 'despite the spectacular lack of encouragement offered by Miss Whiting' (*What's On In London*, 15 March 1957), but the result was a tendency to emote between clenched teeth, and Trewin saw him as 'over-driving the part towards the end, failing to get below the surface of the verse, blurring it by vocal throbs' (*Birmingham Post*, 6 March 1957).

In an assessment tinged perhaps by assumptions about the 'limitations' of a homosexual director, Robert Wraight blamed Helpmann's 'over-production' and failure to grasp what he called the 'essential womanliness of Cleopatra's character' for Whiting's unforthcomingness (*Star*, 6 March 1957). Whiting herself blamed exhausting rehearsals: 'I did not have a great deal of the infinite variety that is needed but, normally, I have a lot of it' (quoted by C. W. Ingham, *Star*, 7 March 1957). What she did have was raven hair and 'the barest bosom seen on the Old Vic for many a day' (H.B., *Kensington News*, 22 March 1957). The *Eastern Daily Press* reviewer thought that 'in expecting our actresses to achieve a totally alien and imaginary passion, we are letting ourselves be misled by Shakespeare's over-painting – and, also, perhaps, by Colonel Nasser's excitability' (11 March 1957). This post-Suez chauvinism was one response to the Englishness debate, which the production had revived. Another was scepticism about the perennial assertion that such passion is 'not in the natures' of English actresses, which one reviewer suspected of causing 'much quiet amusement among those with better opportunities to find out about such things than critics have' (*What's On*). The same reviewer decided 'what they lack is not passion itself but a combination of passion and exhibitionism', a conclusion already reached by Milton Shulman, who claimed that the English regard sex as 'for bottling, not for flaunting' (*Evening Standard*, 6 March 1957). Bottling is often most evident when the English Cleopatra is on the move, and Whiting had 'a bouncing walk and arms that rose and fell as if they were accompanying deep-breathing exercises' (Shulman).[181] Pale-complexioned and beautiful like Leigh, she was small and small-scaled in performance against a large Antony, like Ashcroft, if not in the same class. Like so many of her predecessors, Whiting failed to balance majesty with sensuality, and was more compelling in her final scenes.

Helpmann's was the last production of *Antony and Cleopatra* at the Old Vic before the National Theatre was formed and took over the venue in 1963. The early sixties saw the regrouping of Stratford's Memorial Theatre Company as the Royal Shakespeare Company (1961) as well as the establishment of the National Theatre, and Lamb (*Antony and Cleopatra*, p. 155) claims that this, and the proliferation of provincial repertory, 'radically changed the conditions of Shakespearean production in Britain'; yet the RSC did not produce *Antony and Cleopatra* until 1972 and the National Theatre not until 1987, when it had been in its permanent South Bank home for eleven years, and the three provincial productions of the sixties were undistinguished.[182] The most interesting of the latter was directed by Peter Dews, who had been responsible for the 1963 television series, *The Spread of the Eagle*, 'which reduced parts of *Antony and Cleopatra* to

181 Collier had a similar problem – 'let her once walk about the stage and the illusion is gone' (*Free Lance*, 5 January 1907) – as did Glenda Jackson, who had 'the suburban waddle of a housewife rushing to the supermarket' (Jack Tinker, *Daily Mail*, 11 October 1978).

182 Besides Peter Dews, Bernard Hepton directed it in 1961 for the Birmingham Repertory Theatre, using a revolving stage and starring Tony Steedman and Elizabeth Spriggs, and Frank Hauser in 1965 at the Oxford Playhouse with John Turner and Barbara Jefford. In London, Croft's 1965–6 National Youth Theatre production starred John Nightingale (later Clive Emsley) and the 20 year-old Helen Mirren, who was to play the role again in 1982–3.

popular film terms' (Trewin, *Shakespeare on the English Stage*, p. 243, n.3), together with parts of *Coriolanus* and *Julius Caesar*, and starred the most recent London stage Antony, Keith Michell, with Mary Morris as his Cleopatra.

American interest in the play and the subject was evident in the sixties. Hollywood came to Shakespeare and to the stage in Jack Landau's production of the play at the Festival Theatre, Stratford, Connecticut. With magnificent costumes, an abstract design by Rouben Ter-Arutunian and stars in the form of Robert Ryan and Katharine Hepburn, it was the box-office success of the 1960 American Shakespeare Festival. Hepburn was praised for her passion, both the sensuous and hot-tempered varieties, but Ryan, though he looked the part, had little stage experience and found the verse difficult, and the text was clumsily cut.[183] Two years later Hollywood produced a film as little Shakespearean as it was popular, Joseph Mankiewicz's *Cleopatra*, with Richard Burton and Elizabeth Taylor. The self-referential and appropriating nature of the film industry mirrored the Egyptomania of this famous film. The stars' liaison, begun while they were making the film, and represented as resembling the protagonists' in sexual indulgence, drinking and extravagance, worked wonders, not for their acting, but for the film's publicity.[184] Indeed, the publicists were so successful in identifying the stars with their roles in the popular imagination that the film, and especially Taylor's Cleopatra, has titillated international audiences for over thirty years.[185] In 1966 the new Met opened with what might be seen as an attempt to re-appropriate the subject from popular culture, the first production of Samuel Barber's opera *Antony and Cleopatra*, with a libretto by Franco Zeffirelli after Shakespeare.

When Christopher Plummer and the Melbourne-born actress Zoe Caldwell played the leading roles in Michael Langham's 1967 production at the Festival Theatre, Stratford, Ontario, reviewers accorded them the kind of star status that Hepburn and Ryan, or the English protagonists of 1946, 1951 or 1953 had been given, but this may partly have been because of their supporters' low standard of acting. Langham's production was the major one of the 1960s partly because it was not conceived as a vehicle for stars,

---

183 *Antony and Cleopatra* was apparently chosen at Hepburn's insistence (see Roberta Krensky Cooper, *American Shakespeare Theater*, pp. 64, 69). Landau's production unsurprisingly overshadowed J.H. Crouch's at the Colorado Shakespeare Festival of the same year, in which Molly Riley played a sensitive and versatile Cleopatra: see Samuel L. Leiter (ed.), *Shakespeare Around the Globe*, pp. 18, 27–8.

184 See Hughes-Hallett, *Cleopatra*, pp. 359–61.

185 Clare Higgins's revised wig for the 1993 Caird revival was 'the familiar model, Elizabeth Taylor style', straight and black (Jeremy Kingston, *Times*, 29 May 1993).

and was, in that and other respects, typical of its era. It took further than Helpmann's production the elements they had in common: 'cinematic' technique and an emphasis on power politics.[186] Langham emphasised the primacy of the political circumstances with which the love story is indissolubly linked, and emphasised the game-playing in the lovers' relationship, at the expense of passion, so that there was some doubt about the nature of their love.[187] Plummer seemed clear-sighted about the consequences of his passion and initially jaunty, and Caldwell compensated for her small size, and small-sized sensuality, with her vocal range and impressive technique.[188] The Festival Theatre stage, conceived by British designer Tania Moiseiwitsch as a modern interpretation of the Elizabethan acting area, was a far more satisfactory (and purpose-built) arrangement than the rebuilt Old Vic stage or Byam Shaw's set in 1946: as well as having an inner area and balcony, it went the extra step to establish an intimate relationship between the actors and an audience on three sides. It provided a neutral, flexible and intimate space eminently suited to Langham's use of lighting to approximate filmic techniques in the theatre: he saw the text as a 'film scenario, no less, rich in cross-cuttings, dissolves, close-ups and overlaps',[189] and reviewers generally hailed his success.

Although the plan of the Festival Theatre in Chichester was modelled on that in Ontario, Peter Dews's 1969 production there was conservative compared with Langham's. Cutting his text by some forty minutes' playing time, he used a sombre set by Carl Toms with staircases either side of a platform, placed (like the Motley set in 1946) too far forward. The leading actors, John Clements and Margaret Leighton, were, at 59 and 47, older than most in the wake of Helpmann's production, but there were some decidedly modern

---

186 Lamb (*Antony and Cleopatra*, pp. 155–6) adduces the influence of Berliner Ensemble productions and Jan Kott's interpretations of Shakespeare on the tendency to politicise productions in the sixties and seventies, but I see Helpmann's emphasis on Antony as Roman strategist, and the political tensions of the cold war era, as more tangible influences.

187 In this respect, the production had something in common with Joseph Papp's 1963 New York Shakespeare Festival production in Central Park, in which Colleen Dewhurst's Cleopatra appeared not to love Michael Higgins's Antony (see *Saturday Review*, 6 July 1963); Papp had also directed Dewhurst in 1959 in a 'concert version' for the New York Shakespeare Festival, opposite George C. Scott (see Leiter (ed.), *Shakespeare Around the Globe*, p. 18).

188 Ronald Bryden saw her differently: 'To an extent few Cleopatras dare, she played the royal harlot: sexy, foul-mouthed and funny, itching with desire . . . But she was royal too, with the same animal unselfconsciousness that made her wanton' (*Observer*, 13 September 1967).

189 Quoted in Leiter (ed.), *Shakespeare Around the Globe*, p. 28; I am indebted to Leiter, *ibid.*, pp. 28–9, and Lamb, *Antony and Cleopatra*, pp. 161–2, for this account.

inflexions in their interpretations,[190] with emphasis on the ravages of middle age, its domestic quarrels and its fantasies; the small-scale nature of the performances was unheroic, in the manner of Plummer's and Caldwell's, and Leighton reminded Benedict Nightingale of 'a neurotic society hostess zonked out on tranquillisers and martinis' (*New Statesman*, 20 October 1978). Dews's company was stronger than Langham's, and in particular Keith Baxter, who was to play Antony in Stratford, Ontario in 1976, was widely praised for his reinterpretation of Octavius, as the maturing 'boy' whose hero-worshipping of Antony is transformed into manly vengeance when Octavia is rejected, and who 'turns commandingly for Rome', 'his education completed', at the end (Ronald Bryden, *Observer*, 27 July 1969).

Tutankhamun and the female eunuch: Nunn and the seventies

The last twenty-five years or so have seen a marked increase in the number of productions of the play, mainly in English, though there have been significant ones in translation. One of these was Evgenii Simonov's 1971 production of Boris Pasternak's translation, to mark the fiftieth anniverary of the Vakhtangov Theatre, Moscow, and starring his lead actors, Mikhail Ul'ianov and Iuliana Borisova. At a time when western productions were increasingly emphasising the play's political element, Simonov's reading was almost exclusively political but very different in tenor, in keeping with Soviet political ideology and theatrical practice. Simonov's Antony was a Soviet hero, the man of action committed to old-order honour (as opposed to Caesar's *realpolitik*ing); the decentred Cleopatra was an obstacle to Antony's glory, an untamed and unserious, politically manoeuvring, destabilising, foreign woman threatening male friendship: the situation was graphically rendered by interpolated mimes showing (at the beginning) the earth itself breaking apart and Cleopatra reacting childishly to Antony's gift of a diadem. The staging underlined the interpretation; the permanent set was a half-circle divided into three parts by steps, and Egypt and Rome were represented by emblems on opposite sides, conflict being indicated by the hanging of both emblems. The galley scene was depicted as a climactic moment of male unity and Antony's death as showing both Caesar and Cleopatra how they have missed greatness.[191]

190 See, e.g., Helen Dawson, *Plays and Players*, September 1969, p. 22 and Irving Wardle, *Times*, 24 July 1969.

191 For this account, I am indebted to Irena R. Makaryk, 'Woman Scorned: *Antony and Cleopatra* at Moscow's Vakhtangov Theatre', in Dennis Kennedy (ed.), *Foreign Shakespeare*, pp. 178–94. Makaryk notes earlier Russian productions in 1923, 1934, 1960 and 1961, but says that the play was little produced there because it sat ill with the ruling ideology.

By contrast, the political orientation of Trevor Nunn's 1972 *Antony and Cleopatra* was formally reflected in the contextualisation of the play as one element (together with *Julius Caesar, Coriolanus* and *Titus Andronicus*) in a cycle of Roman plays[192] which examined systems of power, as had Dews's *The Spread of the Eagle* on a smaller scale. Nunn's Roman series could be read pessimistically in the light of seventies' social and political disillusionment (and anti-Vietnam-war demonstrations): Rome's different stages of social and political interplay provided a paradigm of the rise and fall of a 'great' civilisation.[193] Twenty-two years later, Peter Stein was also to offer *Antony and Cleopatra* as part of a cycle: the grouped staging of Shakespeare's Roman plays may well reflect periods of political transition in which ideologies are questioned and patterns of international relations radically altered. In Nunn's cycle there was some continuity of casting – Antony and Octavius were played by the same actors in *Julius Caesar* and *Antony and Cleopatra* – and each play opened with an elaborate procession, 'obligatory at Stratford just now' (Trewin, *Birmingham Post*, 16 August 1972), but for John Elsom 'a firm statement of the age, the social aura and place, and of the presences' which dominated 'this Mediterranean world' (*Observer*, 20 August 1972). Some felt the production was too pictorial, transparently exploiting the recently installed hydraulic equipment under the Stratford stage. The use of moving stage surfaces to establish 'location' (by tilting for marching soldiers, or actually forming a 'galley' or a pyramid-monument), and the creation of separate stage structures for each scene, may have seemed old-fashioned and slow in comparison with the 'filmic' techniques of recent productions,[194] but it was an honest attempt to deal with staging difficulties in terms of the physical conditions of the theatre

192 In the summer months preceding Nunn's Roman season, Michael Kahn staged the play in tandem with *Julius Caesar* for the American Shakespeare Festival, using the same set and the same actors for the triumvirate. In his director's notes, he wrote of the respective triumphs of Octavius and of the protagonists, 'Does not this conflict of ultimate goals of our lives concern us deeply, really *deeply*, today?' (quoted in Cooper, *American Shakespeare Theater*, p. 166). During the same period, Alfred Rossi's Colorado Shakespeare Festival production located Egypt and Rome on opposite sides of the stage, as in Simonov's production (see Leiter (ed.), *Shakespeare Around the Globe*, pp. 18–19).

193 Lamb (*Antony and Cleopatra*, p. 165) sees the series as motivated, in the context of a new interest in the political elements in Shakespeare, by the success of Peter Hall's *The Wars of the Roses* in 1964, but Nunn's series had a grander design. See John Elsom, *Post-War British Theatre*, p. 172.

194 David A. Male's description (*Shakespeare on Stage*, p. 17) of Nunn's approach as 'cinematic' is misplaced; certainly architectural images appeared and disappeared, but in a very concrete and slow-moving way that spoke of stage hydraulics.

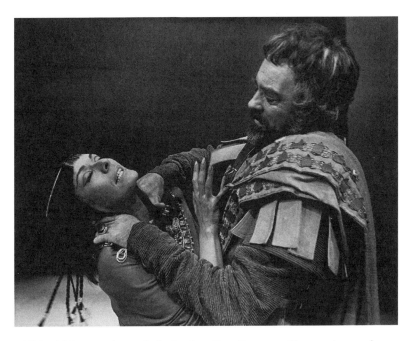

7 Richard Johnson as Antony laying hands on Janet Suzman as Cleopatra in 3.13 of Nunn's RSC production of 1972. Photograph: Reg Wilson.

and to provide 'a formal, clarifying logic' for the action (Elsom). Changing floor levels and lighting clearly differentiated Egypt and Rome, and Nunn used a screen to denote more specific mood changes in each location: in Rome there was a projected map of the empire or a clear blue sky, and in Egypt the projected images of mountains and dissolving clouds in various colours reflected the changeability of Cleopatra herself.

Christopher Morley's glitter of costumes and furnishings reflected a major cultural event: the international Tutankhamun exhibition, which induced Egyptomania and generated block-long queues at the British Museum. Its effects were registered by reviewers, who implied its influence on Nunn's production team and on Guy Woolfenden's score, played on stage 'on flute, harp and great curving brass instruments' that looked as if they had been 'filched' from the exhibition (Charles Lewsen, *Times*, 16 August 1972). The music, with 'flute for fatalism, harp for romantic sadness, brass for power and imperial ambition' (Ray Seaton, *Express Star*, 17 August 1972), helped contrast the locations, but in any case the geopolitical divide was visually enhanced by costume and properties. The Romans' black and white clothing, relieved only by formal purple, and their rigid furniture and stiff deportment accented the imperial principles of duty and discipline, whereas Cleopatra's court, accoutred in pinks, mauves and oranges, moved 'drowsily under billowing Felliniesque canopies' (Michael Billington, *Guardian*, 16 August 1972). Antony and Cleopatra reclined on cushions, whose emblematic associations with lasciviousness would have been familiar to Shakespeare's contemporaries; Cleopatra tickled the supine Antony's ear with her big toe in full view of a consorting stage audience made up of her maids, debauched soldiery and a tittering 'platoon of flabby, shaven-headed eunuchs' bedizened in gold and lapis lazuli (Kenneth Hurren, *Spectator*, 19 August 1972).

For all the Tutankhamunism, some modern notes were struck. Nunn himself remarked, 'you have the whole body of respectable, academic study and complex scholastics behind Shakespeare but you also have to treat [*Antony and Cleopatra*] as a play that has dropped through the letter box' (*Evening Press*, Dublin, 30 August 1972). For some, the mobile extravagance of the Egyptian court resembled the hedonism of the seventies' 'jet set' or the langour of hippie culture, and Billington suspected Antony of seeking 'escape from his royal hooker in a seductive hookah'. Benedict Nightingale identified Janet Suzman's Cleopatra as 'the Ptolemaic equivalent of your modern emancipated woman. You would expect to catch her reading *The Female Eunuch* rather than dallying with male ones' (*New Statesman*, 25 August 1972). Suzman's tawny front was not merely another legacy of the Tutankhamun exhibition, but a sign of her confronting the Egyptianness Shakespeare had given Cleopatra[195] and trying to reconcile it with a modern western (and feminist-influenced) conception of Cleopatra's behaviour not as 'wiles' but as role-playing for sexual and political power. For the feminist reader of the play in performance, Cleopatra's suicide is not merely a patriarchally constructed redemptive act which indicates repentance of sexual and political boundary-crossing. Rather, commitment to love is one element in a decision that includes a desire to resist being marginalised by Caesar (who bartered his sister in a 'redemptive' marriage to Antony), and is about affirming a sense of self or 'integrity of life'.[196] Suzman's Cleopatra offered modern audiences the appeal not only of the liberated woman who lived and died for her own good reasons (laying claim to physical space in the monument and temporal space in the aftermath of

195 See her remarks reported in the *Stratford-upon Avon Herald* (1 September 1972) and the *Daily Express* (9 July 1973). Some reviewers had been lamenting modern English actresses' avoidance of 'dusky' make-up – Ivor Brown over Newcombe (*Observer*, 23 September 1934) and Lacey (*Observer*, 21 April 1935) and Trewin over Whiting (*Birmingham Post*, 6 March 1957).

196 As Webster put it in the final couplet of *The Duchess of Malfi*.

Antony's suicide), but also of the powerful woman who lived out, and died in, her knowledge of the inseparability of sex, gender, power and politics. Her self-affirming enactment made Cleopatra central in the play's theatrical dynamics. Throughout the play, Antony has been irresistibly attracted to her; his being hauled up to her monument as a consequence of her refusal to budge, his dying uncomfortably but willingly among women, shows literally how Cleopatra has drawn him to her. Antony is cleared from the play in preparation for Cleopatra's death, which (in contrast to his) is as painless as she had planned. Her death is concomitantly magnificent and triumphant, not least because it is so evidently an affirmative action. It is another death among women, but, in an ancient royal tradition, she takes her support network with her. And it is an occasion for dressing up – in imperial attire that has to do with majestic Eros rather than the territorial expansionism of armoured Mars.

Hurren thought that because Suzman was South African born, she 'would be able to break through the barrier of innate gentility that has separated so many of our girls from the essence of the character', but she was lithe rather than voluptuous. Her Cleopatra was, despite Peggy Ashcroft's preconceptions, no less intelligent for not being Ptolemaic. The style of her manipulative intelligence, according to Nightingale, had 'little in common with the musky siren of theatrical tradition' and passion served her ulterior purposes, as in the game-playing mode of the Langham production. Her whole performance was moulded by a consciousness that the part was originally written for a boy actor,[197] and the programme notes quoted Granville-Barker's assertion that, because this was so, 'there is not one scene to show the sensual charm that drew Antony to her, and back to her'. Michael Neill (in the Introduction to his edition of the play, p. 52) has described Suzman's Cleopatra as 'the culmination' of the tendency to ironise the play's central relationship with self-conscious theatricality, which he calls a 'deliberate thinning out of the part'. It was probably only a culmination in terms of its reconciliation of the concepts of role-playing and tawniness. It was more a deliberate re-emphasising of the part than a 'thinning out', though one era's solutions are always another's dilutions. Suzman was a 'clever girl tackling a dangerous game and revelling rather too much in her own skill' (Elsom). She used gesture tellingly and, with an excellent vocal range, made her death both poignant and triumphant. Whilst she came short of suggesting greatness, underplaying the moments of rage and uncertainty, hers was 'a performance that suggest[ed] the lines have passed through the actor's imagination' (Billington).

---

197 B.A. Young thought that in manner she 'has given [Cleopatra] a touch of masculinity; she is an Egyptian Elizabeth I' (*Financial Times*, 16 August 1972).

Her Antony, Richard Johnson, was typically English in looking the part without being convincing in it, seeming wooden and tending to shout. Suzman has spoken about Antony as 'in thrall' to Cleopatra and has said that this is 'very difficult, especially for Englishmen' (Pitt, *Shakespeare's Women*, p. 215).[198] Elsom could not believe that this Antony's 'delights were "dolphin-like"' and the *Sunday Telegraph* reviewer was used to seeing 'far more ardent love scenes . . . daily on the platforms of Paddington Station' (20 August 1972). Johnson's appearance was patrician, but his behaviour reflected in a more modern way his late middle age: in Egypt his self-dividedness was apparent in his stooping (as opposed to his upright bearing in Rome) and his desperation was variously manifested in his 'going native' with exotic costume, his 'intensely emotional and passionate' embraces with Cleopatra and his general need for excessive stimulation (Male, *Shakespeare on Stage*, p. 17). Nunn used the stage audience of courtiers and soldiers to emphasise the connection between Antony's political and amorous fortune, and his reliance on their voyeurism as a sexual stimulant: in adversity, the audience dwindled, as did his virility (Lewsen). Johnson was especially good at self-disgust, but that probably had more to do with the traditional forte of English Antonys than with his exhibitionism.

The two major supporting roles were well played.[199] Corin Redgrave, son of a former Antony and former Octavia, and brother of a future Cleopatra, portrayed Octavius in a way that may have been influenced by Baxter's at Chichester, with slowly intensifying hostility to Antony, but Redgrave gave much less emphasis than Baxter to changing relationships, and his Octavius was characterised by 'a dictator's fanaticism burning in his eye' (John Barber, *Daily Telegraph*, 16 August 1972) and venomously sibilant diction. Patrick Stewart's Enobarbus, like Johnson's Antony, was a man divided. In Egypt he wore mufti and lolled among the cushions, but he was plainly torn between loyalty and duty, and cynicism alternated with fascination in his attitude to Cleopatra.

In the television version of Nunn's production, directed by Jon Scoffield, camera-angles replace the hydraulic stage and, as in the stage version, the

198 Potential Antonys of the current generation may see the role as more pro-active. The Northern-Irish-born actor Liam Neeson said in a recent interview that he would like to play Antony the 'ageing warrior' when he is 50: 'The whole body of my work has been supporting female stars. Now I want a bite of the cherry myself' (*Sydney Morning Herald*, 4 February 1995).

199 Michael Neill, in the Introduction to his edition of the play, is perhaps overstating the case in suggesting that the actors 'received more attention than is usual for these roles' because of Johnson's woodennness; reviewers had long recognised the importance of these two roles and had paid their actors due attention when their performance warranted it.

settings are established by properties and costumes: the Egyptian setting, with its scatter cushions, kaftans and fig-eating, looks very seventies-Marrakesh.[200] Occasionally the dialogue is literally illustrated with images – in Philo's opening speech, Caesar's report of the coronation of the lovers (at the beginning of 3.6) and of their mobilising assorted kings for war (at 3.6.70) – but the chief exploitation of filmic technique is in close-ups, which bring forward the power-plays in the galley scene, and particularly suit Suzman's acting style; although she is very much the taunter, the tenderness of some of her smaller gestures helps convey her abiding affection for Antony. Johnson still comes across as rather wooden, but the close-ups also benefit Stewart, whose sparkling eyes are eloquent evidence of his appreciation of Cleopatra, and whose grimaces are the more readily distinguishable from his smiles; possibly, too, the more intimate shots (as much as critical response to his stage performance) discouraged Redgrave from over-exercising his sibilants.

Shortly after Nunn's production was revived at the Aldwych in 1973, the first fully fledged modern dress production of the play opened on a bare semi-open-space stage at the Bankside Globe. Komisarjevsky's and McClintic's productions had modern elements in their costuming, but the Bankside Globe's was comprehensively modern, if eclectic. Cleopatra's clothes ranged in style from the 1920s to 1973, and included cocktail gowns, sheath dresses, fringed robes and a white trouser-suit with red wig; Antony was the soldier playboy in khaki uniform, white silk scarf and flashy ring; a fascistic Caesar wore dark glasses, as did his briefcase-carrying followers; the triumvirate resembled 'a trio of back-stabbing businessmen' and Pompey's army 'a band of Castro guerrillas' (Milton Shulman, *Evening Standard*, 10 August 1973). The production used an 'ingenious set' whose chief novelty was a canvas pyramid 'opening and closing to reveal the Egyptian court' (Nicholas de Jongh, *Plays and Players*, October 1973). Directed by Tony Richardson, this 'full-blast twentieth century version' starred his ex-wife, 'rebel' Vanessa Redgrave, and Julian Glover, and was, said Richardson, 'intended as a comment on power politics today' (*Time*, 20 August 1973). Shulman thought it a 'near-parody production', in which the lovers were 'a squabbling pair of rich, self-indulgent sophisticates' and 'infinite variety is confined to the peevish pouts, the petulant tantrums, the hysterical outbursts of an heiress', though Neil Lyndon felt it 'cop[ed] nicely with scenes of domestic melodrama' (*Listener*, 16 August 1973). Michael Billington was not impressed with 'a scratch company limited to a

---

200 Samuel Crowl, 'A World Elsewhere', pp. 153, 155, notes that the Egyptian scenes are often given a 'hazy texture' and the Roman ones are 'in bright white' and make frequent use of the 'static close-up'.

few weeks' rehearsal' and believed that this production 'of bottomless vul-
garity' ignored the play's cardinal feature: that it constantly relates private
emotions to a precise political background' (*Guardian*, 10 August 1973); in
putting the characters in modern dress, Richardson had not managed to
preserve the distinction between Alexandria and Rome as opposing centres
of culture and power. David Schofield's Octavius was 'a twitching and
sexless neurotic' (Lyndon), Dave King's Enobarbus was deprived of his
'lyricism', Glover's Antony had 'nothing of the decline about it', and
Redgrave's youth robbed her of Cleopatra's 'grand desperation at which
her appropriately lurid costumes hint' (de Jongh); Shulman believed she
acquired 'the dignity of regality' near her death, but Billington, who saw
her as delighting in physical violence, heard her bellow her final speech 'in a
voice increasingly hard and strident'.

The tone of Alf Sjöberg's 1975 Royal Dramatic Theatre production at
the Malarsalen in Stockholm, with Anders Ek and Ulla Sjöblom in the title
roles, was very different. In using a fairly bare stage and sophisticated lighting, and emphasising unheroic role-playing and its blurring of the emotions, Sjöberg's production was typical of its period; but it was less political
than most seventies productions, even if Rolf Skoglund's Octavius was a
representative of the new age of puritanical *realpolitik*, resisted by the
lovers. What was Swedish about it was Sjöberg's reading of Antony's struggles as a process of Strindbergian self-discovery, and his elevation to the
monument by a grotesque and alienated Cleopatra as a redemptive act, followed in turn by her assertion of a sense of freedom despite her existential
isolation.[201]

More straightforward was Robin Phillips's production in the following
year[202] for the Stratford Festival, Canada, starring Keith Baxter and
Maggie Smith, again on an almost bare stage, using a canopied set. The
conflict between desire and duty was clearly depicted in the counter-
pointing of the court and military scenes, both armies being identically costumed in white.[203] In first-rate performances, Baxter gave Antony mythic
stature and Smith was an inspiring Cleopatra of the seventies: one who was
an actor of infinite variety and assured domination, yet vulnerable. Their

---

201 For this account I am indebted to Leiter (ed.), *Shakespeare Around the Globe*,
pp. 32–3.

202 Later in 1976 Frank Dunlop directed a fast-moving Young Vic production with
Michael Graham Cox and Delphine Seyrig, the latter an actor of French origin who
'could give only an alert sketch, never letting the great verse rise and shine' (Trewin,
'Shakespeare in Britain' (1978), p. 220).

203 I am indebted to Leiter (ed.), *Shakespeare Around the Globe*, pp. 33–4 and to Lamb,
Antony and Cleopatra, p. 173, for this account.

relationship became increasingly co-dependent as they lost political power, but their death-scenes were moving in their restraint.

The bare stage of Toby Robertson's Prospect Theatre production at the Edinburgh Festival in 1977[204] (later at the Old Vic and on tour, and revived in modified form in 1978)[205] was offset by Nicholas Georgiadis's sumptuous plumed High Renaissance costumes. Alec McCowen and Dorothy Tutin performed well, but had a higher level of political than of sexual awareness; they were more middle-aged than was then fashionable for the lovers, and seemed incompatible; they had 'their best moments with others' and there seemed to be more affection between Antony and Octavius, and between Octavius and his sister (with a hint of incest) (*Times*, 26 August 1977). Tutin, seeming detached from herself as well as Antony, was best at 'the spoilt teasing bits' (Robert Cushman, *Observer*, 28 August 1977), and her Charmian (Zoe Hicks) and Iras (Suzanne Bertish) were 'middle-aged bitches' (J. W. Lambert, *Sunday Times*, 28 August 1977). McCowen, 'meticulous' when he should have been 'massively careless', seemed 'on distant terms' with Cleopatra. Timothy West, playing the role of Enobarbus as 'a beery ranker instead of the usual staffman' (Cushman), drew the humour from the part, and his watchfulness made 'Antony's decline completely visible'.[206] Derek Jacobi was praised for his 'impressive, calculating precision' as Octavius (*Times*).

Small-scale productions: from Brook to Noble

A 'modern' relationship between the lovers partly characterised by Cleopatra's ironic detachment was also a feature of Peter Brook's 1978 *Antony and Cleopatra* for the RSC in Stratford (revived at the Aldwych in 1979), his last English production.[207] The Brook version disappointed the high expectations of some of its reviewers, eight years after the worldwide success of his *A Midsummer Night's Dream*. He had in the meantime been experimenting with small-scale and minimalist productions in Paris and

---

204 Later in the same year Robert Loper directed an Oregon Shakespeare Festival production, with Elizabeth Huddle and Ted D'Arms in the title roles.

205 It played in repertory ('in contrast') with *All for Love*, in Restoration costume and starring Barbara Jefford and John Turner, who had played the leading roles in Shakespeare's play in Oxford in 1965.

206 West became ill not long after the Festival and was competently replaced by Kenneth Gilbert.

207 In slightly modified form: Glenda Jackson had 'shed her physical excesses', such as 'clawing the carpet' and 'sinking to the ground in a dead faint' (*Guardian*, 10 July 1979), and the Clown was less intrusive (Trewin, 'Shakespeare in Britain' (1980), p. 157).

elsewhere, and the general style of his *Antony and Cleopatra* (and some details, such as the use of the red carpet) reflected his less spectacular recent work. He concentrated on the personal relationships in the play. Like Bridges-Adams in 1931, he wanted to strip it of 'images superimposed by the Victorian era and by the cinema' – and, said his set designer, Sally Jacobs, 'the treasures of Tutankhamun' (quoted in Hunt and Reeves, *Peter Brook*, pp. 224–5). The visual impact of his interest in Artaud, Brecht and Beckett was less obvious in the new Brook style – though the vigilant could point to the blood splashing the translucent panels in 4.7, 'which congeals into a Jackson Pollock war mural' (John Elsom, *Listener*, 19 October 1978) and to the killing of Pacorus; to the clarity of the general ironisation of the lovers' narcissism against a literal backdrop/screen of political violence; and to the horizontal 'hauling' of Antony as signs of his continuing indebtedness to each (respectively). In retrospect Brook's production seems as important as the reviewers had hoped, in its powerful treatment of sexual politics as inseparable from power politics and of the increasing co-dependency of the lovers, for whom the world of power has shrunk to their struggle with each other and themselves. In these interpretative terms, and in its minimalist and small-scale staging, it was both typical of its time and more memorable than its contemporaries. If the 'idiosyncrasy' of the production was less literally colourful and spectacular than had been hoped, it was no less coherent: the set, the costumes, Cleopatra's hairstyle and gestures, challenged expectation to the same end. The uncompromising nature of his approach was reflected in Brook's use of an almost uncut text, played at a fast pace, though still lasting three hours and fifty minutes. The production made a highlight of the Ventidius scene (3.1), hitherto usually cut. Although the violent battle scenes were played behind the screen, Brook had Pacorus killed on stage. As well as bringing to death a character who is already a corpse in the text and who is usually buried by omission, this stage business dramatised a thematic point about the connection between the rulers' drinking orgy on Pompey's galley and the orgy of violence that results from their politicking and erupts into the domestic world normally shielded by the screen. Jacobs's set, a semicircle of translucent perspex panels joined at the top by a sloping skylight, was crucial to the enactment of Brook's conception of the play, making such an abrupt transition from galley to Parthia feasible, as well as representing the conceptual, though not factual, separation of the 'world of relationships' from the battles outside. The translucency of the screen panels meant that 'the figures outside are shadows, as unreal to us as to those who play out the rituals of love and death in the innermost arena of all, which is the human heart' (Bernard Levin, *Sunday Times*, 15 October 1978), but nevertheless 'whatever is happening in the foreground, the blurred images of hovering figures seen through the screen ensures that one has always the whole context of the play in mind' (Ian Stewart, *Country Life*, 23 October 1978). The lighting was straightforward and the stage was kept bare, apart from some severe benches for Roman scenes and some cushions and the red hanging/carpet for the Egyptian ones.

Some critics found it hard to reconcile this bareness with the splendour ascribed to Cleopatra's court in the text: Cleopatra had no throne to reign or die on, and 'there is no attempt to suggest that either Antony or Cleopatra have ever been in charge of more than a few underfurnished rooms in a palace' (Sheridan Morley, *Punch*, 18 October 1978). But, as other reviewers pointed out, the panels of the set and some of the actors' ritualised gestures owed their inspiration to traditional Japanese theatre.[208] Bernard Levin called Alan Howard's 'ritually stylised' suicide 'hara-kiri' and wrote of Glenda Jackson's 'hieratic arm and hand movements, and poses, as formal as the inscription on a stele'. Though in her appearance Jackson was 'a Ptolemaic queen from her cropped black hair to her curled toes' (Benedict Nightingale, *What's On in London*, 13 July 1979), Brook may have intended the Japanese and Egyptian gestures of the production to hint at a post-Hiroshima and post-Vietnam orientalism characterised by a singleminded drive for dominance.[209] Jacobs's striped garments for the Egyptians extended the concept of orientalism in a middle-eastern direction, whilst emphasising Cleopatra's strength of character rather than eastern promise.[210] The design, and Richard Peaslee's music, supported the mode of presentation, where (in the Jacobean convention of the presenter-figure, but discarding the pretext of addressing another character) Philo and Enobarbus delivered many of their speeches downstage, directly to the audience, and the lovers' first entrance was low-key. The lovers' behaviour lacked sensuality, partly because 'direct human affection of the Roman kind

208 See, e.g., Norah Lewis (*Birmingham Evening Mail*, 11 October 1978) and Helen Reid (*Western Daily Press*, 11 October 1978); Michael Billington, commenting on Brook's cinematic technique of fades and dissolves, wrote 'we are closer to the world of Ozu than Cecil B. De Mille' (*Guardian*, 11 October 1978).

209 Peter Jenkins reported Brook as having 'seen the vision of his Cleopatra during the production of *US* when Jackson was doing the Vietnamese lady with a taste for barbecued Buddhists' (*Spectator*, 21 October 1978); Brook's 'vision' is not merely 'the unconscious persistence of the stereotypical *femme fatale* of nineteenth-century oriental fantasy', as Neill suggests (Introduction to his edition, p. 41).

210 For Don Chapman, her first gown accentuated 'her uncompromising features and matelot's arms' (*Oxford Mail*, 11 October 1978); for Norah Lewis, she looked 'impressive in a series of striking costumes' (*Birmingham Evening Mail*, 11 October 1978).

is the one thing [Howard] cannot get' from Jackson (Irving Wardle, *Times*, 11 October 1978), whose great strengths were (like Suzman's) irony and quick-wittedness. Yet Howard and Jackson were 'a visibly crumpled and sexy couple who have evidently spent much of their time together in bed' (Morley) and their encounters had 'a dangerous excitability', in that 'the more defeat comes, the more they become enslaved to passion' (Michael Billington, *Guardian*, 11 October 1978).

Alan Howard, who had been Theseus/Oberon in Brook's *A Midsummer Night's Dream*, was concurrently playing Coriolanus and seemed to some critics too much the 'loner', lacking Antony's magnanimity[211] and more convincing as defeated soldier than as lover; Peter Jenkins wrote of his 'middle-aged despair, his helpless self-loathing as he watches himself let the side down and himself' (*Spectator*, 21 October 1978). J. C. Trewin admired Howard's 'desperately moving voice' (*Birmingham Post*, 11 October 1978), and Don Chapman thought his 'remarkable emotional and vocal power' helped 'suggest the epic nature' of the protagonists' love (*Oxford Mail*, 11 October 1978), but Elsom's view of Howard as soldier-lover was very different: 'an overgrown boy, bragging and playing with himself, under the cold eyes of a sexual nurse'.

Glenda Jackson was generally regarded as more dynamic than the average sexual nurse: 'She gets the lewdness and the sexiness, the sudden flashes of imperiousness, the anxieties of advancing age – all of that, but not that chemical quality which makes her a drug for Antony or any man' (Jenkins). She 'dilute[d] her ruthlessness with spasms of controlled sexuality' (Peter McGarry, *Coventry Evening Telegraph*, 11 October 1978) but her 'danger of succumbing to absolute passion was no closer than Mrs Thatcher's likelihood of weeping at Cabinet meetings' (Milton Shulman, *Evening Standard*, 11 October 1978). Felix Barker saw her as 'an ironic and taunting Cleopatra', but 'passionately in love' with her Antony (*Evening News*, 11 October 1978). Both she and Howard had 'the snap of natural command' (Benedict Nightingale, *New Statesman*, 20 October 1978) and, with an edge to her dark contralto voice, there was no doubt about Jackson's authority, which was sometimes ferociously physicalised, so that 'even Antony is often pummelled by her far from tiny fist' (Billington). Her manner, though not her appearance, reminded Robert Cushman of her television role as Elizabeth I (*Observer*, 15 October 1978). Partly because of the plainnness of her costumes, some reviewers did doubt her regality: B. A. Young thought 'when she assumes majesty, she seems only to be playing a game, even in the serene moments of her suicide' (*Financial Times*, 12 October 1978). Others found 'majesty' in the style of 'a modern crop-

211 See Robert Cushman (*Observer*, 15 October 1978).

haired, kaftaned Cleopatra who speaks the verse magnificently' (Jack Tinker, *Daily Mail*, 11 October 1978), and Trewin, though he wrote of her performance as a 'miniature',[212] called it an 'imperious regal' one.

The warmth many reviewers missed in the lovers was unexpectedly displaced on to the performances of the two major supporting roles by Jonathan Pryce as Octavius and Patrick Stewart as Enobarbus, who was more genial than in Nunn's production, an 'old sweat who has seen it all' but 'enters into Egyptian hedonism with sheer sensual enjoyment' (Billington). Pryce's Octavius was, like some other recent Caesars (Baxter's of 1969 and, to a lesser extent, Redgrave's of 1972), complex and developing; initially gentle and affectionate to his sister, he was 'dazzled by his senior partner, tempted by him into surprising levity: then sobering up in horror, regarding him increasingly as an example to be studied, dreaded and destroyed' (Cushman). Because of Brook's emphasis on 'the whole structure of interlocking needs', Paul Brooke's Lepidus and David Suchet's Pompey 'assume[d] a greater importance than normal' (Elsom). Brook approached the problem of making the play's passion seem convincing by representing a wider and less clearly defined range of sexual emotion and behaviour: his suggestions of homosexuality (especially in the galley scene) were taken up by Adrian Noble; and his emphasis on the unlovely middle-aged quality of the protagonists' sexuality was also to be developed by Peter Hall, John Caird and Peter Zadek. Richard Griffiths's Clown also attracted more than usual attention by unexpected means: he was 'a real red-nosed comedian, who delays [Cleopatra's] grand departure from the world with a series of false exits', using different gaps in the panels (Wardle); some reviewers strongly disapproved of the 'break' in dramatic tension, whilst others accepted it as an updating of standard Jacobean comic tension-heightening technique.

There was also sharp division in the critical responses to the BBC television version, directed by Jonathan Miller in 1981. Small-scale in several senses, it is very reticent, not to say lacklustre, in its performances and in its adaptation to the medium – though there are some nice touches in the staging of Antony's suicide and in Ian Charleson's Octavius, as the puritanical young man with a genuine anxiety about the empire and some warmth of feeling towards Antony, offset by his (very Jacobean) tendency towards rhetorical gesture, mainly in the accusatory or self-righteous modes. The lovers in this production are scarcely more demonstrative than Caesar –

212 Lacey and Ashcroft, who were also dubbed miniaturists, were both small Cleopatras playing to large Antonys, but common ground for all three is an alleged lack of 'voluptuousness' and also (if Jackson's ironic detachment is read thus) of 'tempestuousness'.

indeed, they kiss each other's hands as often as he extends his own – but in moments of anger Colin Blakely shouts and in extreme grief Jane Lapotaire's grimaces are accompanied by heavy aspiration. Of the two she is the more obliquely cast (or miscast), having no trace of sensuality and practically none of regality. She is a Ptolemaic Cleopatra, the only hint of Shakespeare's tawniness being found in the pairing of her women: Charmian (Janet Key) is very fair and Iras (Cassie McFarlane) is black; but Charmian is foregrounded as supportive and Iras is more than usually unobtrusive. The Veronese-style costumes point up the contrast between Rome and Egypt as well as being pleasing to the eye: Roman reticence wears green with modest silver ornaments, whilst Egypt is in pinks and magenta, with lavish gold decoration. Enobarbus (played competently by Emrys James) has a beard style that echoes Antony's, and the colouring and hair-style of Thidias (Harry Waters) echoes his master Caesar's. Cinematic tech-niques are used minimally, as in most of the BBC series; the contrast-in-depth technique often echoes Folio directions, as in the opening scene. Richard David concluded from this production that 'the necessary miniaturisation for TV must be more damaging to *Antony and Cleopatra* than to any other play in the canon',[213] but it is clear from a comparison with the Nunn–Scoffield version that the play can work well in this medium and that the BBC production is wanting in terms of per-formances and dynamics. The earlier version represents open spaces,[214] but in Miller's the emphasis is on interiors: even battlefields are represented by tent interiors (utilitarian white for the Roman camp, a fancier tent in their colours for the Egyptians); but this makes a thematic point about the conse-quences of Antony's wars-within-doors, and the interiorisation is as valid in those terms as that of many nineteenth-century stage productions and some notable ones of the 1970s and 1980s.

Reviewers commented on the televisual or cinematic qualities of one of the latter: Adrian Noble's, starring Michael Gambon and Helen Mirren, at The Other Place, Stratford in 1982 (revived, with modifications, at the Gulbenkian Studio, Newcastle and then the Pit at the Barbican, London). Those who had lamented the lack of grandeur in Brook's production found no consolation in this next RSC *Antony and Cleopatra*, which seems to have

213 'Shakespeare in Miniature: the BBC *Antony and Cleopatra*', in J. C. Bulman and H. R. Coursen (eds.), *Shakespeare on Television*, pp. 139–44. Large-scale Hollywood-style film-making, as represented by Charlton Heston's *Antony and Cleopatra* of 1972 (not commercially released at the time), can be equally 'damaging': for a discussion of the film, see Crowl, 'A World Elsewhere', pp. 157–9.

214 Miller blamed financial necessity for the small-scale nature of the production, but geographical expanses could have been represented cheaply.

been directly influenced by Brook's, but was an attempt to downsize the tragedy further, in accordance with modern anti-heroic attitudes and the exigencies of the studio venue. With the audience seated on three sides, The Other Place provided a bare white linoleum floor (on which a black carpet was placed), a black gallery and black walls – which, together with the shadows produced by lighting designer Leo Leibovici, were used to menacing effect. The Roman scenes were played on the upper level (with colder lighting) and the Egyptian on the lower,[215] whilst the lively homoerotic galley scene was played on both (making points, as Nunn and Brook had done, about male bonding and about the mingling of Roman and Egyptian elements in that scene). Without any processions or fanfares and with 'the squealing bagpipes and muffled drums of George Fenton's score . . . more sparing than usual' (Irving Wardle, *Times*, 15 October 1982), the production moved very quickly, with little sense of majesty. The costumes were austere and uniform-like for the Romans, whilst Cleopatra wore 'extravagant gold' and her women 'multicoloured silk' and 'the renegade Antony wears red leather jerkin and trousers', covered by an Egyptian cloak which he later discarded (Clare Colvin, *Times*, 7 October 1982). Mirren bedaubed herself in dirt in her mourning for Antony and removed all make-up in preparing for her own death. Scarves were a motif in the production, from the lovers' first entrance to the monument scene, their noose-association suggesting 'the killer instinct that lurks in obsessive sexual love' (Victoria Radin, *Observer*, 17 October 1982).

Caught in the noose, Michael Gambon, a 'grizzled, lusthewn soldier given to sudden rushes of blood to the head' (Michael Billington, *Guardian*, 14 October 1982), seemed very large on the small stage, and though literally able to sweep Cleopatra off her feet, in her presence regressed to 'the total sensuous dependence of infancy' (Wardle). The lovers' 'clinches' were 'red hot' (Keith Nurse, *Daily Telegraph*, 14 April 1983), but Gambon was generally thought more convincing as soldier than as lover, his emotion 'often generalised or expressed elliptically' (Stanley Wells, *Times Literary Supplement*, 29 October 1982), and 'we see the two partners losing each

215 Rome and Egypt may have seemed too close at the Other Place, but in an equally anti-heroic (and more politically disillusioned) production at the Nottingham Playhouse in the same year, with Ian McCulloch and Kate O'Mara as the protagonists, they were difficult to distinguish, with all the actors in black and a lot of doubling; nor did the use of a projected cloudscape help, since, unlike that in the Nunn production, it was unchanging. The use of black for costumes (as opposed to the white costuming of the opposing armies in Phillips's 1976 Ontario production or the black decor in Noble's case) might be read as an index of increasing political disenchantment.

8 Helen Mirren as Cleopatra and Michael Gambon as Antony with a dangerous scarf in Noble's 1982 RSC production. Josette Simon as Iras, M. Fitzgerald as Mardian and Sorcha Cusack as Charmian. Photograph: Mark Williamson.

other in the process of losing power' (Wardle), a movement diametrically opposed to that operating in Brook's production. But Noble's lovers, in becoming isolated, were forced to reconsider their identities.

The bare-footed Cleopatra of this production (returning to the role after attempting it at the age of 20 in 1965) was a 'sensuous tigress lording it in figure-hugging shifts in her palace' (Nurse) and 'audiences hungry for spectacle could content themselves with the sight of Helen Mirren's sumptuous and scarcely concealed physique' (Shrimpton, 'Shakespeare Performances', p. 173). With flowing blonde hair, evoking another Anglo-Saxon attitude to female desirability, and complexion redolent of 'a long wet winter in Blackpool', there was 'something over-English about her eroticism' (Benedict Nightingale, *New Statesman*, 29 October 1982). She sported a 'tatty lurex smock' and 'slinky loose-hipped walk' (Radin). Yet, like Jackson, she had undoubted authority: it was established 'by means of lightning emotional reversals' (Wardle) and her dangerousness was manifested 'in flashes of temper' (Gareth Lloyd Evans, *Stratford-upon-Avon Herald*, 29 October 1982). Her underlying insecurity was equally evident: she saw that Antony 'is wriggling off the hook and she is wild to keep him' (Radin). Whilst some reviewers complained of a lack of regality, Billington felt Mirren 'lives like a woman but dies like a queen'.

Cleopatra's attendants shared with her some intimate moments, but they were less straightforwardly supportive than usual: Charmian (Sorcha Cusack) and Iras (Josette Simon), 'overt in a lesbian relationship', 'attempt[ed] to encompass Cleopatra' (Peter McGarry, *Coventry Evening Telegraph*, 14 October 1982); Charmian also gave 'hints of jealousy of Cleopatra and of an eye-fluttering relationship with Antony, which suggests the hot breath of Egyptian intrigue' (Lloyd Evans). The major supporting roles were also given individuality. Penelope Beaumont played Octavia 'with a dignity which rebuts Cleopatra's self-victimisation in the name of love' (Radin); Jonathan Hyde's 'smouldering, sleek-haired, unusually impassioned' Octavius (Billington) managed to let go in the galley scene but was principally 'a Saturnine watcher with the features of an Aztec mask whose silences convey volumes of indignation and regret'. Bob Peck's Enobarbus was 'a grating Thersites-like commentator' who nevertheless found 'voice for high tragic rhetoric' (Wardle) in his death-scene, which some reviewers found the most moving in the production.

Heroic ruins: the myth in the eighties and nineties

If the bare-stage productions following Nunn's seem to have in common an increasing tendency towards ironisation and smallness of scale, there were, from 1983, signs of departure from the prevailing English style, in the use of large-scale images underlining the decay of the heroic, though still emphasising middle-aged fantasy. The new productions may be read partly as reactions against the ironising-out of the epic dimension of the play, but their imaging of decay is hardly an unironic celebration of the heroic. Keith Hack's 1983 Young Vic *Antony and Cleopatra* used a set by Voytek consisting of a gigantic headless statue of a warrior, probably Mars or perhaps Antony, dressed in gold robes, which covered most of the acting area. Changes of locality were indicated by lighting. Keith Baxter, returning to the role of Antony after the Ontario production directed by Robin Phillips (who was again to direct the play in 1985), gave another outstanding rendition, grizzled and swaggering, more varied and pathetic than Gambon's, and middle-aged in the different sense of having 'all the fervour and longing of a man who knows that this grand passion will be his last' (Charles Spencer, *Standard*).[216] Judy Parfitt's auburn-curled[217] Cleopatra seemed

---

216 All reviews of this production are sourced from *London Theatre Record*, 9–22 April 1983, pp. 297–8, 355.

217 She reminded Michael Coveney of 'a pre-Raphaelite Theda Bara' (*Financial Times*), but for Jack Tinker the 'defiant pale make-up and the blaze of auburn curls' concealed 'a frightened woman clutching on to the glories of her own myth' (*Daily Mail*).

modern and skittish: 'her charm might have been purchased at Lucy Clayton and she has a delicious line in smooth bitchery' (Rosalind Carne, *Guardian*); signalling her mood swings vocally, she was best at caprice and command. Brian Deacon's 'most expressive and even attractive' Octavius found 'real emotional force in his disappointment' at the failure of the arranged marriage (Michael Coveney, *Financial Times*) and Barry Stanton's Enobarbus was clubbable, but in Hack's production 'imperial preoccupations' took 'a definite second place' (Carne), the lovers being 'cocooned in their own fantasy even to the last' (Jack Tinker, *Daily Mail*).

Hack's production and the Noble revival ran simultaneously for a time, and Tinker commented, 'so fearful is the scramble for exam success these days that London – thanks to the A-level curriculum – can support not one but two Cleopatras enthroned in splendour just a barge-ride away from each other'. In 1991 no less than three productions of the play were offering, two in London; the fact that Shakespeare is still taught on English syllabuses gives his plays some commercial viability in the right circumstances. By the same token, the paring down of traditional 'literary' elements in school and university courses also means an effective narrowing of the Shakespeare 'canon', especially in terms of theatrical production, and the current stage popularity of *Antony and Cleopatra* almost certainly owes something to the play's generally high reputation in scholarly circles.

By contrast with Hack's, in Robin Phillips's 1985 Chichester production, on an open stage modelled on the one he had used in Ontario in 1976, Daphne Dare's set of gauze boxes and a stepped acting area suited pace but not spectacle, and the contrast between Egypt and Rome was represented only by the wearing of togas. Yet, with his textual excisions Phillips also attempted to shore up heroic ruins: the galley scene went, in the downplaying of power politics, and cuts were made in the last two acts to allow Cleopatra 'to pass out as a stainlessly noble heroine'. In their scenes together, Denis Quilley and Diana Rigg 'translate[d] the majestic affair into a ruthless power struggle', Rigg singleminded in her desire to possess Antony, and Quilley troubled by an 'uneasy conscience' but 'convinced of his own invincible power' (Irving Wardle, *Times*, 16 May 1985) until the naval defeat, when 'his massive body crumple[d]'. But the lovers' relationship looked smaller-scale to John Peter, 'a storm in a teacup', with Rigg's Cleopatra 'a spirited but well-mannered Englishwoman who's liable to fits of temper' (*Sunday Times*, 19 May 1985).[218] The two major supporting roles were played with more complexity. Norman Rodway's Enobarbus was both the 'wholly trustworthy commentator' and the 'rough old trooper' and

218 Rigg was later to play Dryden's Cleopatra (in 1991 at the Almeida Theatre, in Jonathan Kent's production), to which she was considered better suited.

Philip Frank's Octavius was in the more modern tradition, traceable to Baxter's in 1969: 'a nervous, gentle mannered young subaltern gradually evolving into an emperor' (Wardle).

As in Hack's production, a large-scale set imaging decay featured in the Theatr Clwyd production of 1986,[219] directed by Toby Robertson (returning to the play) and Christopher Selbie, and brought from Mold to the Theatre Royal, Haymarket. But Simon Higlett's two-level set, a run-down rotunda with doorways and arches, was little admired: it was useful as a sign of imperial decay or for winching up the bleeding Antony, but (like the Chichester set of the previous year) it blurred the distinction between Rome and Egypt. The Caravaggio-inspired decor used Jacobean-Roman costumes, but singled out the protagonists. Antony dressed for battle as something like a turbanned Turk and Cleopatra was bare-footed like Mirren; 'with short curly red hair . . . in a boyish white outfit, she looks more like a twentieth-century *Guardian* reader than a great Egyptian voluptuary' (Kathy O'Shaughnessy, *Spectator*, 7 June 1986). Whilst Michael Billington was surprised to see Shakespeare return 'very comfortably' to the West End (*Guardian*, 28 May 1986), Francis Wheen was annoyed at the inconsiderate behaviour of the audience (*Sunday Today*, 8 June 1986); some critics complained about the 'provincial' or (as in Phillips's case) 'old-fashioned' nature of the production and the poor standard of support offered by the company. But it gave Vanessa Redgrave her second chance to play Cleopatra, this time opposite Timothy Dalton, and her performance was, for most critics, the main interest. She did not have the aura of political power, but was the self-aware actress (established at the very opening, with the lovers 'romp[ing] around a costume-chest'); 'authoritative, but not regal', she substituted 'nursery sex play' for sensuality and seemed, like Mirren and Rigg, but in a different mode from either, too English (Mary Harron, *Observer*, 1 June 1986). Like Suzman and Jackson, she was witty and vocally strong and, again in the English tradition, her death-scene was impressive, though 'she achieve[d] tragic grandeur on her own terms, facing death as yet another game' (Irving Wardle, *Times*, 28 May 1986). Caesar was played as 'icy, self-contained' by Ken Bones (who looked older than Dalton) and Maecenas and Agrippa operated like servile cabinet ministers (John Peter, *Sunday Times*, 1 June 1986). In relation to this Octavius, to Cleopatra, and to the 'sad joviality' of Robert O'Mahoney's Enobarbus (Peter), Dalton was 'far too young and vigorous and alert', but had the

219 In the same year *Antony and Cleopatra* was produced in China, in Roman dress, as one of a plethora of twenty-five Shakespeare plays, mainly in traditional productions (I am indebted to Murray Levith for this information, communicated to me at the ANZSA Conference in Perth, 1994).

English virtue of being good at self-disgust and emphasised Antony's 'sui-cidal impulse' (Michael Coveney, *Financial Times*, 27 May 1986). He was 'impassioned' 'where necessary', but, in a production which Martin Hoyle saw as 'without the dimension of a world well lost for love', both pro-tagonists gave a 'lightweight but consistent and thought-out performance' (*Plays and Players*, September 1986, p. 31). Two reviewers remarked on an element in the protagonists' relationship which in Peter Hall's production of the following year was to be central: Dalton's Antony was 'a Roman gone so native he resembles some fantasy prince from a Valentino movie' (Jack Tinker, *Daily Mail*, 27 May 1986) and he and Redgrave were 'escapist lovers, prisoners of their own fading fantasies' (Carole Woddis, *City Limits*, 12 June 1986).

Peter Hall's large-scale National Theatre production of 1987, starring Anthony Hopkins and Judi Dench, in the equally large-scale Olivier Theatre, was hailed by most critics as a major success and seen as a worthy successor to the Redgrave–Ashcroft production of 1953: well cast, coher-ent, with plenty of dramatic tension, and placing proper emphasis on verse-speaking; Paul Anderson praised it for not dealing in 'half-thought-out affectation' like so much British Shakespeare (*Tribune*, 24 April 1987). Using a full text with only one interval and lasting four hours, it seemed a little uninnovative, with its dry ice, battles by sound effect, braying trum-pets and standard-bearers rushing down aisles; some critics found the galley scene a little flat. The production was brisk, but hardly novel, in 'cinematically dissolving one scene into another' (Michael Billington, *Guardian*, 11 April 1987). In the entrance of the lovers, where Antony sat on Mardian's shoulders and Cleopatra controlled Mardian by rope, there was a touch of gimickry, but it may have been an allusion to (and ironic reversal of) Antony's piggy-backing Cleopatra in the previous year's Theatr Clwyd production. It certainly literalised Cleopatra's taking the lead in the relationship, as the production emphasised. The decor and costume style was late Renaissance, Veronese being acknowledged by the use of *Mars and Venus Bound by Cupid* on the poster and programme cover, though Alison Chitty's designs were also directly influenced by Mantegna and 'in action, the glittering highlights and bold, leaping shadows suggest the abrupt drama of late Mannerist painters like Caravaggio' (John Peter, *Sunday Times*, 12 April 1987). Chitty's set, in earthy or dried-blood red, used against a cyclorama 'large mobile crumbling colonnades that trundle across the stage at the end of every scene' (Anderson) and took different configurations according to locality, which was also indicated by costume, russets being associated with Egypt and steel blue with Rome. It was a pro-duction that acknowledged the heroic dimensions of the play in a late-

9 Judi Dench as Cleopatra, Miranda Foster as Charmian and asps in Hall's 1987 National Theatre production. Photograph: John Haynes.

eighties way, underlining the discrepancy between aspiration and achievement by casting against type and emphasising the centrality of fantasy in the lovers' relationship: Michael Billington saw it as offering new insight into the way in which the play is 'rooted in prophesy and dream' and in the completion of a pattern, and is 'about two middle-aged people – carnal, deceitful, often sad – seeking in love a reality greater than themselves'.

In keeping with this oblique or ironic approach to heroism via the mid-life crisis, Hopkins and Dench played 'the title roles as if they were not star actors. There is a moving and painful honesty in these performances: they are fleshy, ageing people, both of them attractive and difficult, and they give out a sense of searing, wounded intimacy' (Peter). The protagonists were more convincing in the overweight aspect of their fleshiness than in the carnal one, but as Peter wrote, sexuality was 'not the real bond' between them. Hopkins, whose performance was less universally admired than Dench's, was 'caught in the web not only of *amour* but of time', and enacted the extremity of his desperation at the whipping of the messenger (Steve Grant, *Time Out*, 15 April 1987), losing self-control as he lost his grip on the political situation. Peter Kemp found him 'a portly old cove' lacking charisma (*Independent*, 11 April 1987), Michael Ratcliffe 'an affectionate, exhausted and introspective old lion' (*Observer*, 12 April 1987), Kenneth Hurren 'a boozy and besotted "noble ruin" . . . in whom remnants of bygone greatness obstinately linger' (*Mail on Sunday*, 12 April 1987); for Clive Hirschhorn, he was physically and vocally superb (*Sunday Express*, 12 April 1987), but for Paul Anderson 'so consistently boisterous that he becomes a little tedious'. Robin Ray saw 'brooding restlessness' as at 'the core' of both his and Dench's complementary interpretations; Hopkins's showed itself in 'a physical unquiet born of frustration and despair' and he 'firmly refus[ed] many tempting moments of lyrical beauty in the verse', whereas Dench's was 'the prowling of a feline, dreading the certainty of being caged' (*Punch*, 22 April 1987).

Dench's restlessness was also seen in terms familiar from seventies' reviewing: 'the peevish insecurity of the mistress behind the swagger of the Queen, the crafty calculation and occasional panic, the stagey luxuriatings in her own performances' (Kemp). For Francis King, she was too restless in the first scenes and 'too monotonously plangent' in her grief at the monument (*Sunday Telegraph*, 12 April 1987), but most critics paid tribute to her range, and John Peter read her volatility as 'a constant lust for life, like an animal which is both simple and incomprehensible'. In her cage-dreading animality, 'only the ultimate abandoned carnality elude[d] her' (Hurren); Michael Billington found 'sexual magnetism' in the form of her 'emotional extremism'. Lowen reports that, in the rehearsal period (during which both Hall and Dench consulted Peggy Ashcroft), Dench herself moved from a fear that she was too English for the role to a conviction that 'the play is about middle-aged people', as Hall believed (*Peter Hall*, pp. 22–3, p. 80, pp. 85–6).

The reviewers' general satisfaction with the production also owed something to the sureness with which the two principal supporting roles were played, in terms both of individual performance and of overall coherence.

Hall did not neglect the subtleties of the wider political issues, and Tim Pigott-Smith's Octavius was 'a power-lover who delights in spotting and playing on other men's flaws' (Billington), 'a frigid but choleric politician who dislikes physical contact: devious but self-righteous', who 'will steer Rome towards an arid stability' and whose 'dishonesties are not lost on his followers' (Peter). Michael Bryant's Enobarbus, gruff and 'Cockneyfied' (Kemp), was widely praised but variously read: Billington saw him as delighting 'in aping his master's drinking and womanising', whilst Peter thought his 'powerful feelings' were 'held in check' by his 'sober soldierly manner' and that he was 'the moral touchstone of both the politics and the emotions of the play'.

The most recent major English production of the play was John Caird's for the RSC, with Clare Higgins and Richard Johnson, first offered at Stratford in 1992 and then at the Barbican in the following year.[220] Its reception was more mixed than Hall's, and Caird responded to criticisms by making changes at the Barbican: Cleopatra's many wigs were replaced by one straight black one,[221] the interpolated apotheosis of the lovers was replaced by a lying-in-state, and the Seleucus scene was restored. Like Hall's, the production was large-scale and used a flexible set whose configuration altered with locale: by Sue Blane, its sliding russet-coloured 'great walls and pillars of ancient stone and brick' were 'bathed in a golden light and placed on the side of the stage to allow a panorama of the cerulean sky beyond' in Egypt, whilst 'in Rome they close claustrophobically around the characters' (Charles Spencer, *Daily Telegraph*, 9 November 1992). Few reviewers took exception to the set – though Maureen Paton called it 'Hollywood Egyptian kitsch' (*Daily Express*, 6 November 1992) – but the costumes, in which Martin Esslin detected a Veronese touch (*Plays International*, July–August 1993, p. 17), were viewed as something of a ragbag.

The major difference between Hall's and Caird's approach lay in what Michael Billington called Caird's 'sensuously romantic' quality (*Guardian*, 7 November 1992). Like Brook and Hall, Caird emphasised the middle-aged nature of the lovers' relationship, but he insisted on their transcendence of

---

220 In 1993 Charles Towers directed the play for the Oregon Shakespeare Festival, with Henry Woronicz and Megan Cole in the title parts, using a reduced text that cut the playing time to under three hours, including interval (for details, see A. C. Dessen, 'The Image and the Script', pp. 5–8).

221 In 1992 she first wore 'a long full wig of curly red hair' (George L. Geckle, 'The Power of Desire on Stage', p. 15), but in the course of the play 'change[d] her hair colour more often than she change[d] her mind' (Kirsty Milne, *Sunday Telegraph*, 8 November 1992).

10 Clare Higgins being restrained from stabbing the messenger in Caird's 1992 RSC production. Photograph: Clive Barda.

their limitations, to the extent of an apotheosis in which the wall parted and the lovers embraced in silhouette. In 3.6 Caird staged, during Octavius's angry account of it, the coronation of the lovers (and children) in a tableau reminiscent of Tree's production and which Jeremy Kingston called 'as glittering and sunlit as an Alma-Tadema' (*Times*, 29 May 1993); indeed, for Robert Hewison, the whole production was 'a vast, animated monument, striding majestically towards the nineteenth century' (*Sunday Times*, 8 November 1992). It was not modern enough for Paul Taylor either, in so far as 'it becomes too easy, at the end, to accept the lovers at their own valuation' (*Independent*, 7 November 1992). But for Nicholas de Jongh it was like a modern musical version, with a 'false silver lining' (*Evening Standard*, 6 November 1992), and clearly its 'romantic' nature was in tune with the demand for myth-making theatre (with or without music) current in affluent western or westernised countries. Billington saw Caird's approach as rather closer to Hall's, in so far as 'scene melts filmically into scene' and the audience are reminded that the lovers have 'no future except in the world of their own vivid imagination'. Billington, who had appreciated Hall's emphasis on prophecy and destiny, was one of the few reviewers to approve of the way in which Caird 'cannily reminds us of the tale's tragic destination by making Jasper Britton's Soothsayer a ubiquitous figure who even turns up as the asp-bearing Clown'.

The protagonists' credibility as lovers was also a matter of some dispute; as with Hall's production, most critics found Cleopatra more convincing than Antony. Taylor admired the ability of the lovers to stand back from the myth they were making, 'to burst out laughing at their own magniloquent gestures'. Sensuality was another matter. Johnson was 'an upright elderly party who radiates the sexual magnetism of a retired magistrate' (Hewison) and, though Higgins's 'off-the-shoulder gown almost becomes off-the-breast', and the lovers 'kiss, hug and roll around the floor . . . there is something perfunctory in these displays of affection' (Kingston). Twenty years after being Suzman's Antony, Johnson was, like Antony himself, in a position to contemplate his ability to sustain the role, but most reviewers saw him this time as beginning from a position of sad decline, and his restlessness (unlike Hall's protagonists') was not easily read as a means of characterisation but seemed rather to stem from unease with the part. Like Hopkins, he appeared to some critics to lack charisma, though others saw authority or vanished glory in him; to Spencer, he was a 'grizzled old bear of an Antony, growling with pleasure and painful remorse', but to Taylor 'less of a former warrior than . . . a charming old buffer who would be a boon on the wine committee of the Atheneum'.

Higgins was admired as intelligent, inscrutable, intense, volatile, and not too modern; Billington ranked her with Ashcroft and Dench (*Guardian*, 28 May 1993). More sensual than Dench, her magnetism took a comparable form – 'always alive, always mocking, always aware of the potency of her own self-created myth' – and she gave moving glimpses of Cleopatra's middle-aged vulnerability. She controlled her man by being 'reckless, violent, and impulsive, one minute sprawling all over Antony, the next kneeing him in the chest' (Billington, *Guardian*, 7 November 1992). Whilst to many she seemed less than regal, she spoke the verse better than anyone and developed 'sorrow, seriousness and self-awareness' (de Jongh), though she lacked Cleopatra's 'quivers of ambiguity' after Antony's death (Taylor).

Many reviewers thought the political world of the play either perfunctorily or unsubtly represented, and the verse-speaking unmoving. The major supporting roles were less well played than in Hall's production. John Nettles's Octavius was in the modern mixed mode, though vocally flexible and 'more affable than the usual run' (Jeremy Kingston, *Times*, 29 May 1993): 'a man hungry for triumph' (Billington, *Guardian*, 7 November 1992). Paul Jesson's Enobarbus was not often mentioned in despatches; Malcolm Rutherford dismissed him in Stratford as 'a dull man with a beard'

(*Financial Times*, 7 November 1992), though Kate Kellaway found him 'exceptionally good' at the Barbican (*Observer*, 30 May 1993). Toby Stephens's Pompey and Claire Benedict's Charmian were frequently praised. With her white Charmian, Cleopatra had a black Iras (Susie Lee Hayward); perhaps, as in Miller's BBC version, this pairing was a way of representing her tawniness.

If the phenomenon of Caird's production (for all its lovers' self-consciousness) might be taken to represent a swing against the seventies' and eighties' trend of ironising the lovers, one recent European production, Peter Stein's, seems to confirm that swing, whilst another, Peter Zadek's, offers evidence that Antony and Cleopatra will not necessarily be read at their own valuation in the remainder of the nineties. Stein's 1994 Salzburg Festival production, using his own translation, after Dorothea Tieck, and designed by Dionissis Fotopoulos, was also large-scale, both in terms of its being part of a Roman cycle and as offered in the 'vast arena' of the Felsenreitschule, which Michael Billington saw as a hindrance to pace. Hans Michael Rehberg was a 'tough' and 'soldierly' Antony and Edith Clever a 'self-consciously regal' Cleopatra, but Stein's production shared with Caird's the problem of a lack of 'erotic tension' between the lovers. The production was merely 'cogent' until the last act, when, assisted by a transformation (via the retractable roof) from daylight to 'flame-illuminated darkness', Clever achieved a 'dream-like majesty', 'movingly hungry for death and the prospect of reunion with her Antony. At last one got a glimpse of Stein's real genius . . . for making the historic past seem not like a foreign country but part of our collective memory' (*Guardian Weekly*, 14 August 1994).

Outside the mainstream, 1979–95

In 1979, when small-scale ironising productions were dominant in England, three productions outside Britain took more radical approaches to the play.[222] Two, like Brook's, framed the love story with distancing devices: Robert Colonna's Rhode Island Shakespeare Theatre version set the play, cabaret-style (with pianist on stage throughout) in between-the-wars Berlin, with Charmian and Iras as flappers and Octavius and his supporters in gangster suits, and Senda Koreya's production at the National Theatre, Tokyo, in a translation by Isao Mikami, interpolated three new scenes to emphasise Cleopatra's political motivation.

---

222 I am indebted for these accounts to Leiter (ed.), *Shakespeare Around the Globe*, pp. 19–20.

Estelle Parsons's off-off-Broadway production at the Interart Theatre, New York was more fundamentally radical, since it was partly an expression of the actors' sense of playing from the margins. It was not only modern dress but bilingual: the clash between Egypt and Rome was thrown into high relief by casting Hispanic actors as Romans, speaking their lines in Spanish, and fair actors of Anglo-Saxon origin as the Egyptians, speaking English. Possibly the linguistic contrast dramatised the issue of cultural separateness more cogently than the inversion of the expected power hierarchy dramatised the issue of cultural dominance, though the production clearly offered a local perspective on both issues. The scenes between the lovers, played by Kathleen Gaffney and Francisco Prado, were vividly erotic, and Cleopatra, whose style was 1940s Hollywood, was bare-breasted for her encounter with the asps. If this production was partly a response to racial tensions in the city, so, presumably, was Michael Kahn's 1988 production at the Shakespeare Theatre, Washington, with Franchelle Dorn as Cleopatra and other black actors in the other Egyptian roles. Kahn's production seems to have been the first attempt to 'stress the African nature of Cleopatra's court' in this way, but Dorn's 'naturalistic approach' and unease with the verse contrasted 'so awkwardly with the rather Edwardian orotundity' of Kenneth Haigh as Antony that the Rome–Egypt clash 'often seemed reduced to an indecisive battle of acting styles' (Neill, Introduction to his edition, p. 65).

In 1989 the first black British actor played Cleopatra, but in an 'updated' version of the play, *Cleopatra and Antony*, adapted and directed for the Actors Touring Company by Malcolm Edwards and set in the 1930s. The production was received unenthusiastically, but it has some importance as a radical reinvention of the play for modern purposes, if only because it took to their logical conclusion some notable tendencies in modern mainstream productions. Its agenda was more feminist than racial, though clearly the casting of Cleopatra recognised her otherness in that sense too, as well as reflecting the increasingly multicultural composition and expectations of English-speaking societies, cultures and (to a lesser extent) theatre audiences. Whilst English portayals of Cleopatra since Suzman's had shown signs of the influence of feminism in presenting the queen not as voluptuary or vamp, but in terms of role-playing, sexual politics and power politics, this production presented her as the undisputed protagonist. Mainstream productions of the period tended to treat ironically the notion of history as the actions of great men, but Edwards's production was both feminist and postcolonial in confronting the irony of Cleopatra's being remembered misogynistically when she is one of the few remembered women in history.

Edwards used a text more radically manipulated than any since the main-stream production of 1833; 'unaBridges-Adams' and his contemporaries had changed mainstream thinking, though there was some sign of rethink-ing in Phillips's cuts of 1985.[223] Edwards's version concentrated on Cleopatra by removing most of the political passages and adding episodes from Plutarch, Dryden (including the meeting of Octavia and Cleopatra) and elsewhere, and reducing the cast to five. Pauline Black, 'the ex-Ska singer of the chart-topping band The Selector', 'dealing admirably with the spirally mood changes' of the part, 'more than proved herself as a classical actress in a majestic Shakespearean debut' (Lydia Conway, *Harpers and Queen*, January 1990, p. 32). Jeremy Kingston, reviewing a performance at the Lyric Studio, Hammersmith, thought the enterprise misjudged, but liked the 'intelligence and colour' of some of the verse-speaking, and 'Susan Henry's trim, tight Octavia and Pauline Black's loftily exotic Cleo'; he con-sidered Patrick Wilde 'gravely miscast' as a lightweight Antony (*Times*, 20 May 1989), but the casting, and the doubling of Antony with the Clown, was part of the reorientation of the play.

Yvonne Brewster's 1991 production for the Merseyside Everyman Theatre and Talawa Theatre Company, starring Jeffery Kissoon (who had played Eros and Pompey in Hack's production) and Dona Croll, at the Bloomsbury Theatre, was the first 'all-black' (African, Caribbean and Asian) British production, and their first Shakespeare. It dealt more obliquely with racial tensions, since an all-black cast, like those of main-stream English productions, 'continued to obscure the racial anxieties that contribute so materially to the ambivalent Roman construction of Egyptian difference' in the play (Neill, Introduction to his edition, p. 67), but the nature of the cast stemmed from the formation of the company in response to 'petty racism' (Rick Jones, *Time Out*, 22 May 1991). Helen Turner's set was simple – curved stone promenade and back projection of changing skies, the latter as in Nunn's production – and the costumes were also simple, with Cleopatra and her women in 'cotton shifts and ballet-slippers' and Antony and Octavius in 'identical body-warmers as armour' (Tony Dunn, *Tribune*, 31 May 1991); Annalena McAfee thought the 'richly draped' costumes suggested 'a Biblical fashion shoot' (*Evening Standard*, 20 May 1991). Egypt was represented by cushions and rugs and Rome by metal furniture. The text was pruned and characters amalgamated to suit the small company, and, although the performances were uneven, the pro-

223 Koreya's production of 1979 was more radical in this respect than Phillips's, which suggests that the use of a translated text, particularly in a country with markedly different cultural and theatrical traditions, encourages greater liberties.

duction moved with a broad sweep and great momentum. Like Brook's, the production was more orthodox[224] than expected: it made political intrigue a strong feature; Ben Thomas dominated the political world as a 'ruthless Machiavel' of a Caesar, who had 'his host quietly strangled' at the end of the party on Pompey's galley (Michael Billington, *Guardian*, 20 May 1991). Though it underplayed the 'fatalistic impact' of the love story (Martin Hoyle, *Times*, 18 May 1991) and the protagonists' 'super-heroism' (Dunn), the production nevertheless gave 'the impression of a world too small for the egos of its principal characters' (Jones). Kissoon was physically and vocally powerful, thrillingly so in the battle scenes; his Antony suffered 'an extraordinary loneliness' (Alastair Macaulay, *Financial Times*, 20 May 1991) and fell 'like some wounded grizzled bear'. Croll, 'though spirited, [did] not always catch the lightning changes of tempo demanded by Cleopatra's fiery temperament' (Carole Woddis, *What's On*, 22 May 1991), but was 'funny, sensual, powerful' (Macaulay), yet, like so many others, the production was 'a passion-free zone' (McAfee) because there was no sexual chemistry between the lovers.

The Talawa production used only fifteen actors, and in this period there were several other small companies in England and elsewhere that made do with limited resources and a good deal of doubling in productions that were hardly radical but might be called off-mainstream. In England in the same year[225] Tony Hegarty's fast-moving, judiciously cut and doughtily doubled nine-actor Commonweal Theatre Company's production, first at the Shaw Theatre, London, then on tour, had 'tatty, minimal designs' (Alastair Macaulay, *Financial Times*, 25 April 1991) but clearly contrasted the two power-centres by means of 'panels of Roman numerals and Egyptian hiero-glyphics'. One aspect of the small-scale minimalism was the miming of props, which was less than satisfactory when Antony fell on his sword, but Andrew McDonald's Antony was in any case unheroic and 'somewhat self-satisfied' (Michael Arditti, *Evening Standard*, 31 May 1991). Arditti thought Susan Curnow's Cleopatra lacking in both passion and

224 Critics' and audiences' expectations of unorthodox production and acting styles 'may itself rest upon assumed stereotypes' (Jeffrey Wainwright, *Independent*, 30 April 1991).

225 A third production in 1991, John Adams's at the Birmingham Rep, with Malcolm Tierney and Sylvia Syms, was more mainstream; it used a Napoleonic setting for the Roman scenes, possibly to provide an ironic parallel/contrast with Syms's 'bourgeois self-importance' in her 'more natural and timeless' Egyptian setting. Tierney's voice was 'impressively experienced and varied', but there was 'little chemistry' between the lovers; Simon Dormandy was a complex Octavius (Alastair Macaulay, *Financial Times*, 25 April 1991).

manipulative skills, but Macaulay saw her as majestic and commanding, liked her hieratic postures (reflecting the decor panels) and believed in her intimacy with Antony.

In Australia, where the play has not been popular (but, like elsewhere, more frequently performed in recent times), there have been two experimental productions using small companies.[226] Rex Cramphorn's Playbox Theatre Company's production in 1983, with Lindy Davies and Frank Gallacher in the title roles, used a lot of doubling in the others. At a time when dominant sets were a feature of English productions, his actor-dwarfing set, by Eamon D'Arcy, was more pro-active and decidedly 'post-Brechtian', with three mobile metal platforms on wheels (two with attached spotlights operated by the actors), used 'like battering-rams' to represent the conflict in the battle scenes and draped with curtains to form the monument (Heales and Bartholomeusz, 'Shakespeare in Sydney and Melbourne', pp. 483–4). The set was more memorable than either the interpretation or the performances, but was upstaged at the end by the two four-foot pythons cast as the asps. In 1992 the Sydney Theatre Company mounted a very different experiment, a production 'performed under Elizabethan working conditions' (programme) at the Wharf, directed by Wayne Harrison and Philip Parsons. It was the most ambitious of a series of explorations by Parsons[227] of the Elizabethan repertory system, using a small company of which doubling was expected, a short rehearsal period (though *Antony and Cleopatra* was rehearsed for sixteen days), a raised stage and an equally lit auditorium in which the audience were encouraged to mix freely and take refreshments. John Stanton and Sandy Gore played the protagonists competently, costumes were a mixture of contemporary and historicising, and the platform over the third entrance/tiring-house served as the monument.[228] The brisk production was followed by a jig, emphasising thematic connections, however farcical, with Shakespeare's play.

The most successful recent radical production, both brisk and post-Brechtian (in a wider sense than Cramphorn's) was Peter Zadek's, offered at the King's Theatre in the 1994 Edinburgh Festival, and then in Vienna and Berlin. Zadek approached the play's intermingled love and political stories in a manner that was ironic and postcolonial and used 'alienating' images worthy of Brecht: the production was under the joint auspices of the

226 In addition, in 1977 four members of the Australian Performing Group offered a pared-down version of the play at the Pram Factory Back Theatre, Melbourne.

227 Begun in 1968 with a production of *Dr Faustus*; in the *King Lear* of 1991, the female roles were played by adult males, an experiment the company wisely decided not to repeat in *Antony and Cleopatra*.

228 Hattaway had suggested this as a possibility in *Elizabethan Popular Theatre*, p. 28.

11 The hauling of Antony in Harrison and Parsons's 1992 Sydney Theatre Company production, with John Stanton as Antony, Sandy Gore as Cleopatra and Fiona Press and Laura Keneally as Charmian and Iras. Photograph: Robert McFarlane.

12 Eva Mattes as Cleopatra, dead, in Zadek's 1994 Edinburgh production. Photograph: D. Sillitoe.

Berliner Ensemble and the Wiener Festwochen. It ran for four hours without interval, using a full text in a translation by Elisabeth Plessen, with English surtitles in Edinburgh: the translation's 'determined, provocative modernisation' seems not to have been well received in Berlin (John London, *Plays International*, December 1994, p. 28). It was, unlike Stein's production, fast-moving; the house lights were kept on and Wilfried Minks's set was basically a desert-yellow cyclorama and six chairs. The costumes set the play in a between-wars colonial world, with the Roman rulers in frock coats, top hats and winged collars, the infantry in pith helmets and baggy khaki shorts and Antony 'gone native, in dashing white robes and tea-towel head-dress' over a khaki uniform, looking like Lawrence of Arabia, whilst Cleopatra's court, with its 'scantily clad handmaidens' and the queen 'in a series of knock-out gowns', was 'straight out of some Hollywood epic' (Charles Spencer, *Weekly Telegraph*, 24–30 August 1994). Zadek played up the satirical potential of the galley scene, which 'became a squalid, drunken revel in which world leaders were portrayed as pathetic topers' (Michael Billington, *Country Life*, 25 August 1994). The depiction of military characters and scenes made allusions to the First World War, which John London found a little strained, but which underlined the destructive vanity of powerful leaders. The lovers themselves treated war as 'a kind of capricious game', Antony 'putting on his breast-plate, binoculars and lip-salve in front of vanity mirrors, as if creating his own legend' and Cleopatra regarding war 'largely as an excuse for dressing up in pith helmet and a tight black suit' (Michael Billington, *Guardian Weekly*, 28 August 1994). Spencer called the acting 'magnificent', and Billington called Gert Voss's 'superb Antony' 'a reckless hedonist ready to risk war to satisfy his sexual itch' and Eva Mattes's Cleopatra 'a restless nympho' who 'lives in a state of deluded fantasy about her affair with Antony' (*Guardian Weekly*). Like Nunn and Caird, Zadek underlined the lovers' 'living out their public romance with the exhibitionist relish of Burton and Taylor' (Spencer). Neither acquired 'moral stature' until the end, when Antony realised what he had lost and Cleopatra chose death rather than 'life as a colonial trophy' (Billington, *Guardian Weekly*), but, for all their absurdity, the lovers were 'infinitely preferable to the cold Roman world personified by Veit Schubert's icily calculating Octavius Caesar' (Spencer).

Zadek won a British award for best foreign production, but Vanessa Redgrave's multicultural *Antony and Cleopatra* at the Riverside in 1995 got a very different critical reception. Like Zadek's, her production emphasised the lovers' political motivation, but Redgrave's was considered incoherent, slow-moving and generally badly spoken. Her casting was radical, with a French Vietnamese Charmian in Helene Patarot, 'complete with oo-la-las', a Bosnian Iras in Etela Pardo and a 'mature black American', Paul Butler, as Antony (Clive Hirschhorn, *Sunday Express*, 4 June 1995). Except for Pompey and Lepidus, the Romans were played by black actors and the Egyptians by white ones, an inversion of Shakespeare's white–tawny contrast in Estelle Parsons's manner. Michael Billington wondered whether the production was 'meant to be a deconstruction of classical legend, an attack on Elizabethan–Jacobean colonial adventurism or even a comment on the chaotic new world order and the Balkan tragedy' (*Guardian*, 3 June 1995). Redgrave wanted to 'highlight the contemporary resonance of this powerful political drama, elucidating the personal tragedies within an occupied land' (Benedict Nightingale, *Times*, 6 June 1995). As well as directing and playing Cleopatra, the 58-year-old Redgrave was responsible for the design. Dimly lit, the grim, vast set did not distinguish between Rome and Egypt, and reminded many reviewers of Bosnia: 'Steps, festooned with litter and next to which a beggar sleeps, lead up to a platform hedged by fallen masonry. And a bare, scaffolded gallery with glassless windows is similarly redolent of collapse' (Nicholas de Jongh, *Evening Standard*, 2 June 1995). By contrast, the costumes were 'glorious, with 17th century ruffs, cloaks and jerkins' (Louise Stafford Charles, *What's On*, 7 June 1995). What was missing was passion between the protagonists; and for this some blamed the ulterior motivation given to Cleopatra's 'cold-bloodedly coquettish routine' in captivating Antony (Irving Wardle, *Independent on Sunday*, 4 June 1995), whilst others saw the benign Butler as miscast, 'wander[ing] through the chaos like Santa Claus on Prozac' (Nightingale). Cleopatra, wearing short auburn hair, was intermittently imperious and volatile; Jane Edwardes found it 'a relief not to watch another English actress trying to play a sensuous serpent', but thought her 'a peculiarly upper-crust headmistress with girlish tendencies' (*Time Out*, 7 June 1995). Redgrave remained passionless until her speech over Antony's body, from which point she played 'with the peculiar radiance that makes her such a great actress' (Maureen Paton, *Daily Express*, 5 June 1995). By contrast, David Harewood was a passionate Enobarbus, and reviewers also found consolation in Howard Saddler's 'vigilant, self-possessed Caesar' (de Jongh).

The critics were more than mollified by Northern Broadsides' touring production later in the same year. Whilst Barrie Rutter's directing and playing Antony was not quite a feat to equal Redgrave's, neither was his style anything like the old actor-managers', and his production was praised for the very qualities Redgrave's lacked: pace and sure-footed consistency, with 'sharp, vigorous, Yorkshire-accented and wholly appropriate' verse-speaking. It opened in Halifax 'in the atmospheric Dean Clough vaults – ancient flagstones in the basement of the transformed carpet factory, a brick tunnel, rust-red steel girders' with seating 'traverse-style, on either side of the action'. The two-and-three-quarter-hour production made uncontroversial cuts but added 'humour, lightness and passion' (Michael Coveney, *Observer*, 8 October 1995). On a stage bare except for a draped rostrum with cushions, Egypt was indicated by attendants in orange and red and Rome by functionaries in blue suits; Rutter wore a red shirt and fawn trousers as Antony and Ishia Bennison was Cleopatra in a white lace bodice and coral slacks. The acting was sinewy, with 'no room for displays of sensibility'; 'argument is prized so highly, that in this flinty atmosphere, the poetry suddenly takes flight' (Robert Butler, *Independent on Sunday*, 15 October 1995). The unusual opening, in which boys parodied the lovers, provided 'a sceptical frame' within which Rutter and Bennison were obliged to 'establish the characters' dignity afresh' (Jeffrey Wainwright, *Independent*, 6 October 1995), and did so in unconventional ways. Bennison, 'a hook-nosed, olive-skinned version of Tracey Ullman', 'achieving her dignity through refusing all compromise' (Coveney), eschewed middle-class attitudes and never looked like abandoning Antony; her 'wonderful performance' dominated the play: 'she has no regard for queenliness in the high English fashion, but is coquettish, vulnerable, violent and witty' (Wainwright). Rutter's interpretation of Antony emphasised his association with Hercules and with the god's knack of combining buffoonery with strength (Wainwright);[229] he was a 'pulsating, impetuous Antony' (Coveney), capable of 'gruff tenderness' (Benedict Nightingale, *Times*, 5 October 1995). The protagonists were strongly supported. Dave Hill's Enobarbus wedded 'poetic efflorescence to a head-shaking, cynical decency that places the larger personal and political tragedy in a completely fresh perspective. He's seen it all and watches it happen again' (Coveney). Andrew Cryer was a 'sharp, shrewd' Octavius; Deborah McAndrew's 'neat' Octavia looked 'like a floor manager in a department store' (Nightingale). Three actors doubled parts, John Gully playing Pompey, Eros and Dolabella with distinction. Coveney hailed Rutter's *Antony and Cleopatra* as the first he had 'really enjoyed' because, despite its minimalism, it offered 'the full blast' of the play's 'poetic majesty and brilliance': it was 'the production Peter Brook never achieved'.

Radicalism and reinvention

Michael Billington, reviewing the Zadek production and reaffirming his belief that 'Shakespeare in a foreign tongue . . . becomes an analogue to the original that gives the director new freedom', claimed, 'After this startling, radical, Brechtian re-appraisal, it will be hard to go back to traditional productions in which the ageing lovers are accepted at their own self-satisfied evaluation' (*Guardian Weekly*, 28 August 1994). To date, his prediction has been borne out by Redgrave's and Rutter's productions; but it is easier for a rereading to seem radical if its energies come from outside a local tradition, and the stage history of any play is likely to show successive orthodox clusters within specific theatrical traditions and broader cultures. These orthodox clusters will differ from each other in emphasis and priority, according to prevailing sociological and cultural conditions, and to psychological and commercial need for novelty. If the stage history of *Antony and Cleopatra* is largely one of conservative productions, that is perhaps because the performance demands and complex nature of the play offer sufficient challenges in aesthetic and commercial terms. Given the play's structural tension between the satirical or ironic impulse and the tragic or heroic one, there is potentially an infinite variety of emphases between the two extremes, though reviewers and stage historians are likely (in the interests of strengthening their own emphases, or of struggling with their deadlines)

---

229 Wainwright suggests that Rutter's interpretation was influenced by the Broadsides' project of performing dramatisations of the Hercules myth, and quotes the historian Michael Grant's reference to Hercules as 'the buffoon-like strongman provoking laughter tempered by awe'.

to locate their conceptual clusters at the two polar extremes. In this sense, a traditional production of the play is not so easy to define, except locally in place and time, since every age and place that has a use for the play reinvents its 'History and Her-Story'[230] in its own image, and finds the 'ideal' enactment of that reinvention perpetually elusive.

230 A phrase not first applied to the play by feminist critics, but by the Victorian editor of *Punch*, Francis Burnand, as the subtitle of his travesty.

LIST OF CHARACTERS

MARK ANTONY
OCTAVIUS CAESAR } *triumvirs*
LEPIDUS

CLEOPATRA, *queen of Egypt*
CHARMIAN
IRAS
ALEXAS
MARDIAN, *a eunuch* } *Cleopatra's attendants*
DIOMEDES
SELEUCUS, *Cleopatra's treasurer*

OCTAVIA, *sister of Octavius Caesar and wife of Antony*

DEMETRIUS
PHILO
DOMITIUS ENOBARBUS
VENTIDIUS
SILIUS } *Antony's friends and followers*
CANIDIUS
SCARUS
EROS
DERCETUS
A SCHOOLMASTER, *Antony's* AMBASSADOR *to Caesar*

MAECENAS
AGRIPPA
TAURUS
THIDIAS } *Octavius Caesar's friends and followers*
DOLABELLA
GALLUS
PROCULEIUS

SEXTUS POMPEIUS *or* POMPEY
MENAS
MENECRATES } *Pompey's friends*
VARRIUS

MESSENGERS *to Antony, Octavius Caesar, and Cleopatra*
A SOOTHSAYER
Two SERVANTS *of Pompey*
SERVANTS *of Antony and Cleopatra*
A BOY
SOLDIERS, SENTRIES, GUARDSMEN *of Antony and Octavius Caesar*
A CAPTAIN *in Antony's army*
An EGYPTIAN
A CLOWN *with figs*

*Ladies attending on Cleopatra, eunuchs, servants, soldiers, captains, officers,
silent named characters (Rannius, Lucillius, Lamprius)*

SCENE: *In several parts of the Roman empire*

ANTONY AND CLEOPATRA

In Jacobean performances of the play, pronunciation of characters' names was presumably hybrid, like their costuming. The nineteenth-century vogue for archaeologising the play's Egyptian setting brought a different perspective and a concern for particulars, but directors of this kind of production were so preoccupied with the pictorial that they had little time for the finer details of Shakespeare's text and its delivery. Of Tree's production, which was in some respects the apogee of the movement, one reviewer complained 'No attempt, by the way, was made to give consistency to the pronunciation of proper names. The *u* in *Fulvia* was sounded in the Italian manner, and so was the first *a* in *Cleopatra*; but *Octavia* and the rest were pronounced in the frankest British way' (O.S., *Punch*, 2 January 1907). It is likely that in Shakespeare's day, as in modern productions, actors' regional accents were an additional complication in the matter of pronunciation; in recent times, for example, there has been something of a vogue for Northern English or Scottish Enobarbuses.

Doubling of minor parts was normal practice in Shakespeare's time, and Holmes (*Shakespeare and Burbage*, pp. 191–2) thinks Enobarbus's part was originally doubled with the Clown's. In Garrick's and nineteenth-century productions many liberties were taken with the minor characters: frequently they were combined or substituted and their speeches reassigned, and in Helpmann's production of 1957 some of the minor characters were 'telescoped', with Philo Canidius, Scarus Dercetas, Alexas Diomedes, Euphronius Lamprius and a Soothsayer-Schoolmaster reducing a large cast to a more manageable scale; but recent directors have sometimes used doubling to make thematic points. In Hall's production 'Jeremy Flynn is an affecting Eros, a role enhanced in this production by being given also the lines of the messenger whom Cleopatra terrorises' (Charles Osborne, *Daily Telegraph*, 11 April 1987). In her 1991 Talawa Theatre production, in which characters were 'amalgamated and even unsexed' (Martin Hoyle, *Times*, 18 May 1991), 'Ms Brewster has made a virtue of necessity in merging the cast roster of minor roles so that figures like Thidias and Menas become salutory survivors of the turmoil' (Jeffrey Wainwright, *Independent*, 30 April 1991); in the following year Caird 'reminds us of the tale's tragic destination by making Jasper Britton's Soothsayer a ubiquitous figure who even turns up as the asp-bearing Clown' (Michael Billington, *Guardian*, 7 November 1992). A more radical doubling in the Actors Touring Company's *Cleopatra and Antony* was not read to the actor's advantage: 'Patrick Wilde is gravely miscast as Antony. After his death he reappears as the clown with the asp and is clearly more at home thus than as a colossus' (Jeremy Kingston, *Times,* 20 May 1989). Emma Piper's doubling of Octavia with a 'flirtatious' Charmian in

Hack's 1983 production might be read as an attempt to put Octavia in her amorous place or to contrast Roman and Egyptian supporting roles; Michael Coveney thought the intensity of the relationship between Octavius and his sister 'suffer[ed] slightly' in the process (*Financial Times*, in *London Theatre Record*, 9–22 April 1983, p. 298).

ANTONY AND CLEOPATRA

ACT I, SCENE I

This is one of the key scenes in the play, interpretatively as well as dramatically. T. C. Worsley wrote, in relation to Byam Shaw's 1953 production, 'The success of a production of *Antony and Cleopatra* can be gauged in the first five minutes, for the opening scene plunges us at once into the steaming climate' (*New Statesman*, 7 May 1953). Whether the climate of the opening scene will be steaming is not so certain. The lovers' sexual chemistry is crucial, but the set-designer's inspiration is not always the functioning hot-house: at Iden Payne's production, Ivor Brown 'felt a touch of frost on the Nile' not only because it was an 'English version' but also because of 'that huge stage presenting Cleopatra as in some great columnar vault' (*Observer*, 21 April 1935). In Brook's 1978 production J. C. Trewin saw a glasshouse but little warmth: 'an austere set, like a vacant conservatory opaquely glazed' (*Birmingham Post*, 11 October 1978).

The exoticism of the Egyptian court can be exploited as much for its pictorial appeal as its thematic significance. Extravagance is in either case the keynote. Macready 'judiciously made the description of Cleopatra on the Cydnus the introduction to the whole play' (*Morning Chronicle*, 22 November 1833); in the promptbook, it comes early in the first scene, followed by Philo's 1.1.11–13 and the entrance of the protagonists. His spectacle, however, was disappointing: 'although a brilliant group of dancers and vine-crowned revellers occupied the stage for a few minutes in the first scene, there was nothing else, except the palace and the pyramids, that helped out the ideal of the splendour and costliness and extravagance of the court of Cleopatra. Her attendants were sufficiently commonplace for a burletta. We had no hint of the prodigal woman whose jewels were priceless and numberless, and who squandered the worth of empires to fix the wavering faith of the effeminate Antony – made effeminate by her charms. Miss Phillips' robe was a tarnished garment which your true stage Cleopatra would have trodden underfoot' (*Atlas*, 24 November 1833). Both the Langtry–Wingfield production and Tree's opened with 1.4 and then put Cleopatra's barge on stage for the lovers' entry (Chatterton's had used it for their exit): Victorian and Edwardian directors were inspired by the imperial splendour of another 'great queen' as well as by carefully documented Orientalism. Tree operated, as usual, on a large scale: 'The warm atmosphere of the East is in the cloudless sky, and is reflected in the swarthy faces of the assembled multitude. And what a stage crowd it is! The treasures of Egyptian lore must have been ransacked to enable the costumiers to reproduce those striking dresses. The cheering crowd might have stepped out of Sir Edward Poynter's famous painting of "Israel in Egypt"' (*Leeds Mercury*, 28 December 1906).

Later twentieth-century productions have been less grandiose, and directors have usually been more concerned with the aesthetic arrangement of 'crowds'. Agate 'dislike[d] the Chorus recruited from the canvases of Marcus Stone' in the Cass production of 1934 (*Brief Chronicles*, pp. 177–9), but one reviewer said of Byam Shaw's 1953 production that his 'pictorial groupings of soldiery and slaves, of officers and men, and of court officials are brilliantly composed – probably the best seen at Stratford for a long time' (John Coe, *Bristol Evening Post*, 29 April 1953). In Iden Payne's production 'some of the smaller parts are acted by young men who appear to have swallowed as much of their beards as they had plastered on their faces' (R.C.R., *Birmingham Post*, 16 April 1935). Apart from the scarce-bearded Caesar and the Eunuchs, the male characters probably offered early audiences plenty of scope for physiognomical speculation (dictates of fashion aside, different kinds of beard were associated in Shakespeare's day with particular character traits), and it is likely that in the first performances of the play Enobarbus lived up to his name by wearing a red beard. Three hundred years later, Tree took a detailed interest in the subject, from a historical rather than an emblematic point of view: 'Mr Beerbohm Tree, ever original and no doubt perfectly archaeologically correct, wears, as Mark Antony in *Antony and Cleopatra*, a short fair beard and moustache. And most of those in the exceedingly lengthy cast follow his example and are what Mr Frank Richardson terms "Beavers". The variety of beards – ranging from the "full" adornment of Mr Lyn Harding as Enobarbus, to the curled masterpiece of Mr J. Fisher White as the Soothsayer, and the wooden and wobbly chin pieces of the Egyptians – is astounding and should afford the eminent Whisker Expert above alluded to food for reflection and comment for days to come' (*Pelican*, 2 January 1907).

Agate (*Brief Chronicles*, p. 180), writing about bad music and 'what is left of Victorian taste' in relation to Cass's production of 1934, asked, 'If there is need for a concession to the senses, why not incense?' Incense had contributed to the sense of exotic opulence in such extravagant productions as Abbey's in New York in 1889 and Benson's in 1898, and Tree used it for atmosphere in his opening scene, as did Asche in his Australian touring production. Iden Payne's 'surprisingly pictorial' Stratford production of 1935 was (says Trewin in *Shakespeare on the English Stage*, p. 168) 'a night of fanfares and torches', the naked torches themselves having a certain exoticism because they were permitted in Stratford but banned in London by the LCC. In the following year Komisarjevsky annoyed Agate by 'postpon[ing]' the opening scene 'in favour of a tweeting soothsayer and a pair of gossipy girls' (*Brief Chronicles*, p. 181). Rearranging the opening less radically to try and establish a steamy, rather than a comically bawdy, climate, Helpmann still managed to offend Trewin: 'The curtain rose, and there in the centre of the stage we saw an Alexandrian revel, with Antony's dotage "o'erflowing the measure". At the side of the stage stood Philo … I wait so eagerly for Philo's speech that it annoyed me, at the Vic, to have it blurred' (*Illustrated London News*, 16 March 1957). More recent directors have occasionally used

[1.1] *Enter* DEMETRIUS *and* PHILO

PHILO Nay, but this dotage of our general's
　　　　O'erflows the measure. Those his goodly eyes,
　　　　That o'er the files and musters of the war
　　　　Have glowed like plated Mars, now bend, now turn
　　　　The office and devotion of their view　　　　　　　5
　　　　Upon a tawny front. His captain's heart,
　　　　Which in the scuffles of great fights hath burst
　　　　The buckles on his breast, reneges all temper
　　　　And is become the bellows and the fan
　　　　To cool a gipsy's lust.
Flourish. Enter ANTONY, CLEOPATRA, *her* LADIES [CHARMIAN
and IRAS, *and*] *the train, with eunuchs fanning her*
　　　　　　　　　　　　Look where they come.　　　　　　10
　　　　Take but good note, and you shall see in him
　　　　The triple pillar of the world transformed
　　　　Into a strumpet's fool. Behold and see.

pictorial elements of the 'extra-illustrated' kind to make decidedly thematic points. In Kahn's 1972 production, the lovers made their first entrance on a huge leopardskin litter borne by a dozen bearers, who spent the rest of the scene in deep obeisance, foreheads touching the ground (see Cooper, *American Shakespeare Theater*, p. 169). Nunn's production of the same year inserted before Philo's speech a 'parade of Cleopatra's court', which was read by John Elsom as 'a firm statement of the age, the social aura and place, and of the presences which dominate this Mediterranean world'(*Observer*, 20 August 1972); more specifically, the protagonists were 'dressed as Egyptian god monarchs' (Charles Lewsen, *Times*, 16 August 1972). Brewster's production 'begins stunningly with an ululating chorus dancing on to the impulsive rhythm of a funky Egyptian tune' (Rick Jones, *Time Out*, 22 May 1991). In Caird's 1992 production 'when the play opens, the center panel of terra cotta walls splits open, and Antony and Cleopatra appear upstage, silhouetted in the distance wantoning with each other while Roman soldiers bewail "this dotage of our general's" . . . and the Egyptian servants smile' (Geckle, 'The Power of Desire on Stage', p. 15). Vanessa Redgrave's heavily politicised 1995 production began with 'Mardian reading a modern-prose account of the break-up of the Roman triumvirate' (Alastair Macaulay, *Financial Times*, 5 June 1995), 'the whole play now reduced to a kind of historical dream' (Sheridan Morley, *Spectator*, 10 June 1995). Rutter's production had 'a curious opening, in which boys spoof the lovers from a makeshift stage on a trolley' (Benedict Nightingale, *Times*, 5 October 1995), suggesting 'how the lovers might have been extemporised by the "quick comedians" of Rome who make Cleopatra shudder. This device sets a sceptical frame that allows, for once, the possibility that the ageing lovers are indeed a little ridiculous' (Jeffrey Wainwright, *Independent*, 6 October 1995).

1–13 The play's first audiences presumably understood the naturalistic pretext provided by Demetrius's presence here as part of a convention of presenting, but Brook, in his 1978 production, went out of his way to undercut naturalistic elements in order to emphasise the set-piece nature of these conventions; Trewin wrote that the opening was 'not (as the play used to be) an indulgent romantic orgy . . . Philo's opening fanfare is uttered directly to the house' (*Birmingham Post*, 11 October 1978). In the Nunn–Scoffield television version 'a sense of place is achieved by both camera and sound. Philo's opening "Nay!" is delivered to black and white, helmeted and sober centurions, and cuts to the in-color caperings' of Antony and Cleopatra (Coursen, *Shakespearean Performance*, p. 190); the BBC television version follows the Folio fairly faithfully, except that Canidius and Ventidius are substituted for Philo and Demetrius; the court enters behind them at 10.

6 **a tawny front** See Introduction, pp. 3–4. In Hall's production 'the opening scene immediately established the Rome/Egypt contrast as Philo and Demetrius entered in their buttoned-up Roman outfits to lament Antony's loss of measure; "tawny" was given special emphasis, and the double doors burst open on "gypsy's lust"' (Crowl, *Shakespeare Observed*, p. 95).

9–10a Early audiences were accustomed to viewing emblematically such stage pictures of sensuality, though the verisimilitude of the sensual element is attested to by the Puritans who wrote against the theatre. Modern directors have not always appreciated this – Nunn's 'Stratford programme quotes Harley Granville-Barker's reminder that the original Cleopatra had to be played by a boy, and there is not one scene to show the sensual charm that drew Antony to her, and back to her' (W.H.W., *Birmingham Mail*, 16 August 1972) – and have tended to neglect the ironic relationship between these lines and the following stage direction, passing off *'with eunuchs fanning her'* as an oriental touch. 'Eunuch' here and in 1.2.0 SD does seem to imply oriental costuming in Jacobean production, presumably distinct from that of the 'Egyptian' in 5.1.48 SD. In the Nunn–Scoffield television version, there is an image of Cleopatra flopping backwards on sensuous cushions at this point.

10a SD In 1833 the lovers' entrance was accompanied by dancers. It was preceded by 18 dancers in Phelps's (promptbook), and in 1866 and 1867 *'An Egyptian dance is performed by the Ballet'* at the entrance of the protagonists (Calvert's acting (Lacy's) edition). In Chatterton's production of 1873 'an Egyptian dance is introduced with characteristic effect. The scene is of so striking a nature that Mr Beverly was enthusiastically called for by the audience, an honour also repeated in his favour at the conclusion of the act, which closed with the exhibition of her Majesty's state barge afterwards described by Enobarbus, in which Antony and Cleopatra depart together for the coast' (*Illustrated London News*, 27 September 1873). In the Langtry–Wingfield production, at 13, *'The Queen of Egypt's Barge moves slowly on, having on board Antony and Cleopatra, with their Trains'*; a similar entry was used in Tree's production. In Benson's 1898 production, 'the procession of exquisitely dressed girls, tripping to the sounds of weird music, and waving flowers and garlands, preceding the canopy in which reclined Cleopatra, gracefully attired in rich, soft, clinging garments, suggested at once the Palace of Pleasure in which Marc Antony was being lulled from honour to "the love of Love and her soft hours"' (*Worcestershire Echo*, 20 April 1898). Asche employed a similar entry in his 1912–13 Australian touring production; at the Theatre Royal, Melbourne, he made good use of three flights of steps on the unusually deep stage: 'The Roman Ambassadors waiting for an audience with Antony heard the clash of cymbals and the sound of music in the distance. They turned and looked up-stage. And down these long flights of steps came musicians and dancers and incense-burners, and then a bevy of girls with long ropes of flowers, harnessed as it were to a great wooden platform carried on the shoulders of twenty negro slaves, and on this platform, on a couch rich with coloured cushions, draperies and lion-skins, reposed Cleopatra, habited as Venus, and Antony as Bacchus, with Cupid at their feet, drinking wine and crushing fruit into each other's lips. Following this the courtiers and courtesans of the court, in a state of wild drunkenness. For a moment this procession halted before the Ambassadors, only to proceed, after a few words from Antony, down the steps, laughing and dancing to the music, until all had disappeared below the stage and out of sight, leaving the Ambassadors gazing down after them' (Asche, *Oscar Asche*, p. 142). The procession's downward movement had to be curtailed in other theatres. The 'negro slaves' were necessarily chosen for the strength in their arm; during one performance at the Theatre Royal, Sydney, one of them, a West Indian ex-boxer called Starlight, called out and waved his free arm in acknowledgement of a fan's greeting from the gallery (Bevan, *The Story of the Theatre Royal*, p. 103).

In Atkins's 1922 production, Antony 'entered carrying Cleopatra in his arms' (*Westminster Gazette*, 9 December 1922). In 1953 the lovers 'whirled in a flurry of passion unsatisfied down the long steps bathed in a hot, sandy light' (T. C. Worsley, *New Statesman*, 9 May 1953); in Hepton's of 1961, which opened in half light, the lights were suddenly brought up when the '*flourish*' for the lovers' entrance was heard (Trewin, *Going to Shakespeare*, p. 222). But in Brook's production Trewin complained that 'the entrance of Antony (Alan Howard) and Cleopatra (Glenda Jackson) is almost inconspicuous in the middle of an austere set' (*Birmingham Post*, 11 October 1978). Noble made the lovers' first entrance both dramatic and symbolic; Victoria Radin commented that he 'does a lot with scarves. Cleopatra makes her first entrance tugging on Antony . . . The scarf is a noose, of course, a symbol of the killer instinct that lurks in obsessive sexual love' (*Observer*, 17 October 1982). The Robertson–Selbie entrance set the mood theatrically: Cleopatra 'pulls onstage what appears to be a dressing-up hamper and gleefully opens it to reveal Antony, who is in a sporty mood himself' (Benedict Nightingale, *New Statesman*, 30 May 1986) and 'bounces like a Jack-in-the-box into Cleopatra's arms. Then he gives her a piggy-back' (Kathy O'Shaughnessy, *Spectator*, 7 June 1986); 'she jumps up and quacks like a duck, parodying his wife Fulvia, and then mimicks his own general's stride; he rolls on the floor with her, spanks her, throws her over his shoulder and carries her off' (Nightingale). Jack Tinker commented, 'That dressing-up trunk is no empty device. This Queen of the Nile is a consummate actress, trying on and discarding roles as lesser women try on hats. And although Timothy Dalton's Antony

CLEOPATRA If it be love indeed, tell me how much.
ANTONY There's beggary in the love that can be reckoned.   15
CLEOPATRA I'll set a bourn how far to be beloved.
ANTONY Then must thou needs find out new heaven, new earth.

Enter a MESSENGER

MESSENGER News, my good lord, from Rome.
ANTONY Grates me! The sum.
CLEOPATRA Nay, hear them, Antony.   20
     Fulvia perchance is angry, or who knows

is only too happy to join in the romps, there are moments when you see by the tired way he discards a turbaned headdress or glumly regards his exotic costume that he knows – as all adults must learn – that the time for make-believe is brief' (*Daily Mail*, 27 May 1986). This memorable business seems to have influenced Hall's opening procession in the following year, where the piggy-backing was, in a sense, reversed and related to Cleopatra's control of Antony's entrance, though the power-play was still recognisably playful: 'Cleopatra drags Mardian in on the end of a rope, with Antony sitting on his shoulders, waving a wine-flagon and goblet' (Lowen, *Peter Hall*, p. 33). In 1992 Higgins arrived hopping forty paces (as in 2.2.239), with Johnson puffing alongside. Vanessa Redgrave, in her own 1995 production, wearing 'stiff white dress and short auburn hair, begins, embarrassingly, with a little dance, and presents Cleopatra as a skittish, petulant schemer for whom life and love is all game and role-play' (Nicholas de Jongh, *Evening Standard*, 2 June 1995). A more conventional entrance gives Cleopatra the opportunity to 'tune up' whilst displaying her control: in Bridges-Adams's 1924 production Dorothy Green 'made her first slow entrance, leaning on Antony's leopard-skinned bosom, tuning up her deep incisive voice and feeling Shakespeare's rein with so mettlesome a temper' (H.H., *Observer*, 22 June 1924).

12–13   'Strumpet's' was bowdlerised to 'woman's' in 1833 (promptbook). Baliol Holloway was not transformed: 'rugged, almost harsh in appearance, deeply resonant in speech, and unpolished in action', he seemed 'strangely out of place as a philanderer in the scented courts of Egypt's Queen' (*Birmingham Mail*, 16 July 1924). By contrast, Michael Redgrave's 'fine presence, full voice, and abounding energy enable him to keep the great captain vigorously alive in the strumpet's fool and he makes extraordinarily vivid the instinct of domination at odds with the instinct of sex' (*Times*, 5 November 1953); 'from the first decisive entrance, the *look* of him is so right – a careless laughing and abandoned magnificence . . . This Antony is greedy, weak, but great. His fall is all the greater' (Richard Findlater, *Tribune*, 20 November 1953). Helpmann rearranged the opening scene to dramatise the transformation by showing Michell and Whiting 'dallying as the curtain went up' (Speaight, *Shakespeare on the Stage*, p. 271); the Nunn–Scoffield television version provides an image of Antony capering at this point.

14   Janet Suzman delivered this line 'in a voice that sounds like a cash register' (*Plays and*

If the scarce-bearded Caesar have not sent
His powerful mandate to you, 'Do this, or this;
Take in that kingdom and enfranchise that;
Perform't, or else we damn thee.'   25
ANTONY How, my love?
CLEOPATRA Perchance? Nay, and most like.
You must not stay here longer; your dismission
Is come from Caesar. Therefore hear it, Antony.
Where's Fulvia's process? – Caesar's I would say. Both?   30
Call in the messengers. As I am Egypt's queen,
Thou blushest, Antony, and that blood of thine
Is Caesar's homager; else so thy cheek pays shame
When shrill-tongued Fulvia scolds. The messengers!
ANTONY Let Rome in Tiber melt and the wide arch   35

Players, October 1972); Judi Dench, 'demanding to know the borders of Antony's love',
'tickles, fondles and mocks' him (Milton Shulman, *Evening Standard*, 10 April 1987).

15 Anthony Hopkins spoke this line and his next 'from his perch on Mardian's shoulders which
allowed him to take in the Olivier's substantial space with an expansive gesture' (Crowl,
Shakespeare Observed, p. 95).

17 At this point John Clements studied Margaret Leighton's palm in Dews's production (*Plays
and Players*, September 1969).

18 Here 'Hopkins tumbled down and caught Cleopatra (she was in constant motion during the
first half of the play, and he was always having to reach out to capture and still her) and
playfully wrestled her to the floor ... Antony released his embrace on the word "Rome",
which immediately caused Judi Dench's Cleopatra to become the aggressor as she then
threw her leg over Antony's thigh to prohibit him from escaping her clutches as she taunted
him about his Roman obligations and allegiances' (Crowl, *Shakespeare Observed*, pp.
95–6).

31 **Call ... messengers** At this point in Phelps's production Cleopatra *places her hand on
Antony's shoulders and turns him round, getting back herself to* LC' (promptbook).

31 **As ... queen** Dench straddled Hopkins at this point (Crowl, *Shakespeare Observed*, p. 96).

32–3 **that ... homager** Here Glenda Jackson 'asserted her authority by moving past [Alan
Howard] so as to sit on a cushion centre-right of stage, where she remained, forcing him to
pace agitatedly and guiltily about the stage' (Scott, *Antony and Cleopatra*, p. 52).

35 Nunn introduced some stage business here to emphasise the nature of Antony's
irresponsibility: 'Antony declaims "let Rome in Tiber melt" in the manner of an official
proclamation, cramming an Egyptian wig on the head of a Roman messenger, who retires to
sulk and glare at the great man gone native' (Benedict Nightingale, *New Statesman*, 25
August 1972); in the Nunn–Scoffield television version, Antony pushes a grape into the
messenger's mouth at 54, with similar effect. In 1987 Hopkins 'rolled [Dench] over' at this
line (Crowl, *Shakespeare Observed*, p. 96).

Of the ranged empire fall! Here is my space.
Kingdoms are clay; our dungy earth alike
Feeds beast as man. The nobleness of life
Is to do thus, when such a mutual pair
And such a twain can do't – in which I bind,   40
On pain of punishment, the world to weet
We stand up peerless.
CLEOPATRA   Excellent falsehood!
Why did he marry Fulvia, and not love her?
I'll seem the fool I am not. Antony
Will be himself.
ANTONY   But stirred by Cleopatra.   45
Now, for the love of Love and her soft hours,
Let's not confound the time with conference harsh;
There's not a minute of our lives should stretch
Without some pleasure now. What sport tonight?
CLEOPATRA Hear the ambassadors.
ANTONY   Fie, wrangling queen,   50
Whom everything becomes, to chide, to laugh,

36 **Here . . . space** In 1953 Michael Redgrave 'put his triumphal wreath round [Peggy
Ashcroft's] waist' at this point (Lamb, *Antony and Cleopatra*, p. 152). Richard Johnson points
to the Egyptian ground in the Nunn–Scoffield television version, whilst Anthony Hopkins
interpreted 'space' in updated Jacobean mode: he 'placed his right hand under [Judi
Dench's] thigh and pulled her to him' (Crowl, *Shakespeare Observed*, p. 96).

38–9 **The . . . thus** In an unusual interpretation of these lines, Baxter swung Parfitt into the air
(*Times*, 23 April 1983), but doing thus has usually been read as a more conventional
embrace, in keeping with the stage direction inserted by Pope and later editors. Neither
Macready nor Tree put much energy into the passionate scenes, but modern actors have
usually shown more willingness, if not necessarily more sensuality. Michael Gambon's
'stolid frame is almost too large for the intimacies' but he had 'passionate moments with his
turbulent Cleopatra, effortlessly sweeping her off her feet like some skittish doll' (Gordon
Parsons, *Morning Star*, 18 October 1982). Bernard Levin did not find Howard and Jackson
convincing – 'Even in their embraces, they seem moved less by lust than by what history will
say; though they roll together on the floor, I cannot help feeling that they are only playing
"Last one up's a cissy"' (*Sunday Times*, 15 October 1978) – but for Michael Billington their
response to these lines and to each other was just right: 'From their prolonged and
voluptuous kiss on "The nobleness of life is to do thus" you believe that this Antony and
Cleopatra might have shared a bed as well as the stage' (*Guardian*, 10 July 1979).

49 Following the eighteenth-century editor William Warburton's emendation, Byam Shaw's
1953 production changed 'now' to 'new' here (J. C. Trewin, *John O'London's Weekly*, 15 May
1953), but the Nunn–Scoffield television version makes the original word speak to modern

To weep, whose every passion fully strives
To make itself, in thee, fair and admired!
No messenger but thine, and all alone
Tonight we'll wander through the streets and note   55
The qualities of people. Come, my queen,
Last night you did desire it. [*To the Messenger*] Speak not to
   us.
                          Exeunt [Antony and Cleopatra] with the
                             train, [Charmian, Iras, and eunuchs]
DEMETRIUS Is Caesar with Antonius prized so slight?
PHILO Sir, sometimes when he is not Antony
He comes too short of that great property   60
Which still should go with Antony.
DEMETRIUS   I am full sorry
That he approves the common liar, who
Thus speaks of him at Rome; but I will hope
Of better deeds tomorrow. Rest you happy!
                                     Exeunt

      ears: 'Antony's "now" is a demand for immediate sexual gratification' (Coursen,
      Shakespearean Performance, pp. 191–2). In Brook's production, Howard 'had to move to
      [Jackson], kneel by her and coax her from her mood' here (Scott, *Antony and Cleopatra*, p.
      52).

54   Hopkins 'did not manage to subdue' Dench until this point; he delivered 'No messenger' 'as
      a firm command, slowly shaking his head, and then after a long pause, a quick wink before a
      very tender "but thine"' (Crowl, *Shakespeare Observed*, p. 96).

56   **Come . . . queen** Howard lifted Jackson to her feet here (Scott, *Antony and Cleopatra*,
      p. 52); in Hall's production 'they both swirled through the double doors with Cleopatra in
      the lead flanked, a half pace behind, by Charmian and Iras' (Crowl, *Shakespeare
      Observed*, p. 96).

57   **Speak . . . us** In Richardson's 1973 production, 'Cleopatra rides astride Antony as he
      dismisses the messengers' (Harold Hobson, *Sunday Times*, 12 August 1973); see also the
      commentary at 2.5.22–3a.

58–61   Garrick's production, which substituted Thyreus and Dollabella for Philo and Demetrius in
      this scene, cut these lines and inserted 2.2.200–38a and 243–8a (printed edition). Phelps's
      production cut 58–64 (promptbook).

ACT I, SCENE 2

[1.2] *Enter* ENOBARBUS, *Lamprius, a* SOOTHSAYER, *Rannius,*
Lucillius, CHARMIAN, IRAS, MARDIAN *the Eunuch, and* ALEXAS

CHARMIAN Lord Alexas, sweet Alexas, most anything Alexas,
    almost most absolute Alexas, where's the soothsayer that you
    praised so to th'queen? O, that I knew this husband, which you
    say must charge his horns with garlands!
ALEXAS Soothsayer!   5
SOOTHSAYER Your will?
CHARMIAN Is this the man? – Is't you, sir, that know things?
SOOTHSAYER In nature's infinite book of secrecy
    A little I can read.
ALEXAS [*To Charmian*]   Show him your hand.
ENOBARBUS Bring in the banquet quickly; wine enough   10
    Cleopatra's health to drink.
CHARMIAN [*Giving her hand to the Soothsayer*] Good sir, give me
    good fortune.
SOOTHSAYER I make not, but foresee.
CHARMIAN Pray then, foresee me one.   15
SOOTHSAYER You shall be yet far fairer than you are.
CHARMIAN He means in flesh.
IRAS No, you shall paint when you are old.
CHARMIAN Wrinkles forbid!
ALEXAS Vex not his prescience. Be attentive.   20
CHARMIAN Hush!
SOOTHSAYER You shall be more beloving than beloved.
CHARMIAN I had rather heat my liver with drinking.
ALEXAS Nay, hear him.
CHARMIAN Good now, some excellent fortune! Let me be married   25
    to three kings in a forenoon and widow them all. Let me have a
    child at fifty, to whom Herod of Jewry may do homage. Find me
    to marry me with Octavius Caesar, and companion me with my
    mistress.
SOOTHSAYER You shall outlive the lady whom you serve.   30
CHARMIAN O, excellent! I love long life better than figs.
SOOTHSAYER You have seen and proved a fairer former fortune
    Than that which is to approach.
CHARMIAN Then belike my children shall have no names. Prithee,

how many boys and wenches must I have? 35
SOOTHSAYER If every of your wishes had a womb,
    And fertile every wish, a million.
CHARMIAN Out, fool! I forgive thee for a witch.
ALEXAS You think none but your sheets are privy to your wishes.
CHARMIAN Nay, come, tell Iras hers. 40
ALEXAS We'll know all our fortunes.
ENOBARBUS Mine, and most of our fortunes tonight, shall be –
    drunk to bed.
IRAS [*Giving her hand to the Soothsayer*] There's a palm presages
    chastity, if nothing else. 45
CHARMIAN E'en as the o'erflowing Nilus presageth famine.
IRAS Go, you wild bedfellow, you cannot soothsay.
CHARMIAN Nay, if an oily palm be not a fruitful prognostication, I
    cannot scratch mine ear. Prithee tell her but a workaday fortune.
SOOTHSAYER Your fortunes are alike. 50
IRAS But how, but how? Give me particulars.
SOOTHSAYER I have said.
IRAS Am I not an inch of fortune better than she?

---

0 SD **MARDIAN *the Eunuch* . . .** Some modern actors have played the role as a character part: reviewers praised Roy Byford, 'who lent his bulk with humour to the role' in 1935 (*Yorkshire Post*, 16 April 1935), and in Byam Shaw's 1946 production Olaf Pooley, 'by a flip of yellow eyelids and a terrifying slink of humped shoulders, made a character' out of him (Tynan, *A View of the English Stage*, p. 51) and 'the sense of the flesh and blood of love was pointed' by his 'contrasting shadowy presence' (Stephen Potter, *New Statesman*, 4 January 1947).

1–70 Omitted in 1813 and 1833: Dryden does not include a soothsayer, and in any case such a scene would have been deemed unsuitable because of its bawdy as well as its superfluousness in plotting terms.

3–4 **0 . . . garlands** Omitted for the sake of decency in Phelps's production (promptbook).

26–7 **Let . . . homage** Cut for decency's sake in Phelps's production (promptbook).

30 In the BBC television version, Miller has the protagonists present at the beginning of the scene – 'between Charmian and the Soothsayer in deep focus Antony can be seen caressing Cleopatra as they both half-attentively listen to the fun' – but at this point 'the tone begins to change. Cleopatra's attention momentarily concentrates on the debate, while Enobarbus, unknown to her, whispers in Antony's ear and leads him away to hear the messengers. As the banter continues, Cleopatra realises her lover is missing. She looks around, fidgets and grows more and more impatient, until she breaks up the group on "Saw you my lord?"' (Scott, *Antony and Cleopatra*, pp. 56–7)

34–9 **Prithee . . . wishes** Cut in Garrick's production (printed edition); Phelps's, more punctilious about decency, cut 32–70 (promptbook).

CHARMIAN Well, if you were but an inch of fortune better than I, where would you choose it? 55

IRAS Not in my husband's nose.

CHARMIAN Our worser thoughts heavens mend! Alexas – come, his fortune, his fortune! O, let him marry a woman that cannot go, sweet Isis, I beseech thee, and let her die too, and give him a worse, and let worse follow worse till the worst of all follow him 60 laughing to his grave, fiftyfold a cuckold! Good Isis, hear me this prayer, though thou deny me a matter of more weight; good Isis, I beseech thee!

IRAS Amen, dear goddess, hear that prayer of the people! For, as it is a heart-breaking to see a handsome man loose-wived, so it is a 65 deadly sorrow to behold a foul knave uncuckolded. Therefore, dear Isis, keep decorum, and fortune him accordingly!

CHARMIAN Amen.

ALEXAS Lo now, if it lay in their hands to make me a cuckold, they would make themselves whores but they'd do't. 70

Enter CLEOPATRA

ENOBARBUS Hush, here comes Antony.

CHARMIAN Not he. The queen.

CLEOPATRA Saw you my lord?

ENOBARBUS No, lady.

CLEOPATRA Was he not here? 75

CHARMIAN No, madam.

CLEOPATRA He was disposed to mirth, but on the sudden
    A Roman thought hath struck him. Enobarbus!

ENOBARBUS Madam?

CLEOPATRA Seek him and bring him hither. Where's Alexas? 80

ALEXAS Here at your service. – My lord approaches.

Enter ANTONY, *with a* MESSENGER

CLEOPATRA We will not look upon him. Go with us.
                    Exeunt [all but Antony and the Messenger]

MESSENGER Fulvia thy wife first came into the field.

ANTONY Against my brother Lucius?

MESSENGER Ay; 85
    But soon that war had end, and the time's state
    Made friends of them, jointing their force 'gainst Caesar,
    Whose better issue in the war from Italy
    Upon the first encounter drave them.

ANTONY Well, what worst? 90

MESSENGER The nature of bad news infects the teller.

ANTONY When it concerns the fool or coward. On.
    Things that are past are done, with me. 'Tis thus:

Who tells me true, though in his tale lie death,
I hear him as he flattered.
MESSENGER   Labienus –   95
This is stiff news – hath with his Parthian force
Extended Asia; from Euphrates
His conquering banner shook, from Syria
To Lydia and to Ionia,
Whilst –
ANTONY   Antony, thou wouldst say.
MESSENGER   O, my lord!   100
ANTONY Speak to me home; mince not the general tongue.
Name Cleopatra as she is called in Rome;
Rail thou in Fulvia's phrase, and taunt my faults
With such full licence as both truth and malice
Have power to utter. O, then we bring forth weeds   105
When our quick minds lie still, and our ills told us
Is as our earing. Fare thee well awhile.
MESSENGER At your noble pleasure.   *Exit Messenger*

Enter another MESSENGER[*; a third attends at the door*]

ANTONY From Sicyon, ho, the news! Speak there.
2 MESSENGER The man from Sicyon – is there such an one?   110
3 MESSENGER He stays upon your will.
ANTONY   Let him appear. –
                    [*Exeunt Second and Third Messengers*]
These strong Egyptian fetters I must break,
Or lose myself in dotage.

Enter [a fourth] MESSENGER, *with a letter*

                    What are you?
4 MESSENGER Fulvia thy wife is dead.
ANTONY Where died she?   115
4 MESSENGER In Sicyon.
Her length of sickness, with what else more serious
Importeth thee to know, this bears.
                    [*He gives a letter*]
ANTONY   Forbear me.
                    [*Exit Messenger*]
There's a great spirit gone! Thus did I desire it.
What our contempts doth often hurl from us,   120
We wish it ours again. The present pleasure,
By revolution lowering, does become

---

119 **There's . . . gone** Howard spoke this 'with hollow irony, one caustic eye being fixed on the audience' (Hunt and Reeves, *Peter Brook*, p. 228).

The opposite of itself. She's good, being gone;
The hand could pluck her back that shoved her on.
I must from this enchanting queen break off.   125
Ten thousand harms more than the ills I know
My idleness doth hatch. – How now, Enobarbus!

                    Enter ENOBARBUS

ENOBARBUS What's your pleasure, sir?
ANTONY I must with haste from hence.
ENOBARBUS Why then we kill all our women. We see how mortal an   130
    unkindness is to them; if they suffer our departure, death's the
    word.
ANTONY I must be gone.
ENOBARBUS Under a compelling occasion, let women die. It were
    pity to cast them away for nothing, though between them and a   135
    great cause they should be esteemed nothing. Cleopatra, catching
    but the least noise of this, dies instantly; I have seen her die
    twenty times upon far poorer moment. I do think there is mettle
    in death, which commits some loving act upon her, she hath
    such a celerity in dying.   140
ANTONY She is cunning past man's thought.
ENOBARBUS Alack, sir, no, her passions are made of nothing but
    the finest part of pure love. We cannot call her winds and waters
    sighs and tears; they are greater storms and tempests than
    almanacs can report. This cannot be cunning in her; if it be,   145
    she makes a shower of rain as well as Jove.
ANTONY Would I had never seen her!
ENOBARBUS O sir, you had then left unseen a wonderful piece of
    work, which not to have been blest withal would have discredited
    your travel.   150
ANTONY Fulvia is dead.
ENOBARBUS Sir?
ANTONY Fulvia is dead.
ENOBARBUS Fulvia?
ANTONY Dead.   155
ENOBARBUS Why, sir, give the gods a thankful sacrifice. When it
    pleaseth their deities to take the wife of a man from him, it shows
    to man the tailors of the earth; comforting therein, that when old

---

125 In Vanessa Redgrave's 1995 production, Paul Butler, 'a slow-moving, mellow conqueror and
     lover', spoke this line 'as if reminding himself to get the plumbing mended' (Rhoda Koenig,
     Independent, 3 June 1995).

138–40 **I . . . dying** and 142–50 Garrick's production cut these lines (printed edition), to reduce the
     number of Enobarbus's 'light answers'.

robes are worn out, there are members to make new. If there
were no more women but Fulvia, then had you indeed a cut, and 160
the case to be lamented. This grief is crowned with consolation;
your old smock brings forth a new petticoat, and indeed the tears
live in an onion that should water this sorrow.
ANTONY The business she hath broachèd in the state
      Cannot endure my absence. 165
ENOBARBUS And the business you have broached here cannot
    be without you, especially that of Cleopatra's, which wholly
    depends on your abode.
ANTONY No more light answers. Let our officers
      Have notice what we purpose. I shall break 170
      The cause of our expedience to the queen
      And get her leave to part. For not alone
      The death of Fulvia, with more urgent touches,
      Do strongly speak to us, but the letters too
      Of many our contriving friends in Rome 175
      Petition us at home. Sextus Pompeius
      Hath given the dare to Caesar and commands
      The empire of the sea. Our slippery people,
      Whose love is never linked to the deserver
      Till his deserts are past, begin to throw 180
      Pompey the Great and all his dignities

151   Antony's response here, whilst likely to be intense, is not entirely predictable. In 1927 Wilfrid
     Walter was 'deeply and sincerely moved' (*Stratford-upon-Avon Herald*, 15 July 1927), whilst
     Richard Johnson, in the Nunn–Scoffield television version, initially ruminative, joins
     Enobarbus in laughter at 138, and they both laugh here. The same Enobarbus (Patrick
     Stewart) and a different Antony (Alan Howard) went further in Brook's production, with
     'helpless joyful laughter'; 'the episode brands Patrick Stewart's Enobarbus not (as is usual)
     as the keeper of his general's conscience, but as his junior partner in dissipation' (Robert
     Cushman, *Observer*, 15 October 1978). Brook introduced some business to underline the
     reaction: 'Howard's Antony is only piously regretful at Fulvia's death. Patrick Stewart's
     Enobarbus cheers him up immediately by clasping him around the waist and swinging him
     up into the air. Antony has been let off the hook' (John Elsom, *Listener*, 19 October 1978). In
     the BBC television version, Colin Blakely's Antony is thoughtful, and barely amused at Emrys
     James's levity. In Hall's production Hopkins received the news with 'curt casualness'
     (Michael Coveney, *Financial Times*, 10 April 1987). In Vanessa Redgrave's 1995 production,
     there was much celebration at this point, but Paul Butler, in his performance as Antony, did
     not sustain the impression of 'boldness of spirit' such laughter may be seen to imply (Rhoda
     Koenig, *Independent*, 3 June 1995): see also the commentary at 4.14.125.
156–9   **When . . . new** Cut in Garrick's production (printed edition) and in Phelps's (promptbook).

Upon his son, who – high in name and power,
Higher than both in blood and life – stands up
For the main soldier; whose quality, going on,
The sides o'th'world may danger. Much is breeding,   185
Which, like the courser's hair, hath yet but life
And not a serpent's poison. Say our pleasure,
To such whose place is under us, requires
Our quick remove from hence.
ENOBARBUS I shall do't.   190

                                            [Exeunt]

ACT I, SCENE 3

[1.3] *Enter* CLEOPATRA, CHARMIAN, ALEXAS, *and* IRAS

CLEOPATRA Where is he?
CHARMIAN   I did not see him since.
CLEOPATRA [*To Alexas*]
          See where he is, who's with him, what he does.
          I did not send you. If you find him sad,
          Say I am dancing; if in mirth, report
          That I am sudden sick. Quick, and return.   5
                                                  [*Exit Alexas*]
CHARMIAN Madam, methinks if you did love him dearly,
          You do not hold the method to enforce
          The like from him.
CLEOPATRA   What should I do I do not?
CHARMIAN In each thing give him way. Cross him in nothing.
CLEOPATRA Thou teachest like a fool: the way to lose him.   10
CHARMIAN Tempt him not so too far. I wish, forbear;
          In time we hate that which we often fear.

                    Enter ANTONY

          But here comes Antony.
CLEOPATRA   I am sick and sullen.
ANTONY I am sorry to give breathing to my purpose –
CLEOPATRA Help me away, dear Charmian, I shall fall.   15

---

0 SD **Enter** CLEOPATRA ... Phelps had Glyn *'making a Salaam as she Enters'* (promptbook); in
      the Nunn-Scoffield television version, she enters in her street-wandering outfit.
6–12 There is an opportunity here for a degree of intimacy between Cleopatra and Charmian. In
      Bridges-Adams's production of 1927 Charmian and Iras 'play[ed] up to the caprices of
      Cleopatra with ironical understanding' (K.M.C., *Birmingham Gazette*, 18 July 1927); in Iden
      Payne's the marked change in tone had broader ramifications: 'When she is alone with
      Charmian and Iras she behaves almost as their equal. Only when "company" is present does
      she assume royalty. This reading brings a part which is almost unplayable much more within
      an actress's range' (W. A. Darlington, *Daily Telegraph*, 16 April 1935).
13b   In Phelps's production Cleopatra *'affects to fall into the arms of Charmian'* at this point
      (promptbook); this business was repeated in 1866 and 1867 (Calvert's acting edition).

> It cannot be thus long; the sides of nature
> Will not sustain it.

ANTONY   Now, my dearest queen –

CLEOPATRA Pray you, stand farther from me.

ANTONY   What's the matter?

CLEOPATRA I know by that same eye there's some good news.
> What, says the married woman you may go?   20
> Would she had never given you leave to come!
> Let her not say 'tis I that keep you here.
> I have no power upon you; hers you are.

ANTONY The gods best know –

CLEOPATRA   O, never was there queen
> So mightily betrayed! Yet at the first   25
> I saw the treasons planted.

ANTONY   Cleopatra –

CLEOPATRA Why should I think you can be mine, and true,
> Though you in swearing shake the thronèd gods,
> Who have been false to Fulvia? Riotous madness,
> To be entangled with those mouth-made vows,   30
> Which break themselves in swearing!

ANTONY   Most sweet queen –

CLEOPATRA Nay, pray you, seek no colour for your going,
> But bid farewell and go. When you sued staying,
> Then was the time for words. No going then.
> Eternity was in our lips and eyes,
> Bliss in our brows' bent; none our parts so poor   35
> But was a race of heaven. They are so still,
> Or thou, the greatest soldier of the world,
> Art turned the greatest liar.

ANTONY   How now, lady?

CLEOPATRA I would I had thy inches. Thou shouldst know   40
> There were a heart in Egypt.

ANTONY   Hear me, queen:
> The strong necessity of time commands
> Our services awhile, but my full heart
> Remains in use with you. Our Italy
> Shines o'er with civil swords; Sextus Pompeius   45

17b-18b   In Langham's production, Plummer asked the question 'with an edge to the "dearest" and a faint weariness in the "what's the matter?" ... He didn't believe in her vapors, and neither did she' (Kerr, *Thirty Plays*, p. 164).

33–4   **When ... words** Agate (*Brief Chronicles,* p. 182) transcribed Eugenie Leontovich's pronunciation of these lines as 'Wen you suet staying,/ Den was de time for Wurst.'

40   **I ... inches** Cut in the bowdlerising of the text for Macready's production (promptbook).

Makes his approaches to the port of Rome;
Equality of two domestic powers
Breed scrupulous faction; the hated, grown to strength,
Are newly grown to love; the condemned Pompey,
Rich in his father's honour, creeps apace   50
Into the hearts of such as have not thrived
Upon the present state, whose numbers threaten;
And quietness, grown sick of rest, would purge
By any desperate change. My more particular,
And that which most with you should safe my going,   55
Is Fulvia's death.
CLEOPATRA Though age from folly could not give me freedom,
It does from childishness. Can Fulvia die?
ANTONY She's dead, my queen.
                    [*He offers letters*]
Look here, and at thy sovereign leisure read   60
The garboils she awaked; at the last, best,
See when and where she died.
CLEOPATRA   O most false love!
Where be the sacred vials thou shouldst fill
With sorrowful water? Now I see, I see,
In Fulvia's death how mine received shall be.   65
ANTONY Quarrel no more, but be prepared to know
The purposes I bear, which are, or cease,
As you shall give th'advice. By the fire
That quickens Nilus' slime, I go from hence
Thy soldier, servant, making peace or war   70
As thou affects.
CLEOPATRA   Cut my lace, Charmian, come!

58 **Can ... die** Benedict Nightingale admired 'the capacity for irony Miss Suzman displays with
    her "can Fulvia *die?*" ' (*New Statesman*, 25 August 1972). In 1986 Vanessa Redgrave
    responded by 'giggling loud but chillingly over Fulvia's death' (Jim Hiley, *Listener*, 5 June
    1986).

62b In the productions of 1866 and 1867, Cleopatra here '*scornfully*' returned the letters Antony
    had offered at 62a (Calvert's acting edition). Ruth Ellis commented on Peggy Ashcroft's
    performance of this speech, 'She is genuinely and profoundly shocked by his callousness
    towards his wife, for marriage is not, in her view, a mere political move. He does not offer it
    to her and, though "'tis sweating labour to bear such idleness so near the heart as Cleopatra
    this", the mistake is his' (*Stratford-upon-Avon Herald*, 1 May 1953); the speech is delivered
    ironically by Janet Suzman in the Nunn–Scoffield television version.

71b This detail affirms the view that composite Jacobean-Classical costume was worn in the first
    performances of the play. Granville-Barker, reacting against the 'authenticity' disputes

> But let it be; I am quickly ill, and well,
> So Antony loves.
ANTONY   My precious queen, forbear,
> And give true evidence to his love which stands
> An honourable trial.
CLEOPATRA   So Fulvia told me.   75
> I prithee, turn aside and weep for her,
> Then bid adieu to me, and say the tears
> Belong to Egypt. Good now, play one scene
> Of excellent dissembling, and let it look
> Like perfect honour.
ANTONY   You'll heat my blood. No more.   80
CLEOPATRA You can do better yet; but this is meetly.
ANTONY Now by my sword –
CLEOPATRA   And target. Still he mends.
> But this is not the best. Look, prithee, Charmian,
> How this herculean Roman does become
> The carriage of his chafe.   85
ANTONY I'll leave you, lady.
CLEOPATRA Courteous lord, one word.

associated with Tree's production, commented on this line, 'Careful research might find us an Alexandrian fashion plate of the right period with laces to cut (Sir Arthur Evans has brought us corsets from Knossos), but our conscientiously Egyptian Cleopatras have so far been left laceless and waistless, and the line without meaning' (*Prefaces*, p. 166). In the same spirit, Herbert Farjeon, writing of Edith Evans in 1925, said 'a Cleopatra who asks for her laces to be cut and does not wear laces is not merely un-Elizabethan, but insane' (*Shakespearean Scene*, p. 173); Trewin later quoted Farjeon against Margaret Whiting (*Illustrated London News*, 16 March 1957). Some directors have hoped for salvation in the 'But let it be' of the following line: in Calvert's acting edition, used in 1866 and 1867, '*Attendants hurry to Cleopatra*', but presumably have no time for lace-hunting before '*they retire up*' on Cleopatra's countermand; such scurrying servants are unlikely to distract the Farjeons in an audience. Granville-Barker recommended costumes in the Veronese mode (*Prefaces*, p. 168), a suggestion taken to heart by later directors: Trewin says that in 1931 Bridges-Adams 'caused debate by dressing the play in the modes of Paolo Veronese (Cleopatra in a pink farthingale), as Granville-Barker had proposed and as Harcourt Williams had done lately at the Vic' (*Shakespeare on the English Stage* , p. 138). Recent directors who have followed suit are Miller in the BBC television version (where Charmian reaches for a lace-cutting implement), Hall and Caird; Redgrave's costumes in 1995 were 'all early seventeenth century, with stately stiff bodices, ruffs and farthingales for the women' (Rhoda Koenig, *Independent*, 3 June 1995). In the Nunn–Scoffield television version, Janet Suzman delivers the line as if it is a threadbare tag, not to be taken literally.

> Sir, you and I must part, but that's not it;
> Sir, you and I have loved, but there's not it;
> That you know well. Something it is I would –   90
> O, my oblivion is a very Antony,
> And I am all forgotten.
> ANTONY   But that your royalty
> Holds idleness your subject, I should take you
> For idleness itself.
> CLEOPATRA   'Tis sweating labour
> To bear such idleness so near the heart   95
> As Cleopatra this. But sir, forgive me,
> Since my becomings kill me when they do not
> Eye well to you. Your honour calls you hence;
> Therefore be deaf to my unpitied folly,
> And all the gods go with you! Upon your sword   100
> Sit laurel victory, and smooth success
> Be strewed before your feet!
> ANTONY   Let us go. Come;
> Our separation so abides and flies
> That thou, residing here, goes yet with me,
> And I, hence fleeting, here remain with thee.   105
> Away!

Exeunt

87 During the lovers' quarrel, Helen Mirren 'furiously moves about the almost bare stage until, leaning against a wooden support, she comes near to mental collapse. She pauses while the quiet emotion wells up in her for the most tender expression of her love' in this passage (Scott, *Antony and Cleopatra*, p. 74).

88 'How tender, how beautiful in its groping for a thought to express a feeling is Miss Evans's delivery of [this line]. How she purrs over her libidinous dreams' (Farjeon, *Shakespearean Scene*, pp. 172–3).

89 **Sir . . . loved** Mirren spoke this in a 'lascivious whisper' (*Daily Telegraph*, 14 October, 1982).

91–2a Jackson's delivery of these lines was 'deeply erotic and sensuous' (Hunt and Reeves, *Peter Brook*, p. 228). In Rutter's production, Ishia Bennison and 'her excellent women (Julie Livesey and Deborah McAndrew) interrupt [Antony's] fumbling explanations with bursts of mock applause before Bennison transforms the moment with [this] amazing piece of theatrical sincerity . . . In this realm of female sovereignty, Herculean Antony is a blunderer' (Jeffrey Wainwright, *Independent*, 6 October 1995).

101–2 **smooth . . . feet** Suzman was 'ringingly contemptuous' here (Benedict Nightingale, *New Statesman*, 25 August 1972).

ACT I, SCENE 4

[1.4] *Enter* OCTAVIUS [CAESAR], *reading a letter,* LEPIDUS, *and their train*

CAESAR You may see, Lepidus, and henceforth know,
　　　　It is not Caesar's natural vice to hate
　　　　Our great competitor. From Alexandria
　　　　This is the news: he fishes, drinks, and wastes
　　　　The lamps of night in revel; is not more manlike　　5
　　　　Than Cleopatra, nor the queen of Ptolemy
　　　　More womanly than he; hardly gave audience, or
　　　　Vouchsafed to think he had partners. You shall find there
　　　　A man who is the abstract of all faults
　　　　That all men follow.
LEPIDUS 　　　　　　　I must not think there are　　10
　　　　Evils enough to darken all his goodness.
　　　　His faults in him seem as the spots of heaven,
　　　　More fiery by night's blackness, hereditary
　　　　Rather than purchased, what he cannot change
　　　　Than what he chooses.　　　　　　　　　　　15
CAESAR You are too indulgent. Let's grant it is not
　　　　Amiss to tumble on the bed of Ptolemy,
　　　　To give a kingdom for a mirth, to sit
　　　　And keep the turn of tippling with a slave,
　　　　To reel the streets at noon, and stand the buffet　　20
　　　　With knaves that smells of sweat. Say this becomes him –
　　　　As his composure must be rare indeed
　　　　Whom these things cannot blemish – yet must Antony
　　　　No way excuse his foils when we do bear
　　　　So great weight in his lightness. If he filled　　25
　　　　His vacancy with his voluptuousness,
　　　　Full surfeits and the dryness of his bones
　　　　Call on him for't. But to confound such time
　　　　That drums him from his sport and speaks as loud
　　　　As his own state and ours, 'tis to be chid　　30
　　　　As we rate boys who, being mature in knowledge,
　　　　Pawn their experience to their present pleasure
　　　　And so rebel to judgement.

　　　　　　　　Enter a MESSENGER

LEPIDUS   Here's more news.
MESSENGER Thy biddings have been done, and every hour,
          Most noble Caesar, shalt thou have report   35
          How 'tis abroad. Pompey is strong at sea,
          And it appears he is beloved of those
          That only have feared Caesar. To the ports
          The discontents repair, and men's reports
          Give him much wronged.   [*Exit*]
CAESAR   I should have known no less.   40
          It hath been taught us from the primal state
          That he which is was wished until he were;
          And the ebbed man, ne'er loved till ne'er worth love,
          Comes deared by being lacked. This common body,
          Like to a vagabond flag upon the stream,   45
          Goes to and back, lackeying the varying tide
          To rot itself with motion.

               [*Enter a second* MESSENGER]

MESSENGER Caesar, I bring thee word
          Menecrates and Menas, famous pirates,
          Makes the sea serve them, which they ear and wound   50
          With keels of every kind. Many hot inroads
          They make in Italy; the borders maritime
          Lack blood to think on't, and flush youth revolt.
          No vessel can peep forth but 'tis as soon
          Taken as seen; for Pompey's name strikes more   55
          Than could his war resisted.   [*Exit*]
CAESAR   Antony,
          Leave thy lascivious wassails. When thou once
          Was beaten from Modena, where thou slew'st
          Hirtius and Pansa, consuls, at thy heel
          Did famine follow, whom thou fought'st against,   60
          Though daintily brought up, with patience more
          Than savages could suffer. Thou didst drink
          The stale of horses and the gilded puddle
          Which beasts would cough at. Thy palate then did deign
          The roughest berry on the rudest hedge.   65
          Yea, like the stag when snow the pasture sheets,
          The barks of trees thou browsèd. On the Alps

Cut in 1833 (promptbook); Langtry and Tree began their productions with this scene,
followed by the entrance of the lovers in Cleopatra's barge.

62–4 **Thou . . . at** Cut for decency's sake in Phelps's production (promptbook) and in 1866 and
      1867 (Calvert's acting edition).

It is reported thou didst eat strange flesh,
Which some did die to look on. And all this –
It wounds thine honour that I speak it now –   70
Was borne so like a soldier that thy cheek
So much as lanked not.
LEPIDUS 'Tis pity of him.
CAESAR Let his shames quickly
      Drive him to Rome. 'Tis time we twain   75
      Did show ourselves i'th'field, and to that end
      Assemble we immediate council. Pompey
      Thrives in our idleness.
LEPIDUS   Tomorrow, Caesar,
      I shall be furnished to inform you rightly
      Both what by sea and land I can be able   80
      To front this present time.
CAESAR   Till which encounter,
      It is my business too. Farewell.
LEPIDUS Farewell, my lord. What you shall know meantime
      Of stirs abroad, I shall beseech you, sir,
      To let me be partaker.   85
CAESAR Doubt not, sir, I knew it for my bond.
                              Exeunt [separately]

ACT I, SCENE 5

[1.5] *Enter* CLEOPATRA, CHARMIAN, IRAS, *and* MARDIAN

CLEOPATRA Charmian!
CHARMIAN Madam?
CLEOPATRA Ha, ha! Give me to drink mandragora.
CHARMIAN Why, madam?
CLEOPATRA That I might sleep out this great gap of time   5
    My Antony is away.
CHARMIAN You think of him too much.
CLEOPATRA O, 'tis treason!
CHARMIAN   Madam, I trust not so.
CLEOPATRA Thou, eunuch Mardian!
MARDIAN   What's your highness' pleasure?
CLEOPATRA Not now to hear thee sing. I take no pleasure   10
    In aught an eunuch has. 'Tis well for thee
    That, being unseminared, thy freer thoughts
    May not fly forth of Egypt. Hast thou affections?
MARDIAN Yes, gracious madam.
CLEOPATRA Indeed?   15
MARDIAN Not in deed, madam, for I can do nothing

---

3   In Garrick's production Cleopatra entered *'supporting herself on* Iras' (printed edition);
       Suzman was 'languid, dreaming and sensual. Lying on a couch for [this passage], she
       conveyed the impression of hours of love spent with her warrior' (Scott, *Antony and*
       Cleopatra, p. 50); in the Nunn–Scoffield television version, she is given a full massage by the
       attendants and Charmian, and her voice is charged with sexual emotion; in the BBC
       television version, Lapotaire sounds too sleepy to need mandragora.

10   **Not . . . sing** Presumably the part was played by a trained singer (see also the beginning
       of 2.5), either boy or adult, on the Jacobean stage. In Brewster's production 'the main
       miscalculation is to keep the eunuch upstage in vigorously semaphoring silence through
       many key episodes. Got up to look like Jessye Norman, David Webber deserves better, to
       judge by the mellifluous delivery of his relatively few lines' (Martin Hoyle, *Times*, 18 May
       1991).

16–19a Cut in the bowdlerising of the text for Garrick's (printed edition), Macready's (10b-19a;
       promptbook) and Phelps's (8–19a; promptbook) productions.

16   In McClintic's production, Joseph Wiseman's Mardian, who was 'as thin as a snake' and

But what indeed is honest to be done.
Yet have I fierce affections, and think
What Venus did with Mars.
CLEOPATRA   O Charmian,
Where think'st thou he is now? Stands he, or sits he?   20
Or does he walk? Or is he on his horse?
O happy horse, to bear the weight of Antony!
Do bravely, horse, for wot'st thou whom thou mov'st?
The demi-Atlas of this earth, the arm
And burgonet of men. He's speaking now,   25
Or murmuring 'Where's my serpent of old Nile?'
For so he calls me. Now I feed myself
With most delicious poison. Think on me,
That am with Phoebus' amorous pinches black
And wrinkled deep in time. Broad-fronted Caesar,   30
When thou wast here above the ground I was
A morsel for a monarch. And great Pompey
Would stand and make his eyes grow in my brow;
There would he anchor his aspect, and die
With looking on his life.   35

Enter ALEXAS *from Antony*

ALEXAS Sovereign of Egypt, hail!

'spoke in a hiss', registered 'a lifetime of deprivation' with this line (Tony Randall, Foreword
to Andrews' Everyman edition, p. xv).

22 Milton Shulman said of Glenda Jackson, 'her feelings about him seemed so detached and
even sardonic, one might suspect she actually felt sorry for that horse' (*Evening Standard*,
11 October 1978). Judi Dench delivered the line with 'breathy languor' (Michael Billington,
Guardian, 11 April 1987).

27–8 **Now . . . poison** Referring specifically to this line, Trewin said of Edith Evans in 1946 that
she was 'still matchless in the early wheedlings, rages, languishings' (*Shakespeare on the
English Stage*, p. 204).

28–30 **Think . . . time** These lines (to 35) were cut in Macready's production (promptbook). A
reviewer of Catherine Lacey's performance referred to 'the fear of approaching age, which is
one of the secrets of playing Cleopatra' and compared Lacey's performance with Dorothy
Green's (R.C.R., *Birmingham Post*, 16 April 1935). Peggy Ashcroft said of her 1953
performance, 'though she speaks of being "with Phoebus' amorous pinches black", I believe
that to be an ironical reference to her age – she couples it with "and wrinkled deep in time"'
(*Observer*, 8 October 1978). In the Nunn–Scoffield television version, 'Cleopatra's "wrinkled
deep in time" is spoken into a wrinkled mirror of bronze foil' (Coursen, *Shakespearean
Performance*, p. 192).

CLEOPATRA How much unlike art thou Mark Antony!
　　　　Yet coming from him, that great med'cine hath
　　　　With his tinct gilded thee.
　　　　How goes it with my brave Mark Antony? 　　　　40
ALEXAS Last thing he did, dear queen,
　　　　He kissed – the last of many doubled kisses –
　　　　This orient pearl. His speech sticks in my heart.
CLEOPATRA Mine ear must pluck it thence.
ALEXAS 　　　　　　　　　　　　'Good friend', quoth he,
　　　　'Say the firm Roman to great Egypt sends 　　　　45
　　　　This treasure of an oyster; at whose foot,
　　　　To mend the petty present, I will piece
　　　　Her opulent throne with kingdoms. All the East,
　　　　Say thou, shall call her mistress.' So he nodded,
　　　　And soberly did mount an arm-gaunt steed, 　　　　50
　　　　Who neighed so high that what I would have spoke
　　　　Was beastly dumbed by him.
CLEOPATRA What, was he sad, or merry?
ALEXAS Like to the time o'th'year between the extremes
　　　　Of hot and cold, he was nor sad nor merry. 　　　　55
CLEOPATRA O well-divided disposition! Note him,
　　　　Note him, good Charmian, 'tis the man; but note him.
　　　　He was not sad, for he would shine on those
　　　　That make their looks by his; he was not merry,
　　　　Which seemed to tell them his remembrance lay 　　　　60
　　　　In Egypt with his joy; but between both.
　　　　O heavenly mingle! Be'st thou sad or merry,
　　　　The violence of either thee becomes,
　　　　So does it no man else. – Met'st thou my posts?
ALEXAS Ay, madam, twenty several messengers. 　　　　65
　　　　Why do you send so thick?
CLEOPATRA 　　　　　　　　　　Who's born that day
　　　　When I forget to send to Antony
　　　　Shall die a beggar. Ink and paper, Charmian.
　　　　Welcome, my good Alexas. Did I, Charmian,
　　　　Ever love Caesar so?

37　Judi Dench delivered this with 'cutting humour . . . to an effeminate messenger' (Michael
　　Billington, *Guardian*, 11 April 1987).
55　**he . . . merry** Michael Billington said that Helen Mirren was 'victim rather than the mistress
　　of her passion: a stickish, giddy, mercurial woman . . . when she hears that the absent
　　Antony is both sad and merry she does a rhapsodic little dance ("Oh heavenly mingle") as if
　　finding her own state reflected in his' (*Guardian*, 14 October 1982).
69–78　**Did . . . away** Cut in the bowdlerising of the text for Macready's production (promptbook).

CHARMIAN   O, that brave Caesar!   70
CLEOPATRA Be choked with such another emphasis!
     Say, 'the brave Antony'.
CHARMIAN   The valiant Caesar!
CLEOPATRA By Isis, I will give thee bloody teeth
     If thou with Caesar paragon again
     My man of men.
CHARMIAN   By your most gracious pardon,   75
     I sing but after you.
CLEOPATRA   My salad days,
     When I was green in judgement, cold in blood,
     To say as I said then. But come, away,
     Get me ink and paper.
     He shall have every day a several greeting,   80
     Or I'll unpeople Egypt.

                               Exeunt

70b   At this point in Byam Shaw's 1953 production Cleopatra 'took hold of Charmian's face and pushed her halfway down the steps; when Charmian groveled at Cleopatra's feet, Cleopatra kicked her. One of the queen's flunkies cracked a whip as the scene ended' (Lamb, *Antony and Cleopatra*, p. 152).

76b-7   The age of the actor is perhaps a relevant circumstance in the delivery of these famous lines: see Introduction, pp. 67–8. Parfitt brought 'a delicious dry touch' to them (*Times*, 23 April 1983); Dench uttered them in 'a pensive melancholy . . . at the frank acknowledgement of the passing years' (Michael Billington, *Guardian*, 11 April 1987). In her 1995 production, Vanessa Redgrave 'listens impatiently [to Charmian], pauses long, and then says, "My salad days!" with so dry a mixture of maturity, embarrassment and disdain (the turn of the head so expressive) that we laugh out loud, and forget how the famous line has ever been spoken before' (Alastair Macaulay, *Financial Times*, 5 June 1995).

81   Vanessa Redgrave in 1995 'rattle[d] through' the lines after 76, 'including the big exit line "Or I'll unpeople Egypt"', 'with an astonishingly casual lack of emphasis' (Alastair Macaulay, *Financial Times*, 5 June 1995).

ACT 2, SCENE I

[2.1] *Enter* POMPEY, MENECRATES, *and* MENAS, *in warlike manner*

POMPEY If the great gods be just, they shall assist
    The deeds of justest men.
MENAS   Know, worthy Pompey,
    That what they do delay they not deny.
POMPEY Whiles we are suitors to their throne, decays
    The thing we sue for.
MENAS   We, ignorant of ourselves,   5
    Beg often our own harms, which the wise powers
    Deny us for our good; so find we profit
    By losing of our prayers.
POMPEY   I shall do well.
    The people love me, and the sea is mine;
    My powers are crescent, and my auguring hope   10
    Says it will come to th'full. Mark Antony
    In Egypt sits at dinner, and will make
    No wars without doors. Caesar gets money where
    He loses hearts. Lepidus flatters both,
    Of both is flattered; but he neither loves,   15
    Nor either cares for him.

This and the other Pompey scenes (2.6, 2.7) were omitted by Kemble (following Dryden), Chatterton, Asche in his Australian touring production and the Nunn–Scoffield television version. This scene was cut in Garrick's production (printed edition), in Macready's (promptbook) and in 1866 and 1867 (Calvert's acting edition).

0 SD   Sylvester McCoy in the Robertson–Selbie production 'gives us a Pompey who needs only a wooden leg and a parrot to complete the illusion of naval piracy' (Sheridan Morley, *Punch*, 11 June 1986). In Brewster's production, 'when David Carr's turban-topped Pompey stands surveying the scene, one is put in mind of some proud Abyssinian or Afghan rebel fighter' (Carole Woddis, *What's On*, 22 May 1991). In Caird's 1993 production 'the most imaginative stroke of all is the first sight of Pompey (Toby Stephens) in a storm at sea, standing in the prow of a ship that is nothing but a rippling cloth, while a sailor pulls on a bulging sail' (Jeremy Kingston, *Times*, 29 May 1993).

MENAS   Caesar and Lepidus
    Are in the field. A mighty strength they carry.
POMPEY Where have you this? 'Tis false.
MENAS   From Silvius, sir.
POMPEY He dreams. I know they are in Rome together
    Looking for Antony. But all the charms of love,   20
    Salt Cleopatra, soften thy waned lip!
    Let witchcraft joined with beauty, lust with both,
    Tie up the libertine in a field of feasts,
    Keep his brain fuming. Epicurean cooks,
    Sharpen with cloyless sauce his appetite,   25
    That sleep and feeding may prorogue his honour
    Even till a Lethe'd dullness –

              Enter VARRIUS

                         How now, Varrius?
VARRIUS This is most certain that I shall deliver:
    Mark Antony is every hour in Rome
    Expected. Since he went from Egypt 'tis   30
    A space for farther travel.
POMPEY I could have given less matter
    A better ear. Menas, I did not think
    This amorous surfeiter would have donned his helm
    For such a petty war. His soldiership   35
    Is twice the other twain. But let us rear
    The higher our opinion, that our stirring
    Can from the lap of Egypt's widow pluck
    The ne'er-lust-wearied Antony.
MENAS   I cannot hope
    Caesar and Antony shall well greet together.   40
    His wife that's dead did trespasses to Caesar;
    His brother warred upon him, although, I think,
    Not moved by Antony.
POMPEY   I know not, Menas,
    How lesser enmities may give way to greater.
    Were't not that we stand up against them all,   45
    'Twere pregnant they should square between themselves,
    For they have entertainèd cause enough
    To draw their swords. But how the fear of us
    May cement their divisions and bind up
    The petty difference, we yet not know.   50
    Be't as our gods will have't! It only stands
    Our lives upon to use our strongest hands.
    Come, Menas.
                             Exeunt

[2.2] *Enter* ENOBARBUS *and* LEPIDUS

LEPIDUS Good Enobarbus, 'tis a worthy deed,
    And shall become you well, to entreat your captain
    To soft and gentle speech.
ENOBARBUS   I shall entreat him
    To answer like himself. If Caesar move him,
    Let Antony look over Caesar's head   5
    And speak as loud as Mars. By Jupiter,
    Were I the wearer of Antonio's beard,
    I would not shave't today.
LEPIDUS 'Tis not a time for private stomaching.
ENOBARBUS Every time serves for the matter that is then born in't.   10
LEPIDUS But small to greater matters must give way.
ENOBARBUS Not if the small come first.
LEPIDUS Your speech is passion; but pray you stir
    No embers up. Here comes the noble Antony.

    Enter ANTONY *and* VENTIDIUS [*in conversation*]

ENOBARBUS And yonder Caesar.   15

    Enter CAESAR, MAECENAS, *and* AGRIPPA [*by another door,*
        also in conversation]

ANTONY If we compose well here, to Parthia.
    Hark, Ventidius.
              [*They confer apart*]
CAESAR I do not know, Maecenas. Ask Agrippa.
LEPIDUS Noble friends:
    That which combined us was most great, and let not   20
    A leaner action rend us. What's amiss,
    May it be gently heard. When we debate
    Our trivial difference loud, we do commit
    Murder in healing wounds. Then, noble partners,
    The rather for I earnestly beseech,   25
    Touch you the sourest points with sweetest terms,
    Nor curstness grow to th'matter.
ANTONY   'Tis spoken well.
    Were we before our armies, and to fight,

I should do thus.
               Flourish
CAESAR Welcome to Rome. 30
ANTONY Thank you.
CAESAR Sit.
ANTONY Sit, sir.
CAESAR Nay, then.

Macready's 'acting in the scene of explanation with Caesar of their cause of quarrel, was a specimen of the art carried to its highest pitch of perfection' (*Athenaeum*, 23 November 1833); in 1951 Olivier's Antony was 'a witty piece of work, especially admirable in the earlier scenes of Roman conference' (Ivor Brown, *Observer*, 13 May 1951). Whereas Michael Redgrave had a 'blunt, reluctantly penitent accord with Caesar' in 1953 (Richard Findlater, *Tribune*, 20 November 1953), and Byam Shaw's earlier production of 1946 had used 'naturalistic pauses' (Stephen Potter, *New Statesman*, 4 January 1947), in Helpmann's much-praised meeting of the Triumvirate the 'awkward' pauses were 'adeptly handled' (J. A. Cuddon, *Tablet*, 23 March 1957) and Michell let 'the greatness of the world conqueror show clearly through the man who has for a brief while forgotten Cleopatra and finds a fresh joy in outdoing his rivals, alike in stern wit combats and in nights of revelry' (Anthony Cookman, *Tatler,* 20 March 1957). By contrast, though Plummer in Langham's production 'wore simplicity and truth on his shoulders like epaulets' in this scene, 'our strongest impression was of a man giving the most earnest performance of his life, a performance so well rehearsed that there were almost no traces of technique left in it' (Kerr, *Thirty Plays*, p. 165). The Nunn–Scoffield television version emphasises confrontation and the realities of power: Antony and five battle-hardened supporters in buff are outnumbered by Caesar with ten, 'including a back line of five in Falangist blue. They create an ominous sense of power and context' (Coursen, *Shakespearean Performance*, p. 191) and the mutual suspicion is signalled by circling. One reviewer of Noble's production was troubled by the minimalist set for this scene: 'When the words tell us that the three greatest Princes of the known earth are met in Rome in high conclave, our eyes see them sitting in a hovel, on kitchen chairs against a door marked Push Bar To Open' (*Daily Telegraph*, 14 October 1982). In Vanessa Redgrave's 1995 production, with its strong emphasis on political manoeuvring, 'the power battles and diplomatic jousting of Roman leaders, to the music of a Jew's harp, are intentionally played down' (Nicholas de Jongh, *Evening Standard*, 2 June 1995).

32–4   In Macready's production 'there was one reading which we were certainly astonished to find him adopting. When Octavius and Antony meet in anger in the second act . . . and they seat themselves, Mr Steevens supposed that Antony understood Caesar to assume superiority in bidding him to sit who was his equal, and therefore felt offended; but surely the supposition is *little* in its character, and at variance with the whole subsequent part of the scene, for in it Antony evinces a determined disposition to bear with Caesar, and upon him to throw the whole blame of the quarrel, if quarrel there should be' (*Morning Post*, 22 November 1833).

⸢*They sit*⸣

ANTONY I learn you take things ill which are not so,   35
    Or, being, concern you not.
CAESAR   I must be laughed at
    If or for nothing or a little, I
    Should say myself offended, and with you
    Chiefly i'th'world; more laughed at that I should
    Once name you derogately, when to sound your name   40
    It not concerned me.
ANTONY My being in Egypt, Caesar, what was't to you?
CAESAR No more than my residing here at Rome
    Might be to you in Egypt. Yet if you there
    Did practise on my state, your being in Egypt   45
    Might be my question.
ANTONY   How intend you, 'practised'?
CAESAR You may be pleased to catch at mine intent
    By what did here befall me. Your wife and brother
    Made wars upon me, and their contestation
    Was theme for you; you were the word of war.   50
ANTONY You do mistake your business. My brother never
    Did urge me in his act. I did enquire it,
    And have my learning from some true reports
    That drew their swords with you. Did he not rather
    Discredit my authority with yours,   55
    And make the wars alike against my stomach,
    Having alike your cause? Of this, my letters
    Before did satisfy you. If you'll patch a quarrel,
    As matter whole you have to make it with,
    It must not be with this.
CAESAR   You praise yourself   60
    By laying defects of judgement to me, but
    You patched up your excuses.
ANTONY   Not so, not so.
    I know you could not lack – I am certain on't –
    Very necessity of this thought, that I,
    Your partner in the cause 'gainst which he fought,   65
    Could not with graceful eyes attend those wars
    Which fronted mine own peace. As for my wife,
    I would you had her spirit in such another;
    The third o'th'world is yours, which with a snaffle
    You may pace easy, but not such a wife.   70
ENOBARBUS Would we had all such wives, that the men might go to
  wars with the women!
ANTONY So much uncurbable, her garboils, Caesar,
    Made out of her impatience – which not wanted

Shrewdness of policy too – I grieving grant 75
Did you too much disquiet. For that you must
But say I could not help it.
CAESAR   I wrote to you
When rioting in Alexandria; you
Did pocket up my letters, and with taunts
Did gibe my missive out of audience. 80
ANTONY Sir, he fell upon me ere admitted, then;
Three kings I had newly feasted, and did want
Of what I was i'th'morning. But next day
I told him of myself, which was as much
As to have asked him pardon. Let this fellow 85
Be nothing of our strife; if we contend,
Out of our question wipe him.
CAESAR   You have broken
The article of your oath, which you shall never
Have tongue to charge me with.
LEPIDUS Soft, Caesar! 90
ANTONY No, Lepidus, let him speak.
The honour is sacred which he talks on now,
Supposing that I lacked it. But on, Caesar –
The article of my oath.
CAESAR To lend me arms and aid when I required them, 95
The which you both denied.
ANTONY   Neglected, rather;
And then when poisoned hours had bound me up
From mine own knowledge. As nearly as I may
I'll play the penitent to you, but mine honesty
Shall not make poor my greatness, nor my power 100
Work without it. Truth is that Fulvia,
To have me out of Egypt, made wars here,
For which myself, the ignorant motive, do
So far ask pardon as befits mine honour
To stoop in such a case.
LEPIDUS   'Tis noble spoken. 105
MAECENAS If it might please you to enforce no further
The griefs between ye; to forget them quite
Were to remember that the present need
Speaks to atone you.
LEPIDUS   Worthily spoken, Maecenas.

99–101 **but . . . it** Cut by Nunn, 'to reduce embellishment in Antony's speeches, presenting him . . .
as the straight-forward and pragmatic speaker, politician and soldier' (Scott, *Antony and
Cleopatra*, p. 66).

ENOBARBUS Or, if you borrow one another's love for the instant,   110
    you may, when you hear no more words of Pompey, return it
    again. You shall have time to wrangle in when you have nothing
    else to do.
ANTONY Thou art a soldier only. Speak no more.
ENOBARBUS That truth should be silent I had almost forgot.   115
ANTONY You wrong this presence, therefore speak no more.
ENOBARBUS Go to, then; your considerate stone.
CAESAR I do not much dislike the matter, but
    The manner of his speech; for't cannot be
    We shall remain in friendship, our conditions   120
    So differing in their acts. Yet if I knew
    What hoop should hold us staunch, from edge to edge
    O'th'world I would pursue it.
AGRIPPA Give me leave, Caesar.
CAESAR Speak, Agrippa.   125
AGRIPPA Thou hast a sister by the mother's side,
    Admired Octavia. Great Mark Antony
    Is now a widower.
CAESAR   Say not so, Agrippa.
    If Cleopatra heard you, your reproof
    Were well deserved of rashness.   130
ANTONY I am not married, Caesar. Let me hear
    Agrippa further speak.
AGRIPPA To hold you in perpetual amity,
    To make you brothers, and to knit your hearts

126 In Kemble's production Maecenas and Agrippa were, thought the *Examiner* critic,
    'represented . . . in so ludicrous a style of burlesque, that we feel some surprise that the
    Attorney-General has not taken cognizance of them: not that we think that they intended
    to libel any existing Ministers, but surely Government itself is brought into contempt, and
    becomes a mere farce, when its great managers are so grossly and falsely caricatured' (5
    December 1813). Michael Billington wrote of the Robertson–Selbie production, 'one of its
    few innovative touches is the hint that Antony's marriage to Octavia is a put up job devised
    by two of Caesar's machiavellian followers' (*Guardian*, 28 May 1986); John Peter said
    'Agrippa (Andrew Wheaton) and Maecenas (Christopher Bowen) play their parts with
    servile efficiency. The whole thing is like a well-prepared cabinet meeting.' (*Sunday Times*,
    1 June 1986).
131 **I . . . Caesar** In 1972 Richard Johnson, when in Rome, 'stood straight, and spoke decisively,
    as in the assertive quelling of Octavius' at this line (Thomson, 'No Rome of Safety', pp.
    146–7). Michael Billington said of Michael Gambon's Antony that 'he thinks for about two
    seconds before contracting the fatal marriage' (*Guardian*, 14 October 1982).

With an unslipping knot, take Antony 135
Octavia to his wife, whose beauty claims
No worse a husband than the best of men,
Whose virtue and whose general graces speak
That which none else can utter. By this marriage
All little jealousies, which now seem great, 140
And all great fears, which now import their dangers,
Would then be nothing. Truths would be tales,
Where now half tales be truths. Her love to both
Would each to other and all loves to both
Draw after her. Pardon what I have spoke, 145
For 'tis a studied, not a present thought,
By duty ruminated.

ANTONY   Will Caesar speak?

CAESAR Not till he hears how Antony is touched
With what is spoke already.

ANTONY What power is in Agrippa 150
If I would say, 'Agrippa, be it so',
To make this good?

CAESAR   The power of Caesar, and
His power unto Octavia.

ANTONY   May I never
To this good purpose, that so fairly shows,
Dream of impediment! Let me have thy hand 155
Further this act of grace; and from this hour
The heart of brothers govern in our loves
And sway our great designs!

CAESAR   There's my hand.

[They clasp hands]

A sister I bequeath you whom no brother
Did ever love so dearly. Let her live 160
To join our kingdoms and our hearts; and never

158b SD   Irving Wardle wrote of Brook's production 'The attachment between Alan Howard's Antony
and this Octavius is more than an onerous political duty. There is straightforward human
love between the veteran and the younger man; and after their first parley, each side putting
his point with the slow vigilance of a chess player, the reconciliation is sealed with a
delighted embrace' (*Times*, 11 October 1978); in Caird's 1993 production 'John Nettles is
more affable than the usual run of Octavius Caesars, even giving an uncalculated jump for
joy when he and Antony patch up their quarrel' (Jeremy Kingston, *Times*, 29 May 1993).
However, in Hall's production 'Tim Pigott-Smith plays Octavius as a pasty, virginal
marionette, flinching from contact while actually offering his hand' (Michael Ratcliffe,
Observer, 12 April 1987).

Fly off our loves again!

LEPIDUS Happily, amen!

ANTONY I did not think to draw my sword 'gainst Pompey,
For he hath laid strange courtesies and great
Of late upon me. I must thank him only, 165
Lest my remembrance suffer ill report;
At heel of that, defy him.

LEPIDUS Time calls upon's.
Of us must Pompey presently be sought,
Or else he seeks out us.

ANTONY Where lies he? 170

CAESAR About the Mount Misena.

ANTONY What is his strength by land?

CAESAR Great and increasing;
But by sea he is an absolute master.

ANTONY So is the fame. 175
Would we had spoke together! Haste we for it.
Yet, ere we put ourselves in arms, dispatch we
The business we have talked of.

CAESAR With most gladness,
And do invite you to my sister's view,
Whither straight I'll lead you. 180

ANTONY Let us, Lepidus, not lack your company.

LEPIDUS Noble Antony, not sickness should detain me.

Flourish. Exeunt [Caesar, Antony, Lepidus, and Ventidius].
Enobarbus, Agrippa, Maecenas remain

MAECENAS Welcome from Egypt, sir.

ENOBARBUS Half the heart of Caesar, worthy Maecenas! My honourable friend Agrippa! 185

AGRIPPA Good Enobarbus!

MAECENAS We have cause to be glad that matters are so well
digested. You stayed well by't in Egypt.

ENOBARBUS Ay, sir, we did sleep day out of countenance, and made
the night light with drinking. 190

MAECENAS Eight wild boars roasted whole at a breakfast, and but
twelve persons there. Is this true?

ENOBARBUS This was but as a fly by an eagle. We had much more
monstrous matter of feast, which worthily deserved noting.

MAECENAS She's a most triumphant lady, if report be square to her. 195

ENOBARBUS When she first met Mark Antony, she pursed up his
heart upon the river of Cydnus.

183–99 Cut in Garrick's production, which omitted the rest of this scene, transposing 200–38a and
243–8a to 1.1 (printed edition).

AGRIPPA There she appeared indeed, or my reporter devised well
    for her.
ENOBARBUS I will tell you.   200
    The barge she sat in, like a burnished throne
    Burned on the water. The poop was beaten gold;
    Purple the sails, and so perfumèd that
    The winds were lovesick with them. The oars were silver,

200   At this point in Hall's production Michael Bryant 'came round and sat confidently in Antony's
    chair' (Crowl, *Shakespeare Observed*, p. 98).

201–50 This speech was inserted, with bridging lines, at 1.1.58 in Garrick's production (printed
    edition), and delivered by Thyreus, 'probably, because Thyreus had been cast to one of his
    special favourites, Charles Holland, a serious actor of much talent, while Enobarbus was
    allotted to Berry, apparently a minor comedian' (Winter, *Shakespeare*, pp. 434–5). In 1813
    the first half of the speech, mixed with the second half of Dryden's version, was given to
    Antony in Kemble's 4.3, a scene in which Ventidius tries to persuade Antony to leave
    Cleopatra (printed text). Bach's 1937 production, using an adaptation by William Strunk Jr
    which was especially damaging to Enobarbus, gave the barge-speech to a first-act
    messenger (Leiter, *Encyclopedia, 1930–1940*, p. 38).

      On Shakespeare's stage, where geographical location was unspecific and properties used
    sparingly and often symbolically, such descriptive passages had an obvious function, but in
    Victorian and Edwardian 'pictorial' productions they must have seemed almost superfluous.
    Famous lines like these could be treated as an elocutionary set-piece: 'Ryder was a roarer'
    (Mullin, *Victorian Actors and Actresses*, p. 400), but in Chatterton's production his 'delivery
    of the famous description extorted plaudits from the house' (*Illustrated London News*, 27
    September 1873). Lyn Harding displayed his 'elocutionary power' (*Dundee Advertiser*, 28
    December 1906) in Tree's production, and 'received a deserved ovation after his spirited
    delivery of the famous description' (*Manchester Dispatch*, 28 December 1906); Collier
    wrote that his speech was 'the great success of the evening' (*Harlequinade*, p. 185) and
    Hesketh Pearson remarked 'here again Tree was eclipsed in his own theatre, and there were
    occasions when the audience shouted for Harding so lustily that the lights in the house went
    up and the National Anthem was played' (*Beerbohm Tree*, p. 133). There was, however, the
    potential problem of a mismatch between Enobarbus's description and the barge itself,
    which illustrative directors insisted on putting on stage; either because, as in the case of
    Tree's production, 'the actual vessel, which we see in the first act, is not that described by
    Enobarbus' (J.J.N., *Guardian*, 2 January 1907), or because the quality of Enobarbus's
    response seemed inadequate: in Eytinge's production, 'the tableau showing Cleopatra's
    barge . . . was beautiful, but the representative of Enobarbus [G. B. Waldron], who gave a
    low-comedy performance of that fine part . . . described that gorgeous vessel . . . much as a
    bovine rustic might do, descanting on a new canal boat' (Winter, *Shakespeare*, p. 459).

In modern productions, actors and their directors have wrestled with the problem of an appropriate tone for the delivery of lines which are so well known that they are apt to sound like quotations. There has been a tendency away from a 'freshness' that underplays Enobarbus's cynicism to a more self-conscious approach that emphasises either the satirical commentator or the conspirator in debauchery, and confronts the problem of 'quotations' by using direct address, pseudo-ham acting, or proprietorial pride. In Bridges-Adams's production of 1921, Holloway 'caught just the right blend of cynicism and stoicism. His speaking, too, was good, and he made even the "quotations" sound natural – which is no mean test' (F.A.C., *Birmingham Gazette*, 25 April 1921). Agate thought that in Leigh's 1925 production Neil Porter 'succeeded in delivering the most threadbare tag in Shakespeare as though it were newly minted in his mind' (*Brief Chronicles,* p. 176), and the 1927 Enobarbus, George Skillan, surprisingly succeeded in being unselfconscious in the famous speech: 'When this Enobarbus stormed his way agitatedly through Shakespeare's lines he was unintelligible; when he forgot the conventional trick of "recitation", as in the description of Cleopatra's barge, the golden poop and the purple sails of which he spoke were both music and pictures in words' (*Times*, 13 July 1927). In 1930 Ralph Richardson 'gave the Cydnus speech naturally, not as a set-piece' (Crosse, *Shakespearean Playgoing*, p. 67), whilst in 1931 Randle Ayrton gave Enobarbus 'a rare and salty humour – how excellently he contrives to give the true under-current of satire to the famous "description of Cleopatra's barge"!' (*Birmingham Post*, 8 June 1931). Also the Enobarbus of Iden Payne's production, Ayrton made 'the superbly natural delivery of the speech about Cleopatra's barge' (R.C.R., *Birmingham Post*, 16 April 1935) a function of characterisation: 'The famous descriptions of Cleopatra lost none of their poetic beauty by being delivered as essentially in character with the rough soldier' (P.D.H., *Leamington Chronicle*, 19 April 1935). By contrast, in Komisarjevsky's production Leon Quartermaine, 'by turning the bluff soldier into the silky diplomat, was utterly and entirely wrong from the first syllable of the part to the last' (Agate, *Brief Chronicles*, p. 184). Tristan Rawson, in 1945, 'excellent in "plainness", joviality and moving in death' (Ruth Ellis, *Stratford-upon-Avon Herald*, 24 April 1945), was 'imperfectly aware that he is also a great descriptive reporter' (*Times*, 25 April 1945). In 1951 Norman Wooland 'seemed resolved not to share the beauty with us' (Harold Hobson, *Sunday Times*, 13 May 1951), whereas in 1953 Harry Andrews delivered 'the great description with a fine relish and . . . a rough soldierliness' (T. C. Worsley, *New Statesman*, 7 May 1953). In 1957 Derek Godfrey 'spoke the famous Cydnus speech finely, without ever going out of character or giving it the air of a set piece' (Byrne, 'The Shakespeare Season', p. 476). Patrick Stewart's Enobarbus in Nunn's production was a 'modern' combination of cynicism and response to Cleopatra's charms that Jacobeans might have felt comfortable with – 'The "barge" speech, though spoken in soldierly tones, betrayed a profound sense of the power of Cleopatra's invading charms' (Male, *Shakespeare on Stage*, p. 28) – but he was a little lacking in old-fashioned elocutionary technique in the barge speech, 'which was last night heralded by a gross preparatory slowing of pace' (Charles Lewsen, *Times*, 16 August 1972). In the

Which to the tune of flutes kept stroke, and made 205
The water which they beat to follow faster,
As amorous of their strokes. For her own person,

Nunn–Scoffield television version the heralding of the speech by distant barking dogs and the ironic tone of Agrippa's responses barely diminish the effect of the narrator's enthusiasm, though they do frame it. In Brook's production, Patrick Stewart, 'who does not reduce Enobarbus to a single purple patch', delivered 'a great deal of the Barge speech' 'directly to the house' (J. C. Trewin, *Birmingham Post*, 11 October 1978); Robert Cushman wrote of his 'proprietorial "I will tell you", as who should say, you ain't heard nothing yet' (*Observer*, 15 October 1978). In the BBC television version, Emrys James delivers the speech casually, though he does suspend his eating and drinking for it. Bob Peck, in Noble's production, 'plays Enobarbus as a puritan satirist' (Stanley Wells, *Times Literary Supplement*, 29 October 1982); Victoria Radin considered he 'strangely trounces Enobarbus's famous lines on the barge' (*Observer*, 17 October 1982), whilst Gordon Parsons thought he 'is picturing a great ham performance in his famous barge description speech' (*Morning Star*, 18 October 1982); according to Male (*Shakespeare on Stage*, p. 28), it 'still enthralled his listeners'. In the Robertson–Selbie production, Ian Stewart found Robert O'Mahoney credible in his nostalgia for glorious moments – 'Enobarbus, a wry commentator on the weakness of Antony, nevertheless stirs one with his memories of shared glories in a fine rendering of the most purple of this play's many purple passages' (*Country Life*, 12 June 1986) – but Irving Wardle thought he intended his hyperbole to have a specifically political function: 'it is not an aria but an angry rebuke to the two Roman idiots who proposed the idea of marrying Antony to Octavia in the first place' (*Times*, 28 May 1986). In Hall's production, when Michael Bryant 'begins his famous speech about Cleopatra's barge, it is in the casual tones of an old sweat reporting what he has seen: as he continues, he gets carried into an imaginative trance from which he has to be roused' (Michael Billington, *Guardian*, 11 April 1987). Renu Setna's delivery of the barge speech in Brewster's production got a mixed response; Michael Billington thought he made 'every syllable . . . gleam' (*Guardian,* 20 May 1991), but Tony Dunn heard it differently: 'Brewster throws away, wilfully it seems, the super-heroism. Renu Setna's Enobarbus chews as remorselessly through the beauty of [the barge speech] as through the rest of the part' (*Tribune*, 31 May 1991). In Caird's 1993 production Paul Jesson 'doesn't lean on the poetry; his urgent enthusiasm makes us see every detail of the barge, silver oars and all, as if for the first time' (Kate Kellaway, *Observer*, 30 May 1993). In Rutter's production, 'when Dave Hill, as a weary seen-it-all Enobarbus, tells Agrippa and Maecenas of the barge Cleopatra sat in, it's no purple passage: they've asked him, so he'll tell them' (Robert Butler, *Independent on Sunday*, 15 October 1995).

205 In 1987 Bryant 'used his hands to imitate the silver oars' here (Crowl, *Shakespeare Observed*, p. 98).

It beggared all description: she did lie
In her pavilion – cloth of gold, of tissue –
O'erpicturing that Venus where we see 210
The fancy outwork nature. On each side her
Stood pretty dimpled boys, like smiling Cupids,
With divers-coloured fans, whose wind did seem
To glow the delicate cheeks which they did cool,
And what they undid did.

AGRIPPA   O rare for Antony! 215

ENOBARBUS Her gentlewomen, like the Nereides,
So many mermaids, tended her i'th'eyes,
And made their bends adornings. At the helm
A seeming mermaid steers. The silken tackle
Swell with the touches of those flower-soft hands, 220
That yarely frame the office. From the barge
A strange invisible perfume hits the sense
Of the adjacent wharfs. The city cast
Her people out upon her; and Antony,
Enthroned i'th'market-place, did sit alone, 225
Whistling to th'air, which, but for vacancy,
Had gone to gaze on Cleopatra too,
And made a gap in nature.

AGRIPPA   Rare Egyptian!

ENOBARBUS Upon her landing, Antony sent to her,
Invited her to supper. She replied, 230
It should be better he became her guest,
Which she entreated. Our courteous Antony,
Whom ne'er the word of 'No' woman heard speak,
Being barbered ten times o'er, goes to the feast,
And for his ordinary pays his heart 235
For what his eyes ate only.

AGRIPPA   Royal wench!
She made great Caesar lay his sword to bed;
He ploughed her, and she cropped.

ENOBARBUS   I saw her once
Hop forty paces through the public street,

---

207 **For ... person** Bryant 'threw his right leg over the chair's arm as he launched into' this
section (Crowl, *Shakespeare Observed*, p. 98).

238–42 Cut, presumably in the interests of decorum, in Garrick's production, (in the process of
inserting the barge speech in 1.1; printed edition) and in Phelps's (promptbook).

239 Bryant 'leaned forward to become wondrously confidential' at this point (Crowl,
Shakespeare Observed, p. 98).

And having lost her breath, she spoke, and panted, 240
That she did make defect perfection
And, breathless, power breathe forth.
MAECENAS Now Antony must leave her utterly.
ENOBARBUS Never. He will not.
     Age cannot wither her, nor custom stale 245
Her infinite variety. Other women cloy
The appetites they feed, but she makes hungry
Where most she satisfies. For vilest things
Become themselves in her, that the holy priests
Bless her when she is riggish. 250
MAECENAS If beauty, wisdom, modesty can settle
The heart of Antony, Octavia is
A blessèd lottery to him.
AGRIPPA   Let us go.
Good Enobarbus, make yourself my guest
Whilst you abide here.
ENOBARBUS   Humbly, sir, I thank you. 255
               Exeunt

246 **Her infinite variety** One reviewer of Byam Shaw's 1953 production wished Harry Andrews would 'summon more poetry to voice' at this point (*Western Daily Press*, 30 April 1953). In Langham's production, William Hutt, after a pause, 'inflected "infinite" in such a way as to suggest . . . that he had seen the repertoire of moods and despaired of ever seeing the end of it' (Kerr, *Thirty Plays*, p. 166).

247–8 **but . . . satisfies** Bryant 'slowly leaned back into the chair to savor' this notion (Crowl, *Shakespeare Observed*, p. 98).

248–50 **For . . . riggish** Cut in Garrick's production, in the process of transposing the barge speech to 1.1 (printed edition), and in the bowdlerising of the text for Phelps's (promptbook). In Hall's production 'a long pause after [these lines] caught all three men in rapt contemplation of Enobarbus's vision of the Egyptian queen' (Crowl, *Shakespeare Observed*, pp. 98–9).

252–3 **Octavia . . . him** Hall's 'Enobarbus responded with a smile and a knowing laugh, and all three exited shaking their heads with the understanding that the marriage and thus the peace between Antony and Octavius was doomed' (Crowl, *Shakespeare Observed*, p. 99).

ACT 2, SCENE 3

[2.3] *Enter* ANTONY, CAESAR, OCTAVIA *between them*

ANTONY The world, and my great office, will sometimes
      Divide me from your bosom.
OCTAVIA   All which time
      Before the gods my knee shall bow my prayers
      To them for you.
ANTONY   Good night, sir. My Octavia,
      Read not my blemishes in the world's report.   5

Omitted in Garrick's production, where 38b-40a were inserted at 2.7.121 (printed edition), and in 1866 and 1867 (Calvert's acting edition).

0 SD In Shakespeare's day the function of such flanked entries derived from the emblematic tradition, sometimes heavily qualified by irony, as in the entrance of Richard III between two bishops, and here the stage picture of concord has been ironically foreshadowed by Enobarbus's memorable tribute to the fascination of Cleopatra. Kemble omitted the scene (printed text). Frank Harris said of Maud Cressall in Tree's version, 'She is lachrymose in the play, and she was lachrymose on the stage; but she was very pretty, and charmingly gowned, and that is all we have any right to expect of Octavia' (*Vanity Fair*, 2 January 1907); in Bridges-Adams's production of 1927, however, Octavia was a fuller presence: Esme Biddle 'lets us see by her passivity that Octavia is but a pawn in the game. How sweet natured and how motherly she makes her, how full of suppressed emotion; yet allows her to lack just the one thing that drew Antony away to Egypt – the art of trading upon her sex' (*Stratford-upon-Avon Herald*, 15 July 1927). In the Nunn–Scoffield television version, Octavia (Judy Cornwell) is equally affectionate to both men; in Brook's production Jonathan Pryce's Octavius had a demonstrative relationship with his sister and a complex one with Antony, and the flanked entry was an eloquent, if updated, stage image: 'at the beginning [he] still hero-worships Antony, and is nervously thrilled to be able to marry him off to Octavia, the beloved sister he tends to fondle or (quaintly) massage whenever she emerges from cold-storage' (Benedict Nightingale, *New Statesman*, 20 October 1978).

5 For Richard Findlater, Michael Redgrave's delivery of this line indicated his 'compassion' for Octavia (*Tribune*, 20 November 1953); 'his promise of constancy to Octavia, on the very heels of his passionate parting with Cleopatra, seemed credible, even honest' (N.T., *Royal Leamington Spa Courier*, 1 May 1953); Redgrave was married to the production's Octavia, Rachel Kempson.

           I have not kept my square, but that to come
           Shall all be done by th'rule. Good night, dear lady.
OCTAVIA Good night, sir.
CAESAR Good night.

                                   Exit [with Octavia]

          Enter SOOTHSAYER

ANTONY Now, sirrah: you do wish yourself in Egypt?   10
SOOTHSAYER Would I had never come from thence, nor you thither!
ANTONY If you can, your reason?
SOOTHSAYER I see it in my motion, have it not in my tongue; but yet
     hie you to Egypt again.
ANTONY Say to me, whose fortunes shall rise higher,   15
           Caesar's or mine?
SOOTHSAYER Caesar's.
           Therefore, O Antony, stay not by his side.
           Thy daemon – that thy spirit which keeps thee – is
           Noble, courageous, high unmatchable,   20
           Where Caesar's is not. But near him thy angel
           Becomes afeard, as being o'erpowered; therefore
           Make space enough between you.
ANTONY   Speak this no more.
SOOTHSAYER To none but thee; no more but when to thee.
           If thou dost play with him at any game,   25
           Thou art sure to lose; and of that natural luck
           He beats thee 'gainst the odds. Thy lustre thickens
           When he shines by. I say again, thy spirit
           Is all afraid to govern thee near him;
           But, he away, 'tis noble.
ANTONY   Get thee gone.   30
           Say to Ventidius I would speak with him.

                              Exit [Soothsayer]

           He shall to Parthia. – Be it art or hap,
           He hath spoken true. The very dice obey him,
            And in our sports my better cunning faints
           Under his chance. If we draw lots, he speeds;   35
           His cocks do win the battle still of mine
           When it is all to naught, and his quails ever
           Beat mine, inhooped, at odds. I will to Egypt;
           And though I make this marriage for my peace,
           I'th'East my pleasure lies.

          Enter VENTIDIUS

O, come, Ventidius. 40
You must to Parthia; your commission's ready.
Follow me and receive't.

Exeunt

40a 'Mr Tree goes out, kissing a ring on his finger and shouting in a stage whisper: "Cleopatra,
Cleopatra". This is "business," but it is not Shakespeare' (*Morning Post*, 28 December,
1906). In Michael Redgrave's mouth the line was 'ecstatic yet uneasy' (Richard Findlater,
Tribune, 20 November 1953).

ACT 2, SCENE 4

[2.4] *Enter* LEPIDUS, MAECENAS, *and* AGRIPPA

LEPIDUS Trouble yourselves no further. Pray you hasten
    Your generals after.
AGRIPPA   Sir, Mark Antony
    Will e'en but kiss Octavia, and we'll follow.
LEPIDUS Till I shall see you in your soldiers' dress,
    Which will become you both, farewell.
MAECENAS   We shall,   5
    As I conceive the journey, be at th'Mount
    Before you, Lepidus.
LEPIDUS   Your way is shorter;
    My purposes do draw me much about.
    You'll win two days upon me.
MAECENAS, AGRIPPA   Sir, good success!
LEPIDUS Farewell.   10
                          Exeunt

Omitted by Garrick (printed edition), Phelps (promptbook), in 1866 and 1867 (Calvert's acting edition) and by Helpmann. Trewin approved of the way in which Helpmann's staging connected the lovers' longings: 'Mr Helpmann must always get me to remember how as Antony (in Rome) cries "I' the east my pleasure lies", Cleopatra is already approaching from the Alexandrian side of the stage. For a few seconds there they are, as it were sharing the world between them. Then Antony is gone, and Cleopatra turns to the business of the scene, "Give us some music ; music, moody food of us that trade in love"' (*Illustrated London News*, 16 March 1957). Brook omitted the scene: Patrick Stewart, playing Enobarbus, said 'we never could understand why it was there' (quoted in Hunt and Reeves, *Peter Brook*, p. 225).

ACT 2, SCENE 5

[2.5] *Enter* CLEOPATRA, CHARMIAN, IRAS, *and* ALEXAS

CLEOPATRA Give me some music; music, moody food
    Of us that trade in love.
ALL   The music, ho!

Enter MARDIAN *the eunuch*

CLEOPATRA Let it alone. Let's to billiards. Come, Charmian.
CHARMIAN My arm is sore. Best play with Mardian.
CLEOPATRA As well a woman with an eunuch played   5
    As with a woman. Come, you'll play with me, sir?
MARDIAN As well as I can, madam.
CLEOPATRA And when good will is showed, though't come too short,
    The actor may plead pardon. I'll none now.
    Give me mine angle; we'll to the river. There,   10
    My music playing far off, I will betray
    Tawny-finned fishes. My bended hook shall pierce
    Their slimy jaws, and as I draw them up

1–2a Dorothy Green's delivery of these lines in 1924 could have been 'enriched by a bolder sensual colour' (*Times*, 16 July 1924).

5–6 **As . . . woman** The way in which these lines were delivered and received in Noble's production reflected changing social attitudes to other sexualities; Peter McGarry said of the 1982 version: 'Charmian and Iras are overt in a lesbian relationship and attempt to encompass Cleopatra. She is unsure of her feelings there, as she is towards the motherly protectiveness of her eunuch' (*Coventry Evening Telegraph*, 14 October 1982). Of the 1983 version, Clare Colvin observed 'The protective attitude of Cleopatra's maids towards the unhappy Eunuch, who is all too aware in the sensual atmosphere of what he has missed, and the Eunuch in turn comforting Cleopatra when she hears of Antony's marriage, all reflect a pervading female influence [in Egypt]' (*Times*, 14 April 1983). In Caird's 1992 production Clare Higgins was not averse to 'dallying with Mardian (played by Nick Holder with a very high-pitched voice)' (Geckle, 'The Power of Desire on Stage', p. 16).

10–15a In Nunn's production Cleopatra lay 'on a great keyhole-shaped bed' for her recollections (Charles Lewsen, *Times*, 16 August 1972); in the television version, she mimes the angling, just as Isabella Glyn is doing in the print of 1849. Lapotaire also mimes the fishing in the BBC television version.

> I'll think them every one an Antony
> And say, 'Aha! You're caught.'
> CHARMIAN   'Twas merry when   15
> You wagered on your angling, when your diver
> Did hang a salt fish on his hook, which he
> With fervency drew up.
> CLEOPATRA   That time? – O times! –
> I laughed him out of patience; and that night
> I laughed him into patience, and next morn,   20
> Ere the ninth hour, I drunk him to his bed;
> Then put my tires and mantles on him, whilst
> I wore his sword Philippan.
>
> *Enter a* MESSENGER
>
>   O, from Italy!
> Ram thou thy fruitful tidings in mine ears,
> That long time have been barren.

15a   In 1946 Edith Evans 'stroked the line' with 'cloyless complacency' (Tynan, *A View of the English Stage*, p. 50).

15b–23   Noble's production was notable for 'the transitions of emotion effortlessly effected between . . . her affectionate jesting with her women and her subsequent ferocity with the messenger who brings news of Antony's marriage to Octavia' (Stanley Wells, *Times Literary Supplement*, 29 October 1982).

22–3a   To the Jacobean ear, as well as being titillatingly erotic, this image was doubtless emblematic of subversion. Recent directors, notably Brook and Hall, have emphasised the grotesquerie and fantasising of middle-aged love and may have regretted that the image is heard but not seen. The postmodern ear is also postcolonial and likely to hear Cleopatra's recollection as a key to the series of subversions of Roman military triumph on stage, and it is not surprising that there have been visual allusions to the crossdressing in modern productions. Peggy Ashcroft recalled 'When I played it at Oxford, Antony and Cleopatra changed into each other's cloaks and coats while they were speaking . . . to identify more closely with each other' (*Observer*, 8 October 1978). In the first scene of Nunn's production 'Cleopatra playfully wields Antony's sword and he simpers like a maid in reply' (Jeremy Kingston, *Punch*, 23 August 1972); in the Nunn–Scoffield television version an image of Cleopatra, wearing Antony's helmet, holding his sword and riding him like a horse, is one of those illustrating Philo's opening speech.

23b–108a   The play's first audiences may have thought, as did a reviewer of Kemble's production, that Shakespeare modelled Cleopatra's behaviour here on the home life of his own late queen: 'Shakespeare had a living and striking authority in the Queen Elizabeth, who, though undoubtedly a woman of high spirit, and capable at least of prating about magnanimity as fluently as if she knew its nature, was yet debased by a thousand meannesses and littlenesses: and was besides, like her image Cleopatra, much given to cuffing and kicking her attendants' (*Examiner*, 5 December 1813). In Kemble's production, Cleopatra's violent acts were suppressed (printed edition), and one reviewer wrote of the scene in Macready's production, 'if acted now literally, according to the old stage directions, [it] would appear coarse and vulgar, as well as violent: this was properly curtailed both in the word and the action. The state of society and manners was formerly different, and if Queen Elizabeth could give Lord Essex a box on the ear in her Court, Cleopatra might be allowed to "harry" a messenger on the stage' (*Morning Chronicle*, 22 November 1833). In 1849, without any violent action, Glyn gave a memorable rendition of 'the spiteful rage with which she receives the news of Octavia's marriage, and which would vent itself with oriental cruelty on the messenger' (*Spectator*, 27 October 1849). The 1866 and 1867 productions restored some physical violence to the messenger scene, allowing Cleopatra to strike Mardian (who was substituted for the messenger, as in 1849) once and to draw her knife (Calvert's acting edition). In 1898, when the part of the messenger was combined with that of Diomedes, the scene was Constance Benson's 'one great moment . . . In this there was an approach to the requisite tragic power' (*Stratford-upon-Avon Herald*, 15 April 1898). Indisputably one of the most dramatic scenes in the play, in this century it has not usually been 'curtailed', and has almost invariably brought even reticent Cleopatras to violent life. In Tree's production, Collier's 'onslaught on the messenger . . . is thrilling in savage, passionate intensity and energy, and was greeted with rapture by the audience' (*Athenaeum*, 5 January 1907). In 1909, however, Julia Marlowe evinced 'no royalty' and 'in the passages of tempestuous rage was merely fractious' (Winter, *Shakespeare*, p. 467). Margaret Whiting also disappointed in this scene, as in others: 'So badly did this performance fall flat that I found myself admiring . . . the warm, sincere acting of the messenger, James Culliford' (F.G.B, *Plays and Players*, April 1957). But Tynan liked the 'deep entreating of her voice' in Whiting's rendition (*Observer*, 10 March 1957), and certainly the scene can be played for an emotional intensity beyond that of Cleopatra's fury. In 1921 Dorothy Green rose 'to her greatest height in the scene of sheer fury wherein she learns from the messenger of Antony's marriage to Octavia' (*Times*, 25 April 1921) and in 1924 she 'suggest[ed] the tigerish fury of a disappointed autocrat' in encompassing 'the whole range of tragic acting' (*Birmingham Mail*, 16 July 1924). In 1953 Peggy Ashcroft was 'able within the privacy of her retinue to turn for a moment into an old disillusioned woman on hearing the news of Antony's marriage to Octavia' (*Times*, 29 April 1953); shortly afterwards, 'she took the hapless messenger by the hair and threw him down the stairs' (Lamb, *Antony and Cleopatra*, p. 152). Janet Suzman's 'outrage with the messenger . . . was not as credible as in other productions since her conception of the role was more calculated than tempestuous' (Scott, *Antony and Cleopatra*, p. 51). Suzman also resorts to hair-pulling in the Nunn–Scoffield television version, where, with an update of Garrick's fright-wig, the tawny messenger's hair, initially pinned in a tight-curled 'Afro' hairstyle, is standing on end by the time she has finished with

MESSENGER   Madam, madam –   25
CLEOPATRA Antonio's dead! If thou say so, villain,
       Thou kill'st thy mistress; but well and free,
       If thou so yield him, there is gold, and here
       My bluest veins to kiss – a hand that kings
       Have lipped, and trembled kissing.   30
MESSENGER First, madam, he is well.
CLEOPATRA Why, there's more gold. But, sirrah, mark, we use
       To say the dead are well. Bring it to that,
       The gold I give thee will I melt and pour
       Down thy ill-uttering throat.   35
MESSENGER Good madam, hear me.
CLEOPATRA Well, go to, I will.
       But there's no goodness in thy face, if Antony
       Be free and healthful – so tart a favour
       To trumpet such good tidings! If not well,   40
       Thou shouldst come like a Fury crowned with snakes,
       Not like a formal man.
MESSENGER   Will't please you hear me?
CLEOPATRA I have a mind to strike thee ere thou speak'st.
       Yet if thou say Antony lives, is well,
       Or friends with Caesar, or not captive to him,   45
       I'll set thee in a shower of gold and hail
       Rich pearls upon thee.
MESSENGER   Madam, he's well.
CLEOPATRA   Well said.
MESSENGER And friends with Caesar.
CLEOPATRA   Thou'rt an honest man.
MESSENGER Caesar and he are greater friends than ever.

him. Lapotaire pulls the messenger's ears, rather than his hair, in the BBC television version, as did Higgins in Caird's messenger scene, which was was both violent and 'hilariously funny' (Geckle, 'The Power of Desire on Stage', p. 16); Alan Cox 'gets a lot of humour out of a diplomatic messenger' (Michael Billington, *Guardian*, 28 May 1993) and Clare Higgins 'plays her part feelingly, especially when enraged, and reminds us that Cleopatra was more than a touch insecure' (Kate Kellaway, *Observer*, 30 May 1993). In Rutter's production, Ishia Bennison's 'streetwise' 'reaction to unappealing news is to thump the messenger in the solar plexus, half-suffocate him with a cushion and then run at him with a knife' (Benedict Nightingale, *Times*, 5 October 1995).

34–5 In the Brook revival of 1979 Glenda Jackson put 'much more than the usual venom into th[is] threat'; she showed 'a natural bent for cruelty' (Benedict Nightingale, *What's on in London*, 13 July 1979).

48b Glenda Jackson tickled the messenger under the chin here (Scott, *Antony and Cleopatra*, p. 52).

CLEOPATRA Make thee a fortune from me.
MESSENGER   But yet, madam –   50
CLEOPATRA I do not like 'But yet'; it does allay
　　　The good precedence. Fie upon 'But yet'!
　　　'But yet' is as a gaoler to bring forth
　　　Some monstrous malefactor. Prithee, friend,
　　　Pour out the pack of matter to mine ear,   55
　　　The good and bad together: he's friends with Caesar,
　　　In state of health, thou say'st, and, thou say'st, free.
MESSENGER Free, madam? No! I made no such report.
　　　He's bound unto Octavia.
CLEOPATRA   For what good turn?
MESSENGER For the best turn i'th'bed.
CLEOPATRA   I am pale, Charmian.   60
MESSENGER Madam, he's married to Octavia.
CLEOPATRA The most infectious pestilence upon thee!
　　　　　　Strikes him down

50a Lillie Langtry unclasped some jewels to reward the messenger, but later struck him in the
　　face with them (see Sprague, *Shakespeare and the Actors*, p. 331). In Nunn's production 'the
　　scared Messenger . . . clings to the gold bracelet Cleopatra thrust on him when she supposed
　　his news was good' (Jeremy Kingston, *Punch*, 23 August 1972).

60a This and the previous half-line were cut in the bowdlerising of the text for Garrick's
　　production (printed edition), Phelps's (promptbook) and for those of 1866 and 1867
　　(Calvert's acting edition). In Brook's production this line 'caused initial movement, not from
　　the Queen, but from Charmian. As the messenger confirmed his story Cleopatra exploded,
　　crossing from her stool to grab him by the hair. Charmian in her concern moved downstage-
　　right, where she knelt looking towards, and thus focusing attention on, the two characters
　　centre-stage. The scene accelerated. Cleopatra kicked the messenger, dragged him about
　　the stage by the hair, shaking him in her rage' (Scott, *Antony and Cleopatra*, p. 52).

62 In 1953 Peggy Ashcroft was 'a queen throughout, even when spitting her curses on innocent
　　messengers' (P.R., *Western Daily Press*, 30 April 1953).

62 SD In 1898 'Cleopatra's rage was terrible, and the slave who brought the dire intelligence was
　　passionately struck down. Charmian's interposition saved his life' (*Birmingham Daily Post*,
　　15 April 1898). To a reviewer of Tree's version, 'knocking him clean over with a straight one
　　from the right' was 'an unbecoming exhibition of brute strength' (*Weekly Times and Echo*,
　　30 December 1906), but recent Cleopatras have followed Constance Collier's lead: Helen
　　Mirren 'socks in the jaw the hapless messenger' (Victoria Radin, *Observer*, 17 October 1982),
　　Judi Dench was 'highly dangerous' when she 'fell[ed]' the messenger 'with a right hook'
　　(Michael Billington, *Guardian*, 11 April 1987) and Clare Higgins 'shifts in a twinkling from
　　rapture to rage, giving him a right upper cut and a boot in the belly before screeching after
　　him with a dagger. And then, equally suddenly, she is in tears and holding the poor wretch's
　　head on her lap' (Benedict Nightingale, *Times*, 7 November 1992).

MESSENGER Good madam, patience.
CLEOPATRA   What say you?
                              Strikes him
                                                      Hence,
          Horrible villain, or I'll spurn thine eyes
          Like balls before me! I'll unhair thy head!   65
                    She hales him up and down
          Thou shalt be whipped with wire, and stewed in brine,
          Smarting in ling'ring pickle!
MESSENGER   Gracious madam,

63b SD   Constance Collier again gave the lead in inventiveness, showing 'vigour and grip (as Mr
     Quartermaine's poor neck must remember to its sorrow)' (*Illustrated Sporting and
     Dramatic News*, 12 January 1907); Richardson's 1973 modern-dress production had Vanessa
     Redgrave 'brandishing a Coke bottle' (Milton Shulman, *Evening Standard*, 10 August 1973);
     Helen Mirren 'is pampering the messenger of Antony's marriage with cushions and drinks
     before flying at his eyes with outstretched nails' (Irving Wardle, *Times*, 15 October 1982).

65 SD   Jacobean audiences would not have been unduly surprised to see a menial haled up and
     down; 'haling' was the rough treatment the low-born could expect in public in being
     dragged to prison or the gallows. Modern actors and directors have tended to seek more
     modern and local equivalents for Cleopatra's 'haling'. A reviewer said of Constance Collier,
     'the turbulent passion of the incident in which she indulges in a game of jiu-jitsu with the
     luckless messenger, who tells her that Antony has married Octavia, let us into the secret of
     her heart' (*Daily Mail*, 28 December 1906); Dorothy Green in 1921 'all but strangles him in
     her madness' (*Times*, 25 April 1921), Janet Suzman 'wildly and passionately drubs the
     messenger' (Benedict Nightingale, *New Statesman*, 25 August 1972), whilst for Helen Mirren
     the news 'brings on a fit of almost certifiable hysteria' (Michael Billington, *Guardian*, 14
     October 1982). Judi Dench 'haul[ed] the messenger . . . across the full width of Alison
     Chitty's rust-red, brick-red, blood-red Olivier stage by his hair' (David Nathan, *Jewish
     Chronicle*, 17 April 1987), though 'she never quite (even when punching messengers) gets
     what is terrible and beautiful in Cleopatra: the repose of her effortless sense of power'
     (Barbara Everett, *Times Literary Supplement*, 24 April 1987). The lucklessness of the
     messenger has made some reviewers concerned for the actor's safety. Catherine Lacey,
     whilst disappointing some at this point in the play, convinced at least one reviewer and
     perhaps one actor: 'She gives him a thorough good thrashing with a whip. To-night she
     cannot but have actually hurt Mr Neil Porter, who played the part admirably' (*Morning Post*,
     16 April 1935). Claire Luce was also enthusiastic: 'Will Clement Hamelin as the slave
     messenger (another small part well done) survive Cleopatra's man-handling till the end of
     the season?' (J.H.B., *Evesham Journal*, 5 May 1945). See also the references to Jackson at
     2.5.60 and Higgins at 2.5.62 SD.

67b–75   Cut, with all the references to Cleopatra's physical violence, in Phelps's production; at 67a,

I that do bring the news made not the match.
CLEOPATRA Say 'tis not so, a province I will give thee
And make thy fortunes proud. The blow thou hadst 70
Shall make thy peace for moving me to rage,
And I will boot thee with what gift beside
Thy modesty can beg.
MESSENGER He's married, madam.
CLEOPATRA Rogue, thou hast lived too long! *Draw a knife*
MESSENGER Nay then, I'll run.
What mean you, madam? I have made no fault. *Exit* 75
CHARMIAN Good madam, keep yourself within yourself.
The man is innocent.
CLEOPATRA Some innocents scape not the thunderbolt.
Melt Egypt into Nile, and kindly creatures
Turn all to serpents! Call the slave again. 80
Though I am mad, I will not bite him. Call!
CHARMIAN He is afeard to come.
CLEOPATRA I will not hurt him.
[*The Messenger is sent for*]

'*Alexas comes down and urges Mardian* [who was substituted for the messenger] *off*'
(promptbook).

74a SD This threat need not seem empty. In 1866 and 1867 Charmian caught the queen's arm when
she drew (Calvert's acting edition). Tree turned the knife into two scimitars in the hands of
others – 'the comic handling of Cleopatra's messenger by two black slaves armed with
scimitars, in the second act, came perilously near to spoiling a dramatic scene' (*Sportsman*,
28 December 1906) – but Glenda Jackson 'drew a knife from the folds of the messenger's
own clothes' (Scott, *Antony and Cleopatra*, p. 52) and threw it at the messenger's 'rapidly
disappearing back' (Benedict Nightingale, *What's on in London*, 13 July 1979); Jane
Lapotaire also throws it after the messenger, but without deliberate aim, in the BBC
television version. See also the reference to Higgins at 2.5.62 SD. Vanessa Redgrave, in her
1995 production, chased the messenger with a spear (Benedict Nightingale, *Times*, 6 June
1995).

82b SD A reviewer of Bridges-Adams's 1927 production objected to his 'allow[ing] the messenger . . .
to re-enter Cleopatra's presence of his own accord, although he has run away, and is,
according to Charmian, when he does not answer to her beckoning, "afeared to come". He
is surely too far off to hear the "serpent of old Nile's" words when she says, "I will not hurt
him", and would, one is convinced, not approach unless assured by Charmian or Iras that he
could do so with impunity . . . Mr John Laurie's Messenger is also delightful. How the man
can use his eyes!' (*Stratford-upon-Avon Herald*, 15 July 1927). Throughout the scene the
messenger's emotions can find expression in his eyes, and actors have made the most of the

These hands do lack nobility, that they strike
A meaner than myself, since I myself
Have given myself the cause.

Enter the MESSENGER *again*

                          Come hither, sir.   85
Though it be honest, it is never good
To bring bad news. Give to a gracious message
An host of tongues, but let ill tidings tell
Themselves when they be felt.
MESSENGER I have done my duty.   90
CLEOPATRA Is he married?
I cannot hate thee worser than I do
If thou again say 'Yes'.
MESSENGER   He's married, madam.
CLEOPATRA The gods confound thee, dost thou hold there still?
MESSENGER Should I lie, madam?
CLEOPATRA   O, I would thou didst,   95
So half my Egypt were submerged and made
A cistern for scaled snakes! Go, get thee hence.
Hadst thou Narcissus in thy face, to me
Thou wouldst appear most ugly. He is married?
MESSENGER I crave your highness' pardon.
CLEOPATRA   He is married?   100

opportunity at least since Tree's 'cowering, yet frank and determined, Messenger (a part played with admirable skill, and an effective display of the whites of the eyes, by Mr Charles Quartermaine)' (*Stage*, 3 January 1907).

83–5a   Collier's 'rage was convincing and her speaking of the[se] lines . . . was finely effective' (*Academy*, 5 January 1907); Claire Luce's delivery of the lines was 'simply and delicately moving' (*Stage*, 26 April 1945); Peggy Ashcroft was 'not simply the offended beauty wounded in her vanity, but the woman cut to the heart by the betrayal of a vital relationship. To hear Miss Ashcroft say: "These hands do lack nobility . . ." is to hear Cleopatra remembering what the wife of Antony should be, and "I am paid for't now" pricks the heart. So she paves the way for "Husband, I come . . ." in the last great pageant of immortality' (Ruth Ellis, *Stratford-upon-Avon Herald*, 1 May 1953).

85b   Glenda Jackson 'pressed his head close to her in despair before pacing up and down the stage in her frustration' (Scott, *Antony and Cleopatra*, p. 52). In Brewster's production Dona Croll 'captures the Egyptian dish's violent changeability not least in the way she first beats then butters up the hapless messenger' (Michael Billington, *Guardian*, 20 May 1991). See also the reference to Higgins at 2.5.62 SD.

100b   Helen Mirren 'sadly doubles herself up, holding her stomach as she moans' these words (Scott, *Antony and Cleopatra*, p. 74).

MESSENGER Take no offence that I would not offend you;
      To punish me for what you make me do
      Seems much unequal. He's married to Octavia.
CLEOPATRA O, that his fault should make a knave of thee,
      That art not what thou'rt sure of! Get thee hence.   105
      The merchandise which thou hast brought from Rome
      Are all too dear for me. Lie they upon thy hand,
      And be undone by 'em!
                                      [Exit Messenger]
CHARMIAN   Good your highness, patience.
CLEOPATRA In praising Antony, I have dispraised Caesar.
CHARMIAN Many times, madam.   110
CLEOPATRA I am paid for't now. Lead me from hence;
      I faint. O Iras, Charmian! – 'Tis no matter.
      Go to the fellow, good Alexas. Bid him
      Report the feature of Octavia, her years,
      Her inclination. Let him not leave out   115
      The colour of her hair. Bring me word quickly.
                               [Exit Alexas]
      Let him for ever go! – Let him not, Charmian.
      Though he be painted one way like a Gorgon,
      The other way's a Mars. *[To Mardian]* Bid you Alexas
      Bring me word how tall she is. – Pity me, Charmian,   120
      But do not speak to me. Lead me to my chamber.
                                    Exeunt

109–11 **In . . . now** Cut in Phelps's production (promptbook).

111 **I . . . now** See the comment on Ashcroft's performance at 2.5.83. Whiting's exit, 'weeping and surrounded by her women, was entirely feminine and a nice contrast to the next episode' (Lamb, *Antony and Cleopatra*, p. 159).

112 Glenda Jackson 'fell to her knees' here, 'but shook Charmian and Iras from her as they tried to help' (Scott, *Antony and Cleopatra*, p. 53).

117 With these words Jackson 'hugged her companion. There was no panic now but intense compassion' (Scott, *Antony and Cleopatra*, p. 53).

ACT 2, SCENE 6

[2.6] *Flourish. Enter* POMPEY [*and*] MENAS *at one door, with Drum and Trumpet; at another,* CAESAR, LEPIDUS, ANTONY, ENOBAR-BUS, MAECENAS, AGRIPPA, *with Soldiers marching*

POMPEY Your hostages I have, so have you mine,
 And we shall talk before we fight.
CAESAR   Most meet
 That first we come to words, and therefore have we
 Our written purposes before us sent,
 Which if thou hast considered, let us know   5
 If 'twill tie up thy discontented sword
 And carry back to Sicily much tall youth
 That else must perish here.
POMPEY   To you all three,
 The senators alone of this great world,
 Chief factors for the gods: I do not know   10
 Wherefore my father should revengers want,
 Having a son and friends, since Julius Caesar,
 Who at Philippi the good Brutus ghosted,
 There saw you labouring for him. What was't
 That moved pale Cassius to conspire? And what   15
 Made th'all-honoured, honest Roman, Brutus,
 With the armed rest, courtiers of beauteous freedom,
 To drench the Capitol, but that they would
 Have one man but a man? And that is it
 Hath made me rig my navy, at whose burden   20
 The angered ocean foams, with which I meant

<hr>

This, with the other Pompey scenes, was cut by Kemble, Chatterton, Asche in his Australian touring production and the Nunn–Scoffield television version.

1–83 Cut in Garrick's production (printed edition); the remainder of the scene (except 88–101) was set on board Pompey's galley and joined with the next.

14–16 **What . . . Brutus** In Caird's 1992 production 'Richard Johnson's Antony is a bit of a bluff roarer but at least he has an aura of vanished glory: he frets impatiently when Pompey starts tactlessly going on about pale Cassius and honest Brutus' (Michael Billington, *Guardian*, 7 November 1992).

To scourge th'ingratitude that despiteful Rome
Cast on my noble father.

CAESAR   Take your time.

ANTONY Thou canst not fear us, Pompey, with thy sails.
We'll speak with thee at sea. At land thou know'st   25
How much we do o'ercount thee.

POMPEY   At land indeed
Thou dost o'ercount me of my father's house;
But since the cuckoo builds not for himself,
Remain in't as thou mayst.

LEPIDUS   Be pleased to tell us –
For this is from the present – how you take   30
The offers we have sent you.

CAESAR   There's the point.

ANTONY Which do not be entreated to, but weigh
What it is worth embraced.

CAESAR   And what may follow
To try a larger fortune.

POMPEY   You have made me offer
Of Sicily, Sardinia; and I must   35
Rid all the sea of pirates; then, to send
Measures of wheat to Rome. This 'greed upon,
To part with unhacked edges and bear back
Our targes undinted.

CAESAR, ANTONY, LEPIDUS   That's our offer.

POMPEY   Know then
I came before you here a man prepared   40
To take this offer. But Mark Antony
Put me to some impatience. Though I lose
The praise of it by telling, you must know,
When Caesar and your brother were at blows,
Your mother came to Sicily, and did find   45
Her welcome friendly.

ANTONY   I have heard it, Pompey,
And am well studied for a liberal thanks
Which I do owe you.

POMPEY   Let me have your hand.
               [*They shake hands*]
I did not think, sir, to have met you here.

42–57   **Though … Lepidus**   Cut in Phelps's production (promptbook).

48b SD   In Brook's production David Suchet's Pompey 'begins with loudly unselfconfident blustering and then seizes Antony's patronising hand of friendship with intense relief' (Irving Wardle, *Times*, 11 October 1978).

ANTONY The beds i'th'East are soft; and thanks to you, 50
     That called me timelier than my purpose hither,
     For I have gained by't.
CAESAR   Since I saw you last,
     There's a change upon you.
POMPEY   Well, I know not
     What counts harsh fortune casts upon my face,
     But in my bosom shall she never come 55
     To make my heart her vassal.
LEPIDUS   Well met here.
POMPEY I hope so, Lepidus. Thus we are agreed.
     I crave our composition may be written
     And sealed between us.
CAESAR   That's the next to do.
POMPEY We'll feast each other ere we part, and let's 60
     Draw lots who shall begin.
ANTONY   That will I, Pompey.
POMPEY No, Antony, take the lot. But, first or last,
     Your fine Egyptian cookery shall have
     The fame. I have heard that Julius Caesar
     Grew fat with feasting there. 65
ANTONY You have heard much.
POMPEY I have fair meanings, sir.
ANTONY And fair words to them.
POMPEY Then so much have I heard.
     And I have heard Apollodorus carried – 70
ENOBARBUS No more of that. He did so.
POMPEY   What, I pray you?
ENOBARBUS A certain queen to Caesar in a mattress.
POMPEY I know thee now. How far'st thou, soldier?
ENOBARBUS   Well,
     And well am like to do, for I perceive
     Four feasts are toward.
POMPEY   Let me shake thy hand. 75
     I never hated thee. I have seen thee fight
     When I have envied thy behaviour.
ENOBARBUS   Sir,
     I never loved you much, but I ha' praised ye
     When you have well deserved ten times as much
     As I have said you did.
POMPEY   Enjoy thy plainness; 80
     It nothing ill becomes thee.
     Aboard my galley I invite you all.
     Will you lead, lords?
CAESAR, ANTONY, LEPIDUS Show's the way, sir.

POMPEY   Come.

Exeunt. Enobarbus and Menas remain

MENAS [*Aside*] Thy father, Pompey, would ne'er have made this
    treaty. – You and I have known, sir.   85

ENOBARBUS At sea, I think.

MENAS We have, sir.

ENOBARBUS You have done well by water.

MENAS And you by land.

ENOBARBUS I will praise any man that will praise me, though it   90
    cannot be denied what I have done by land.

MENAS Nor what I have done by water.

ENOBARBUS Yes, something you can deny for your own safety: you
    have been a great thief by sea.

MENAS And you by land.   95

ENOBARBUS There I deny my land service. But give me your hand,
    Menas. If our eyes had authority, here they might take two thieves
    kissing.

MENAS All men's faces are true, whatsome'er their hands are.

ENOBARBUS But there is never a fair woman has a true face.   100

MENAS No slander, they steal hearts.

ENOBARBUS We came hither to fight with you.

MENAS For my part, I am sorry it is turned to a drinking. Pompey
    doth this day laugh away his fortune.

ENOBARBUS If he do, sure he cannot weep't back again.   105

MENAS You've said, sir. We looked not for Mark Antony here. Pray
    you, is he married to Cleopatra?

ENOBARBUS Caesar's sister is called Octavia.

MENAS True, sir. She was the wife of Caius Marcellus.

ENOBARBUS But she is now the wife of Marcus Antonius.   110

MENAS Pray ye, sir?

ENOBARBUS 'Tis true.

MENAS Then is Caesar and he for ever knit together.

ENOBARBUS If I were bound to divine of this unity, I would not
    prophesy so.   115

MENAS I think the policy of that purpose made more in the marriage
    than the love of the parties.

ENOBARBUS I think so, too. But you shall find the band that seems
    to tie their friendship together will be the very strangler of their
    amity: Octavia is of a holy, cold, and still conversation.   120

---

50 **The . . . soft** In Caird's 1992 production Richard Johnson was 'heavy handed in politics and
    avuncular in love: when he says [this line] he might be recommending the Alexandria Hilton'
    (Robert Hewison, *Sunday Times*, 8 November 1992).

60–81 **and . . . thee** Cut in Phelps's production (promptbook).

MENAS Who would not have his wife so?

ENOBARBUS Not he that himself is not so, which is Mark Antony.
He will to his Egyptian dish again. Then shall the sighs of Octavia
blow the fire up in Caesar, and, as I said before, that which is the
strength of their amity shall prove the immediate author of their 125
variance. Antony will use his affection where it is. He married
but his occasion here.

MENAS And thus it may be. Come, sir, will you aboard? I have a
health for you.

ENOBARBUS I shall take it, sir. We have used our throats in Egypt. 130

MENAS Come, let's away.

Exeunt

ACT 2, SCENE 7

According to H. Neville Davies ('Jacobean *Antony and Cleopatra*', p. 141), the galley scene got its impetus from the 1606 festivities in which James I and Christian of Denmark feasted on board ship; if this is so, audiences at the first performances may have found additional topical interest in this partly satirical scene of 'the banquetting sovereigns of the world as drunk as cobblers', as one reviewer of Phelps's production put it (*Illustrated London News*, 27 October 1849). In the same politico-satirical spirit, Peter Hall asked his actors 'for an image of excess: "As if, after Yalta, Stalin is stuffed with food, Churchill reeling about . . ."' (Lowen, *Peter Hall*, p. 17).

Kemble cut the galley scene with the character of Pompey (printed edition). Macready's production kept the scene but cut the revelry. Chatterton, omitting Pompey, replaced the galley scene with a celebration of Antony and Octavia's marriage: 'The scene is in Rome, and a festival is supposed to take place in honour of the wedding of Antony and Octavia, in which we are treated with four processions, and a new song, the music composed by Mr W. C. Levey, words from Shakespeare, sung by Miss Banks and a choir of thirty boys, which was honoured with an encore, and followed by a ballet, called the path of flowers, the principal dancer being Mdlle. A. Gedda' (*Illustrated London News*, 27 September 1873). Asche eliminated the galley scene, with Pompey, in his Australian touring production, as does the Nunn–Scoffield television version, where, as in Chatterton's production, the party is retained as a post-nuptial celebration. Phillips's 1985 Chichester production, which de-emphasised the play's political elements, omitted the galley scene.

Other directors have been happy enough with the opportunities offered by Shakespeare's scene, but until Helpmann's production, most of them concentrated on the rollicking. Of Phelps's production one reviewer wrote 'Mr Phelps, in particular, aided the pictorial, by his well-studied bacchanalian attitudes' (*Illustrated London News*, 27 October 1849); the *Examiner* critic thought 'the drunken revel in Pompey's galley was overdone; but the intention of the scene had been thoroughly understood by Mr Phelps, and its breadth of execution at least roused the audience to a very hearty strain of enjoyment, highly useful at that point of the acted play' (27 October 1849). The 1866 and 1867 productions had '*laughter and shouts – dance of* Bacchanals, *and the Act closes upon a tableau of wild hilarity*' (Calvert's acting edition). In Benson's 1898 production, 'a very notable and striking scene was that on Pompey's galley, where all the great generals meet in a happy carouse, and finish up with the song – "Come, thou monarch . . .", and join in a sort of drunken dance' (*Worcester Daily Times*, 16 April 1898). The galley in Tree's production was predictably lavish – 'Mr Tree throws himself into the part with his usual energy, and in the

Bacchanalian Soirée on board the millionaire Pompey's galley, he enters thoroughly into the sport of the thing' (*Pelican*, 2 January 1907) – but Frank Harris felt alienated: 'The drunken scene was hideously exaggerated: it quickly degenerated into a bestial scene that would have suited Commodus or Caligula, but not this Caesar. Shakespeare condemns the whole scene through the mouth of Caesar, and Mr Tree exaggerates the animality of it, and makes it a brutish revel from beginning to end' (*Vanity Fair*, 2 January 1907). Brutish or not, Tree was not content with Shakespeare's drunken dance, but devised a shipboard ballet. The *Daily Mail* critic – 'the much-advertised "ballet" on board Pompey's galley resolved itself into a rather feeble little skip' (28 December 1906) – was less impressed than the reviewer from *The Stage*: 'The scene of revelry ... is graced by the presence of a body of dancing girls, arrayed almost in Coan purple, who perform an intoxicating dance (arranged by Carlo Coppi) upon the lower deck of a vessel as substantial in appearance as the Ship in Mr Tree's production of *The Tempest*' (3 January 1907).

In Bridges-Adams's production of 1921 the galley scene was one of 'the most striking', and the 'reaction of the principal characters under wine was admirably varied' (F.A.C., *Birmingham Gazette*, 25 April 1921). In Iden Payne's 'the painted cloth of Pompey's galley was so garish in colouring that it was difficult for the actors to achieve their proper importance against such a background' (P.D.H., *Leamington Chronicle*, 19 April 1935) and 'the carousal on the barge was rather a waterish revel' (Ivor Brown, *Observer*, 21 April 1935). In Jean-Louis Barrault's 1945 production at the Comédie-Française, the galley scene, 'perfect as it is in balance and grouping, introduces an element of *grand spectacle* which diverts the attention and ... breaks the spell' (Fluchère, 'Shakespeare in France', p. 123), but in Byam Shaw's 1946 production 'the excesses of the feast scene were given point by the presence of a wonderfully lean-and-hungry looking Caesar' (Stephen Potter, *New Statesman*, 4 January 1947) and the Caesar, Michael Goodliffe, 'held aloof from the revels' in a 'self-conscious way' (Crosse, *Shakespearean Playgoing*, p. 151). Venezky named this as one of Olivier's 'memorable' scenes in Benthall's production ('Current Shakespearian Productions', p. 336), but the *Times* critic said 'at the drinking bout he is least effective' (12 May 1951); Byam Shaw set a good pace in 1953: 'when the captains carouse aboard the galley, he keeps the guests briskly a-riot' (T.C.K., *Birmingham Post*, 29 April 1953), but Marius Goring's Caesar was 'the spectre at the feast' (E.R.A., *Nottingham Guardian*, 30 April 1953).

Helpmann's production in 1957 recognised the structural significance of the scene, as of 2.2. Anthony Cookman (*Tatler*, 20 March 1957) praised the way in which Helpmann 'paid great attention' to this 'crucial' scene and in which Keith Michell showed Antony's renewed pleasure in 'outdoing his rivals'. Nunn's galley scene was in the mode of 'rugger-club rowdiness' (B. A. Young, *Financial Times*, 16 August 1972); J. W. Lambert found it 'brilliantly frightful' (*Sunday Times*, 20 August 1972). In the Nunn–Scoffield television version the rowdy celebration, which seems mainly to be concerned with male bonding and drinking as a test of manhood, 'is not on Pompey's galley but is a bachelor party *after* the wedding, a placement in time that does not suggest Antony's eagerness to be with his new wife'

[2.7] *Music plays. Enter two or three* SERVANTS *with a banquet*

1 SERVANT Here they'll be, man. Some o'their plants are ill-rooted
    already; the least wind i'th'world will blow them down.
2 SERVANT Lepidus is high-coloured.
1 SERVANT They have made him drink alms-drink.

(Coursen, *Shakespearean Performance*, p. 192). Brook's galley scene 'works, like some of
the best scenes in *Evita*, by going on just the vital bit longer and more intensely than you
would think possible. (Richard Peaslee's music, here and throughout, has unusual
distinction)' (Robert Cushman, *Observer*, 15 October 1978) and by using mechanical means
and character interaction to show how the structure of society itself collapses: 'he can lower
a red carpet for the monument, or raise a dun-coloured one, to tip the revellers on
Pompey's galley into a drunken sprawl' (John Elsom, *Listener*, 19 October 1978). Impending
change and betrayal were also suggested in Hall's production by the designer's allusion to
the symbolic conventions of Renaissance painting: 'To create Chitty's *Last Supper* image,
three trestles make up a table facing the audience, with stools positioned along the upstage
side' (Lowen, *Peter Hall*, p. 17). In Brewster's production her 'most original touch is her
interpretation of Octavius Caesar as not just a cold calculator but a murderous pragmatist.
At the end of the scene aboard Pompey's galley he has his host quietly strangled and later
sees his political partner, Lepidus, taken into custody. The former idea runs clean against the
text . . . But one forgives it since Octavius is marvellously played by Ben Thomas' (Michael
Billington, *Guardian,* 20 May 1991). Pompey was stabbed at the end of the scene in Vanessa
Redgrave's 1995 production, where 'Enobarbus takes it upon himself to kill' him (Jane
Edwardes, *Time Out*, 7 June 1995) and Lepidus, suddenly struck blind, was left 'blundering
helplessly about with a white stick'. Benedict Nightingale asked 'Does Redgrave really think
that men who get blind drunk end up blind sober?' (*Times*, 6 June 1995). Rutter's galley
scene was 'defiantly northern in character. Pompey's party takes place to the
accompaniment of Lepidus on skiffle and Enobarbus on guitar, and the drink comes in
bottles of brown or maybe pale ale from a red plastic container embossed with the name of
Scottish and Newcastle Breweries' (Benedict Nightingale, *Times*, 5 October 1995).

0 SD On the Jacobean stage, two or three servants would have sufficed because the portable
banquet was a stock property, with additional items brought out as and when required. The
hautboys who play '*under the stage*' in 4.3 may well have provided the music here, either on
the stage or '*aloft*'. In Hack's 1983 production 'the boozers provide their own music and the
remaining sound effects are by Stephen Gilbert – an eerie, doom-ridden barrage of organ
and percussion' (Rosalind Carne, *Guardian*, in *London Theatre Record*, 9–22 April 1983, p.
297).

4–15 Cut in Garrick's production (printed edition); Phelps's cut 10–15 (promptbook) and 1–15
were omitted in 1866 and 1867 (Calvert's acting edition).

2 SERVANT As they pinch one another by the disposition, he cries 5
out, 'No more', reconciles them to his entreaty, and himself to
the drink.

1 SERVANT But it raises the greater war between him and his
discretion.

2 SERVANT Why, this it is to have a name in great men's fellowship. 10
I had as lief have a reed that will do me no service as a partisan
I could not heave.

1 SERVANT To be called into a huge sphere, and not to be seen to
move in't, are the holes where eyes should be, which pitifully
disaster the cheeks. 15

A sennet sounded. Enter CAESAR, ANTONY, POMPEY, LEPIDUS,
AGRIPPA, MAECENAS, ENOBARBUS, MENAS, *with other Captains*
[*and a* BOY]

ANTONY [*To Caesar*] Thus do they, sir: they take the flow o'th'Nile
By certain scales i'th'Pyramid; they know,
By the height, the lowness, or the mean if dearth
Or foison follow. The higher Nilus swells,
The more it promises; as it ebbs, the seedsman 20
Upon the slime and ooze scatters his grain,
And shortly comes to harvest.

LEPIDUS You've strange serpents there.

ANTONY Ay, Lepidus.

LEPIDUS Your serpent of Egypt is bred now of your mud by the 25
operation of your sun; so is your crocodile.

15 SD Ceremonial trumpet calls alerted Jacobean audiences to the arrival of the politically
powerful: the Folio directions do not distinguish carefully between the sennet, traditionally
associated with the entry of a group of important people, as here, and the flourish, usually
associated with individual entries or exits, but used for multiple ones in this play (see, e.g.,
1.1.10 SD, 2.2.182 SD; 2.7.127 SD is rather boisterous, in the aftermath of the carousing). The
entrance in Phelps's production has '*Enobarbus leading Lepidus*' (promptbook); in Brook's
'the drunken world leaders enter[ed] with . . . faintly exaggerated tip-toe care' (Michael
Billington, *Guardian*, 11 October 1978). Noble's production dispensed with flamboyant
fanfares and processions, 'demonstrat[ing] that the text can be no less fascinating as
chamber music than as grand opera' (Stanley Wells, *Times Literary Supplement*, 29 October
1982).

25–6 In Iden Payne's production, 'Mr Kay Souper made a nice donnish figure of poor Lepidus'
(Ivor Brown, *Observer*, 21 April 1935); in Byam Shaw's of 1953, Donald Pleasence had 'an
excellent scene in which he gives the drunken Lepidus the immemorial, fatuous wisdom
of the intoxicated' (Harold Hobson, *Sunday Times*, 3 May 1953).

ANTONY They are so.

POMPEY Sit – and some wine. A health to Lepidus!

[*They sit and drink*]

LEPIDUS I am not so well as I should be, but I'll ne'er out.

ENOBARBUS Not till you have slept; I fear me you'll be in till then.   30

LEPIDUS Nay, certainly, I have heard the Ptolemies' pyramises are
   very goodly things. Without contradiction I have heard that.

MENAS [*Aside to Pompey*] Pompey, a word.

POMPEY [*Aside to Menas*]   Say in mine ear, what is 't?

MENAS (*Whispers in 's ear*) Forsake thy seat, I do beseech thee, captain,
   And hear me speak a word.   35

POMPEY [*Aside to Menas*] Forbear me till anon. – This wine for
   Lepidus!

LEPIDUS What manner o'thing is your crocodile?

ANTONY It is shaped, sir, like itself, and it is as broad as it hath
   breadth. It is just so high as it is, and moves with it own organs. It
   lives by that which nourisheth it, and the elements once out of it,   40
   it transmigrates.

LEPIDUS What colour is it of?

ANTONY Of it own colour too.

26, 31   **crocodile, pyramises** In Tree's version, 'Mr Norman Forbes plays a low comedy Roman
      Sportsman, who wreathes his brow with flowers, and looking on the wine when it is red,
      experiences a not unnatural difficulty in giving clear expression to such words as
      "crocodiles" and "pyramids"' (*Pelican*, 2 January 1907). Esmond Knight's Lepidus has a
      similar problem in the BBC television version.

28   In Tree's production, 'when Pompey casually cries "Sit" in the galley scene, Lepidus flops on
      the floor' (H. Hamilton Fyfe, *Pall Mall Gazette*, 2 January 1907).

33b   In Tree's version 'Mr Julian L'Estrange made an excellent Pompey; but if he will look at the
      part again he will not talk as if he were drunk when his friend Menas counsels him to cut the
      cable and make himself the master of the world' (Frank Harris, *Vanity Fair*, 2 January 1907);
      'Lepidus . . . supplied the "comic relief" in the gallery scene quite cleverly, his business with
      the ballet girls "at back", while Menas was making his proposals of assassination to Pompey,
      being very funny indeed' (*Era*, 29 December 1906). In Komisarjevsky's production, 'As
      Menas, Mr Lawrence Anderson elected for a gum-chewing gangster of our own day' (Agate,
      Brief Chronicles, p. 184).

36   **This . . . Lepidus** A reviewer of Tree's production protested 'Lepidus plays the chief comic
      part. But surely it is carrying realism too far to spit wine out on to the stage, by way of
      indicating that he cannot drink any more' (*Evening News*, 28 December 1906).

38–41   'Out of this passage [Tree] coaxed a fantastic humour' (*Speaker*, 2 January 1907). Kate
      Kellaway was generally disappointed with Richard Johnson in Caird's 1993 production but
      said 'he *is* good at crocodile impersonations' (*Observer*, 30 May 1993).

LEPIDUS 'Tis a strange serpent.

ANTONY 'Tis so, and the tears of it are wet. 45

CAESAR Will this description satisfy him?

ANTONY With the health that Pompey gives him, else he is a very
    epicure.

                      [Menas whispers again]

POMPEY *[Aside to Menas]* Go hang, sir, hang! Tell me of that? Away!
    Do as I bid you. – Where's this cup I called for? 50

MENAS *[Aside to Pompey]* If for the sake of merit thou wilt hear me,
    Rise from thy stool.

POMPEY *[Aside to Menas]*   I think thou'rt mad.

          [He rises, and they walk aside]

                                The matter?

MENAS I have ever held my cap off to thy fortunes.

POMPEY Thou hast served me with much faith. What's else to say? –
    Be jolly, lords.

ANTONY   These quicksands, Lepidus, 55
    Keep off them, for you sink.

          [Menas and Pompey speak aside]

MENAS Wilt thou be lord of all the world?

POMPEY   What say'st thou?

MENAS Wilt thou be lord of the whole world? That's twice.

POMPEY How should that be?

MENAS   But entertain it,
    And, though thou think me poor, I am the man 60
    Will give thee all the world.

POMPEY   Hast thou drunk well?

MENAS No, Pompey, I have kept me from the cup.
    Thou art, if thou dar'st be, the earthly Jove.
    Whate'er the ocean pales or sky inclips
    Is thine, if thou wilt ha't.

POMPEY   Show me which way. 65

MENAS These three world-sharers, these competitors,
    Are in thy vessel. Let me cut the cable,
    And when we are put off, fall to their throats.
    All there is thine.

POMPEY   Ah, this thou shouldst have done
    And not have spoke on't! In me 'tis villainy; 70

---

62 In Hall's production, 'the hardheaded clarity of Michael Carter's Menas, who alone has
    abstained, stands out' (Lowen, *Peter Hall*, p. 111).

66–9a In Noble's production, 'Menas's suggestion to Pompey that he bump off these triple rulers
    of the world flits by so fast that the vulnerability of power is never fully grasped' (Michael
    Billington, *Guardian*, 14 October 1982).

In thee't had been good service. Thou must know,
'Tis not my profit that does lead mine honour;
Mine honour, it. Repent that e'er thy tongue
Hath so betrayed thine act. Being done unknown,
I should have found it afterwards well done,   75
But must condemn it now. Desist, and drink.
                    [*He returns to the feast*]
MENAS [*Aside*] For this, I'll never follow thy palled fortunes more.
        Who seeks and will not take when once 'tis offered
        Shall never find it more.
POMPEY   This health to Lepidus!
ANTONY Bear him ashore. I'll pledge it for him, Pompey.   80
ENOBARBUS Here's to thee, Menas!
                    [*They drink*]
MENAS   Enobarbus, welcome!
POMPEY Fill till the cup be hid.
ENOBARBUS There's a strong fellow, Menas.
        [*He points to the Servant who carries off Lepidus*]
MENAS   Why?
ENOBARBUS   A bears
        The third part of the world, man; see'st not?
MENAS The third part, then, is drunk. Would it were all,   85
        That it might go on wheels!
ENOBARBUS Drink thou; increase the reels.
MENAS Come.
POMPEY This is not yet an Alexandrian feast.
ANTONY It ripens towards it. Strike the vessels, ho!   90

---

77 **For this** Menas delivered these words '*looking contemptibly after him*' in Garrick's
    production (printed edition).

78–9a Cut in Phelps's production (promptbook).

83a In Tree's version Lepidus was carried out by Antony and Caesar with the aid of Pompey
    and Enobarbus; that exit and the dances, claimed one reviewer, 'furnishe[d] the only bit
    of comedy of the evening' (*Truth*, 2 January 1907).

90 **Strike . . . ho** In Phelps's production '*they rise and wave their goblets as striking them*'
    (promptbook); in 1866 and 1867 the revellers also showed their eagerness for refills: '*They
    all rise and come forward, waving their goblets*' at 89 (Calvert's acting edition). In Benson's
    1912 production, 'Mr Benson's Mark Antony had its trifling blemishes. He poured a great
    deal more wine, for instance, into his helmet in the galley scene than ever he drank out of it,
    but property cups are dangerous things' (*Birmingham Daily Post*, 24 April 1912). A similar
    lack of verisimilitude characterised Bridges-Adams's galley scene in 1924: 'There was a
    tendency to bombast in one or two of these lesser military, and we could have wished that

Here's to Caesar.
CAESAR   I could well forbear't.
    It's monstrous labour when I wash my brain
    And it grow fouler.
ANTONY   Be a child o'th'time.
CAESAR Possess it, I'll make answer;
    But I had rather fast from all, four days,   95
    Than drink so much in one.
ENOBARBUS [*To Antony*]   Ha, my brave emperor,
    Shall we dance now the Egyptian Bacchanals,
    And celebrate our drink?
POMPEY Let's ha't, good soldier.
ANTONY Come, let's all take hands,   100
    Till that the conquering wine hath steeped our sense
    In soft and delicate Lethe.
ENOBARBUS   All take hands.
    Make battery to our ears with the loud music,
    The while I'll place you; then the boy shall sing.
    The holding every man shall bear as loud   105
    As his strong sides can volley.
    Music plays. Enobarbus places them hand in hand

the wine in Pompey's galley had been of a more cheerful red. It was, however, a hot night to revel with empty cups, and we scarcely blame this supper party, though it did seem rather self-consciously hilarious' (*Times*, 16 July 1924).

91a   In the Nunn–Scoffield television version, Antony's delivery of 'Caesar' is drawn out and mocking (and repeated by his followers as they echo his toast).

94-6a   Caesar's preference for abstemiousness was cut in Garrick's production (printed edition) and in Phelps's (91b–96a; promptbook).

96b-8   In Brook's production, 'Enobarbus is not a semi-detached observer to the revels, but a hotblooded participant, somebody who eggs Antony on, rather than restrains him' (John Elsom, *Listener*, 19 October 1978).

106 SD   Kahn's 1972 production featured, among the carousing, a male bellydance (see Cooper, *American Shakespeare Theater*, p. 169). Antony's followers are the dancers in the Nunn–Scoffield television version, and when they catch Caesar up in their revelry, he is rescued by his guard's closing ranks around him. In Brook's production, 'a boy singer is rather suggestively whirled around Antony's waist like an Apache dancer; pillows are flung and benches overturned as the dancers circle the stage in leaps and bounds like minor Baryshnikovs; and eventually the floor cloth rises into the air and becomes a huge sail to the furls of which Antony precariously clings. It is a magnificent piece of voluptuous staging' (Michael Billington, *Guardian*, 11 October 1978). In Noble's 1982 version, 'the song is performed on the upper level by a nearly naked, curiously pallid youth while his seniors

The Song

BOY [*Sings*] Come thou monarch of the vine,
     Plumpy Bacchus with pink eyne!
     In thy fats our cares be drowned,
     With thy grapes our hairs be crowned.   110
ALL   Cup us till the world go round,
         Cup us till the world go round.
CAESAR What would you more? Pompey, good night. Good brother,
     Let me request you off. Our graver business
     Frowns at this levity. Gentle lords, let's part;   115
     You see we have burnt our cheeks. Strong Enobarb
     Is weaker than the wine, and mine own tongue
     Splits what it speaks. The wild disguise hath almost
     Anticked us all. What needs more words? Good night.
     Good Antony, your hand.
POMPEY   I'll try you on the shore.   120
ANTONY And shall, sir. Give's your hand.
POMPEY   O Antony,
     You have my father's house. But what? We are friends.
     Come down into the boat.

dance below him, after which he swallow-dives into their upraised arms and ends up consoling Enobarbus. As Pompey, Clive Wood strips off his shirt, revealing his well-known ginger chest-hairs, and kisses Antony. There is a suggestion that the abundant sexuality of these warriors seeks satisfaction whatever the circumstances' (Stanley Wells, *Times Literary Supplement*, 29 October 1982).

110 At this point in Phelps's production '*characters leave go hands and turn riotously for their goblets gesticulating and using every means to impart hilarity to the scene*' (promptbook).

114 **Let . . . off** Ken Bones, in the Robertson–Selbie production, 'excels at repressed menace, as when he is soon out-drunk, out-danced and humiliated in the carousing scene, out of his element in the robust merry-making (a man's world, the army). He strides off angrily; a dangerous enemy has been made' (Martin Hoyle, *Plays and Players*, September 1986). In Hall's production, 'after they have danced "the Egyptian bacchanals" [Hopkins] falls to the ground, pulling down Tim Pigott-Smith and, satyr-like, entangling limbs with him. (This gives Caesar ample cause for [this line])' (Lowen, *Peter Hall*, p. 110).

115–19 **Gentle . . . all** Cut in Phelps's production (promptbook).

116–17 **Strong . . . wine** In preparation for these lines in Brook's production, Enobarbus 'fell off a bench, pulling it on top of him and embracing it' (Hunt and Reeves, *Peter Brook*, p. 230).

121a **And . . . sir** At this point, Garrick's production inserted 2.3.38b–40a ('I will to Egypt . . . my pleasure lies'), in an aside (printed edition).

121a–3a **Give's . . . boat** In Noble's 1983 revival, the masculinity of Rome found 'release' in 'orgiastic

ENOBARBUS   Take heed you fall not.
                       [*Exeunt all but Enobarbus and Menas*]
              Menas, I'll not on shore.
MENAS   No, to my cabin.
              These drums, these trumpets, flutes! What!   125
              Let Neptune hear we bid a loud farewell
              To these great fellows. Sound and be hanged, sound out!
                       Sound a flourish, with drums
ENOBARBUS Hoo! says a. There's my cap.
                       [*He flings his cap in the air*]
MENAS Hoo! Noble captain, come.
                                                              Exeunt

drinking parties, where, in the heat of the moment, Antony [Michael Gambon] and
Pompeius (Clive Wood) fall into an almost homosexual clinch' (Clare Colvin, *Times*, 14 April
1983). In the 1983 production at the Young Vic, Keith Baxter 'left the scene hoisting Octavius
. . . in one hand and his host in the other' (*Times*, 23 April 1983).

123b   Emrys James collapses drunkenly as he says this in the BBC television version.

128   In Phelps's production '*All the characters are enwreathed*' for this scene and at the end of it
       '*they throw up their wreathes &c making a noisy demonstration of mirth*' (promptbook).

ACT 3, SCENE I

[3.1] *Enter* VENTIDIUS, *as it were in triumph* [*with* SILIUS, *and other Romans, Officers, and Soldiers*], *the dead body of Pacorus borne before him*

VENTIDIUS Now, darting Parthia, art thou struck, and now
         Pleased Fortune does of Marcus Crassus' death
         Make me revenger. Bear the king's son's body
         Before our army. Thy Pacorus, Orodes,
         Pays this for Marcus Crassus.
SILIUS   Noble Ventidius,   5

In the first performances Pacorus's body is likely to have been carried on a litter (see the commentary at 5.2.350). Granville-Barker appreciated 'the contrasting of the soldiers at their duty with the rulers at their drinking bout' and 'the dramatic value to the spectator of the quick shift' (*Prefaces*, p. 121), but this scene was usually cut from the time of Garrick until Brook's production in 1978, though Nunn's included it in the 1973 Aldwych revival (promptbook). Noble omitted it in 1982, as does the BBC television version. Of its omission in Benthall's production, Rylands said it 'spares Antony a sorry mark of shabbiness' ('Festival Shakespeare', p. 141). Bernard Levin wrote of Brook's production, 'the scene is set in a plastic shell. Inside is a world of relationships; outside, battle. Twice the "real" world makes its presence felt; once when the enemy outside pelts the walls of the shell with great gobbets of blood, and again when the Parthian war scene (usually cut) erupts through the gaps in the screen to defile the sanctuary itself . . . for in the text of this scene Pacorus is already dead; Mr Brook has him butchered before our eyes, just when we have been feasting with the quatuorvirs on Pompey's galley . . . and the abruptness of the transition makes the point with shocking violence' (*Sunday Times*, 15 October 1978). John Elsom commented further on the thematic point made by running 'Pompey's party, dangerous and erotic in its brutal comradeliness, into the battle on Syria's plains, another kind of orgy altogether . . . Brook runs the two scenes together, as if one were the extension of the other; but without Jacobs's set, this elision would have seemed cumbersome' (*Listener*, 19 October 1978). Another reviewer liked the 'inspired use of droning music to sustain tension. This resolved into a euphoric drunken Roman romp cutting suddenly into a horrifying murder scene with crashing timpani' (*Kentish Mercury*, 19 July 1979). In Zadek's production in Edinburgh, the 'stupefying bender' on Pompey's galley was 'instantly followed' by this scene, 'show[ing] us the grim reality of war: we get blood-smirched victors, suspended corpses and the melancholy strain of an harmonica' (Michael Billington, *Guardian Weekly*, 28 August 1994).

Whilst yet with Parthian blood thy sword is warm,
The fugitive Parthians follow. Spur through Media,
Mesopotamia, and the shelters whither
The routed fly. So thy grand captain, Antony,
Shall set thee on triumphant chariots and   10
Put garlands on thy head.
VENTIDIUS   O Silius, Silius,
I have done enough. A lower place, note well,
May make too great an act. For learn this, Silius:
Better to leave undone than by our deed
Acquire too high a fame when him we serve's away.   15
Caesar and Antony have ever won
More in their officer than person. Sossius,
One of my place in Syria, his lieutenant,
For quick accumulation of renown,
Which he achieved by th'minute, lost his favour.   20
Who does i'th'wars more than his captain can
Becomes his captain's captain; and ambition,
The soldier's virtue, rather makes choice of loss
Than gain which darkens him.
I could do more to do Antonius good,   25
But 'twould offend him, and in his offence
Should my performance perish.
SILIUS Thou hast, Ventidius, that
Without the which a soldier and his sword
Grants scarce distinction. Thou wilt write to Antony?   30
VENTIDIUS I'll humbly signify what in his name,
That magical word of war, we have effected:
How with his banners and his well-paid ranks
The ne'er-yet-beaten horse of Parthia
We have jaded out o'th'field.
SILIUS   Where is he now?   35
VENTIDIUS He purposeth to Athens, whither, with what haste
The weight we must convey with's will permit,
We shall appear before him. – On, there; pass along!
                                                        Exeunt

ACT 3, SCENE 2

[3.2] *Enter* AGRIPPA *at one door,* ENOBARBUS *at another*

AGRIPPA What, are the brothers parted?
ENOBARBUS They have dispatched with Pompey; he is gone.
   The other three are sealing. Octavia weeps
   To part from Rome; Caesar is sad; and Lepidus
   Since Pompey's feast, as Menas says, is troubled   5
   With the green-sickness.
AGRIPPA   'Tis a noble Lepidus.
ENOBARBUS A very fine one. O, how he loves Caesar!
AGRIPPA Nay, but how dearly he adores Mark Antony!
ENOBARBUS Caesar? Why, he's the Jupiter of men.
AGRIPPA What's Antony? The god of Jupiter.   10
ENOBARBUS Spake you of Caesar? How, the nonpareil!
AGRIPPA O Antony, O thou Arabian bird!
ENOBARBUS Would you praise Caesar, say 'Caesar', go no further.
AGRIPPA Indeed, he plied them both with excellent praises.
ENOBARBUS But he loves Caesar best; yet he loves Antony: 15
   Hoo! Hearts, tongues, figures, scribes, bards, poets, cannot
   Think, speak, cast, write, sing, number, hoo!
   His love to Antony. But as for Caesar,
   Kneel down, kneel down, and wonder.
AGRIPPA   Both he loves.
ENOBARBUS They are his shards, and he their beetle.
   [*Trumpets within*]
             So;   20
   This is to horse. Adieu, noble Agrippa.
AGRIPPA Good fortune, worthy soldier, and farewell.

   Enter CAESAR, ANTONY, LEPIDUS, *and* OCTAVIA

ANTONY No further, sir.
CAESAR You take from me a great part of myself;
   Use me well in't. – Sister, prove such a wife   25
   As my thoughts make thee, and as my farthest bond

Omitted in Garrick's production (printed edition), Phelps's (promptbook) and in 1866 and
1867 (Calvert's acting edition).

Shall pass on thy approof. – Most noble Antony,
Let not the piece of virtue which is set
Betwixt us as the cement of our love
To keep it builded, be the ram to batter 30
The fortress of it; for better might we
Have loved without this mean, if on both parts
This be not cherished.

ANTONY   Make me not offended
In your distrust.

CAESAR   I have said.

ANTONY   You shall not find,
Though you be therein curious, the least cause 35
For what you seem to fear. So the gods keep you,
And make the hearts of Romans serve your ends!
We will here part.

CAESAR Farewell, my dearest sister, fare thee well.
The elements be kind to thee, and make 40
Thy spirits all of comfort! Fare thee well.

OCTAVIA My noble brother! [*She weeps*]

ANTONY The April's in her eyes; it is love's spring,
And these the showers to bring it on. – Be cheerful.

OCTAVIA [*To Caesar*] Sir, look well to my husband's house; and – 45

CAESAR What, Octavia?

OCTAVIA   I'll tell you in your ear.
[*She whispers to Caesar*]

ANTONY Her tongue will not obey her heart, nor can
Her heart inform her tongue – the swansdown feather,
That stands upon the swell at the full of tide,
And neither way inclines. 50

ENOBARBUS [*Aside to Agrippa*] Will Caesar weep?

AGRIPPA [*Aside to Enobarbus*] He has a cloud in's face.

ENOBARBUS [*Aside to Agrippa*]
He were the worse for that were he a horse,
So is he being a man.

39–67b In Byam Shaw's 1953 production, 'Mr Goring, with his close-cropped hair, pale face, and
clipped authoritative delivery, wore the mantle of distinction whenever he came upon the
stage, and his touching farewell to his sister Octavia, played with a touch of plaintive
sweetness by Rachel Kempson, remains a haunting memory' (C.L.W., *Birmingham Mail*, 29
April 1953).

46b SD In Hall's production Caesar's relationship with Octavia 'was presented as absolutely loving
and tender; in fact, with such a strong emotional subtext that their famous "swan's-down
feather" unspoken conversation in 3.2 was almost painful to watch in its intimacy' (Crowl,
Shakespeare Observed, p. 99).

AGRIPPA [*Aside to Enobarbus*] Why, Enobarbus,
    When Antony found Julius Caesar dead, 55
    He cried almost to roaring; and he wept
    When at Philippi he found Brutus slain.
ENOBARBUS [*Aside to Agrippa*]
    That year, indeed, he was troubled with a rheum;
    What willingly he did confound, he wailed,
    Believe't, till I wept too.
CAESAR   No, sweet Octavia, 60
    You shall hear from me still; the time shall not
    Outgo my thinking on you.
ANTONY   Come, sir, come,
    I'll wrestle with you in my strength of love.
    Look, here I have you [*Embracing him*]; thus I let you go,
    And give you to the gods.
CAESAR   Adieu. Be happy! 65
LEPIDUS Let all the number of the stars give light
    To thy fair way!
CAESAR   Farewell, farewell!
         Kisses Octavia
ANTONY   Farewell!
        Trumpets sound. Exeunt [in separate groups]

63–5a   In the Nunn–Scoffield television version Caesar's body-language is eloquent: in this scene
      he has wrapped his cloak around himself defensively and here he recoils from Antony's
      embrace.

ACT 3, SCENE 3

[3.3] *Enter* CLEOPATRA, CHARMIAN, IRAS, *and* ALEXAS

If Shakespeare did model Cleopatra's behaviour in the first messenger scene (2.5) on Queen Elizabeth's, it is just possible that he was influenced in his writing of this second messenger scene by accounts of Elizabeth's questions in 1564 about the features and style of Mary Queen of Scots (see Neale, *Queen Elizabeth*, p. 131); but a useful early nineteenth-century corrective to such speculation is Byron's remark, provoked by Kemble's production, 'and the questions about Octavia – it is woman all over' (*'Alas! the Love of Women!'*, vol. III, p. 207). The second messenger scene was omitted in Macready's production (*Morning Chronicle*, 22 November 1833) and in Phelps's (promptbook). In Louis Calvert's production of 1897 it was added to the first, as it was in Tree's, where one reviewer liked the contrast between 'the volcanic passion' and 'the subsequent curiosity' (*Stage*, 3 January 1907). Whilst one critic thought that 'in the second part of the scene, where Cleopatra asks the messenger for a description of Octavia's appearance, she lacked the woman's indescribable fascination of voice and gesture which makes that swift change of mood charming' (*Academy*, 5 January 1907), another admired Collier's facial gestures 'when, with forced smile, she sought to wring from the messenger's lips words of detraction' and said she used with 'admirable art the facial expression necessary to convey to the audience the conflicting emotions which, like angry waves, were rushing with torrential violence through her distracted mind' (*Northern Advertiser*, 29 December 1906). In the Nunn–Scoffield television version, Cleopatra's studied composure is represented by her sitting on her throne, wearing black with gold jewellery (in contrast with the first messenger scene, where she is lolling in a caftan on cushions when the messenger enters); the messenger's delivery is understandably hesitant in this scene. Mirren, in Noble's production, showed 'a mixture of contempt and rage' (Steve Grant, *Plays and Players*, December 1982). In the Robertson–Selbie production, 'the first intimation . . . Miss Redgrave gives us of Cleopatra's ambivalence and unpredictability comes with the barbed wit of her response to the messenger's description of Antony's new wife Octavia' (Ian Stewart, *Country Life*, 12 June 1986); Redgrave wore 'a decorous wig to learn of Octavia's points; the welcome bad report means that the security hair-piece can be dispensed with' (Michael Coveney, *Financial Times*, 27 May 1986). In Caird's 1992 production Alan Cox 'stands out as a hilarious messenger, his face a hapless SOS as he tries to second-guess Cleopatra's prejudices and so avoid a beating' (Paul Taylor, *Independent*, 7 November 1992).

CLEOPATRA Where is the fellow?
ALEXAS   Half afeard to come.
CLEOPATRA Go to, go to.

Enter the MESSENGER *as before*

                         Come hither, sir.
ALEXAS   Good majesty,
      Herod of Jewry dare not look upon you
      But when you are well pleased.
CLEOPATRA   That Herod's head
      I'll have; but how, when Antony is gone,   5
      Through whom I might command it? – Come thou near.
MESSENGER Most gracious majesty!
CLEOPATRA   Didst thou behold Octavia?
MESSENGER Ay, dread queen.
CLEOPATRA   Where?
MESSENGER   Madam, in Rome.
      I looked her in the face, and saw her led
      Between her brother and Mark Antony.   10
CLEOPATRA Is she as tall as me?
MESSENGER   She is not, madam.
CLEOPATRA Didst hear her speak? Is she shrill-tongued or low?
MESSENGER Madam, I heard her speak. She is low-voiced.
CLEOPATRA That's not so good. He cannot like her long.
CHARMIAN Like her? O Isis! 'Tis impossible.   15
CLEOPATRA I think so, Charmian. Dull of tongue, and dwarfish. –
      What majesty is in her gait? Remember
      If e'er thou look'st on majesty.
MESSENGER   She creeps:
      Her motion and her station are as one.
      She shows a body rather than a life,   20
      A statue than a breather.
CLEOPATRA   Is this certain?
MESSENGER Or I have no observance.
CHARMIAN   Three in Egypt
      Cannot make better note.
CLEOPATRA   He's very knowing,
      I do perceive't. There's nothing in her yet.

---

16 **Dull ... dwarfish** Mrs Siddons 'drew herself up to a most imperial and queen-like dignity'
in delivering 16–18a in her public readings of the play (*Morning Chronicle*, 22 November
1833). In 1953 Peggy Ashcroft 'missed the malice' in this line (Philip Hope-Wallace, *Time &
Tide*, 8 May 1953); in 1986 Vanessa Redgrave 'revels in the humour of the woman's
complacent view of Antony's new wife' (John Barber, *Daily Telegraph*, 24 May 1986).

> The fellow has good judgement.

CHARMIAN   Excellent.   25
CLEOPATRA Guess at her years, I prithee.
MESSENGER   Madam,
> She was a widow –
CLEOPATRA   Widow? Charmian, hark.
MESSENGER And I do think she's thirty.
CLEOPATRA Bear'st thou her face in mind? Is't long or round?
MESSENGER Round, even to faultiness.   30
CLEOPATRA For the most part, too, they are foolish that are so. –
> Her hair, what colour?
MESSENGER   Brown, madam, and her forehead
> As low as she would wish it.
CLEOPATRA   There's gold for thee.
> Thou must not take my former sharpness ill.
> I will employ thee back again; I find thee   35
> Most fit for business. Go make thee ready;
> Our letters are prepared.
>   [*Exit Messenger*]
CHARMIAN   A proper man.
CLEOPATRA Indeed, he is so. I repent me much
> That so I harried him. Why, methinks, by him,
> This creature's no such thing.
CHARMIAN   Nothing, madam.   40
CLEOPATRA The man hath seen some majesty, and should know.
CHARMIAN Hath he seen majesty? Isis else defend,
> And serving you so long!
CLEOPATRA I have one thing more to ask him yet, good Charmian –
> But 'tis no matter; thou shalt bring him to me   45
> Where I will write. All may be well enough.
CHARMIAN I warrant you, madam.
>   *Exeunt*

28 Janet Achurch gave the messenger 'a terrible look' here (Shaw, *Plays and Players*, p. 191);
    in 1986 Vanessa Redgrave's response was more self-aware, 'giving her attendants a deadly
    look when she hears her rival is only 30, and mocking her own jealousy' (Mary Harron,
    Observer, 1 June 1986). Judi Dench 'rushe[d] for the door in affronted dignity' at this point
    (Michael Billington, *Guardian*, 11 April 1987), whereas Edith Clever responded with a 'fretful
    scratching of her ear as she learns of Octavia's age' in Stein's production (Michael Billington,
    Guardian Weekly, 14 August 1994). The messenger laughs as he says this in the BBC
    television version, but suddenly stops on seeing Cleopatra's response.

ACT 3, SCENE 4

[3.4] *Enter* ANTONY *and* OCTAVIA

ANTONY Nay, nay, Octavia, not only that –
　　　That were excusable, that and thousands more
　　　Of semblable import – but he hath waged
　　　New wars 'gainst Pompey, made his will and read it
　　　To public ear, spoke scantly of me.　　　　　　　　　5
　　　When perforce he could not
　　　But pay me terms of honour, cold and sickly
　　　He vented them, most narrow measure lent me;
　　　When the best hint was given him, he not took't,
　　　Or did it from his teeth.
OCTAVIA　　　　　　　　　O my good lord,　　　　　　10
　　　Believe not all, or, if you must believe,
　　　Stomach not all. A more unhappy lady,
　　　If this division chance, ne'er stood between,
　　　Praying for both parts.
　　　The good gods will mock me presently,　　　　　　15
　　　When I shall pray, 'O, bless my lord and husband!',

Omitted by Garrick (printed edition), Phelps (promptbook) and in 1866 and 1867 (Calvert's acting edition), and in Helpmann's production 'the vital scenes wherein Antony abandons Octavia were cut' (Kenneth Tynan, *Observer*, 10 March 1957). Tree predictably introduced further business in this scene: 'we know [Cleopatra] is still in his voluptuous thoughts at Athens by his flinging her letter over his head in a kind of schoolboy ecstasy' (H. Hamilton Fyfe, *Pall Mall Gazette*, 2 January 1907). In the Nunn–Scoffield television version, Antony is sitting at a table with letters, and Octavia tries unsuccessfully to calm him by caressing his neck; her 'efforts at affection obviously make Antony wish to shrug her off and contrast with the sensuously confident slide of Cleopatra's arms over Antony's shoulders' (Coursen, *Shakespearean Performance*, p. 192). The setting is a surprisingly intimate one in the BBC television version, with Octavia in bed and Antony sitting on the edge of the bed; presumably this is one of the occasions on which Antony forebears the getting of a lawful race. In Noble's 1982 production 'Penelope Beaumont plays [Caesar's] unfortunate sister with a dignity which rebuts Cleopatra's self-victimisation in the name of love' (Victoria Radin, *Observer*, 17 October 1982).

Undo that prayer by crying out as loud,
'O, bless my brother!' Husband win, win brother,
Prays and destroys the prayer; no midway
'Twixt these extremes at all.

ANTONY   Gentle Octavia,   20
Let your best love draw to that point which seeks
Best to preserve it. If I lose mine honour,
I lose myself; better I were not yours
Than yours so branchless. But, as you requested,
Yourself shall go between's. The meantime, lady,   25
I'll raise the preparation of a war
Shall stain your brother. Make your soonest haste;
So your desires are yours.

OCTAVIA   Thanks to my lord.
The Jove of power make me, most weak, most weak,
Your reconciler! Wars 'twixt you twain would be   30
As if the world should cleave, and that slain men
Should solder up the rift.

ANTONY When it appears to you where this begins,
Turn your displeasure that way, for our faults
Can never be so equal that your love   35
Can equally move with them. Provide your going;
Choose your own company and command what cost
Your heart has mind to.

                                  Exeunt

ACT 3, SCENE 5

[3.5] *Enter* ENOBARBUS *and* EROS, [*meeting*]

ENOBARBUS How now, friend Eros?
EROS There's strange news come, sir.
ENOBARBUS What, man?
EROS Caesar and Lepidus have made wars upon Pompey.
ENOBARBUS This is old. What is the success?   5
EROS Caesar, having made use of him in the wars 'gainst Pompey,
     presently denied him rivality, would not let him partake in the
     glory of the action; and, not resting here, accuses him of letters
     he had formerly wrote to Pompey; upon his own appeal seizes
     him. So the poor third is up, till death enlarge his confine.   10
ENOBARBUS Then, world, thou hast a pair of chaps, no more;
     And throw between them all the food thou hast,
     They'll grind the one the other. Where's Antony?
EROS He's walking in the garden – thus – and spurns
     The rush that lies before him; cries, 'Fool Lepidus!'   15
     And threats the throat of that his officer
     That murdered Pompey.
ENOBARBUS   Our great navy's rigged.
EROS For Italy and Caesar. More, Domitius:
     My lord desires you presently. My news
     I might have told hereafter.
ENOBARBUS   'Twill be naught,   20
     But let it be. Bring me to Antony.
EROS   Come, sir.

                                                              Exeunt

Cut by Garrick (printed edition), in 1866 and 1867 (Calvert's acting edition) and by Nunn:
Jeremy Kingston wrote 'I query his decision to cut so abruptly from Antony's farewell to
Octavia in Athens to the revelation (in Rome) of the amazing things he has subsequently
done on silver thrones in Alexandria' (*Punch*, 23 August 1972). Also cut by Brook, after being
rehearsed for six weeks (Hunt and Reeves, *Peter Brook*, p. 225).

14 **thus** Delivered '*folding his arms*' in Phelps's production (promptbook).

ACT 3, SCENE 6

[3.6] *Enter* AGRIPPA, MAECENAS, *and* CAESAR

CAESAR Contemning Rome, he has done all this and more
      In Alexandria. Here's the manner of 't:
      I'th'market-place, on a tribunal silvered,
      Cleopatra and himself in chairs of gold
      Were publicly enthroned; at the feet sat   5
      Caesarion, whom they call my father's son,
      And all the unlawful issue that their lust
      Since then hath made between them. Unto her
      He gave the stablishment of Egypt, made her
      Of lower Syria, Cyprus, Lydia,   10
      Absolute queen.
MAECENAS   This in the public eye?
CAESAR I'th'common show-place, where they exercise.
      His sons he there proclaimed the kings of kings:
      Great Media, Parthia, and Armenia
      He gave to Alexander; to Ptolemy he assigned   15
      Syria, Cilicia, and Phoenicia. She
      In th'habiliments of the goddess Isis
      That day appeared, and oft before gave audience –
      As 'tis reported – so.

1–19   In the Nunn–Scoffield television version, 'Caesar's stark Rome cuts back and forth from his complaint to hazy close-ups of Cleopatra, Antony, and Cesarion, all in cloth-of-gold Eastern habiliments. This sequence reminds us of Philo's opening commentary, but it raises the odds in that it is spoken by Caesar and shows Antony and Cleopatra clothed as divinities' (Coursen, *Shakespearean Performance*, pp. 192–3). In the BBC television version, Charleson's Jacobean-style rhetorical gestures come into their own in this passage: his accusatory index finger is especially telling. Cinematic techniques seem to have influenced Caird's production at this point, though in terms of stage history, it looked behind them to Tree's pictorialism: Jeremy Kingston described Caird's effect as 'a tableau in the background, as glittering and sunlit as an Alma-Tadema' (*Times*, 29 May 1993), Cleopatra 'appearing magnificently regal in her goddess Isis outfit silhouetted in the background with Antony and their several children as Octavius disgustedly recounts their sexual and political sins'

MAECENAS Let Rome be thus informed. 20
AGRIPPA Who, queasy with his insolence already,
    Will their good thoughts call from him.
CAESAR The people knows it, and have now received
    His accusations.
AGRIPPA   Who does he accuse?
CAESAR Caesar, and that having in Sicily 25
    Sextus Pompeius spoiled, we had not rated him
    His part o'th'isle. Then does he say he lent me
    Some shipping, unrestored. Lastly, he frets
    That Lepidus of the triumvirate
    Should be deposed, and, being, that we detain 30
    All his revenue.
AGRIPPA   Sir, this should be answered.
CAESAR 'Tis done already, and the messenger gone.
    I have told him Lepidus was grown too cruel,
    That he his high authority abused
    And did deserve his change. For what I have conquered, 35
    I grant him part; but then in his Armenia
    And other of his conquered kingdoms I
    Demand the like.
MAECENAS   He'll never yield to that.

(Geckle, 'The Power of Desire on Stage', p. 16). Paul Taylor's remark that the 'populous golden procession . . . decisively proves, among other things, that the amorous pair were no pioneers of family planning' (*Independent*, 7 November 1992) recalls Constance Collier's reaction to Tree's decision to put the children on stage here: 'He loved historical facts and had discovered that Cleopatra had five children. This appealed to his whimsical, fantastic mind. What was my horror to find myself in the procession, looking most lovely, followed by this brood! . . . The splendid, passionate Queen was ridiculous with a large family. The domestic point of view of Cleopatra seemed utterly incongruous' (*Harlequinade*, p. 186). Placing his interval 'at this unusual moment in 3.6', Caird 'obviously wants the spectators to take this tableau of Antony and Cleopatra and the now irreconcilable Octavius with them. After twenty minutes, we are introduced to a continuation of 3.6' (Geckle, 'The Power of Desire on Stage', p. 16).

5–8 **at . . . them** and 13–16 Phelps's production eliminated reference to the children in cutting these lines (promptbook).

32 **'Tis done** In Tree's version Basil Gill was 'a little too loud at times' and 'shouted' these words 'as though he were in a heroic passion' (*Morning Post*, 28 December 1906).

33 In the Nunn–Scoffield television version, Corin Redgrave delivers this line 'as a joke that evokes derisive Roman laughter in a world where to do good is only dangerous folly' (Coursen, *Shakespearean Performance*, p. 194).

CAESAR Nor must not then be yielded to in this.

Enter OCTAVIA *with her train*

OCTAVIA Hail, Caesar, and my lord! Hail, most dear Caesar! 40
CAESAR That ever I should call thee castaway!
OCTAVIA You have not called me so, nor have you cause.
CAESAR Why have you stol'n upon us thus? You come not
      Like Caesar's sister. The wife of Antony
      Should have an army for an usher and 45
      The neighs of horse to tell of her approach
      Long ere she did appear. The trees by th'way
      Should have borne men, and expectation fainted,
      Longing for what it had not. Nay, the dust
      Should have ascended to the roof of heaven, 50
      Raised by your populous troops. But you are come
      A market maid to Rome, and have prevented
      The ostentation of our love, which, left unshown,
      Is often left unloved. We should have met you
      By sea and land, supplying every stage 55
      With an augmented greeting.
OCTAVIA   Good my lord,
      To come thus was I not constrained, but did it
      On my free will. My lord, Mark Antony,
      Hearing that you prepared for war, acquainted
      My grievèd ear withal, whereon I begged 60
      His pardon for return.
CAESAR   Which soon he granted,
      Being an abstract 'tween his lust and him.
OCTAVIA Do not say so, my lord.
CAESAR   I have eyes upon him,
      And his affairs come to me on the wind.
      Where is he now? 65
OCTAVIA My lord, in Athens.
CAESAR No, my most wrongèd sister, Cleopatra
      Hath nodded him to her. He hath given his empire
      Up to a whore, who now are levying
      The kings o'th'earth for war. He hath assembled 70

47–51 **The . . . troops,** 53–6 **which . . . greeting,** 79–102 Cut in the Nunn–Scoffield television version.

68–9 **He . . . whore** Cut in the bowdlerising of the text for Phelps's production (promptbook); the following 'who' was changed to 'they'.

70–8 **He . . . sceptres** The list of kings was cut by Garrick (printed edition) and Phelps (promptbook) and in the BBC television version. The Nunn–Scoffield version provides

Bocchus, the King of Libya; Archelaus,
Of Cappadocia; Philadelphos, King
Of Paphlagonia; the Thracian king, Adallas;
King Manchus of Arabia; King of Pont;
Herod of Jewry; Mithridates, King   75
Of Comagene; Polemon and Amyntas,
The Kings of Mede and Lycaonia,
With a more larger list of sceptres.
OCTAVIA Ay me most wretched,
That have my heart parted betwixt two friends   80
That does afflict each other!
CAESAR   Welcome hither.
Your letters did withhold our breaking forth
Till we perceived both how you were wrong led
And we in negligent danger. Cheer your heart;
Be you not troubled with the time, which drives   85
O'er your content these strong necessities,
But let determined things to destiny
Hold unbewailed their way. Welcome to Rome,
Nothing more dear to me. You are abused
Beyond the mark of thought, and the high gods,   90
To do you justice, makes his ministers
Of us and those that love you. Best of comfort,
And ever welcome to us.
AGRIPPA Welcome, lady.
MAECENAS Welcome, dear madam.   95
Each heart in Rome does love and pity you;
Only th'adulterous Antony, most large
In his abominations, turns you off
And gives his potent regiment to a trull
That noises it against us.
OCTAVIA   Is it so, sir?   100
CAESAR Most certain. Sister, welcome. Pray you
Be ever known to patience. My dear'st sister!
                                        Exeunt

images of the kings, whose unprepossessing persons we have previously sighted in
Cleopatra's court.
102 In Hall's production 'Sally Dexter is a suppressed Octavia, white-faced with fury' (Michael
Coveney, *Financial Times*, 10 April 1987) and Tim Pigott-Smith's 'clutching embrace of
Octavia, on which the production fades for its interval, is more passionate than anything
Antony ever rises to' (Peter Kemp, *Independent*, 11 April 1987).

[3.7] *Enter* CLEOPATRA *and* ENOBARBUS

CLEOPATRA I will be even with thee, doubt it not.
ENOBARBUS But why, why, why?
CLEOPATRA Thou hast forspoke my being in these wars,
    And say'st it is not fit.
ENOBARBUS   Well, is it, is it?
CLEOPATRA If not denounced against us, why should not we   5
    Be there is person?
ENOBARBUS [*Aside*]   Well, I could reply.
    If we should serve with horse and mares together,
    The horse were merely lost; the mares would bear
    A soldier and his horse.
CLEOPATRA   What is't you say?

Hall's second half began here: 'the audience is plunged stereophonically into the midst of battle, with characters making urgent entrances and exits up and down the aisles' (Charles Osborne, *Daily Telegraph*, 11 April 1987).

0 SD   For this scene in 1889 the gauzily costumed Cora Brown-Potter wore a plumed helmet and a breastplate enamelled blue (Shattuck, *Shakespeare on the American Stage*, vol. II, p. 122), whilst in 1936 Eugenie Leontovich sported 'a Roman helmet, a golden breastplate, and a slashed skirt of forget-me-not blue satin' (Agate, *Brief Chronicles,* p. 183). In Nunn's production Janet Suzman 'looked formidable, sword at her side, her metallic skirt glittering in the light' (Scott, *Antony and Cleopatra*, p. 50). Judy Parfitt's battle dress in Hack's production of 1983 was less formidable than fantastic: 'when Cleopatra girds herself in an ornamental breast plate for the final battle it is as much to do with the reality of her plight as Marie Antoinette dressing up as a shepherdess had to do with The Good Life' (Jack Tinker, *Daily Mail*, in *London Theatre Record*, 9–22 April 1983, p. 335). In 1992 Clare Higgins 'arrives wearing a gold breastplate and black harem pants with a black cockaded helmet and silver baubles clanking as she moves, and, sitting on a chair covered with a leopard skin, she proceeds to get a manicure as she speaks with Enobarbus about going to war' (Geckle, 'The Power of Desire on Stage', p. 16). Eva Mattes's Cleopatra, in Zadek's Edinburgh production, 'treats war largely as an excuse for dressing up in pith helmet and a tight black suit' (Michael Billington, *Guardian Weekly*, 28 August 1994).

6b–9a   Cut in the bowdlerising of the text for Phelps's production (promptbook).

ENOBARBUS Your presence needs must puzzle Antony,   10
    Take from his heart, take from his brain, from's time
    What should not then be spared. He is already
    Traduced for levity, and 'tis said in Rome
    That Photinus, an eunuch, and your maids
    Manage this war.
CLEOPATRA   Sink Rome, and their tongues rot   15
    That speak against us! A charge we bear i'th'war,
    And as the president of my kingdom will
    Appear there for a man. Speak not against it;
    I will not stay behind.

            Enter ANTONY *and* CANIDIUS

ENOBARBUS   Nay, I have done.
    Here comes the emperor.
ANTONY   Is it not strange, Canidius,   20
    That from Tarentum and Brundusium
    He could so quickly cut the Ionian Sea
    And take in Toryne? – You have heard on't, sweet?
CLEOPATRA Celerity is never more admired
    Than by the negligent.
ANTONY   A good rebuke,   25
    Which might have well becomed the best of men,
    To taunt at slackness. Canidius, we will fight
    With him by sea.
CLEOPATRA   By sea, what else?
CANIDIUS   Why will
    My lord do so?
ANTONY   For that he dares us to't.
ENOBARBUS So hath my lord dared him to single fight.   30
CANIDIUS Ay, and to wage this battle at Pharsalia,
    Where Caesar fought with Pompey. But these offers,
    Which serve not for his vantage, he shakes off,
    And so should you.
ENOBARBUS   Your ships are not well manned.
    Your mariners are muleteers, reapers, people   35
    Ingrossed by swift impress; in Caesar's fleet
    Are those that often have 'gainst Pompey fought.
    Their ships are yare, yours heavy. No disgrace

19a SD   In keeping with his production's emphasis on Antony's association with Hercules, Rutter
      'dons the Nemean lion's skin' for the battle scenes (Jeffrey Wainwright, *Independent*, 6
      October 1995).

> Shall fall you for refusing him at sea,
> Being prepared for land.
ANTONY   By sea, by sea.   40
ENOBARBUS Most worthy sir, you therein throw away
> The absolute soldiership you have by land,
> Distract your army, which doth most consist
> Of war-marked footmen, leave unexecuted
> Your own renownèd knowledge, quite forgo   45
> The way which promises assurance, and
> Give up yourself merely to chance and hazard
> From firm security.
ANTONY   I'll fight at sea.
CLEOPATRA I have sixty sails, Caesar none better.
ANTONY Our overplus of shipping will we burn,   50
> And with the rest full-manned, from th'head of Actium
> Beat th'approaching Caesar. But if we fail,
> We then can do't at land.

Enter a MESSENGER

>   Thy business?
MESSENGER The news is true, my lord; he is descried.
> Caesar has taken Toryne.   55
ANTONY Can he be there in person? 'Tis impossible;
> Strange that his power should be. Canidius,
> Our nineteen legions thou shalt hold by land,
> And our twelve thousand horse. We'll to our ship.
> Away, my Thetis!

Enter a SOLDIER

>   How now, worthy soldier?   60
SOLDIER O noble emperor, do not fight by sea;
> Trust not to rotten planks. Do you misdoubt
> This sword and these my wounds? Let th'Egyptians
> And the Phoenicians go a-ducking; we
> Have used to conquer standing on the earth   65
> And fighting foot to foot.

40b   Robert Cushman said of Alan Howard in Brook's production that he 'gets Antony's madness
(suicidal) in his determination to fight "by sea, by sea", which words he burns up'
(*Observer*, 15 October 1978); Michael Billington wrote of Howard's 'fervour of someone
hungry for honour' at this point (*Guardian*, 11 October 1978).

60b   Olivier was 'dallying' with Leigh 'instead of listening to his soldiers' arguments against
fighting at sea' (Venezky, 'Current Shakespearian Productions', p. 336).

ANTONY   Well, well, away!
                    Exeunt Antony, Cleopatra, and Enobarbus
SOLDIER By Hercules, I think I am i'th'right.
CANIDIUS Soldier, thou art; but his whole action grows
           Not in the power on't. So our leader's led,
           And we are women's men.
SOLDIER   You keep by land   70
           The legions and the horse whole, do you not?
CANIDIUS Marcus Octavius, Marcus Justeius,
           Publicola, and Caelius are for sea,
           But we keep whole by land. This speed of Caesar's
           Carries beyond belief.   75
SOLDIER While he was yet in Rome,
           His power went out in such distractions as
           Beguiled all spies.
CANIDIUS   Who's his lieutenant, hear you?
SOLDIER They say, one Taurus.
CANIDIUS   Well I know the man.

                    Enter a MESSENGER

MESSENGER The emperor calls Canidius.   80
CANIDIUS With news the time's in labour, and throws forth
           Each minute some.
                                                    Exeunt

ACT 3, SCENE 8

[3.8] *Enter* CAESAR [*and* TAURUS] *with his army, marching*

CAESAR Taurus!
TAURUS My lord?
CAESAR Strike not by land; keep whole. Provoke not battle
    Till we have done at sea. Do not exceed
    The prescript of this scroll.
               [*He gives a scroll*]
                       Our fortune lies   5
  Upon this jump.

                                    Exeunt

Cut in Phelps's production (promptbook) and in 1866 and 1867 (Calvert's acting edition).

ACT 3, SCENE 9

[3.9] *Enter* ANTONY *and* ENOBARBUS

ANTONY Set we our squadrons on yond side o'th'hill,
            In eye of Caesar's battle, from which place
            We may the number of the ships behold
            And so proceed accordingly.

                                                    Exeunt

Cut by Phelps (promptbook) and in 1866 and 1867 (Calvert's acting edition).

[3.10] CANIDIUS *marcheth with his land army one way over the stage, and* TAURUS *the lieutenant of Caesar the other way. After their going in is heard the noise of a sea fight*

Alarum. Enter ENOBARBUS

ENOBARBUS Naught, naught, all naught! I can behold no longer.
 Th'Antoniad, the Egyptian admiral,
 With all their sixty, fly and turn the rudder.
 To see't mine eyes are blasted.

Enter SCARUS

SCARUS   Gods and goddesses,

0 SD **CANIDIUS . . . *other way.*** Passing 'over the stage' on the Jacobean stage is now generally understood to mean entering by one door, making a broad sweep of the stage and exiting by another door, though Nicoll ('"Passing over the Stage"', pp. 47–55) thought it meant crossing the width of the stage by steps to and from the yard, and Sprinchorn ('An Intermediate Level', *Theatre Notebook*, 46, pp. 73–94, and *Theatre Notebook*, 48, pp. 51–2) posits a permanent raised platform at the rear of the stage for such crossings. The modern equivalent in Hall's production left one critic unmoved by the 'braying of trumpets and marching of Roman soldiers with banners up and down the aisles and across the stage, which produces an effect like the breaks on commercial television' (Della Couling, *Tablet*, 2 May 1987).

0 SD **After . . . *fight*** J. C. Trewin called this 'the most puzzling direction in the First Folio' and quoted Granville-Barker's response (in *Prefaces*, p. 144) to Stuart-Jones's suggestion that on the Jacobean stage it implied 'the sound of the galley-sweeps breaking': 'I fancy that a hurly-burly flavoured with Avasts, Belays, and other such sea-phrases from the landsman's vocabulary would be a likelier refuge in a difficulty for the prompter and his staff. But there may have been some recognised symbolism of a sea-fight.' Trewin also cited a critic's account of Kemble's 'determined pump-and-tub battle': 'The encounter of real combatants required gallies of a size that impeded all their movements, and the whole scene gave us the idea of unwieldy and unpicturesque confusion' (*Birmingham Post*, 13 March 1957). Chatterton's production ended Act 3 with a rousing naval battle: 'the appearance of two contending galleys and the heartiness with which their respective crews showered arrows

```
                   All the whole synod of them!
ENOBARBUS                              What's thy passion?                         5
SCARUS  The greater cantle of the world is lost
                   With very ignorance. We have kissed away
                   Kingdoms and provinces.
ENOBARBUS                              How appears the fight?
SCARUS  On our side like the tokened pestilence,
                   Where death is sure. Yon ribaudred nag of Egypt –              10
                   Whom leprosy o'ertake! – i'th'midst o'th'fight,
                   When vantage like a pair of twins appeared
                   Both as the same, or rather ours the elder,
                   The breeze upon her, like a cow in June,
                   Hoists sail and flies.
ENOBARBUS                   That I beheld.                                         15
                   Mine eyes did sicken at the sight, and could not
                   Endure a further view.
SCARUS                              She once being loofed,
                   The noble ruin of her magic, Antony,
                   Claps on his sea wing, and, like a doting mallard,
```

on each other raised the audience on Saturday to a state of excitement which would not be calmed till Mr Chatterton came before the curtain' (*Times*, 22 September 1873). In Iden Payne's production, 'the battering rams and other engines of war in the later battle scenes so impressed and distracted the audience that it was hard to hear what the actors were saying' (P.D.H., *Leamington Chronicle*, 19 April 1935), whilst Fluchère thought Jean-Louis Barrault's 'pantomime of the sea-fight' in his 1945 Comédie-Française production 'badly spoils the tragedy' ('Shakespeare in France', p. 123). In Byam Shaw's production of 1953 there was an 'eerily echoing cavern of sound that made almost superfluous Enobarbus's cry of despair at the chaos of the disastrous sea fight' (N.T., *Royal Leamington Spa Courier*, 1 May 1953). Trewin, unhappy with the 'unwieldy and unpicturesque confusion' created by this scene in 'some contemporary Shakespeare revivals', approved of the way in which Helpmann 'manages with Gordon Jacob's music and an empty stage' (*Birmingham Post*, 13 March 1957). Of Brook's production Bernard Levin wrote, 'for the sea-fight we hear only the rise and fall of a mighty wave, and see only the solitary figure of Enobarbus, silhouetted with his back to us outside the magic circle, looking out on desolation' (*Sunday Times*, 15 October 1978); Trewin enthused,'"noise of a sea-fight" is a frenzy of sound able to suggest anything we care to imagine' (*Lady*, 19 July 1979). In Rutter's production 'the two sides stand either end of the hall, wearing plain uniforms, like rival companies of refuse collectors. One side wears orange, the other blue. The battle is a percussive one. They hammer threateningly on oil barrels and plastic containers (orange and blue, too). When an orange guy crosses the hall and drums with the blue guys, we all know Antony's lost' (Robert Butler, *Independent on Sunday*, 15 October 1995).

Leaving the fight in height, flies after her.   20
I never saw an action of such shame.
Experience, manhood, honour, ne'er before
Did violate so itself.
ENOBARBUS   Alack, alack!

Enter CANIDIUS

CANIDIUS Our fortune on the sea is out of breath,
And sinks most lamentably. Had our general   25
Been what he knew himself, it had gone well.
O, he has given example for our flight
Most grossly by his own!
ENOBARBUS Ay, are you thereabouts? Why then good night indeed.
CANIDIUS Toward Peloponnesus are they fled.   30
SCARUS 'Tis easy to't, and there I will attend
What further comes.
CANIDIUS   To Caesar will I render
My legions and my horse. Six kings already
Show me the way of yielding.
ENOBARBUS   I'll yet follow
The wounded chance of Antony, though my reason   35
Sits in the wind against me.

                              [*Exeunt separately*]

ACT 3, SCENE 11

[3.11] *Enter* ANTONY *with* ATTENDANTS

ANTONY Hark! The land bids me tread no more upon't;
     It is ashamed to bear me. Friends, come hither.
     I am so lated in the world that I
     Have lost my way for ever. I have a ship
     Laden with gold. Take that, divide it; fly,   5
     And make your peace with Caesar.
ALL   Fly? Not we.
ANTONY I have fled myself, and have instructed cowards
     To run and show their shoulders. Friends, begone.

Macready's 'best scene' was 'when he throws himself on the ground' here (*Morning Chronicle*, 22 November 1833). Beerbohm Tree, too, 'was at his best' in this scene: 'Here he gave some idea of the great man's dejection, of his anger, and of the temporary revival of his old self, with its epicurean carelessness of the world' (*Morning Post*, 28 December 1906); 'he acted with a pathetic dignity that was the one inspired moment of the evening' (*Sportsman*, 28 December 1906). In Asche's Australian touring production, Antony made his speech not merely before his '*attendants*', but the whole army (promptbook). Olivier made 'a superbly managed entrance . . . when he winds his way in through the pillars, bowed with shame' (T. C. Worsley, *New Statesman*, 19 May 1951). In Nunn's production 'the canopy of the court was displayed fallen from the skies, the luxurious cushions were displaced and Antony appeared broken, at one with the deranged set' (Scott, *Antony and Cleopatra*, p. 66). Under Brook's direction 'both Octavius and Pompey look up to Antony as a senior partner by whom they have always felt outclassed. Antony shares this view: hence the incredulity on both sides when he meets his first defeat. Mr Howard collapses and covers his eyes, unable to contemplate the unbelievable humiliation. As for Octavius, he begins from that moment to lose his innocent charm and develop into the icy calculating demigod of the later scenes' (Irving Wardle, *Times*, 11 October 1978).

1 Johnson shudders here in the Nunn–Scoffield television version; in Brook's production, Howard delivered this passage 'down stage in little light while his attendants waited in the obscurity beyond the screens' (Hunt and Reeves, *Peter Brook*, p. 226); Gambon spoke this line in 'soft tones' (Scott, *Antony and Cleopatra*, p. 75); in Hack's production, Baxter was 'horribly moving' in this passage (*Times*, 23 April 1983).

8–11 **Friends . . . it** Cut in Phelps's production (promptbook).

I have myself resolved upon a course
Which has no need of you. Begone.   10
My treasure's in the harbour. Take it. O,
I followed that I blush to look upon!
My very hairs do mutiny, for the white
Reprove the brown for rashness, and they them
For fear and doting. Friends, begone. You shall   15
Have letters from me to some friends that will
Sweep your way for you. Pray you, look not sad,
Nor make replies of loathness. Take the hint
Which my despair proclaims. Let that be left
Which leaves itself. To the seaside straightway!   20
I will possess you of that ship and treasure.
Leave me, I pray, a little. Pray you now,
Nay, do so, for indeed I have lost command.
Therefore I pray you. I'll see you by and by.
                    [*Exeunt Attendants. Antony*] *sits down*

Enter CLEOPATRA *led by* CHARMIAN, [IRAS], *and* EROS

EROS Nay, gentle madam, to him, comfort him.   25

8–53a   Cut by Kemble (printed edition).

12   In Brook's production, Howard spoke the line 'with the sunken head of one corroded by shame' (Michael Billington, *Guardian*, 11 October 1978).

13–15   **My . . . doting** Cut in Macready's production, possibly because, like James Anderson forty years later (when, however, the lines were not cut), he was wearing 'the conventional black wig of heavy tragedy' (*Athenaeum*, 27 September 1873).

15–19   **You . . . proclaims** Cut in Phelps's production (promptbook).

23   Richard Findlater said of Michael Redgrave, 'it is an unforgettable moment of tragedy when he speaks his own epitaph, "I have lost command" and, in a waste of shame, "I have offended reputation, A most unnoble swerving"' (*Tribune*, 20 November 1953). John Barber remarked that Howard's 'moving "Indeed, I have lost command" summarises the whole character' as conceived in Brook's production (*Daily Telegraph*, 10 July 1979).

24 SD   **[*Exeunt Attendants. Antony*] *sits down*** Garrick 'Thr[ew] *himself on a Couch*' in his production (printed text).

25   Michael Billington said of Janet Suzman in Nunn's production, 'she is also good on tiny detail such as instinctive recoil on seeing Antony paralysed by defeat after Actium' (*Guardian*, 16 August 1972); in the television version, Antony and Cleopatra weep separately, almost rivals in grief, until her women lead the queen over to Antony at this point. In Brook's production 'Iras and Charmian almost forced [Cleopatra] on stage . . . As she saw [Antony] she attempted to escape but was prevented by her women' (Scott, *Antony and Cleopatra*, p. 54).

IRAS Do, most dear queen.

CHARMIAN Do. Why, what else?

CLEOPATRA Let me sit down. O Juno!

ANTONY No, no, no, no, no.

EROS See you here, sir?   30

ANTONY O fie, fie, fie!

CHARMIAN Madam!

IRAS Madam, O good empress!

EROS Sir, sir!

ANTONY Yes, my lord, yes. He at Philippi kept   35
    His sword e'en like a dancer, while I struck
    The lean and wrinkled Cassius, and 'twas I
    That the mad Brutus ended. He alone
    Dealt on lieutenantry, and no practice had
    In the brave squares of war. Yet now – no matter.   40

CLEOPATRA Ah, stand by.

EROS   The queen, my lord, the queen.

IRAS Go to him, madam, speak to him.
    He's unqualitied with very shame.

CLEOPATRA Well then, sustain me. O!

EROS Most noble sir, arise. The queen approaches.   45
    Her head's declined, and death will seize her but
    Your comfort makes the rescue.

ANTONY I have offended reputation,
    A most unnoble swerving.

EROS   Sir, the queen.

ANTONY O, whither hast thou led me, Egypt? See   50
    How I convey my shame out of thine eyes
    By looking back what I have left behind
    'Stroyed in dishonour.

40 **Yet . . . matter** In 1849 Samuel Phelps '*thr[ew] his head on table*' here (promptbook).

46–9,51–3a Cut by Nunn, to give Antony a 'directness of approach . . . as he broke through to the essentials of the situation' (Scott, *Antony and Cleopatra*, p. 66).

48–9a See Findlater on Michael Redgrave, quoted at 3.11.23.

50 Tree 'was at his best when Antony . . . was filled with shame and remorse and, meeting his temptress, cried in the bitterness of his heart' this line (*Lloyds*, 30 December 1906). In 1972 Richard Johnson was 'leaden-footed, miserably moaning: "Whither hast thou led me, Egypt", [Janet Suzman] crawling on all fours, adrift in tears' (Michael Owen, *Evening Standard*, 16 August 1972); in Noble's 1982 production Antony wore 'another of her neckcloths when he learns of his defeat' (Victoria Radin, *Observer*, 17 October 1982; see Radin on scarf-nooses, quoted at 1.1.10).

50 **See** Garrick suited the action to the word by '*starting up*' here (printed text).

CLEOPATRA   O my lord, my lord,
        Forgive my fearful sails! I little thought
        You would have followed.
ANTONY   Egypt, thou knew'st too well   55
        My heart was to thy rudder tied by th'strings,
        And thou shouldst tow me after. O'er my spirit
        Thy full supremacy thou knew'st, and that
        Thy beck might from the bidding of the gods
        Command me.
CLEOPATRA   O, my pardon!
ANTONY   Now I must   60
        To the young man send humble treaties, dodge
        And palter in the shifts of lowness, who
        With half the bulk o'th'world played as I pleased,
        Making and marring fortunes. You did know
        How much you were my conqueror, and that   65
        My sword, made weak by my affection, would
        Obey it on all cause.
CLEOPATRA   Pardon, pardon!
ANTONY Fall not a tear, I say; one of them rates
        All that is won and lost. Give me a kiss.
                        [*They kiss*]
        Even this repays me. – We sent our schoolmaster;   70
        Is a come back? – Love, I am full of lead. –
        Some wine within there, and our viands! Fortune knows
        We scorn her most when most she offers blows.
                                                                    Exeunt

55b–7   Robert Butler wrote of this moment in Rutter's production, 'Who needs scenery, props,
        background music or lighting cues? None of them can rival the visual grandeur of Antony
        (Barrie Rutter) spelling out to Cleopatra (Ishia Bennison) as a matter of fact why he had to
        follow her from battle' (*Independent on Sunday*, 15 October 1995).

  60b   Glenda Jackson was 'wonderfully alive from the neck up but, until things are going really
        badly, hardly moves her body at all . . . there is nothing to prepare us for the exaggerated
        amount of prostration, distraction, contortion and carpet-clawing that follows the defeat at
        Actium' (Ian Stewart, *Country Life*, 23 October 1978). Others shared this view of the carpet-
        clawing and it was dropped in the 1979 revival (see Michael Billington, *Guardian*, 10 July
        1979). In the Robertson–Selbie production 'the spectacle of Antony in full but bloodstained
        oriental garb, dragging his Queen across the floor is not more easily forgotten than his one
        telling moment of paralytical indecisiveness in battle' (Ian Stewart, *Country Life*, 12 June
        1986).

68–73   Cut in performance in 1866 (Unidentified newspaper review, pasted into Beck's copy of the
        play in the NY Public Library), though not in Calvert's acting edition, which directs the lovers

to '*rush into each other's arms*' at 69.

68–9 Richard Findlater appreciated 'the idolatry in mutual shame' of Redgrave's uttering of these lines to Ashcroft in 1953 (*Tribune*, 20 November 1953).

69 SD This is a crucial moment for the protagonists to show their love, but not all have risen to the occasion: William Archer said Eleanora Duse, who did not have the excuse of being English, 'kisses like a canary-bird' (*1893*, pp. 175–6). A modern canary is Jane Lapotaire in the BBC television version, who kisses Antony's hand here; in the Talawa Theatre production, 'one of the most chaste productions on record', Antony at this point set about 'politely bussing Cleopatra's palm' (Michael Billington, *Guardian*, 20 May 1991).

ACT 3, SCENE 12

[3.12] *Enter* CAESAR, AGRIPPA, [THIDIAS], *and* DOLABELLA, *with others*

CAESAR Let him appear that's come from Antony.
    Know you him?
DOLABELLA   Caesar, 'tis his schoolmaster –
    An argument that he is plucked, when hither
    He sends so poor a pinion of his wing,
    Which had superfluous kings for messengers   5
    Not many moons gone by.

              Enter AMBASSADOR *from Antony*

CAESAR   Approach and speak.
AMBASSADOR Such as I am, I come from Antony.
    I was of late as petty to his ends
    As is the morn-dew on the myrtle leaf
    To his grand sea.
CAESAR   Be't so. Declare thine office.   10
AMBASSADOR Lord of his fortunes he salutes thee, and
    Requires to live in Egypt; which not granted,
    He lessens his requests, and to thee sues
    To let him breathe between the heavens and earth
    A private man in Athens. This for him.   15
    Next, Cleopatra does confess thy greatness,
    Submits her to thy might, and of thee craves
    The circle of the Ptolemies for her heirs,
    Now hazarded to thy grace.
CAESAR   For Antony,
    I have no ears to his request. The queen   20

Omitted in 1866 and 1867 (Calvert's acting edition).

7–10a   Garrick substituted the Soothsayer for the Ambassador here (printed text); Phelps followed suit, but cut lines 8–10 (promptbook). Helpmann also made the substitution, to which Trewin objected, as he did to 'the dry, gritty enunciation' of these lines (*Illustrated London News*, 16 March 1957).

12–15   **which . . . Athens** Cut in Phelps's production (promptbook).

Of audience nor desire shall fail, so she
From Egypt drive her all-disgracèd friend
Or take his life there. This if she perform
She shall not sue unheard. So to them both.
AMBASSADOR Fortune pursue thee!
CAESAR   Bring him through the bands.   25
                                   [*Exit Ambassador, attended*]
[*To Thidias*] To try thy eloquence now 'tis time. Dispatch.
From Antony win Cleopatra. Promise,
And in our name, what she requires; add more,
From thine invention, offers. Women are not
In their best fortunes strong, but want will perjure   30
The ne'er-touched vestal. Try thy cunning, Thidias.
Make thine own edict for thy pains, which we
Will answer as a law.
THIDIAS   Caesar, I go.
CAESAR Observe how Antony becomes his flaw,
And what thou think'st his very action speaks   35
In every power that moves.
THIDIAS   Caesar, I shall.
                                   Exeunt

33b, 36b   Exaggerated respect for Caesar can affect Thidias's tone even here; B. A. Young said that in
Nunn's production Calvin Lockhart 'speaks his first two lines . . . as if they were invocations
to Isis' (*Financial Times*, 16 August 1972).

ACT 3, SCENE 13

[3.13] *Enter* CLEOPATRA, ENOBARBUS, CHARMIAN, *and* IRAS

CLEOPATRA What shall we do, Enobarbus?
ENOBARBUS   Think, and die.
CLEOPATRA Is Antony or we in fault for this?
ENOBARBUS Antony only, that would make his will
    Lord of his reason. What though you fled
    From that great face of war, whose several ranges   5
    Frighted each other? Why should he follow?
    The itch of his affection should not then
    Have nicked his captainship, at such a point,
    When half to half the world opposed, he being
    The merèd question. 'Twas a shame no less   10
    Than was his loss, to course your flying flags
    And leave his navy gazing.
CLEOPATRA   Prithee, peace.

    Enter the AMBASSADOR, *with* ANTONY

ANTONY Is that his answer?
AMBASSADOR Ay, my lord.
ANTONY The queen shall then have courtesy, so she   15
    Will yield us up.
AMBASSADOR   He says so.
ANTONY   Let her know't. –
    To the boy Caesar send this grizzled head,
    And he will fill thy wishes to the brim
    With principalities.
CLEOPATRA   That head, my lord?
ANTONY To him again. Tell him he wears the rose   20
    Of youth upon him, from which the world should note
    Something particular. His coin, ships, legions,
    May be a coward's, whose ministers would prevail
    Under the service of a child as soon
    As i'th'command of Caesar. I dare him therefore   25
    To lay his gay caparisons apart
    And answer me declined, sword against sword,
    Ourselves alone. I'll write it. Follow me.
             [*Exeunt Antony and Ambassador*]

ENOBARBUS [*Aside*] Yes, like enough, high-battled Caesar will
    Unstate his happiness and be staged to th'show   30
    Against a sworder! I see men's judgements are
    A parcel of their fortunes, and things outward
    Do draw the inward quality after them
    To suffer all alike. That he should dream,
    Knowing all measures, the full Caesar will   35
    Answer his emptiness! Caesar, thou hast subdued
    His judgement too.

Enter a SERVANT

SERVANT   A messenger from Caesar.
CLEOPATRA What, no more ceremony? See, my women,
    Against the blown rose may they stop their nose
    That kneeled unto the buds. – Admit him, sir.   40
                                  [*Exit Servant*]
ENOBARBUS [*Aside*] Mine honesty and I begin to square.
    The loyalty well held to fools does make
    Our faith mere folly; yet he that can endure
    To follow with allegiance a fall'n lord
    Does conquer him that did his master conquer   45
    And earns a place i'th'story.

Enter THIDIAS

CLEOPATRA   Caesar's will?
THIDIAS Hear it apart.
CLEOPATRA   None but friends. Say boldly.
THIDIAS So haply are they friends to Antony.
ENOBARBUS He needs as many, sir, as Caesar has,
    Or needs not us. If Caesar please, our master   50
    Will leap to be his friend. For us, you know
    Whose he is we are, and that is Caesar's.
THIDIAS So.
    Thus then, thou most renowned: Caesar entreats
    Not to consider in what case thou stand'st   55
    Further than he is Caesar.
CLEOPATRA   Go on: right royal.
THIDIAS He knows that you embrace not Antony

25–8 **I . . . alone** In Brook's production Alan Howard 'turns his single-combat challenge to
Octavius into a wild, self-consciously absurd boast' (Bernard Levin, *Sunday Times*, 15
October 1978).

31–4 **I . . . alike** Cut in Phelps's production (promptbook) and in 1866 (Unidentified newspaper
review, pasted into Beck's copy of the play in the NY Public Library).

As you did love, but as you feared him.
CLEOPATRA   O!
THIDIAS The scars upon your honour therefore he
        Does pity as constrainèd blemishes,   60
        Not as deserved.
CLEOPATRA   He is a god and knows
        What is most right. Mine honour was not yielded,
        But conquered merely.
ENOBARBUS [*Aside*]   To be sure of that,
        I will ask Antony. Sir, sir, thou art so leaky
        That we must leave thee to thy sinking, for   65
        Thy dearest quit thee.   *Exit Enobarbus*
THIDIAS   Shall I say to Caesar
        What you require of him? For he partly begs
        To be desired to give. It much would please him
        That of his fortunes you should make a staff
        To lean upon. But it would warm his spirits   70
        To hear from me you had left Antony
        And put yourself under his shroud,
        The universal landlord.
CLEOPATRA   What's your name?
THIDIAS My name is Thidias.
CLEOPATRA   Most kind messenger,
        Say to great Caesar this in deputation: 75
        I kiss his conqu'ring hand. Tell him I am prompt
        To lay my crown at's feet, and there to kneel.
        Tell him, from his all-obeying breath I hear
        The doom of Egypt.
THIDIAS   'Tis your noblest course.
        Wisdom and fortune combating together,   80
        If that the former dare but what it can,
        No chance may shake it. Give me grace to lay
        My duty on your hand.
            [*He kisses her hand*]
    CLEOPATRA Your Caesar's father oft,

63a   Glyn *'goes up to her women'* at this point in Phelps's production (promptbook); Suzman
      delivers the line with at least a touch of irony in the Nunn–Scoffield television version. In
      Ishia Bennison's delivery in Rutter's production, 'we hear in that "merely" that not only can
      she match them all man for man in pride and energy, she inhabits a different sphere – "fire
      and air" indeed' (Jeffrey Wainwright, *Independent*, 6 October 1995).
84   Mrs Yates's *'giving her Hand'* at this point in Garrick's production (printed text) may have
      signalled encouragement beyond mere assent. Clare Higgins seemed 'shrewd enough to
      know when it is diplomatic to invoke her affair with Caesar's father' (Michael Billington,
      Guardian, 7 November 1992).

When he hath mused of taking kingdoms in,   85
Bestowed his lips on that unworthy place,
As it rained kisses.

Enter ANTONY *and* ENOBARBUS

ANTONY   Favours? By Jove that thunders!
   What art thou, fellow?
THIDIAS   One that but performs
   The bidding of the fullest man, and worthiest
   To have command obeyed.
ENOBARBUS [*Aside*]   You will be whipped.   90
ANTONY [*Calling for Servants*]
   Approach, there! – Ah, you kite! – Now, gods and devils,
   Authority melts from me. Of late, when I cried 'Ho!',
   Like boys unto a muss kings would start forth
   And cry 'Your will?' – Have you no ears? – I am
   Antony yet.

Enter Servants

                        Take hence this jack and whip him.   95
ENOBARBUS [*Aside*] 'Tis better playing with a lion's whelp
   Than with an old one dying.
ANTONY   Moon and stars!
   Whip him. Were't twenty of the greatest tributaries
   That do acknowledge Caesar, should I find them

87a At this point Thyreus knelt and kissed her hand in Phelps's production (promptbook) and in
      1866 and 1867 (Calvert's acting edition); in Robertson's production of 1977–8 Thidias '*kisses
      her hand again; & arm*' (promptbook).

87b In the Nunn–Scoffield television version, Ben Kingsley's Thidias, who has sat on Cleopatra's
      bed and wooingly kissed her palm, turns to find Antony standing over them. In Brook's
      production Thidias 'stood and slowly backed away downstage right in recognition of his
      fault' (Scott, *Antony and Cleopatra*, p. 68). 'Helen Mirren plays the Thidias episode as a
      strumpet, seductively lying against Charmian's back whilst, glancing at the entering Antony,
      she teases him by blatantly flirting with Caesar's man. Antony's answer is to strike her to the
      floor and later straddle her as [if] she were a whore' (Scott, *Antony and Cleopatra*, p. 74).

95   Antony orders the whipping of Caesar's messenger ostensibly on the grounds that he has
      taken liberties with majesty's person (100), and he tells the servants to 'tug him away' (104);
      Cleopatra's personally 'haling' the messenger at 2.5.65 is an intervention that she quickly
      regrets (2.5.83), and on the Jacobean stage Antony would not have been likely to 'hale'
      Thidias himself, as in some modern productions. In Macready's production 'the anger which
      the jealous lover feels when he discovers Caesar's messenger profaning with his lips the
      hand of Cleopatra' was 'forcibly expressed' (*Times*, 22 November 1833). One of Tree's

So saucy with the hand of she here – what's her name   100
Since she was Cleopatra? Whip him, fellows,
Till like a boy you see him cringe his face
And whine aloud for mercy. Take him hence.
THIDIAS Mark Antony –
ANTONY   Tug him away! Being whipped,
Bring him again; this jack of Caesar's shall   105
Bear us an errand to him.
                              Exeunt [Servants] with Thidias
[*To Cleopatra*] You were half blasted ere I knew you. Ha?
Have I my pillow left unpressed in Rome,
Forborne the getting of a lawful race,
And by a gem of women, to be abused   110
By one that looks on feeders?
CLEOPATRA Good my lord –
ANTONY You have been a boggler ever.

reviewers remarked on 'the savagery of his words and acting when he causes Caesar's
messenger to be whipped' (*Daily Mail*, 28 December 1906), and forty years later Godfrey
Tearle was also memorably violent: 'his anger jerked and shook through his body like a
spasm, and he leapt across the stage to grab the messenger by the neck. He shook him like
a dog shakes a rat' (*Daily Express*, 21 December 1946). In 1951 the *Times* critic admired
Olivier's 'savage jealousy' (12 May 1951). T. C. Worsley considered this one of Michael
Redgrave's 'masterly' 'big scenes' of 'passion and guilt', and liked the way 'the interpretation
was superbly maintained' until Antony's suicide (*New Statesman*, 7 May 1953). In Brook's
production, Antony 'violently manhandled Thidias' (Male, *Shakespeare on Stage*, p. 20) and
in the BBC television version he grabs him by the hair and chin, whilst Noble saw 'Antony's
thrashing of the slave after Actium as being symbolic of a huge sexual rage:"A lot of mature
love has a very ugly side to it", he says. "There's nothing particularly romantic about it; it can
be absolutely disgusting to look at"' (Richard Ingham, *Times,* 2–8 April 1983).

96–7a   In the Nunn–Scoffield television version Enobarbus says these lines 'directly to a Thidias
who is led off to be whipped' (Coursen, *Shakespearean Performance*, p. 192); the BBC
television version follows suit. In Brook's production Antony, 'moving from one side to the
other and then up and down centre, [gave] the impression of an agitated lion wounded
on one side by Caesar's man and on the other more grievously by his love'. At this point
Enobarbus 'took Thidias's hand', and 'delivered [him] to the soldiers' at 101 (Scott, *Antony
and Cleopatra*, pp. 68–9).

100   **what's . . . name** In the BBC television version, Blakely delivers this in a decidedly
colloquial manner, appropriate to Antony's anger.

109–10   **Forborne . . . women** Cut in the bowdlerising of the text for Phelps's production
(promptbook).

113   Anthony Hopkins 'reserves a distance still from her, raising his hand at the end to define

But when we in our viciousness grow hard –
O, misery on't! – the wise gods seel our eyes,   115
In our own filth drop our clear judgements, make us
Adore our errors, laugh at's while we strut
To our confusion.
CLEOPATRA   O, is't come to this?
ANTONY I found you as a morsel cold upon
Dead Caesar's trencher; nay, you were a fragment   120
Of Cneius Pompey's, besides what hotter hours,
Unregistered in vulgar fame, you have
Luxuriously picked out. For I am sure,
Though you can guess what temperance should be,
You know not what it is.
CLEOPATRA   Wherefore is this?   125
ANTONY To let a fellow that will take rewards
And say 'God quit you!' be familiar with
My playfellow, your hand, this kingly seal
And plighter of high hearts! O, that I were
Upon the hill of Basan, to outroar   130
The hornèd herd! For I have savage cause,
And to proclaim it civilly were like
A haltered neck which does the hangman thank
For being yare about him.

Enter a SERVANT *with* THIDIAS

                    Is he whipped?
SERVANT Soundly, my lord.   135
ANTONY Cried he? And begged a pardon?
SERVANT He did ask favour.
ANTONY [*To Thidias*] If that thy father live, let him repent
Thou wast not made his daughter; and be thou sorry
To follow Caesar in his triumph, since   140

---

old Nile as "a boggler ever"' (Michael Coveney, *Financial Times*, 10 April 1987).

119–20 **I ... trencher** Antony is strongly contemptuous and physically violent in the
Nunn–Scoffield television version; in Brewster's production 'Jeffery Kissoon's Antony and
Dona Croll's Cleopatra spend a lot of time on the floor, largely because there is neither
throne nor couch for them to recline on'; at these lines 'Antony wrestles Cleopatra to the
ground, as he accuses her' (Tony Dunn, *Tribune*, 31 May 1991).

129–34a **O ... him** Cut in Garrick's production (printed text). In 1925 Holloway 'had not sufficient
power, pace, and excitement for the passage ... Antony here out-roared the horned herd
too much like a bull who is not sure of his next line' (Agate, *Brief Chronicles*, p. 176).

136–43 **Cried ... on't** Cut in 1866 and 1867 (Calvert's acting edition).

Thou hast been whipped for following him. Henceforth
The white hand of a lady fever thee;
Shake thou to look on't. Get thee back to Caesar.
Tell him thy entertainment. Look thou say
He makes me angry with him; for he seems 145
Proud and disdainful, harping on what I am,
Not what he knew I was. He makes me angry,
And at this time most easy 'tis to do it,
When my good stars that were my former guides
Have empty left their orbs and shot their fires 150
Into th'abysm of hell. If he mislike
My speech and what is done, tell him he has
Hipparchus, my enfranchèd bondman, whom
He may at pleasure whip, or hang, or torture,
As he shall like to quit me. Urge it thou. 155
Hence with thy stripes, begone!
                    Exeunt [Servant and] Thidias
CLEOPATRA   Have you done yet?
ANTONY Alack, our terrene moon is now eclipsed,
    And it portends alone the fall of Antony.
CLEOPATRA I must stay his time.
ANTONY To flatter Caesar would you mingle eyes 160
    With one that ties his points?
CLEOPATRA   Not know me yet?
ANTONY Cold-hearted toward me?
CLEOPATRA   Ah, dear, if I be so,
    From my cold heart let heaven engender hail,
    And poison it in the source, and the first stone
    Drop in my neck; as it determines, so 165

141 The 'stripes' on Thidias's back are bloodily in evidence in the Nunn–Scoffield and BBC
     television versions. At this point in Brook's production 'Antony grabbed the man and lifted
     him to his feet only to throw him down again' at 143. He kicked Thidias at 154 (Scott, *Antony
     and Cleopatra*, p. 69). In Caird's 1992 production the whipping was 'particularly fearsome
     and bloody' (Geckle, 'The Power of Desire on Stage', p. 16).

146–7 **harping . . . was** Richard Johnson looks hard at Cleopatra in a long pause after 'I am' in
     the Nunn–Scoffield television version, and in 1992 he struck 'a moment of real pathos' by
     making the same pause (Michael Billington, *Guardian*, 7 November 1992); 'Higgins starts
     crying, and Johnson immediately embraces her. And what is so good here is that we just do
     not know if Cleopatra was going to betray Antony' (Geckle, 'The Power of Desire on Stage',
     p. 16).

147–51 **He . . . hell** Cut in Phelps's production (promptbook).

151–5 **If . . . thou** Cut in 1866 and 1867 (Calvert's acting edition).

Dissolve my life! The next Caesarion smite,
Till by degrees the memory of my womb,
Together with my brave Egyptians all,
By the discandying of this pelleted storm
Lie graveless till the flies and gnats of Nile   170
Have buried them for prey!
ANTONY   I am satisfied.
Caesar sits down in Alexandria, where
I will oppose his fate. Our force by land
Hath nobly held; our severed navy too
Have knit again, and fleet, threat'ning most sea-like.   175
Where hast thou been, my heart? Dost thou hear, lady?
If from the field I shall return once more
To kiss these lips, I will appear in blood;
I and my sword will earn our chronicle.
There's hope in't yet.   180
CLEOPATRA ·That's my brave lord!
ANTONY I will be treble-sinewed, hearted, breathed,
And fight maliciously. For when mine hours
Were nice and lucky, men did ransom lives
Of me for jests; but now I'll set my teeth   185
And send to darkness all that stop me. Come,
Let's have one other gaudy night. Call to me
All my sad captains. Fill our bowls once more;

171b These words were delivered after a '*slight pause*' in Phelps's production; in response,
       '*Cleopatra rushe*[*d*] *into his arms*' (promptbook); in Brook's production, Howard and
       Jackson 'embraced, Antony bringing her to kneel by him' (Scott, *Antony and Cleopatra*,
       p. 69).
181   Suzman seals her approval and their reconciliation with a touch of her fist to Antony's cheek
       in the Nunn–Scoffield television version; she repeats the gesture in the arming scene.
182   In Benson's 1898 production 'the changes in Antony's fierce moods were well depicted by
       Mr Benson, alternating with his love for Cleopatra and his despair and detestation of himself
       and his Queen, as in the scene where, in a fury of rage, he reproaches her with playing into
       Caesar's hands; and then almost at a word from her, his anger ceases, and the old spirit
       rises: "I will be treble-sinewed . . . midnight bell"' (*Worcestershire Echo*, 20 April 1898).
187   **Let's . . . night** In Nunn's production this line 'has a splendid drive, clearly underscored by
       the fact that neither sexual ecstasy nor military greatness is any more possible to Antony'
       (Charles Lewsen, *Times*, 16 August 1972). In Brook's production Alan Howard 'swings from
       his rage at the messenger who dares to kiss Cleopatra's hand to a forced euphoria at the
       prospect of her birthday party' (Bernard Levin, *Sunday Times*, 15 October 1978).
187–8 **Call . . . captains** Holloway 'did not get the full pathos' out of these lines in 1925 (Agate,
       Brief Chronicles, p. 176); Komisarjevsky cut them (Agate, *Brief Chronicles*, p. 183); and in

Let's mock the midnight bell.
CLEOPATRA   It is my birthday.
    I had thought t'have held it poor; but since my lord   190
    Is Antony again, I will be Cleopatra.
ANTONY We will yet do well.
CLEOPATRA [*To Attendants*] Call all his noble captains to my lord.
ANTONY Do so; we'll speak to them, and tonight I'll force
    The wine peep through their scars. Come on, my queen,   195
    There's sap in't yet. The next time I do fight
    I'll make Death love me, for I will contend
    Even with his pestilent scythe.
                                Exeunt [all but Enobarbus]
ENOBARBUS Now he'll outstare the lightning. To be furious
    Is to be frighted out of fear, and in that mood   200
    The dove will peck the estridge; and I see still
    A diminution in our captain's brain
    Restores his heart. When valour preys on reason,
    It eats the sword it fights with. I will seek
    Some way to leave him.   *Exit*   205

1946 Byam Shaw ruined them by 'making [Antony] say them as he mounts the stairs' (Agate, *Sunday Times*, 29 December 1946), though in delivering them Tearle did show 'a flicker of the old spirit' (*Times*, 21 December 1946).

190–1   **but . . . Cleopatra** Michael Billington wrote of this point in Brook's production, 'Cleopatra spins around like a child seeing how far it can go without being sick and together she and Antony roll around the floor in berserk abandon. The more defeat comes, the more they become enslaved to passion' (*Guardian*, 11 October 1978). Robert Cushman saw the business differently in the London revival: Glenda Jackson 'goes into a brief whirling-dervish routine presumably meant to represent the conventional idea of eastern promise. But after a couple of twirls she gives it up; she really cannot play the Cleopatra game any more' (*Observer*, 15 July 1979).

194–5   **tonight . . . scars** Cut by Komisarjevsky (Agate, *Brief Chronicles,* p. 183); the lines were ruined for Agate in 1946 by being spoken (like 187–8) whilst Antony mounted the stairs (*Sunday Times*, 29 December 1946).

197–8   Howard and Jackson stopped 'rolling joyfully downstage together' at this point and 'he lifted Cleopatra on to his shoulders' (Scott, *Antony and Cleopatra*, p. 70). Hopkins spoke the lines 'with a swashbuckling bravura that moves one to tears' (Michael Billington, *Guardian*, 11 April 1987).

198 SD   Chatterton's 'third act concludes with the naval battle between the Romans and the Egyptians, in which the latter were defeated' (*Illustrated London News*, 27 September 1873). In Helpmann's, 'when Antony led Cleopatra off in triumph . . . it looked for all the world as though it was to make an honest woman of her, and a sentimentally happy ending seemed

imminent. The sombre heroics of the play were accordingly lost' (F.G.B., *Plays and Players*, April 1957).

199–205 Cut in 1866 and 1867 (Calvert's acting edition).

199 **Now . . . lightning** In Brook's production Patrick Stewart spoke this line 'in admiration, even though followed by his realistic plan for desertion' (Robert Cushman, *Observer*, 15 October 1978).

[4.1] *Enter* CAESAR, AGRIPPA, *and* MAECENAS, *with his army,*
Caesar reading a letter

CAESAR He calls me boy, and chides as he had power
　　　　To beat me out of Egypt. My messenger
　　　　He hath whipped with rods, dares me to personal combat,
　　　　Caesar to Antony. Let the old ruffian know
　　　　I have many other ways to die, meantime　　　　　　　　5
　　　　Laugh at his challenge.
MAECENAS　　　　　　　　　　　Caesar must think,
　　　　When one so great begins to rage, he's hunted
　　　　Even to falling. Give him no breath, but now
　　　　Make boot of his distraction. Never anger　　　　　　　10
　　　　Made good guard for itself.
CAESAR　　　　　　　　　　　　　　　Let our best heads

Cut in Garrick's production (printed text).

1　**he ... boy** Some Octaviuses have not seemed boyish: Charles Dickens wrote to Wilkie
　　Collins about John Bradshaw in Douglass's production, 'A man much heavier than Mark (in
　　the actual scale, I mean), and about twenty years older, played Caesar. When he came on
　　with a map of London – pretending it was a scroll and making believe to read it – and said,
　　"He calls me Boy" – a howl of derision arose from the audience which you probably heard
　　in the dark, without knowing what occasioned it' (4 March 1855, in *Letters*, vol. II, p. 638.) In
　　Brook's production, Jonathan Pryce turns the Folio's '*reading a letter*' 'into a long running
　　entry' (Michael Billington, *Guardian*, 10 July 1979); in 1978 'he enters whirling [the letter]
　　around in a state of delirious frenzy' (Michael Billington, *Guardian*, 11 October 1978); '"He
　　calls me boy," he cries exultantly on receiving Antony's craziest message (and using it as a
　　paper kite): as who should say, he's really blown it now' (Robert Cushman, *Observer*, 15
　　October 1978); in 1979 'he bears the insulting missive aloft and extends the final noun into a
　　shout of rage' (Michael Billington, *Guardian*, 10 July 1979).

4–6　**Let ... challenge** Ian Charleson laughs hollowly at this point in the BBC television version;
　　John Nettles's Octavius, 'a cool-headed and cold-blooded blond Aryan-type', 'sums up his
　　attitude to Antony' in these lines in Caird's 1992 production (Geckle, 'The Power of Desire on
　　Stage', p. 16), where the dialogue was 'eclipsed by downstage ministrations' to the whipped
　　Thidias (Dessen, 'The Image and the Script', p. 5).

Know that tomorrow the last of many battles
We mean to fight. Within our files there are,
Of those that served Mark Antony but late,
Enough to fetch him in. See it done, 15
And feast the army; we have store to do't,
And they have earned the waste. Poor Antony!

Exeunt

17 **Poor Antony** 'For this most cinematic play Brook also uses a technique of fades and dissolves so that one moment melts into another often with great poignancy. No sooner has Octavius at the end of one scene cried "poor Antony" than we see the tottering hero entering for the next propped up by Enobarbus' (Michael Billington, *Guardian,* 11 October 1978). In the Talawa Theatre production Ben Thomas's Octavius was 'a ruthless Machiavel who, even when he laments Antony's decline, reminds one of Max Beerbohm's point that pity is half-sister to contempt' (Michael Billington, *Guardian,* 20 May 1991).

[4.2] *Enter* ANTONY, CLEOPATRA, ENOBARBUS, CHARMIAN, IRAS, ALEXAS, *with others*

ANTONY He will not fight with me, Domitius?
ENOBARBUS No.
ANTONY Why should he not?
ENOBARBUS He thinks, being twenty times of better fortune,
    He is twenty men to one.
ANTONY   Tomorrow, soldier,   5
    By sea and land I'll fight. Or I will live
    Or bathe my dying honour in the blood
    Shall make it live again. Woo't thou fight well?
ENOBARBUS I'll strike, and cry 'Take all.'
ANTONY   Well said. Come on!
    Call forth my household servants. Let's tonight   10

        Enter three or four SERVITORS

    Be bounteous at our meal. – Give me thy hand,
    Thou hast been rightly honest – so hast thou –
    Thou – and thou – and thou. You have served me well,
    And kings have been your fellows.
CLEOPATRA [*Aside to Enobarbus*]   What means this?
ENOBARBUS [*Aside to Cleopatra*]
    'Tis one of those odd tricks which sorrow shoots   15
    Out of the mind.
ANTONY   And thou art honest too.
    I wish I could be made so many men,
    And all of you clapped up together in
    An Antony, that I might do you service
    So good as you have done.
ALL   The gods forbid!   20
ANTONY Well, my good fellows, wait on me tonight:
    Scant not my cups, and make as much of me
    As when mine empire was your fellow too,
    And suffered my command.
CLEOPATRA [*Aside to Enobarbus*]   What does he mean?
ENOBARBUS [*Aside to Cleopatra*]
    To make his followers weep.

ANTONY   Tend me tonight;   25
    May be it is the period of your duty.
    Haply you shall not see me more, or if,
    A mangled shadow. Perchance tomorrow
    You'll serve another master. I look on you
    As one that takes his leave. Mine honest friends,   30
    I turn you not away, but, like a master
    Married to your good service, stay till death.
    Tend me tonight two hours, I ask no more,
    And the gods yield you for't!
ENOBARBUS   What mean you, sir,
    To give them this discomfort? Look, they weep,   35
    And I, an ass, am onion-eyed. For shame,
    Transform us not to women.
ANTONY   Ho, ho, ho!
    Now the witch take me if I meant it thus!
    Grace grow where those drops fall! My hearty friends,
    You take me in too dolorous a sense,   40
    For I spake to you for your comfort, did desire you
    To burn this night with torches. Know, my hearts,
    I hope well of tomorrow, and will lead you
    Where rather I'll expect victorious life
    Than death and honour. Let's to supper, come,   45
    And drown consideration.
                                Exeunt

Cut in Garrick's production (printed text), in Phelps's (promptbook) and in 1866 and 1867
(Calvert's acting edition).

1   In the Robertson–Selbie production 'Dalton is no "old ruffian". In fact, when Caesar refuses
    single combat his perplexity is almost adolescent' (Jim Hiley, *Listener*, 5 June 1986).

10–46 The 'indispensable farewell to the household servants' was cut in Helpmann's production
    (Kenneth Tynan, *Observer*, 10 March 1957). Michael Billington wrote of Anthony Hopkins's
    performance, 'but what I shall remember most is Mr Hopkins's false gaiety – and
    overpowering inward grief – in the short scene where he bids farewell to his servants. From
    that point on, the knowledge of death sits on Antony' (*Guardian*, 11 April 1987).

ACT 4, SCENE 3

[4.3] *Enter a Company of* SOLDIERS

1 SOLDIER Brother, good night. Tomorrow is the day.
2 SOLDIER It will determine one way. Fare you well.
        Heard you of nothing strange about the streets?
1 SOLDIER Nothing. What news?
2 SOLDIER Belike 'tis but a rumour. Good night to you.   5
1 SOLDIER Well, sir, good night.

              They meet other SOLDIERS

2 SOLDIER Soldiers, have careful watch.
3 SOLDIER And you. Good night, good night.
       They place themselves in every corner of the stage
2 SOLDIER Here we; and if tomorrow
        Our navy thrive, I have an absolute hope   10
        Our landmen will stand up.
1 SOLDIER 'Tis a brave army, and full of purpose.
        Music of the hautboys is under the stage
2 SOLDIER Peace, what noise?
1 SOLDIER List, list!
2 SOLDIER Hark!   15
1 SOLDIER Music i'th'air.
3 SOLDIER Under the earth.
4 SOLDIER It signs well, does it not?
3 SOLDIER No.
1 SOLDIER Peace, I say! What should this mean?   20
2 SOLDIER 'Tis the god Hercules, whom Antony loved,
        Now leaves him.
1 SOLDIER   Walk. Let's see if other watchmen
        Do hear what we do.
2 SOLDIER How now, masters?
            [*They*] *speak together*
ALL How now? How now? Do you hear this?   25
1 SOLDIER Ay, is't not strange?
3 SOLDIER Do you hear, masters? Do you hear?
1 SOLDIER Follow the noise so far as we have quarter.
        Let's see how it will give off.
ALL Content. 'Tis strange.   30
                       Exeunt

This scene seems to be at variance with modern taste, though it was something of a favourite with Trewin. It was cut by Garrick, Kemble, Macready, Phelps and in 1866 and 1867. Asche, in his Australian touring production, replaced it with one of the court the morning after the night of revels, stirring only after three blasts of a herald's trumpet (promptbook). Agate (*Brief Chronicles,* p. 184) favourably contrasts Cass's depiction of this scene in 1934 (in a manner consistent with the Folio stage directions and the implications of the dialogue) with Komisarjevsky's, who had ''Tis the god Hercules' 'said at high noon by a soothsayer'. Trewin (*Shakespeare on the English Stage*, p. 139) says that Williams's treatment of the scene in 1930 acknowledged his debt to Benson's 1912 production; Atkins cut it in 1945 (J. C.Trewin, *Observer*, 29 April 1945). Trewin thought Byam Shaw's 1953 rendition had 'little of the atmosphere of midnight dread' (*Illustrated London News*, 16 May 1953), but in Helpmann's production 'among many good effects was a wonderful moment after the second interval when the god abandoned Antony' (H.G.M., *Theatre World*, April 1957). The scene is cut in the BBC television version, but in Noble's 1982 production, it was 'played on the upper level, the music supplied by humming from characters below, left sleeping from the previous scene' (Stanley Wells, *Times Literary Supplement*, 29 October 1982), the characters in question being 'the lovers and their entourages stretched out in slumber after that "one other gaudy night"' (Michael Coveney, *Financial Times*, 14 October 1982). In Brewster's production the scene was cut and 21–2a 'just muttered on the run by Eros as part of the stage-bustle before the battle'; Tony Dunn remarked, 'a small cast often dictates the cutting of those important Shakespeare scenes . . . where soldiers or servants comment on the actions of the great and represent a larger, more common world below the élites, but one which the élites ignore at their peril. This production throws away the greatest of such moments' (*Tribune*, 31 May 1991). In Rutter's production, which emphasised Antony's association with Hercules, the scene was 'magically staged' (Jeffrey Wainwright, *Independent*, 6 October 1995).

12 SD This is a helpfully specific indication of Jacobean staging for a supernatural scene, which recalls that of the better-known swearing scene in *Hamlet*, 1.5, where the 'old mole' moves around under the stage. Cass's production had memorably 'unearthly music' (Agate, *Brief Chronicles,* p. 184), but in Caird's, 'the noise under the stage was nothing special, indeed was less distinctive than many other sound effects in the show' and was 'superseded' as a sign of mystery by the ubiquitous soothsayer; the noise was cut in Towers's production (Dessen, 'The Image and the Script', p. 5).

[4.4] *Enter* ANTONY *and* CLEOPATRA *with* [CHARMIAN *and*] *others* [*attending*]

ANTONY Eros! Mine armour, Eros!
CLEOPATRA   Sleep a little.
ANTONY No, my chuck. Eros, come, mine armour, Eros!

Enter EROS [*with armour*]

Come, good fellow, put thine iron on.
If fortune be not ours today, it is
Because we brave her. Come.
CLEOPATRA   Nay, I'll help too.   5
What's this for?
          [*She tries to help arm him*]
ANTONY   Ah, let be, let be! Thou art
The armourer of my heart. False, false; this, this.
CLEOPATRA Sooth, la, I'll help. Thus it must be.
ANTONY   Well, well,
We shall thrive now. Seest thou, my good fellow?
Go, put on thy defences.
EROS   Briefly, sir.   10
CLEOPATRA Is not this buckled well?
ANTONY   Rarely, rarely.

0 SD   Trewin said of Helpmann's production, 'I have to remember here one of the most magically
simple, simply magical, moments I have known at the Vic in recent years: the moment when
day dawns over the palace of Alexandria, and slowly, those obelisks are tinged with the rose
of morning. Eros sleeps by Antony's armour. Then, with the rising sun, Antony and
Cleopatra come out to face the new day, the new hope' (*Illustrated London News*, 16 March
1957). For Gert Voss's Antony in Zadek's Edinburgh production, 'even war itself becomes a
kind of capricious game: he costumes himself for conflict, putting on his breast-plate,
binoculars and lip-salve in front of vanity mirrors, as if creating his own legend' (Michael
Billington, *Guardian Weekly*, 28 August 1994).

5b   See the comment on Suzman's gesture at 3.13.181. In 1992 Clare Higgins 'continues to amuse
Antony and us as she helps to dress him in his armor' (Geckle, 'The Power of Desire on
Stage', p. 16).

He that unbuckles this, till we do please
To doff't for our repose, shall hear a storm.
Thou fumblest, Eros, and my queen's a squire
More tight at this than thou. Dispatch. O love,   15
That thou couldst see my wars today, and knew'st
The royal occupation, thou shouldst see
A workman in't.

     Enter an armed SOLDIER

     Good morrow to thee; welcome.
Thou look'st like him that knows a warlike charge.
To business that we love we rise betime   20
And go to't with delight.
SOLDIER   A thousand, sir,
Early though't be, have on their riveted trim
And at the port expect you.
    Shout. Trumpets flourish

    Enter CAPTAINS *and* SOLDIERS

CAPTAIN The morn is fair. Good morrow, general.
ALL Good morrow, general.
ANTONY   'Tis well blown, lads.   25
This morning, like the spirit of a youth
That means to be of note, begins betimes.
So, so. Come, give me that. This way. Well said.
Fare thee well, dame. Whate'er becomes of me,
This is a soldier's kiss.
     [He kisses her]
     Rebukable,   30
And worthy shameful check it were, to stand
On more mechanic compliment. I'll leave thee
Now like a man of steel. – You that will fight,
Follow me close. I'll bring you to't. Adieu.
    Exeunt [Antony, Eros, Captains, and Soldiers]

18b–23 Cut, with the stage direction for the soldier's entrance, in Phelps's production
   (promptbook).

28 **Come . . . way** In Calvert's acting edition, used in 1866 and 1867, Cleopatra *'gives shield the
   wrong way'* at this point.

30a A soldier's kiss, whilst less leisurely than those deployed in wars-within-doors, might be his
   last; Paul Butler's looked like mere lip service in Vanessa Redgrave's 1995 production, where
   he gave 'the queen a perfunctory peck as if he was going off to catch the 8.30 train' (Michael
   Billington, *Guardian*, 3 June 1995).

CHARMIAN Please you retire to your chamber?
CLEOPATRA   Lead me.   35
     He goes forth gallantly. That he and Caesar might
     Determine this great war in single fight!
     Then Antony – but now – Well, on.

                                                            Exeunt

38   Edith Clever held her 'hands raised, palms outwards, in silent prayer, as Antony goes off to
     war' in Stein's production (Michael Billington, *Guardian Weekly*, 14 August 1994).

ACT 4, SCENE 5

[4.5] *Trumpets sound. Enter* ANTONY *and* EROS[, *a* SOLDIER *meeting them*]

SOLDIER The gods make this a happy day to Antony!
ANTONY Would thou and those thy scars had once prevailed
       To make me fight at land!
SOLDIER   Hadst thou done so,
       The kings that have revolted, and the soldier
       That has this morning left thee, would have still   5
       Followed thy heels.
ANTONY   Who's gone this morning?
SOLDIER   Who?
       One ever near thee. Call for Enobarbus,
       He shall not hear thee, or from Caesar's camp
       Say 'I am none of thine.'
ANTONY   What sayest thou?
SOLDIER   Sir,
       He is with Caesar.
EROS   Sir, his chests and treasure   10
       He has not with him.
ANTONY   Is he gone?
SOLDIER   Most certain.
ANTONY Go, Eros, send his treasure after. Do it.
       Detain no jot, I charge thee. Write to him –
       I will subscribe – gentle adieus and greetings;
       Say that I wish he never find more cause   15
       To change a master. O, my fortunes have
       Corrupted honest men. Dispatch. – Enobarbus!
                               Exeunt

Enobarbus's desertion was omitted in Kemble's production (printed text).

12–17   In Caird's production 'Johnson is a grizzled bear of a man, gruff but often hunched in gait, already blasted, yet his voice modulates to a gentle, almost sweet nobility' for this passage (Jeremy Kingston, *Times*, 29 May 1993).

16–17   **O . . . men** In Brook's production Alan Howard made these lines 'wry, not heartbroken' (Bernard Levin, *Sunday Times*, 15 October 1978).

17   **Enobarbus** Jeffery Kissoon, in the Talawa Theatre production, was 'particularly good in his sunset period, uttering a rafter-echoing cry of "Enobarbus"' (Michael Billington, *Guardian*, 20 May 1991).

ACT 4, SCENE 6

[4.6] *Flourish. Enter* AGRIPPA, CAESAR, *with* ENOBARBUS, *and*
DOLABELLA

CAESAR Go forth, Agrippa, and begin the fight.
      Our will is Antony be took alive;
      Make it so known.
AGRIPPA Caesar, I shall.   [*Exit*]
CAESAR The time of universal peace is near.   5
      Prove this a prosp'rous day, the three-nooked world
      Shall bear the olive freely.

                Enter a MESSENGER

MESSENGER   Antony
      Is come into the field.
CAESAR   Go charge Agrippa
      Plant those that have revolted in the van,
      That Antony may seem to spend his fury   10
      Upon himself.
                    Exeunt [all but Enobarbus]
ENOBARBUS Alexas did revolt and went to Jewry on
      Affairs of Antony, there did dissuade
      Great Herod to incline himself to Caesar
      And leave his master Antony. For this pains,   15
      Caesar hath hanged him. Canidius and the rest
      That fell away have entertainment but
      No honourable trust. I have done ill,
      Of which I do accuse myself so sorely
      That I will joy no more.

             Enter a SOLDIER *of Caesar's*

SOLDIER   Enobarbus, Antony   20
      Hath after thee sent all thy treasure, with
      His bounty overplus. The messenger
      Came on my guard, and at thy tent is now
      Unloading of his mules.
ENOBARBUS I give it you.   25
SOLDIER Mock not, Enobarbus,
      I tell you true. Best you safed the bringer

Out of the host; I must attend mine office,
Or would have done't myself. Your emperor
Continues still a Jove. *Exit* 30

ENOBARBUS I am alone the villain of the earth,
And feel I am so most. O Antony,
Thou mine of bounty, how wouldst thou have paid
My better service when my turpitude
Thou dost so crown with gold! This blows my heart. 35
If swift thought break it not, a swifter mean
Shall outstrike thought; but thought will do't, I feel.
I fight against thee? No, I will go seek
Some ditch wherein to die. The foul'st best fits
My latter part of life. *Exit* 40

12–40   Omitted, with the previous desertion scene, in Kemble's production (printed edition).

ACT 4, SCENE 7

[4.7] *Alarum. Drums and Trumpets. Enter* AGRIPPA *[and others]*

AGRIPPA Retire! We have engaged ourselves too far.
  Caesar himself has work, and our oppression
  Exceeds what we expected.

                                    Exeunt

  Alarums. Enter ANTONY, *and* SCARUS *wounded*

SCARUS O my brave emperor, this is fought indeed!
  Had we done so at first, we had droven them home   5
  With clouts about their heads.
ANTONY   Thou bleed'st apace.
SCARUS I had a wound here that was like a T,
  But now 'tis made an H.
         [Sound retreat] far off
ANTONY   They do retire.
SCARUS We'll beat 'em into bench-holes. I have yet
  Room for six scotches more.   10

                Enter EROS

EROS They are beaten, sir, and our advantage serves
  For a fair victory.
SCARUS   Let us score their backs
  And snatch 'em up as we take hares, behind!
  'Tis sport to maul a runner.
ANTONY   I will reward thee
  Once for thy sprightly comfort and tenfold   15
  For thy good valour. Come thee on.
SCARUS I'll halt after.

                                    Exeunt

Cut in Phelps's production (promptbook) and in 1866 and 1867 (Calvert's acting edition).

9–10 **I ... more** To avoid the impression of drinking on duty, Scarus made what Trewin called a
'discrete' emendation to 'notches' in Byam Shaw's 1953 production (*Illustrated London
News*, 16 May 1953); Stephen Williams could scarcely believe his ears: 'did the soldier Scarus
substitute the word "notches" in my favourite Shakespearean line ... ?' (*Evening News*, 29
April 1953).

ACT 4, SCENE 8

[4.8] *Alarum. Enter* ANTONY *again in a march;* SCARUS, *with others*

ANTONY We have beat him to his camp. Run one before,
And let the queen know of our gests.
                                        [*Exit a Soldier*]
                              Tomorrow,
Before the sun shall see's, we'll spill the blood
That has today escaped. I thank you all,
For doughty-handed are you, and have fought   5
Not as you served the cause, but as't had been
Each man's like mine; you have shown all Hectors.
Enter the city, clip your wives, your friends,
Tell them your feats, whilst they with joyful tears
Wash the congealment from your wounds and kiss   10
The honoured gashes whole.

        Enter CLEOPATRA, [*with Attendants*]

                [*To Scarus*] Give me thy hand;
To this great fairy I'll commend thy acts,
Make her thanks bless thee. [*To Cleopatra*] O thou day
    o'th'world,
Chain mine armed neck; leap thou, attire and all,
Through proof of harness to my heart, and there   15
Ride on the pants triumphing!
                [*They embrace*]
CLEOPATRA   Lord of lords,

---

0 SD   In Phelps's production, Antony was preceded by '*4 officers, 4 trophies, 21 troops 3 abreast*' (promptbook); in Calvert's acting edition, used in 1866 and 1867, Antony, Scarus and Officers '*are met by procession of Dancing Girls, Egyptians, &c*'.

11a SD   In Phelps's production, Cleopatra and attendants were accompanied by '*12 Amazonian guards*' and '*6 Egyptian guards*' (promptbook); Calvert's acting edition, used in 1866 and 1867, follows suit. In 1946 Edith Evans 'stood with arms uplifted on the upper stage, while Antony and his victorious soldiers cheered her from below' (Crosse, *Shakespearean Playgoing*, p. 151).

O infinite virtue, com'st thou smiling from
The world's great snare uncaught?
ANTONY My nightingale,
We have beat them to their beds. What, girl, though grey
Do something mingle with our younger brown, yet ha' we   20
A brain that nourishes our nerves and can
Get goal for goal of youth. Behold this man;
Commend unto his lips thy favouring hand. –
Kiss it, my warrior.
> [*Scarus kisses Cleopatra's hand*]
He hath fought today
As if a god in hate of mankind had   25
Destroyed in such a shape.
CLEOPATRA I'll give thee, friend,
An armour all of gold; it was a king's.
ANTONY He has deserved it, were it carbuncled
Like holy Phoebus' car. Give me thy hand.
Through Alexandria make a jolly march;   30
Bear our hacked targets, like the men that owe them.
Had our great palace the capacity
To camp this host, we all would sup together
And drink carouses to the next day's fate,
Which promises royal peril. Trumpeters,   35
With brazen din blast you the city's ear;
Make mingle with our rattling taborins,
That heaven and earth may strike their sounds together,
Applauding our approach.
> [*Trumpets sound.*] *Exeunt*

17–18 **com'st ... uncaught** In Nunn's production 'there is a world of radiant wonder charging' these lines (Jeremy Kingston, *Punch*, 23 August 1972); in Hall's it was the protagonists' 'only moment of mutuality, of union in this life ... Hall allowed this moment to be held and cherished, burnished with the glow of evening torches surrounding the lovers as they exit to the applause of heaven and earth' (Crowl, *Shakespeare Observed*, p. 98).

19–20 **grey ... brown** James Anderson's black wig must have been seen to disadvantage here by audiences increasingly expectant of pictorial realism; see the commentary at 3.11.13–15.

39 SD The triumphant exit of the protagonists was made much of in Phelps's production; in similar style, in 1866 and 1867, their triumph was attended by 'Dancing Girls, *twelve* Amazons ... Scarus, Charmian, Iras, Alexas, Mardian, Diomede, Menecrates, Eros, Egyptian Troops, *Roman trophies*, Roman Officers, *twenty-one* Troops, *three abreast*' (Calvert's acting edition).

ACT 4, SCENE 9

[4.9] *Enter a* SENTRY *and his Company* [*of* WATCH]. ENOBARBUS
follows

SENTRY If we be not relieved within this hour,
　　　　We must return to th'court of guard. The night
　　　　Is shiny, and they say we shall embattle
　　　　By th'second hour i'th'morn.
1 WATCH　　　　　　　　　　This last day was
　　　　A shrewd one to's.
ENOBARBUS　　　　　　O, bear me witness, night –　　　　5
2 WATCH What man is this?
1 WATCH　　　　　　　　Stand close and list him.
　　　　　　　　[*They stand aside*]
ENOBARBUS Be witness to me, O thou blessèd moon,
　　　　When men revolted shall upon record
　　　　Bear hateful memory: poor Enobarbus did
　　　　Before thy face repent.
SENTRY　　　　　　　　Enobarbus?　　　　　　　10
2 WATCH Peace! Hark further.
ENOBARBUS O sovereign mistress of true melancholy,
　　　　The poisonous damp of night disponge upon me,
　　　　That life, a very rebel to my will,
　　　　May hang no longer on me. Throw my heart　　15

7–23a　Enobarbus's suicide was omitted in Kemble's production (printed text); Chatterton's kept this
speech but had Enobarbus '*exit* R.H.' at 18 rather than killing himself (Halliday's edition).
Whatever the emphasis in their characterisation, most actors of Enobarbus have died with at
least a touch of pathos. In Benson's production of 1898, 'it was a touching scene to hear [Lyall
Swete] breathe out his sorrow to the cold moon' (*Stratford-upon-Avon Herald*, 15 April
1898). In Bridges-Adams's production of 1921, Baliol Holloway threatened to upstage Antony
by being 'in the moment of his death . . . a much more majestic figure'; he 'depicted very
cleverly the sufferings of the friend who, having deserted the cause, realises his error and
atones for it by his death' (*Times*, 25 April 1921). 'Mr Tristan Rawson, a little lacking in the
astringency Randle Ayrton once gave to Enobarbus', found 'a true pathos at the end' of
Atkins's 1945 production (J. C. Trewin, *Observer*, 29 April 1945), but in Benthall's production,
Norman Wooland 'lack[ed] the hard-bitten realism of the role, and he die[d] like a

Against the flint and hardness of my fault,
Which, being dried with grief, will break to powder
And finish all foul thoughts. O Antony,
Nobler than my revolt is infamous,
Forgive me in thine own particular,   20
But let the world rank me in register
A master-leaver and a fugitive.
O Antony! O Antony!   [*He dies*]
1 WATCH   Let's speak to him.
SENTRY Let's hear him, for the things he speaks
May concern Caesar.
2 WATCH   Let's do so. But he sleeps.   25
SENTRY Swoons rather, for so bad a prayer as his
Was never yet for sleep.
1 WATCH   Go we to him.
                    [*They approach Enobarbus*]
2 WATCH Awake, sir, awake. Speak to us.

broken-hearted schoolgirl rather than a Stoic Roman soldier' (Venezky, 'Current Shakespearian Productions', p. 336). In the Nunn–Scoffield television version, Stewart's death is low-profile: he sobs his speech lying flat on his back, whilst dogs howl (just as they barked before his barge speech). The exceptions to the general rule of pathos have been Dave King in Richardson's 1973 production, who sought to 'extinguish the character's anguish or confusion by giving him a contemporary American nihilism' (Nicholas de Jongh, *Plays and Players*, October 1973), and Patrick Stewart in Brook's production, 'a marvellously mellow Enobarbus, a genial voluptuary who actually dies with a smile, thinking of those gaudy nights with his tutor Antony' (Benedict Nightingale, *New Statesman*, 20 October 1978). In Hack's production, 'Barry Stanton plays Enobarbus as a bluff, clubbable figure, which makes his later lonely misery particularly touching' (Charles Spencer, *Standard*, in *London Theatre Record*, 9–22 April 1983, p. 298), and Michael Coveney thought Bob Peck's death at least as moving as either of the protagonists' in Noble's 1983 revival (*Financial Times*, 15 April 1983). At Enobarbus's death in Caird's 1992 production, the Soothsayer, played by Jasper Britton, 'appears in the background and does a *danse macabre* with swords' (Geckle, 'The Power of Desire on Stage', p. 16). In Vanessa Redgrave's 1995 production, David Harewood made Enobarbus's death doubly moving because of the imaginative force of his admiration for Antony: 'his loyalty and love for Antony appears inviolable. And when he betrays that trust, we really do believe that his soul might break in two. Through his eyes, just for a fleeting moment, we believe that our Antony has all the stature with which Shakespeare's words endow him' (Louise Stafford Charles, *What's On*, 7 June 1995).

22   Harry Andrews was impressive here in Byam Shaw's 1953 production, as 'overcome by Antony's generosity, broken in heart and spirit' (C.J., *Wolverhampton Express*, 29 April 1953).

1 WATCH Hear you, sir?
SENTRY   The hand of death hath raught him.
                        Drums afar off
                Hark, the drums demurely wake the sleepers.   30
                Let us bear him to th'court of guard;
                He is of note. Our hour is fully out.
2 WATCH Come on, then. He may recover yet.
                                        Exeunt [with the body]

23a SD   In Phelps's production, Enobarbus *'dies on his face'* and is turned over at 29a
         (promptbook).

  29a   Here the speaker tried to rouse Enobarbus by *'shaking him'* in Garrick's production
         (printed edition).

ACT 4, SCENE 10

[4.10] *Enter* ANTONY *and* SCARUS, *with their army*

ANTONY Their preparation is today by sea;
      We please them not by land.
SCARUS   For both, my lord.
ANTONY I would they'd fight i'th'fire or i'th'air;
      We'd fight there too. But this it is: our foot
      Upon the hills adjoining to the city   5
      Shall stay with us – order for sea is given;
      They have put forth the haven –
      Where their appointment we may best discover
      And look on their endeavour.

                                                Exeunt

Cut in Calvert's acting edition, used in 1866 and 1867.

ACT 4, SCENE 11

[**4.11**] *Enter* CAESAR *and his army*

CAESAR But being charged, we will be still by land –
        Which, as I take't, we shall, for his best force
        Is forth to man his galleys. To the vales,
        And hold our best advantage.

Exeunt

Cut in Calvert's acting edition, used in 1866 and 1867. In Brook's production, Antony and Scarus remained on stage, standing still, while Octavius spoke his lines (Hunt and Reeves, *Peter Brook*, p. 226).

ACT 4, SCENE 12

[4.12] *Enter* ANTONY *and* SCARUS

ANTONY Yet they are not joined. Where yond pine does stand
       I shall discover all. I'll bring thee word
       Straight how 'tis like to go.   *Exit*
          Alarum afar off, as at a sea fight
SCARUS   Swallows have built
       In Cleopatra's sails their nests. The augurers
       Say they know not, they cannot tell, look grimly,   5
       And dare not speak their knowledge. Antony
       Is valiant, and dejected, and by starts
       His fretted fortunes give him hope and fear
       Of what he has and has not.

              Enter ANTONY

ANTONY   All is lost!
       This foul Egyptian hath betrayèd me.   10
       My fleet hath yielded to the foe, and yonder
       They cast their caps up and carouse together
       Like friends long lost. Triple-turned whore! 'Tis thou
       Hast sold me to this novice, and my heart
       Makes only wars on thee. Bid them all fly;   15
       For when I am revenged upon my charm,
       I have done all. Bid them all fly. Begone!
                     [Exit Scarus]
       O sun, thy uprise shall I see no more.
       Fortune and Antony part here; even here
       Do we shake hands. All come to this? The hearts   20
       That spanieled me at heels, to whom I gave

1–9a   Cut in Calvert's acting edition, used in 1866 and 1867.

9b   Garrick spoke this after entering '*hastily*' in his production (printed edition). In Byam Shaw's
    production of 1953, Michael Redgrave's 'sigh echoe[d] the uttermost depths of dejection'
    (*Morning Advertiser*, 6 May 1953), whereas in Brook's production Alan Howard spoke the
    line 'with a broad smile on his face' (Bernard Levin, *Sunday Times*, 15 October 1978) and in
    Noble's of 1982 Michael Gambon cried the words 'like a conquering hero, and sounded to
    be made of steel when he claimed to be full of lead' (*Daily Telegraph*, 14 October 1982).

Their wishes, do discandy, melt their sweets
On blossoming Caesar; and this pine is barked
That overtopped them all. Betrayed I am.
O, this false soul of Egypt! This grave charm,   25
Whose eye becked forth my wars and called them home,
Whose bosom was my crownet, my chief end,
Like a right gipsy hath at fast and loose
Beguiled me to the very heart of loss.
What, Eros, Eros!

           Enter CLEOPATRA

           Ah, thou spell! Avaunt!   30
CLEOPATRA Why is my lord enraged against his love?
ANTONY Vanish, or I shall give thee thy deserving
And blemish Caesar's triumph. Let him take thee
And hoist thee up to the shouting plebeians!
Follow his chariot, like the greatest spot   35
Of all thy sex; most monster-like be shown
For poor'st diminutives, for dolts, and let
Patient Octavia plough thy visage up
With her preparèd nails!

                     Exit Cleopatra
           'Tis well thou'rt gone,
If it be well to live. But better 'twere   40
Thou fell'st into my fury, for one death
Might have prevented many. Eros, ho!
The shirt of Nessus is upon me. Teach me,

30a SD In the Nunn–Scoffield television version, Cleopatra 'materialises' here 'as if sent by a
      mocking god of love' (Coursen, *Shakespearean Performance*, p. 192); Antony makes to
      strangle her and throws her to the ground. Cleopatra's appearance is equally sudden in the
      BBC television version, but Antony takes out his violence on the bedlinen.
  33 **Let . . . thee** Blakely turns this into a prayer by clasping his hands in the BBC television
      version, and the buzzing of a fly (presumably a Jacobean flesh-fly) is heard accompanying
      Antony's sense of fatal betrayal; the buzzing culminates at Antony's suicide.
  34 In Garrick's production, 'plebeians' was accented on the first syllable, as it was in
      Shakespeare's day ('plébeians', printed edition). In Phelps's production, Antony seized
      Cleopatra *'by the arm'* here; she strove to *'extricate herself'* from his *'grasp'* and succeeded
      at 39a, exiting *'hastily'* (promptbook).
  43 **The . . . me** Richard Findlater noted Michael Redgrave's 'emphasis' on this line in Byam
      Shaw's 1953 production (*Tribune*, 20 November 1953). This and other classical allusions have
      often been cut in recent productions (Scott, *Antony and Cleopatra*, p. 71), presumably
      because directors think they will be lost on modern audiences. Hall did not cut it, but

Alcides, thou mine ancestor, thy rage.
Let me lodge Lichas on the horns o'th'moon,   45
And with those hands that grasped the heaviest club
Subdue my worthiest self. The witch shall die.
To the young Roman boy she hath sold me, and I fall
Under this plot. She dies for't. Eros, ho!   *Exit*

'Hopkins makes it sound like the grumbling of someone who's got into the wrong togs at the Rugby Club' (Peter Kemp, *Independent*, 11 April 1987).

47   **The . . . die** At this point in 1992, Caird extra-literalised Antony's name-calling: Cleopatra 'appears silently with the Soothsayer behind her' (Geckle, 'The Power of Desire on Stage', p. 16).

ACT 4, SCENE 13

[4.13] *Enter* CLEOPATRA, CHARMIAN, IRAS, [*and*] MARDIAN

CLEOPATRA Help me, my women! O, he's more mad
      Than Telamon for his shield; the boar of Thessaly
      Was never so embossed.
CHARMIAN   To th'monument!
      There lock yourself and send him word you are dead.
      The soul and body rive not more in parting   5
      Than greatness going off.
CLEOPATRA   To th'monument!
      Mardian, go tell him I have slain myself.
      Say that the last I spoke was 'Antony',
      And word it, prithee, piteously. Hence, Mardian,
      And bring me how he takes my death. To th'monument!   10
                                          Exeunt

Zoe Caldwell, in Langham's production, 'was happiest when . . . she spread rumors of her death – so that she could be told precisely how Antony took the news. Antony was her audience, even more than he was her lover' (Kerr, *Thirty Plays*, pp. 165–6). In the Nunn–Scoffield television version, the eunuchs come into their own here: their screeching and other signs of panic immediately establish a sense of hysteria in Cleopatra's court. In Brook's production, Antony remained from the previous scene, 'down stage, prostrated in grief, his outstretched arms on the two brass stools, while Cleopatra and her entourage played [the scene] up stage, beyond the screens' (Hunt and Reeves, *Peter Brook*, p. 226).

ACT 4, SCENE 14

[4.14] *Enter* ANTONY *and* EROS

ANTONY Eros, thou yet behold'st me?
EROS   Ay, noble lord.
ANTONY Sometime we see a cloud that's dragonish,
　　　　A vapour sometime like a bear or lion,
　　　　A towered citadel, a pendent rock,
　　　　A forkèd mountain, or blue promontory   5
　　　　With trees upon't that nod unto the world
　　　　And mock our eyes with air. Thou hast seen these signs;
　　　　They are black vesper's pageants.
EROS   Ay, my lord.
ANTONY That which is now a horse, even with a thought
　　　　The rack dislimns and makes it indistinct   10
　　　　As water is in water.

Kemble's production used a passage from Dryden, in which Ventidius replaces Eros (printed edition). In Macready's, George Bennett as Eros 'made his fidelity look real, and as it were wholly drawn out in the extremity of the occasion, by grasping the hands of his lord with energy, and covering them with convulsive kisses, clasping his knees, and gazing up with the spirit's devotion towards his averted face. The very familiarity of the action was a commentary upon the desperate fortunes of the moment, which drew the devoted follower still closer to the bosom of his sovereign' (*Atlas*, 24 November 1833). In Phelps's production, the scene was set carefully with '*Egyptian Screens – backed by a lower terrace or garden – dwarf wall across painted as Balustrade in 4th Entrance*' (promptbook). Trewin said of Benson's acting, 'It was Antony in his scene with Eros and not Cleopatra in her last scene with her dying lover, who drew the tears of the house' (*Benson*, pp. 96–7). In Bridges-Adams's production of 1927 Wilfrid Walter was 'deeply and sincerely moved . . . when the faithful Eros relieves him of his armour and trappings just before his death' (*Stratford-upon-Avon Herald*, 15 July 1927). In Atkins's 1945 production, 'Eros is well spoken by David Peel, who bears his part nobly in one of the most beautiful scenes ever written' (Ruth Ellis, *Stratford-upon-Avon Herald*, 24 April 1945). Philip Hope-Wallace commented on a staging problem, and what he saw as a misplaced emphasis, in Byam Shaw's production of 1953: 'And with so small an Eros, surely he should stand above Antony on those convenient steps? Antony could never have expected a death wound from that angle? Mr Redgrave in this scene produced a clinical study of a man wincing away from a pain he had expected but

EROS It does, my lord.

ANTONY My good knave Eros, now thy captain is
    Even such a body. Here I am Antony,
    Yet cannot hold this visible shape, my knave.
    I made these wars for Egypt, and the queen, 15
    Whose heart I thought I had, for she had mine –
    Which whilst it was mine had annexed unto't
    A million more, now lost – she, Eros, has
    Packed cards with Caesar and false-played my glory
    Unto an enemy's triumph. 20
    Nay, weep not, gentle Eros; there is left us
    Ourselves to end ourselves.

Enter MARDIAN

                  O, thy vile lady!
    She has robbed me of my sword.

MARDIAN   No, Antony,
    My mistress loved thee, and her fortunes mingled
    With thine entirely.

ANTONY   Hence, saucy eunuch, peace! 25
    She hath betrayed me and shall die the death.

hadn't in fact felt . . . But that seems to me not the point in that scene' (*Time and Tide*, 8 May 1953). Brook's production made much of the drama of the suicide, both that of Antony's expectation of a fatal stroke from Eros and that of his preparation to kill himself, the frame of reference being the popular form of Japanese theatre, Kabuki: after Antony's 'voluptuous caress of the blade that will kill him and his hand in hand walk with his servant Eros prefiguring his celestial encounter with Cleopatra' (Michael Billington, *Guardian*, 11 October 1978), he 'sits cross-legged, hands folded, for the fatal sword-stroke that never comes' (Bernard Levin, *Sunday Times*, 15 October 1978). In the BBC television version, Antony kneels in expectation of beheading.

2–14   Trewin thought Michael Redgrave 'passes too easily over certain speeches' such as this one, 'though, in his odd way, he finds unexpected treasure in others' (*Illustrated London News*, 16 May 1953). The speech is cut in the Nunn–Scoffield television version.

19   **false-played . . . glory** At this point in Phelps's production, '*Eros turns aside as weeping*' (promptbook).

22b–34   Cut in Phillips's 1985 Chichester production, in the process of 'ennobling' Cleopatra's character.

23   In the Nunn–Scoffield television version, Antony has been swordless since his defeat; Brook's production marked this as the point of 'Antony's final resignation when he hurls his sword clear across the back of the stage' (B. A. Young, *Financial Times*, 12 October 1978). The line is given edge by being addressed to the eunuch Mardian; in Towers's 1993

MARDIAN Death of one person can be paid but once,
            And that she has discharged. What thou wouldst do
            Is done unto thy hand. The last she spake
            Was 'Antony, most noble Antony!'   30
            Then in the midst a tearing groan did break
            The name of Antony; it was divided
            Between her heart and lips. She rendered life
            Thy name so buried in her.
ANTONY   Dead, then?
MARDIAN   Dead.
ANTONY Unarm, Eros. The long day's task is done,   35
            And we must sleep. [*To Mardian*] That thou depart'st hence
            ·   safe
            Does pay thy labour richly; go.
                                                            Exit Mardian
                                    Off, pluck off!
                        [*Eros unarms him*]
            The sevenfold shield of Ajax cannot keep
            The battery from my heart. O, cleave, my sides!
            Heart, once be stronger than thy continent;   40
            Crack thy frail case! Apace, Eros, apace!
            No more a soldier. Bruisèd pieces, go;
            You have been nobly borne. – From me awhile.
                                                            Exit Eros
            I will o'ertake thee, Cleopatra, and
            Weep for my pardon. So it must be, for now   45
            All length is torture; since the torch is out,
            Lie down and stray no farther. Now all labour
            Mars what it does; yea, very force entangles
            Itself with strength. Seal then, and all is done.
            Eros! – I come, my queen. – Eros! – Stay for me.   50
            Where souls do couch on flowers, we'll hand in hand,

production, where Mardian was omitted and replaced here by 'an impressive male servant',
the effect was lost (Dessen, 'The Image and the Script', p. 5).

35–104   T. C. Worsley regarded Michael Redgrave's performance here as 'magnificent', 'passion and
guilt fighting it out desperately till the last' (*New Statesman*, 7 May 1953).

42   **Bruisèd ... go** 'Hopkins took his long unarming at a deliberate pace, pausing to kiss his
"bruised pieces" as he passed them on to Eros' (Crowl, *Shakespeare Observed*, pp. 99–100).

50–1   **Stay ... flowers** Olivier spoke these and the following lines in a 'charged dry-throbbing
voice that holds all ecstasy, all yearning' (Trewin, *A Play To-night*, pp. 86–7), but Philip
Hope-Wallace thought Michael Redgrave 'seemed throttled ... just where a clear ringing
sustained note (logical or illogical) is all one wants' (*Time and Tide*, 8 May 1953).

And with our sprightly port make the ghosts gaze.
Dido and her Aeneas shall want troops,
And all the haunt be ours. – Come, Eros, Eros!

Enter EROS

EROS What would my lord?
ANTONY   Since Cleopatra died   55
    I have lived in such dishonour that the gods
    Detest my baseness. I, that with my sword
    Quartered the world, and o'er green Neptune's back
    With ships made cities, condemn myself to lack
    The courage of a woman – less noble mind   60
    Than she which by her death our Caesar tells
    'I am conqueror of myself.' Thou art sworn, Eros,
    That when the exigent should come – which now
    Is come indeed – when I should see behind me
    Th'inevitable prosecution of   65
    Disgrace and horror, that on my command
    Thou then wouldst kill me. Do't. The time is come.
    Thou strik'st not me, 'tis Caesar thou defeat'st.
    Put colour in thy cheek.
EROS   The gods withhold me!
    Shall I do that which all the Parthian darts,   70
    Though enemy, lost aim and could not?
ANTONY   Eros,
    Wouldst thou be windowed in great Rome and see
    Thy master thus with pleached arms, bending down
    His corrigible neck, his face subdued
    To penetrative shame, whilst the wheeled seat   75
    Of fortunate Caesar, drawn before him, branded
    His baseness that ensued?
EROS   I would not see't.
ANTONY Come, then, for with a wound I must be cured.
    Draw that thy honest sword, which thou hast worn

53–4 **Dido . . . ours** Trewin wrote of 'the hush when [Olivier] spoke' these lines (*Shakespeare on the English Stage*, p. 219) and said 'for me, Olivier's Antony, arms out-flung as he speaks [these lines] is still my picture of the man at whose death even Caesar cried' (*John O'London's Weekly*, 15 May 1953).

55–62a, 68–9a, 83–7, 88b–93a Cut by Nunn, to indicate 'the servant's swift suicide in the face of Antony's stern resolution' (Scott, *Antony and Cleopatra*, p. 67).

71b–7a Hopkins 'kissed and cradled Eros in his arms as he envisioned . . . his treatment in Rome' (Crowl, *Shakespeare Observed*, p. 100).

>   Most useful for thy country.
> EROS   O, sir, pardon me!   80
> ANTONY When I did make thee free, swor'st thou not then
>   To do this when I bade thee? Do it at once,
>   Or thy precedent services are all
>   But accidents unpurposed. Draw, and come.
> EROS Turn from me then that noble countenance   85
>   Wherein the worship of the whole world lies.
> ANTONY Lo thee! [*He turns from him*]
> EROS My sword is drawn.
> ANTONY   Then let it do at once
>   The thing why thou hast drawn it.
> EROS   My dear master,
>   My captain, and my emperor, let me say   90
>   Before I strike this bloody stroke, farewell.
> ANTONY 'Tis said, man, and farewell.
> EROS Farewell, great chief. Shall I strike now?
> ANTONY   Now, Eros.
> EROS (*Kills himself*)
>   Why, there then! Thus I do escape the sorrow
>   Of Antony's death.
> ANTONY   Thrice nobler than myself!   95
>   Thou teachest me, O valiant Eros, what
>   I should, and thou couldst not. My queen and Eros
>   Have by their brave instruction got upon me
>   A nobleness in record. But I will be
>   A bridegroom in my death and run into't   100
>   As to a lover's bed. Come then, and Eros,

84 **Draw . . . come** In Calvert's acting edition, used in 1866 and 1867, Antony *'throws himself open to the blow'* here.

93b SD In Phelps's production, Eros *'falls on his sword'*, *'throwing it convulsively at the feet of Antony, as he staggers back & falls. Antony starts round in amazement'* (promptbook); 'the beauty of the surprise struck the audience into stillness for an instant, and was followed by a burst of sustained applause' (*Examiner*, 27 October 1849). In 1866 and 1867 (Calvert's acting edition) and in 1873 (Halliday's edition) the convulsions were used, but *'falls on his sword'* became *'stabs himself with the sword'*, and the *Athenaeum* critic found that unsatisfactory in Chatterton's production, since 'falling on a sword is a more easily realizable form of suicide than thrusting the weapon with a violent effort into the side' (27 September 1873). In the Nunn–Scoffield television version, Antony covers his eyes as his black Eros (Joe Marcell) holds the blade in striking position close to Antony before turning it on himself.

99–101 **But . . . bed** Garrick's production had Antony *'taking* Eros' *Sword'* for his own suicide and *'running on it'* (printed edition); presumably Garrick discarded his own sword when he

Thy master dies thy scholar. To do thus
I learned of thee.
                    [*He falls on his sword*]
                    How, not dead? Not dead?
The guard, ho! O, dispatch me!

Enter a [Company of the] GUARD, *[one of them* DERCETUS]

1 GUARD What's the noise?   105
ANTONY I have done my work ill, friends.
        O, make an end of what I have begun!
2 GUARD The star is fall'n.
1 GUARD And time is at his period.
ALL Alas, and woe!   110
ANTONY Let him that loves me strike me dead.
1 GUARD Not I.
2 GUARD Nor I.
3 GUARD Nor anyone.
                    Exeunt [all the Guard but Dercetus]
DERCETUS Thy death and fortunes bid thy followers fly.   115
        This sword but shown to Caesar with this tidings
        Shall enter me with him.
                    [*He takes up Antony's sword*]

                    Enter DIOMEDES

unarmed. In 1849 Phelps spoke these lines *'taking up the sword thrown down by Eros'*
(promptbook). In the Robertson–Selbie production 'this welcoming of death is ecstatically
undertaken by Dalton, who disrobes joyfully to his loincloth' (Michael Coveney, *Financial
Times*, 27 May 1986).

103b Olivier 'flung his sword from him as he wounded himself only to find, when not dead, that
     he could no longer reach it and therefore had to call for help' (Scott, *Antony and Cleopatra*,
     p. 64). In Helpmann's production, Keith Michell 'rushed upon his sword clumsily. When it
     fell from his hand he remained upright for a moment expecting to crash forward into death
     until the terrible realization came upon him' (Clarke, *Shakespeare at the Old Vic*, n.p.). In
     the Nunn–Scoffield television version, a white curtain falls down over Antony's wound as he
     stabs himself, in what may possibly be an allusion to the white cloth on which ritual suicides
     are committed in Kabuki theatre. In Brook's production, Antony, having waited cross-legged
     for Eros's blow, 'commits his own hara-kiri in a no less ritually stylised manner' (Bernard
     Levin, *Sunday Times*, 15 October 1978). In the BBC television version, Antony falls on his
     sword kneeling on the bed, a nice emblematic touch, as is the buzzing of the flesh-fly (see
     the commentary at 4.12.33). Antony's bungling his suicide can produce an unlooked-for
     response; Geckle reported that it 'elicited laughs from the audience the night I saw [Caird's
     1992] production' ('The Power of Desire on Stage', p. 16).

DIOMEDES Where's Antony?
DERCETUS There, Diomed, there.
DIOMEDES Lives he? Wilt thou not answer, man?   120
                              [*Exit Dercetus*]
ANTONY Art thou there, Diomed? Draw thy sword and give me
          Sufficing strokes for death.
DIOMEDES   Most absolute lord,
          My mistress Cleopatra sent me to thee.
ANTONY When did she send thee?
DIOMEDES   Now, my lord.
ANTONY   Where is she?
DIOMEDES Locked in her monument. She had a prophesying fear   125
          Of what hath come to pass. For when she saw –
          Which never shall be found – you did suspect
          She had disposed with Caesar, and that your rage
          Would not be purged, she sent you word she was dead;
          But fearing since how it might work, hath sent   130
          Me to proclaim the truth, and I am come,
          I dread, too late.
ANTONY Too late, good Diomed. Call my guard, I prithee.
DIOMEDES What ho, the emperor's guard! The guard, what ho!
          Come, your lord calls.   135

          Enter four or five of the GUARD *of Antony*

ANTONY Bear me, good friends, where Cleopatra bides.
          'Tis the last service that I shall command you.
1 GUARD Woe, woe are we, sir, you may not live to wear
          All your true followers out.
ALL   Most heavy day!
ANTONY Nay, good my fellows, do not please sharp fate   140
          To grace it with your sorrows. Bid that welcome
          Which comes to punish us, and we punish it,
          Seeming to bear it lightly. Take me up.
          I have led you oft; carry me now, good friends,

---

125 **Locked . . . monument** In 1897 Calvert gave a short burst of laughter at this point (Shaw,
     Plays and Players, p. 193), and in Hall's production 'Mr Hopkins was at his best as Antony lay
     dying, greeting with ironic laughter the realization that Cleopatra's reported death had been
     just another of her lies to test his affection' (Charles Osborne, *Daily Telegraph*, 11 April
     1987). In Vanessa Redgrave's 1995 production, Paul Butler also laughed here, as he had at
     the news of Fulvia's death, but his laughter seemed out of keeping with the quieter nature of
     'the rest of the performance' (Rhoda Koenig, *Independent*, 3 June 1995).
138–43 **Woe . . . lightly** Cut in Phelps's production (promptbook).

And have my thanks for all. 145

Exeunt, bearing Antony [and Eros]

145 SD This was managed with '*Soldiers bearing and supporting Antony on a shield*' in 1866 and 1867 (Calvert's acting edition).

ACT 4, SCENE 15

[4.15] *Enter* CLEOPATRA *and her Maids aloft, with* CHARMIAN *and*
IRAS

CLEOPATRA O Charmian, I will never go from hence.
CHARMIAN Be comforted, dear madam.
CLEOPATRA   No, I will not.
    All strange and terrible events are welcome,
    But comforts we despise. Our size of sorrow,
    Proportioned to our cause, must be as great   5
    As that which makes it.

Enter [*below*] DIOMEDES

              How now? Is he dead?

In 1833 Antony and Cleopatra died in the same scene, as they did in the Australian touring productions of Asche (1912–13) and Wilkie (1927–8). Some reviewers of pictorial versions of the play were impatient with the deaths of the lovers. In Chatterton's production 'the interminable agonies of Antony, for such in the presentation they seemed, rendered altogether ineffective the death scene of Cleopatra' (*Athenaeum*, 27 September 1873), which was 'spoiled by theatrical affectations necessitated by new stage arrangements' (*Illustrated London News*, 27 September 1873). Turn-of-the-century critics tended to regard the deaths of both protagonists as occupying too much playing time. In Benson's production of 1898 'it is in the last act of the play that "dragging" is perceptible, and Mr Benson will, doubtless, in future representations . . . see the desirability of condensing the "dying" scenes. These are unduly prolonged' (*Stratford-upon-Avon Herald*, 22 April 1898); in Tree's version 'if anything could have prevented the full fruition of the triumph it would have been the inordinate length of the closing act, which occupied over an hour and five minutes, mainly devoted to a series of suicides in each of which the intending defunct took "an unconscionable time in dying"' (*Birmingham Daily Mail*, 28 December 1906). Critical dissatisfaction with Shakespeare's treatment of the lovers' deaths has been more subdued in recent times, though Agate, writing about Leigh's production of 1925, said 'so long an interval between the dying of the two protagonists is certain to make for anti-climax' (*Brief Chronicles*, p. 174), and Michael Billington, praising the pace of the Talawa Theatre production, complained of 'Shakespeare's interminably protracted conclusion (give me Dryden any day)' (*Guardian*, 20 May 1991).

DIOMEDES His death's upon him, but not dead.
　　　　Look out o'th'other side your monument;
　　　　His guard have brought him thither.

　　　Enter [below] ANTONY, *and the* GUARD *[bearing him]*

CLEOPATRA O sun,   10
　　　　Burn the great sphere thou mov'st in; darkling stand
　　　　The varying shore o'th'world! O Antony,
　　　　Antony, Antony! Help, Charmian, help, Iras, help!
　　　　Help friends below! Let's draw him hither.
ANTONY   Peace!
　　　　Not Caesar's valour hath o'erthrown Antony,   15
　　　　But Antony's hath triumphed on itself.
CLEOPATRA So it should be, that none but Antony
　　　　Should conquer Antony, but woe 'tis so!

9 SD　The Folio stage direction does not specify Antony's manner of entry, though 4.14.136,143,144
　　　and 4.15.9 all indicate that he is no longer on his feet. A litter or a chair may have been used
　　　in early performances; if so, such a property may also have been used in the hauling which
　　　follows. Kemble paid scant regard to Cleopatra's security arrangements and avoided the
　　　hauling simply by having Antony enter Cleopatra's monument, *'supported by the Guard'*
　　　(printed edition); Wilkie's Australian touring production in 1927–8 followed suit. In 1833 and
　　　1873 Cleopatra went to Antony, as in Dryden. In 1849 Phelps managed by means of a scene
　　　change at 19 to the interior of the monument, where Cleopatra and Charmian are
　　　'discovered leading forward Antony' (promptbook). In 1866 and 1867 the guard carry
　　　Antony in *'on a shield'* and *'place him on couch'* in the monument before leaving (Calvert's
　　　acting edition). In the Langtry–Wingfield production, Antony died offstage, though his body
　　　was later brought in for Cleopatra's death-scene. In Hack's 1983 production 'they made such
　　　a business of carting Keith Baxter's half-dead Antony off the scene that when they brought
　　　him back down the same steps past the audience, the journey couldn't help looking wasted,
　　　so that having to winch him up to the Monument for Cleopatra's last blessing looked more
　　　cumbersome than ever' (Eric Shorter, *Daily Telegraph*, in *London Theatre Record*, 9–22
　　　April 1983, p. 298). Brook departed from tradition to make a point: 'Antony is defeated
　　　twice; he then fails to kill himself. It is a terrible ignoble mess: and in showing it to be
　　　precisely that, with Mr Howard finally stumbling towards the monument in an unbelieving
　　　daze, the production deliberately forfeits any aspirations to the heroic' (Irving Wardle,
　　　Times, 11 October 1978).

13　　Avoiding the hauling, Phelps's production inserted 35–38 ('Had . . . fools') after 'Antony,
　　　Antony!' and, among other minor changes, substituted 'We must draw him up' for 'Let's
　　　draw him hither' (promptbook).

15–18　Cut in Phelps's production (promptbook).

ANTONY I am dying, Egypt, dying; only
       I here importune death awhile, until   20
       Of many thousand kisses the poor last
       I lay upon thy lips.
CLEOPATRA   I dare not, dear –
       Dear my lord, pardon – I dare not,
       Lest I be taken. Not th'imperious show
       Of the full-fortuned Caesar ever shall   25
       Be brooched with me. If knife, drugs, serpents, have
       Edge, sting, or operation, I am safe.
       Your wife Octavia, with her modest eyes
       And still conclusion, shall acquire no honour
       Demuring upon me. But come, come, Antony –   30
       Help me, my women – we must draw thee up.
       Assist, good friends.
ANTONY   O, quick, or I am gone.
       [They begin lifting]
CLEOPATRA Here's sport indeed! How heavy weighs my lord!
       Our strength is all gone into heaviness,
       That makes the weight. Had I great Juno's power,   35
       The strong-winged Mercury should fetch thee up
       And set thee by Jove's side. Yet come a little;
       Wishers were ever fools. O, come, come, come!
       They heave Antony aloft to Cleopatra

19   Antony delivered the line *'falling C'* in Phelps's production (promptbook).

22b–39 **I . . . welcome** Cut in the avoidance of the hauling in Phelps's production (promptbook).
       22b–29a were cut to bolster Cleopatra's staunchness in Robertson's production of 1977–8
       and Phillips's 1985 Chichester production.

38 SD Scholars of the Jacobean stage have usually been concerned about the logistics of lifting
       Antony to the gallery above the rear of the stage, which presumably represented Cleopatra's
       vantage-point in the monument; the 'problem' is compounded by the perceived need to
       take him over the gallery balustrade (an additional three feet in height; some have hoped
       for a hinged section) 'into' the monument, and two consequent practical issues: how
       Cleopatra remains visible and audible while lamenting over the corpse, and how Antony's
       body is removed at the end of the scene (the Folio direction is *'Exeunt, bearing of Anthonies
       body'*). Andrew Gurr (*Shakespearean Stage*, p. 137), probably thinking the gallery too
       problematic, says that a monument is likely to have been one of the 'special properties' at
       the Globe, but this is an old notion that begs many questions about the staging of the scene.
       Evert Sprinchorn ('An Intermediate Level', *Theatre Notebook*, 46, pp. 73–94, and 48, pp.
       51–2) believes that theatres of the period had a permanent raised platform in front of the
       tiring house and that (presumably at the Globe) Antony was winched through the floor of
       the balcony; there is no reason why private theatres should not have shared this feature, but

an 'intermediate level' would seem to have as many drawbacks as advantages. If Rees ('An Elizabethan Eyewitness', pp. 92–3) is right, and Daniel's 1607 description of Antony twice suspended on the way up is a reflection of a performance of Shakespeare's play, it is possibly also an indication that hauling mechanisms or methods have caused difficulty from the start, whatever the height of the upper playing area. Reading Daniel via Rees will probably lead to the conclusion that the King's Men used a block and tackle with a sling made of 'rowles of taffety' (presumably representing women's garments or monument soft furnishings), and perhaps (as Lamb suggests in *Antony and Cleopatra*, p. 183) made theatrical capital out of the need for pauses for adjustment in the hauling process. Certainly Daniel's 'pale Antonius, showring out his blood / On th'under lookers, which there gazing stood' sounds like Jacobean staging (perhaps making a theatrical point out of the practicalities of managing a bladder of blood whilst being hoisted), though it is as well to remember that this detail is in Plutarch and is not alluded to in Shakespeare's text. Lamb (*Antony and Cleopatra*, p. 185) comments in passing on the connection between Cleopatra's 'mercurial nature' and Antony's being left dangling, and Jacobean audiences may well have seen emblematic significance in the stage picture of Antony's death among women. Thomson ('Antony and Cleopatra, Act 4 Scene 16', pp. 79–90) thinks the awkwardness of the procedure intentional and supported linguistically by the punning on heaviness, and emphasises the emblematic associations of the lifting with the power of love (and, less explicitly, with the wheel of fortune). Thomson also makes the attractive suggestion that Antony was not meant to be taken over the gallery balustrade, but lowered again to the stage (at 64–70): given the thematic value of additional awkwardness and the need, in any case, for strong-armed boy and adult actors, this makes practical sense in terms both of the visibility of the lamenting Cleopatra and the Folio's '*exeunt*'.

For the hoisting in Garrick's production, 'Cleopatra, *and her Women, throw out certain Tackle; into which the People below put* Antony, *and he is drawn up*' (printed edition). In Benson's 1898 production, where the monument was a large set (Lamb, *Antony and Cleopatra*, p. 89), the women 'used to lower strips of linen which guards wound round Antony, and raising him on the butt end of their halberds, helped [them] to hoist him over the balcony. This was no easy task' (Constance Benson, *Mainly Players*, pp. 158–9). Tree, also using linen but not halberd-butts, employed diversionary tactics and a scene change to manage the hoisting: 'the Empress and her attendants are made to look from a window in Cleopatra's monument and stretch their arms down to the dying Antony as if they would lift him from the shoulders of those who are bearing him away' (*Daily News*, 28 December 1906); the hauling 'had been done behind the curtain while the audience was being distracted by a little diversion in "Caesar's Camp" just over the footlights. Judging by the noise that went on behind I should say the hoisting was done by a very primitive hand-crane' (O.S., *Punch*, 2 January 1907); 'As the lights go out we see the body being hoisted upwards to the window; then, by a quick change, we are transported to the interior of the monument, and once more see Antony being lifted inwards through the open window, and brought to the couch to receive Cleopatra's farewell. It was a clever bit of stage work, which gave a complete and satisfactory impression without any lack of verisimilitude' (*Telegraph*, 28 December 1906). In Asche's Australian touring production, Antony was helped up to the stage through a trap door (promptbook). In Atkins's 1922 production, Wilfrid Walter 'had to lie on his back throughout two scenes' (Lamb, *Antony and Cleopatra*, p. 108), whilst in Komisarjevsky's, the dying Antony was carried to the rear of Cleopatra's tomb 'so that he was invisible at the back of the stage and Cleopatra's back was to us as he spoke his last words' (*New English Weekly*, 22 October 1936). Agate commented on Komisarjevsky's production, 'here the playgoer's induced simplicity comes in. Why, he asks, go to all that trouble when from the spot where Antony has fallen to the top of the monument there is a perfectly good staircase of six steps only? I am afraid this production is one of those cases in which what is wanted is a little less imagination and a few more scene-shifters' (*Brief Chronicles*, p. 182). Of Atkins's 1945 production, with its traverse curtains and music between the scenes, one critic wrote, 'Note how simply the producer overcomes the old problem . . . of lifting the body of Antony 10 or 12 feet high into the monument. No struggling with ropes; no scene changing here to ruin a good speech or a smooth performance' (J.H.B., *Evesham Journal*, 5 May 1945). In the Nunn–Scoffield television version, soldiers lift Antony while standing on his litter, which is lifted by other soldiers. Brook decided that 'with no split-level pretences the dying Antony can simply be hauled horizontally to Cleopatra wrapped in her and her women's scarves' (Robert Cushman, *Observer*, 15 October 1978). In the BBC television version, the ledge of the monument is no higher than the soldiers' heads, so that the linen slings used for the lifting seem superfluous, and in Phillips's 1985 Chichester production the monument was 'set on stage level and Antony is hoisted into it up three piffling little steps' (Irving Wardle, *Times*, 16 May 1985). Other modern productions have used specially constructed monuments to try and minimise the hauling difficulties: Bridges-Adams had a monument-platform concealed behind a seven-foot traverse curtain for his 1921 OUDS production (Lamb, *Antony and Cleopatra*, p. 110); Benthall's of 1951 (which was also used in the alternately running *Caesar and Cleopatra*) had a platform little more than six feet high; of Caird's in 1992 Geckle wrote that 'the monument's actually descending to the level of the stage is a *trompe l'oeil* effect gone awry' ('The Power of Desire on Stage', p. 16).

The lifting of Antony was read symbolically as elevation in Sjöberg's 1975 Stockholm production, where Cleopatra 'raise[d] up her Antony from the lowliness of the earth's surface to his final redemption' (Leiter (ed.), *Shakespeare Around the Globe*, p. 33). Since Byam Shaw's 1953 production, women's scarves have sometimes been used for the lifting, as much for symbolic as for naturalistic reasons; Noble's production, in a theatrical spirit akin to the Jacobean, made a noose symbol out of necessity 'in the blood-stained cloth with which [Cleopatra] hauled the dying Antony up to the monument' (Victoria Radin, *Observer*, 17 October 1982), and in Hall's 'Antony was hauled up to her in a great net. "Ah ha! Y'are caught" and "com'st thou from the world's great snare uncaught?" were surely the text's

And welcome, welcome! Die when thou hast lived;
Quicken with kissing. Had my lips that power,   40
Thus would I wear them out.
    [*She kisses him*]

images which inspired Hall's staging here. The space on the ledge was cramped and awkward, but fitting as an image of how much the vast world of this play has shrunk' (Crowl, *Shakespeare Observed*, p. 100). In the Robertson–Selbie production of the previous year, critics were surprised by Antony's scantily clad and bloody state. Jack Tinker related it to the dressing-up trunk at the lovers' entrance: 'all the disguises have gone and the game is not only over but up. Miss Redgrave soaks her tunic in his blood and the grief etched on her face is even more eloquent than Shakespeare's words' (*Daily Mail*, 27 May 1986). Many reviewers saw reference to Christian iconography in Antony's being 'winched up to a balcony, naked and bleeding in a loin-cloth, like a crucifixion', to the arms of 'Cleopatra, austere at this point in a bloodstained shift and shorn hair, like a Christian martyr' (Mary Harron, *Observer*, 1 June 1986). Rather than viewing the protagonists as love's martyrs, other critics focussed on the image of Antony's slaughter: 'a Christ-like carcase in a loin-cloth, his greatness reduced to a poor remnant of bleeding meat' (John Barber, *Daily Telegraph*, 24 May 1986), 'lifted up to Cleopatra's monument in the wierdest, most arresting way I've ever seen: three-quarters naked, one-quarter disembowelled, and vertically, by means of a rope attached to a wrist. He dangles like a piece of meat from a Bacon painting' (Benedict Nightingale, *New Statesman*, 30 May 1986).

 Critics have been quick to notice the absurdities generated by the practical problems. One said of Bridges-Adams's production of 1924, 'the dying Antony was carried in and "slewed up" to a sort of window casement, where I was afraid his subsequent corpse would fall off!' (*Referee*, 22 June 1924). For one critic, Brook's horizontal method made Antony's death 'ludicrous by his being dragged along the floor by what looks like lengths of ticking, hauled by Cleopatra and her companions instead of being "drawn up to a higher level". This scene only underlines the producer's insistence on playing everything at floor level' (P.B., *Worcester Journal*, 19 October 1978); Francis King remarked 'if there is to be no visual magic – even when Cleopatra and her women are dragging Antony up on to the monument, all of them are, for some reason, on the same level – then a strong verbal magic should compensate' (*Sunday Telegraph*, 15 July 1979). In the preview of Hall's production, 'having tied a rope round Hopkins' considerable girth, the guards wrestled ineffectually with a pulley for fully two minutes. The audience's merriment at the sight of Hopkins stuck six feet from the ground was such that a guardsman was forced to cry: "Pray be silent"' (P.H.S., *Times*, 6 April 1987) and John London wrote of Zadek's Berlin production, 'the extended acrobatic struggle with which the dying Antony is lifted "aloft" to Cleopatra produces more than a titter in the audience' (*Plays International*, December 1994, p. 28).

41 In 1889 Cora Brown-Potter, 'as she bent over the dying Antony . . . tore open her bodice,

ALL A heavy sight!
ANTONY I am dying, Egypt, dying.
     Give me some wine, and let me speak a little.
CLEOPATRA No, let me speak, and let me rail so high   45
     That the false huswife Fortune break her wheel,
     Provoked by my offence.
ANTONY   One word, sweet queen:
     Of Caesar seek your honour, with your safety. O!
CLEOPATRA They do not go together.
ANTONY   Gentle, hear me.
     None about Caesar trust but Proculeius.   50
CLEOPATRA My resolution and my hands I'll trust,
     None about Caesar.
ANTONY The miserable change now at my end
     Lament nor sorrow at, but please your thoughts

exposing the flesh-colored silk cloths covering her bosom' (Shattuck, *Shakespeare on the American Stage*, vol. II, p. 123). In the BBC television version, this line seems hyperbolic on Lapotaire's lips, since her kisses are always perfunctory, though she does at least kiss Antony on the lips here. John Barber thought Suzman's kisses 'business-like rather than passionate' (*Daily Telegraph*, 16 August 1972); in the television version her last kiss is tender rather than either business-like or passionate; the wind, which has been howling as Antony is hauled up, 'whips Suzman's hair as she tries to quicken her Antony with kissing' (Crowl, 'A World Elsewhere', p. 155). The literal-minded may have found Glenda Jackson more credible here – 'At [Antony's] death, the two of them clutch and cuddle and laugh . . . a last-gasp attempt to recapture their pristine rapture' (Benedict Nightingale, *What's On in London*, 13 July 1979) – or Helen Mirren, whose 'clinches are red hot' (Keith Nurse, *Daily Telegraph*, 14 April 1983).

42   Cut in Phelps's production, where there was no hauling (promptbook); also cut by Helpmann and by Robertson, presumably to prevent an inappropriate response to anticipated lifting difficulties. The omission did not help in 1957: 'there was even mirth when his dying frame was hoisted perilously into the monument. This business should certainly be omitted' (J. A. Cuddon, *Tablet*, 23 March 1957). Seasoned critics may be more anticipatory than most; Trewin wrote of the hauling in Byam Shaw's 1953 production, 'I was in distracting agony lest he should crash' (*John O'London's Weekly*, 15 May 1953). At the Hall preview, 'When he finally made it, and was greeted by Cleopatra with the words "A heavy sight", the entire Olivier broke into applause' (P.H.S., *Times*, 6 April 1987).

43   In Komisarjevsky's production, 'nothing is seen save the backs of the hauling women, while Antony's broken: "I am dying, Egypt, dying!" has to be shouted at the top of his lungs by an actor in obviously excellent vocal condition' (Agate, *Brief Chronicles*, p. 182). Harold Hobson saw Julian Glover's Antony in Richardson's production as 'peevishly interrupting Cleopatra's

In feeding them with those my former fortunes,   55
Wherein I lived the greatest prince o'th'world,
The noblest; and do now not basely die,
Not cowardly put off my helmet to
My countryman – a Roman by a Roman
Valiantly vanquished. Now my spirit is going;   60
I can no more.
CLEOPATRA   Noblest of men, woo't die?

chatter to say "I am dying, Egypt, dying" as if she would not otherwise have noticed'
(*Sunday Times*, 12 August 1973). In Brook's production, the famous line was given a twist
consonant with the play's widespread Jacobean punning on 'dying' in the sexual sense: '"I
am dying, Egypt, dying", Mr Howard complains at his consort's continued appetite for his
body' (Irving Wardle, *Times*, 11 October 1978). Scott (*Antony and Cleopatra*, p. 75) says
Gambon made this line 'a matter-of-fact statement rather than a moment of great emotion';
Rosalind Carne was impressed in Gambon's death-scene by the 'steady look from beneath
those distinctive, hooded eyelids. He has an extraordinary quality of concentrated
impassivity . . . dropping to a low pitch of stunned detachment in the moments before death'
(*Guardian*, 14 April, 1983), whilst Francis King was not: 'he acquits himself like a Gilbert and
Sullivan tenor unexpectedly called on to sing Tristan' (*Sunday Telegraph*, 17 October 1982).
Rutter's interpretation may have owed something to both Howard and Gambon, but was
delivered more colloqially as 'I'm dying, Egypt' (see Michael Coveney, *Observer*, 8 October
1995 and Robert Butler, *Independent on Sunday*, 15 October 1995); 'When the dying Antony
is hauled over the wire mesh of the Monument, he finds himself stuck and smothered by
Cleopatra. At that point Rutter's "let me speak a little" comes across as a polite version of
"gerroff", and amused the first-night audience more than it should' (Benedict Nightingale,
Times, 5 October 1995).

61a   Antony '*sinks*' at this point in Garrick's production (printed edition). Tree did manage a little
more: 'Even in dying Mr Tree introduces extra "business". Cleopatra kisses him as he lies on
a couch and seems dead. He returns the kiss, rolls over Cleopatra's body on to the floor, and
is then content to be dead' (*Morning Post*, 28 December 1906); 'I think it regrettable that
Antony should have rolled off the bed when he expired, because the ladies had a lot of
difficulty, even with the help of Mardian (who was not supposed to be there) in getting him
back again. They had not really quite recovered from the exhausting process of hauling him
up through the window' (O.S., *Punch*, 2 January 1907). In Asche's Australian touring
production, Antony '*kisses Cleopatra and falls backward and behind trap. Head R*'
(promptbook). In Komisarjevsky's production, 'the moaning of the women', 'affected in its
melodiousness', 'spoilt the realism of Antony's death' (*New English Weekly*, 22 October
1936); likewise 'Antony's death [was] lost in wailing and moaning' in Helpmann's (*Nursing
Times*, 15 March 1957), whereas in Nunn's production the grief was memorably
concentrated in Cleopatra's cry: 'Miss Suzman arches her elegantly-black-wigged head to

Hast thou no care of me? Shall I abide
In this dull world, which in thy absence is
No better than a sty? O see, my women:

                                  [*Antony dies*]

The crown o'th'earth doth melt. My lord!   65
O, withered is the garland of the war;
The soldier's pole is fall'n! Young boys and girls
Are level now with men; the odds is gone,
And there is nothing left remarkable
Beneath the visiting moon. [*She starts to faint*]   70

the skies and lets out a heart-wringing cry of grief that comes from every fibre of her body.
I can hear its echo yet' (Michael Owen, *Evening Standard*, 16 August 1972).

65   In the Nunn–Scoffield television version, the wind 'whistles plaintively in counterpoint to
[Suzman's] huge scream after "My lord" when she realises that Antony has died' (Crowl, 'A
World Elsewhere', p. 155). 'Mirren scream[ed] a bit' on this line (Michael Coveney, *Financial
Times*, 14 October 1982); Dench delivered it 'as one great extended cry with the word "earth"
stretched out to seeming infinity' (Crowl, *Shakespeare Observed*, p. 100).

66–8   **O . . . men** Charles Morgan's phonetic transcription in *The Times* (16 October 1936) of
Leontovich's pronunciation of these lines ('O weederdee degarlano devar / Desolderspo
lees falln: young boisenguls / Alefelnow wimen') is famous and made these perhaps the
best-known lines in the play in 1936. Agate (*Brief Chronicles*, p. 182) alluded to it, and so did
Trewin in reviewing Helpmann's production twenty-one years later: 'Many people show
their age when they whisper to themselves or to a neighbour . . . the phrase, "O weederdee
degarlano devar", a line of gibberish that takes us, across twenty years, to a performance
still barbed in the incredulous mind' (*Illustrated London News*, 16 March 1957); see the
commentary at 1.3.33–4. In Langham's production, 'as her Antony's dead head fell back on
her arm', Zoe Caldwell 'launched into' these lines 'in a crooning howl, like a wolf baying at
the moon. The theatre throbbed with wild, furious desolation' (Ronald Bryden, *Observer*, 13
September 1967). In Hall's production, Dench brought 'an embittered despair' to this speech
(Charles Osborne, *Daily Telegraph*, 11 April 1987).

67–70 **Young . . . moon** In Bridges-Adams's 1924 production, Dorothy Green delivered these lines
'broken with grief, whereas they should be spoken as by one in a trance' (R.C.R.,
Birmingham Post, 17 July 1924).

70 SD The Folio has no stage direction; Rowe supplied '*She faints.*' 'Cleopatra *swoons*' in Garrick's
production (printed edition). In Phelps's production '*She falls in a burst of grief on Antony*'
(promptbook) and 71–4 were cut; Calvert's acting edition, used in 1866 and 1867, has the
same direction. Janet Suzman said of the direction to faint, 'It's erroneous, but I can see why
it was put in. Charmian and Iras try to rouse her and when she next speaks it's on a
completely new level . . . it was only then that she realised the truth of her love for [Antony]'
(Pitt, *Shakespeare's Women*, p. 217).

CHARMIAN O, quietness, lady!
IRAS She's dead too, our sovereign.
CHARMIAN Lady!
IRAS Madam!
CHARMIAN O madam, madam, madam!   75
IRAS Royal Egypt! Empress!
                    [*Cleopatra stirs*]
CHARMIAN Peace, peace, Iras.
CLEOPATRA No more but e'en a woman, and commanded
               By such poor passion as the maid that milks
               And does the meanest chares. It were for me   80
               To throw my sceptre at the injurious gods,
               To tell them that this world did equal theirs
               Till they had stol'n our jewel. All's but naught;
               Patience is sottish, and impatience does
               Become a dog that's mad. Then is it sin   85
               To rush into the secret house of death
               Ere death dare come to us? How do you, women?
               What, what, good cheer! Why, how now, Charmian?
               My noble girls! Ah, women, women! Look,
               Our lamp is spent, it's out. Good sirs, take heart.   90
               We'll bury him; and then, what's brave, what's noble,
               Let's do't after the high Roman fashion
               And make death proud to take us. Come, away.
               This case of that huge spirit now is cold.
               Ah, women, women! Come, we have no friend   95
               But resolution and the briefest end.
                    Exeunt, [*those above*] *bearing off Antony's body*

83–9 **All's . . . girls** Cut in Phelps's production (promptbook).

90   **Our . . . out** Here Suzman makes as if to close Antony's eyes in the Nunn–Scoffield television version.

95–6 **no . . . end** In Phelps's production, Glyn spoke the lines '*Kneeling C, and with her arms extended aloft as invoking the protection of the Gods – Charmian and Iras in great despondency*' (promptbook); Calvert's acting edition, used in 1866 and 1867, follows suit. In the Nunn–Scoffield television version, Suzman's strong jaw underlines her determination at this point.

96 SD Capell was the first editor to suggest the removal of the body by those above, and it was done thus in Garrick's production (printed edition). Unless Antony is raised and then lowered again (possibly the original staging, but not one embraced by directors since its proposal in 1989), the guard have been superfluous since the heaving of Antony aloft; they may be given a ceremonial function at the end of the scene, but that involves a conceptual

opening of the monument door, which Cleopatra has earlier refused. Helpmann seized on the ceremonial solution, inspired by his own success in removing Hamlet's body with a flourish at the end of that play: 'Robert Helpmann's production is vividly pictorial (and his admirers will recognise a distinct echo of the sensational *Hamlet* in the way that Antony's body is borne round the stage on the shoulders of the soldiers)' (G.M.P., *Croydon Advertiser*, 14 June 1957).

ACT 5, SCENE I

[5.1] *Enter* CAESAR, AGRIPPA, DOLABELLA, MAECENAS,
[GALLUS, PROCULEIUS,] *with his council of war*

CAESAR Go to him, Dolabella, bid him yield;
　　　　Being so frustrate, tell him, he mocks
　　　　The pauses that he makes.
DOLABELLA 　　　　　　　　Caesar, I shall.　　　　[*Exit*]

　　　　Enter DERCETUS, *with the sword of Antony*

CAESAR Wherefore is that? And what art thou that dar'st
　　　　Appear thus to us?
DERCETUS 　　　　　　I am called Dercetus.　　　　5
　　　　Mark Antony I served, who best was worthy
　　　　Best to be served. Whilst he stood up and spoke
　　　　He was my master, and I wore my life
　　　　To spend upon his haters. If thou please
　　　　To take me to thee, as I was to him　　　　10
　　　　I'll be to Caesar; if thou pleasest not,
　　　　I yield thee up my life.
CAESAR 　　　　　　　　What is't thou say'st?
DERCETUS I say, O Caesar, Antony is dead.
CAESAR The breaking of so great a thing should make
　　　　A greater crack. The round world　　　　15
　　　　Should have shook lions into civil streets
　　　　And citizens to their dens. The death of Antony
　　　　Is not a single doom; in the name lay
　　　　A moiety of the world.
DERCETUS 　　　　　　　　He is dead, Caesar,
　　　　Not by a public minister of justice,　　　　20
　　　　Nor by a hirèd knife; but that self hand
　　　　Which writ his honour in the acts it did
　　　　Hath, with the courage which the heart did lend it,
　　　　Splitted the heart. This is his sword;

Omitted in 1866 and 1867 (Calvert's acting edition).

20–1　**Not . . . knife** Cut in Phelps's production (promptbook), where Dercetus's part was given to Menas.

                    [*He offers the sword*]

I robbed his wound of it. Behold it stained 25
With his most noble blood.
CAESAR   Look you sad, friends?
The gods rebuke me, but it is tidings
To wash the eyes of kings.
AGRIPPA   And strange it is
That nature must compel us to lament
Our most persisted deeds.
MAECENAS   His taints and honours 30
Waged equal with him.
AGRIPPA   A rarer spirit never
Did steer humanity; but you gods will give us
Some faults to make us men. Caesar is touched.
MAECENAS When such a spacious mirror's set before him,
He needs must see himself.
CAESAR   O Antony, 35
I have followed thee to this; but we do launch
Diseases in our bodies. I must perforce
Have shown to thee such a declining day,
Or look on thine; we could not stall together
In the whole world. But yet let me lament 40
With tears as sovereign as the blood of hearts
That thou, my brother, my competitor
In top of all design, my mate in empire,
Friend and companion in the front of war,
The arm of mine own body, and the heart 45
Where mine his thoughts did kindle – that our stars,
Unreconciliable, should divide
Our equalness to this. Hear me, good friends –

24 SD   In the BBC television version, Ian Charleson not only takes the emblematic bloody sword (which has cured Antony with a wound), he weeps over it and, withdrawing from the others, holds its hilt to his face. In Noble's production, Jonathan Hyde 'breaks down when he takes the death weapon in his hands' (Irving Wardle, *Times*, 14 October 1982).

28a   In Nunn's production, Corin Redgrave's 'tears on hearing of Antony's death may be crocodile tears – the man is incapable of any others – but they are oddly moving all the same' (W.T., *Nottingham Evening Post*, 16 August 1972). In Miller's BBC television version, Charleston 'holds back the tears at Octavia's departure but allows them to fall freely at Antony's death, while still he probes his mind to discover why it had to happen in this way' (Scott, *Antony and Cleopatra*, p. 72). Tim Piggott-Smith was 'hit hard (and was not play-acting for public consumption)' in Hall's production (Dessen, 'The Image and the Script', pp. 7–8).

30b–35a   Cut in Phelps's production (promptbook).

Enter an EGYPTIAN

But I will tell you at some meeter season.
The business of this man looks out of him;   50
We'll hear him what he says. – Whence are you?
EGYPTIAN A poor Egyptian yet, the queen my mistress,
            Confined in all she has, her monument,
            Of thy intents desires instruction,
            That she preparedly may frame herself   55
            To th'way she's forced to.
CAESAR   Bid her have good heart.
            She soon shall know of us, by some of ours,
            How honourable and how kindly we
            Determine for her; for Caesar cannot live
            To be ungentle.
EGYPTIAN   So the gods preserve thee!   *Exit* 60
CAESAR Come hither, Proculeius. Go and say
            We purpose her no shame. Give her what comforts
            The quality of her passion shall require,
            Lest, in her greatness, by some mortal stroke
            She do defeat us; for her life in Rome   65
            Would be eternal in our triumph. Go,
            And with your speediest bring us what she says
            And how you find of her.
PROCULEIUS   Caesar, I shall.   *Exit Proculeius*
CAESAR Gallus, go you along.
                                                [Exit Gallus]
                        Where's Dolabella,
            To second Proculeius?
ALL   Dolabella!   70
CAESAR Let him alone, for I remember now
            How he's employed. He shall in time be ready.
            Go with me to my tent, where you shall see

48 SD   This seems to imply some attempt in Jacobean production at exotic costuming for the
         Egyptian males; Caesar's question at 51 need not be understood geographically.

73   **Go with me to my tent** In the BBC television version, these words are addressed to
      Dercetus, as the sword-bringer; so, too, in Caird's and Towers's productions, which used
      'the same group of actors who attend Caesar in 5.1 to storm Cleopatra's monument in 5.2',
      leaving Dercetus as 'the only figure still available'. In Hall's production, however, Octavius's
      words were addressed to 'an older, statesman-like' Agrippa, who nodded, but distanced
      himself from Caesar's 'vengeful choices' by exiting in a different direction in anticipation of
      his absence in the last scene (Dessen, 'The Image and the Script', pp. 7–8).

69b,70b–7 Cut in the Nunn–Scoffield television version.

How hardly I was drawn into this war,
How calm and gentle I proceeded still 75
In all my writings. Go with me and see
What I can show in this.

Exeunt

ACT 5, SCENE 2

[5.2] *Enter* CLEOPATRA, CHARMIAN, IRAS, *and* MARDIAN

CLEOPATRA My desolation does begin to make
    A better life. 'Tis paltry to be Caesar;
    Not being Fortune, he's but Fortune's knave,
    A minister of her will. And it is great
    To do that thing that ends all other deeds,   5
    Which shackles accidents and bolts up change,
    Which sleeps, and never palates more the dung,
    The beggar's nurse and Caesar's.

Enter [to the gates of the monument] PROCULEIUS

PROCULEIUS Caesar sends greeting to the Queen of Egypt,
    And bids thee study on what fair demands   10
    Thou mean'st to have him grant thee.
CLEOPATRA   What's thy name?
PROCULEIUS My name is Proculeius.
CLEOPATRA   Antony
    Did tell me of you, bade me trust you, but
    I do not greatly care to be deceived
    That have no use for trusting. If your master   15
    Would have a queen his beggar, you must tell him
    That majesty, to keep decorum, must
    No less beg than a kingdom. If he please
    To give me conquered Egypt for my son,
    He gives me so much of mine own as I   20
    Will kneel to him with thanks.
PROCULEIUS   Be of good cheer;
    You're fall'n into a princely hand. Fear nothing.

---

0 SD   In the Jacobean theatre, however Antony's corpse was removed, Cleopatra, Iras and
      Charmian had plenty of time, during 5.1, to get to the main stage by the usual means
      available to those '*aloft*' (presumably internal stairs). The generally unlocalised use of stage
      areas permitted the temporary naming of specific areas for specific purposes but did not
      insist on a constricting 'consistency'; thus rapid transitions could be managed between
      'interiors' and 'exteriors'. In 1898 Benson, working within very different conventions, staged
      Cleopatra's death, like Antony's, on top of the monument.

Make your full reference freely to my lord,
Who is so full of grace that it flows over
On all that need. Let me report to him   25
Your sweet dependency, and you shall find
A conqueror that will pray in aid for kindness
Where he for grace is kneeled to.
CLEOPATRA   Pray you tell him
I am his fortune's vassal, and I send him
The greatness he has got. I hourly learn   30
A doctrine of obedience, and would gladly
Look him i'th'face.
PROCULEIUS   This I'll report, dear lady.
Have comfort, for I know your plight is pitied
Of him that caused it.

[Some of the Guard come behind Cleopatra and seize her]

You see how easily she may be surprised.   35
Guard her till Caesar come.
IRAS   Royal queen!
CHARMIAN O Cleopatra! Thou art taken, queen.
CLEOPATRA Quick, quick, good hands. *[Drawing a dagger]*
PROCULEIUS   . Hold, worthy lady, hold!
            [He seizes and disarms her]
Do not yourself such wrong, who are in this
Relieved, but not betrayed.

34 SD   On the Jacobean stage there was no need to represent in a literal fashion the 'scaling' of the
        monument by Caesar's soldiers; presumably they simply entered in the manner of scalers
        (stealthily), from one of the usual entry doors. Later directors, however, have had to
        contend with conventions and assumptions influenced by realism. Garrick's production
        concentrated on the plausibility of the surprise element: 'Gallus *maintains Converse with*
        Cleopatra. *Re-enter, into the Monument, from behind*, Proculeius, *and Soldiers, hastily*'
        (printed edition). Phelps's was preoccupied with the mechanics of scaling: at 28a, '*Gallus
        and 2 Soldiers appear at back lowering a Ladder by which they stealthily descend on to the
        Stage. Throw back bar of grated door and let in Proculeius and 2 guards and exits himself
        at grated door*'; the '*noise of bolt*' was heard at 34 (promptbook); similar business was used
        in 1866 and 1867 (Calvert's acting edition). Sheridan Morley wrote of the Robertson–Selbie
        production, 'soldiers from Rome capture Cleopatra in an unusually plausible rope-ladder
        attack' (*Punch*, 11 June 1986). In Caird's production there was 'a sudden invasion of SAS-
        style Roman soldiers, abseiling down from the flies on ropes' (Charles Spencer, *Daily
        Telegraph*, 9 November 1992) and Cesarion was in the monument, 'so that he could be
        taken away as a hostage' (Dessen, 'The Image and the Script', p. 5).

CLEOPATRA   What, of death too,   40
     That rids our dogs of languish?
PROCULEIUS   Cleopatra,
     Do not abuse my master's bounty by
     Th'undoing of yourself. Let the world see
     His nobleness well acted, which your death
     Will never let come forth.
CLEOPATRA   Where art thou, Death?   45
     Come hither, come! Come, come, and take a queen
     Worth many babes and beggars.
PROCULEIUS   O, temperance, lady!
CLEOPATRA Sir, I will eat no meat, I'll not drink, sir;
     If idle talk will once be necessary
     I'll not sleep, neither. This mortal house I'll ruin,   50
     Do Caesar what he can. Know, sir, that I
     Will not wait piniored at your master's court,
     Nor once be chastised with the sober eye
     Of dull Octavia. Shall they hoist me up
     And show me to the shouting varletry   55
     Of censuring Rome? Rather a ditch in Egypt
     Be gentle grave unto me! Rather on Nilus' mud
     Lay me stark nak'd and let the water-flies
     Blow me into abhorring! Rather make
     My country's high pyramides my gibbet   60
     And hang me up in chains!
PROCULEIUS   You do extend
     These thoughts of horror further than you shall
     Find cause in Caesar.

Enter DOLABELLA

DOLABELLA   Proculeius,
     What thou hast done thy master Caesar knows,
     And he hath sent for thee. For the queen,   65
     I'll take her to my guard.

56–7   **Rather . . . me** In 1866, Adelaide Calvert spoke this passage 'with thrilling power'
(unidentified newspaper review, pasted into Beck's copy of the play in the NY Public
Library); Judi Dench delivered the lines as a 'furious cry of indignation' (Michael Ratcliffe,
Observer, 12 April 1987).

60   **pyramides** William Archer 'implore[d]' Janet Achurch 'not to be led astray by a misprint in
the ordinary editions, but to follow the Folio and the metre' here (*1897*, p. 72), and Agate
said Mary Newcombe ought to give the word 'its four syllables' (*Brief Chronicles*, p. 179).

61a   Suzman mimes this condition in the Nunn–Scofield television version.

PROCULEIUS   So, Dolabella,
  It shall content me best. Be gentle to her.
  [*To Cleopatra*] To Caesar I will speak what you shall please,
  If you'll employ me to him.
CLEOPATRA   Say I would die.
                                   Exit Proculeius [with Soldiers]
DOLABELLA Most noble empress, you have heard of me?   70
CLEOPATRA I cannot tell.
DOLABELLA   Assuredly you know me.
CLEOPATRA No matter, sir, what I have heard or known.
  You laugh when boys or women tell their dreams;
  Is't not your trick?
DOLABELLA   I understand not, madam.
CLEOPATRA I dreamt there was an emperor Antony.   75
  O, such another sleep, that I might see
  But such another man!
DOLABELLA   If it might please ye –
CLEOPATRA His face was as the heav'ns, and therein stuck
  A sun and moon, which kept their course and lighted
  The little O, the earth.
DOLABELLA   Most sovereign creature –   80
CLEOPATRA His legs bestrid the ocean; his reared arm
  Crested the world; his voice was propertied
  As all the tunèd spheres, and that to friends;
  But when he meant to quail and shake the orb,
  He was as rattling thunder. For his bounty,   85
  There was no winter in't; an autumn 'twas
  That grew the more by reaping. His delights
  Were dolphin-like; they showed his back above
  The element they lived in. In his livery
  Walked crowns and crownets; realms and islands were   90
  As plates dropped from his pocket.
DOLABELLA   Cleopatra –

73–4 Cut in Phelps's production (promptbook).
75–91a Adelaide Calvert's delivery of this eulogy was 'touching' (unidentified newspaper review,
  pasted into Beck's copy of the play in the NY Public Library); Claire Luce delivered the first
  line with 'pathos rather than triumph' (Ruth Ellis, *Stratford-upon-Avon Herald*, 24 April
  1945). Noble's production interpreted 'Cleopatra's famous hymn to Antony' as 'a dream-like
  fantasy' (Michael Billington, *Guardian*, 14 October 1982) and Judi Dench delivered it 'with
  the intensity of someone recounting a dream' (Michael Billington, *Guardian*, 11 April 1987).
  In what was the high point of her 1995 production, Vanessa Redgrave shed her robes to utter
  'the speech of a woman dazed with shock yet every inch a queen' (Rhoda Koenig,

CLEOPATRA Think you there was or might be such a man
      As this I dreamt of?
DOLABELLA   Gentle madam, no.
CLEOPATRA You lie up to the hearing of the gods.
      But if there be nor ever were one such,   95
      It's past the size of dreaming. Nature wants stuff
      To vie strange forms with fancy; yet t'imagine
      An Antony were Nature's piece 'gainst fancy,
      Condemning shadows quite.
DOLABELLA   Hear me, good madam:
      Your loss is as yourself, great; and you bear it   100
      As answering to the weight. Would I might never
      O'ertake pursued success but I do feel,
      By the rebound of yours, a grief that smites
      My very heart at root.
CLEOPATRA   I thank you, sir.
      Know you what Caesar means to do with me?   105
DOLABELLA I am loath to tell you what I would you knew.
CLEOPATRA Nay, pray you, sir.
DOLABELLA   Though he be honourable –
CLEOPATRA He'll lead me then in triumph.
DOLABELLA Madam, he will, I know't.

   Flourish. Enter PROCULEIUS, CAESAR, GALLUS, MAECENAS,
                and others of his train

Independent, 3 June 1995): 'The way Miss Redgrave exquisitely speaks Cleopatra's eulogy, in slow, entranced contemplation of grief and loss, signals the fact that in dying, Antony has at last made the queen aware of her capacity for genuine feeling' (Nicholas de Jongh, *Evening Standard*, 2 June 1995).

87–8   **His . . . dolphin-like** In Brewster's production, Dona Croll spoke these lines 'in liquid phrases', holding them 'out . . . to the light with relish' (Alastair Macaulay, *Financial Times*, 20 May 1991).

90–1   **realms . . . pocket** Michael Billington remarked that Glenda Jackson 'trie[d] to circumvent the rhetoric by a hyper-realism' and here 'trie[d] to imitate the image instead of accepting it for what it is' (*Guardian*, 11 October 1978).

93b   Helen Mirren 'crumples into tears when Dolabella denies the validity of her dream' (Stanley Wells, *Times Literary Supplement*, 29 October 1982).

102–4a   **but . . . root** In Caird's 1993 revival, Dominic Masham 'introduced the fascinating nuance that he, in trying to console [Cleopatra] for her grief, actually makes love to her, and that, as a result of her yielding to him for a moment, he is moved to reveal the secret of his master's intentions' (Martin Esslin, *Plays International*, July-August 1993).

09 SD–89 SD   The meeting of Caesar and Cleopatra was omitted in Kemble's, Macready's and

ALL Make way there! Caesar!   110
CAESAR Which is the Queen of Egypt?
DOLABELLA It is the emperor, madam.
                              Cleopatra kneels
CAESAR Arise, you shall not kneel.

Chatterton's productions, and in Tree's 'the omission of [Cleopatra's] overtures to [Octavius]
at the end of the play loses one more facet of her amazing character, and makes her death-
scene a sentimentality instead of a passage of grandeur following on one of degradation'
(*Manchester Guardian*, 29 December 1906).

111   This line seems, on the face of it, an impertinence on Caesar's part: Agate (in *Brief
Chronicles*, p. 184) says that in 1936 Ellis Irving 'preferred a forthright rendering of that
polished snake, Octavius; this honest manly fellow would never have conceived the
impertinent [line]'. Early audiences would probably have expected Cleopatra to seem
queenly in bearing, if not in costume or circumstance; but here she is captive and desolate,
and cannot be expected to radiate majesty. Glenda Jackson said in an interview, 'Queens
aren't queens because of the clothes they wear. It's as much the way others on the stage
react to you as the way you look' (*Guardian*, 2 July 1979). Some actresses have not been
queenly enough, either here or elsewhere, for their critics: Agate said of Edith Evans in 1925,
apropos of this line, 'indeed, the jade is never very easily distinguished from her attendants'
(*Brief Chronicles*, p. 175); in 1935 Catherine Lacey differentiated clearly between the queen's
private and public roles (see the quotation at 1.3.6–12); and Claire Luce, considered better at
seduction than royal presence, 'makes of Cleopatra a fascinating gamine . . . she can never
give a passionate grandeur to Cleopatra' (E.F., *News Chronicle*, 24 April 1945). The line is
interpreted more literally than usual in the Nunn–Scoffield television version, where
Cleopatra's misery has her crouched on the ground in a foetal position, and her attendants
crouched in obeisance to Caesar, when he enters; it is cut in the BBC television version.
Noble's production also gave the queen's appearance symbolic value at the expense of
majesty: Helen Mirren 'appears in black, her face besmirched, dragging a bloodstained
blanket. Her refusal to be led in triumph is immensely dignified . . . while never allowing us
to lose sight of her vulnerable femininity' (Stanley Wells, *Times Literary Supplement*, 29
October 1982). In 1983 Judy Parfitt's regality was aggressively modern; she made Cleopatra
'into a glamorous society belle, impressive and defiantly regal, but strangely modern in her
mannerisms' (Rosalind Carne, *Guardian*, in *London Theatre Record*, 9–22 April 1983, p.
297).

112 SD In Byam Shaw's 1953 production, Cleopatra descended the four steps from her throne to
kneel '*right down*' to Caesar (promptbook); in Nunn's production the queen crawled on her
hands and knees to Octavius; she kisses his foot in the television version, and his hand
at 189.

I pray you, rise. Rise, Egypt.
CLEOPATRA [*Rising*]   Sir, the gods
            Will have it thus. My master and my lord   115
            I must obey.
CAESAR   Take to you no hard thoughts.
            The record of what injuries you did us,
            Though written in our flesh, we shall remember
            As things but done by chance.
CLEOPATRA   Sole sir o'th'world,
            I cannot project mine own cause so well   120
            To make it clear, but do confess I have
            Been laden with like frailties which before
            Have often shamed our sex.
CAESAR   Cleopatra, know
            We will extenuate rather than enforce.
            If you apply yourself to our intents,   125
            Which towards you are most gentle, you shall find
            A benefit in this change; but if you seek
            To lay on me a cruelty by taking
            Antony's course, you shall bereave yourself
            Of my good purposes and put your children   130
            To that destruction which I'll guard them from
            If thereon you rely. I'll take my leave.
CLEOPATRA And may through all the world! 'Tis yours, and we,
            Your scutcheons and your signs of conquest, shall
            Hang in what place you please. Here, my good lord.   135
                    [*She offers him a scroll*]
CAESAR You shall advise me in all for Cleopatra.
CLEOPATRA This is the brief of money, plate, and jewels
            I am possessed of. 'Tis exactly valued,
            Not petty things admitted. Where's Seleucus?

                    [*Enter* SELEUCUS]

114b–15 **Sir ... thus** Janet Suzman's 'sense of vocal detail is matched in simple physical effect when, looking at Octavius's proffered hand, she clearly compares it in her mind with the hand of Antony' (Charles Lewsen, *Times*, 16 August 1972). In the Talawa Theatre production, Dona Croll, hitherto 'all playfulness and flirtatious irony with her conqueror, Octavius Caesar', at this point 'realises *he* is playing with *her*' (Martin Hoyle, *Times*, 18 May 1991).

139–78a **Where's ... pitied** Cut by Phelps (from line 133 to line 187), by the Australian touring productions of Asche (1912–13) and Wilkie (1927–8), and by Atkins in 1945, when Trewin commented, 'None will miss Cleopatra's undignified brawl with Seleucus' (*Observer*, 29 April 1945). Byam Shaw kept it in 1953 (Leech, 'Stratford 1953', p. 464), but not in in 1946 (Trewin, *Shakespeare on the English Stage*, p. 204); Benthall also cut it in 1951, to make

SELEUCUS Here, madam. 140
CLEOPATRA This is my treasurer. Let him speak, my lord,
    Upon his peril, that I have reserved
    To myself nothing. Speak the truth, Seleucus.
SELEUCUS Madam, I had rather seal my lips
    Than to my peril speak that which is not. 145
CLEOPATRA What have I kept back?
SELEUCUS Enough to purchase what you have made known.
CAESAR Nay, blush not, Cleopatra. I approve
    Your wisdom in the deed.
CLEOPATRA   See, Caesar! O, behold
    How pomp is followed! Mine will now be yours, 150
    And should we shift estates yours would be mine.
    The ingratitude of this Seleucus does
    Even make me wild. – O slave, of no more trust
    Than love that's hired! What, goest thou back? Thou shalt
    Go back, I warrant thee! But I'll catch thine eyes 155
    Though they had wings. Slave, soulless villain, dog!
    O rarely base!
CAESAR   Good queen, let us entreat you.
CLEOPATRA O Caesar, what a wounding shame is this,
    That thou vouchsafing here to visit me,
    Doing the honour of thy lordliness 160
    To one so meek, that mine own servant should
    Parcel the sum of my disgraces by
    Addition of his envy! Say, good Caesar,
    That I some lady trifles have reserved,
    Immoment toys, things of such dignity 165
    As we greet modern friends withal, and say

Cleopatra's suicide 'appear to follow hard upon the death of her lord' (Rylands, Festival Shakespeare', p. 141), as did the Nunn–Scoffield and BBC television versions, and Phillips's 1985 Chichester production. Caird cut it in 1992, but 'the vital scene where Cleopatra's tax fiddle is exposed by her treasurer' was restored in the 1993 revival (Michael Billington, *Guardian*, 28 May 1993). Brook included it, 'not as an episode of deception, but as one emphasising [Cleopatra's] defeat' (Scott, *Antony and Cleopatra*, p. 55). In 1924 Dorothy Green 'simply rants at the Egyptian who tells Caesar that she is concealing from him some of her treasures' (R.C.R., *Birmingham Post*, 17 July 1924), but Glenda Jackson 'kicks her treasurer right around the stage' (Michael Billington, *Guardian*, 11 October 1978); Helen Mirren was 'reduced to frantic humiliation by the embarrassed confessions of her treasurer' (Irving Wardle, *Times*, 15 October 1982).

157 Mrs Yates articulated her anger by '*flying at*' Seleucus in Garrick's production; Caesar 'entreat[ed]' her by '*interposing*' himself between them (printed edition).

Some nobler token I have kept apart
For Livia and Octavia, to induce
Their mediation, must I be unfolded
With one that I have bred? The gods! It smites me   170
Beneath the fall I have. *[To Seleucus]* Prithee, go hence,
Or I shall show the cinders of my spirits
Through th'ashes of my chance. Wert thou a man,
Thou wouldst have mercy on me.

CAESAR   Forbear, Seleucus.

[Seleucus withdraws]

CLEOPATRA Be it known that we, the greatest, are misthought   175
For things that others do; and when we fall,
We answer others' merits in our name,
Are therefore to be pitied.

CAESAR   Cleopatra,
Not what you have reserved nor what acknowledged
Put we i'th'roll of conquest. Still be't yours;   180
Bestow it at your pleasure, and believe
Caesar's no merchant, to make prize with you
Of things that merchants sold. Therefore be cheered.
Make not your thoughts your prisons. No, dear queen,
For we intend so to dispose you as   185
Yourself shall give us counsel. Feed and sleep.
Our care and pity is so much upon you
That we remain your friend; and so adieu.

CLEOPATRA My master, and my lord!

CAESAR   Not so. Adieu.

Flourish. Exeunt Caesar and his train

CLEOPATRA He words me, girls, he words me, that I should not   190
Be noble to myself. But hark thee, Charmian.

[She whispers to Charmian]

189 This is a good opportunity for Caesar to indicate, by body language, that he does not find
Cleopatra's submission seductive. Tim Pigott-Smith, in Hall's production, gave an excellent
conventional reading of the part, as 'a frigid but choleric politician who dislikes physical
contact: devious but self-righteous' (John Peter, *Sunday Times*, 12 April 1987).

190 **He . . . me** Helen Mirren's 'former spirit shows itself in . . . the comedy with which she
invests her comment on Caesar's exit' (Stanley Wells, *Times Literary Supplement*, 29
October 1982); 'she suddenly passed on . . . from an extremity of violent grief to a serene
perception of her fate' (Shrimpton, 'Shakespeare Performances', p. 173). In Brewster's
production, Dona Croll's 'temper is splendid' at this point (Alastair Macaulay, *Financial
Times*, 20 May 1991).

IRAS Finish, good lady. The bright day is done,
    And we are for the dark.
CLEOPATRA   Hie thee again.
    I have spoke already, and it is provided;
    Go put it to the haste.
CHARMIAN   Madam, I will.   195

Enter DOLABELLA

DOLABELLA Where's the queen?
CHARMIAN   Behold, sir.   [*Exit*]
CLEOPATRA   Dolabella!
DOLABELLA Madam, as thereto sworn by your command,
    Which my love makes religion to obey,
    I tell you this: Caesar through Syria
    Intends his journey, and within three days   200
    You with your children will he send before.
    Make your best use of this. I have performed
    Your pleasure and my promise.
CLEOPATRA   Dolabella,
    I shall remain your debtor.
DOLABELLA   I your servant.
    Adieu, good queen. I must attend on Caesar.   205
CLEOPATRA Farewell, and thanks.
                              Exit [*Dolabella*]
    Now, Iras, what think'st thou?
    Thou an Egyptian puppet shall be shown
    In Rome as well as I. Mechanic slaves
    With greasy aprons, rules, and hammers shall
    Uplift us to the view. In their thick breaths,   210
    Rank of gross diet, shall we be enclouded
    And forced to drink their vapour.
IRAS   The gods forbid!
CLEOPATRA Nay, 'tis most certain, Iras. Saucy lictors
    Will catch at us like strumpets, and scald rhymers
    Ballad us out o'tune. The quick comedians   215
    Extemporally will stage us and present
    Our Alexandrian revels; Antony

192 In 1930 Joan Harben was praised 'for her skill in showing the timid courage of Iras in the
    final scene' (Crosse, *Shakespearean Playgoing*, p. 68), and a reviewer of Byam Shaw's
    production of 1953 approved of Iras's 'laying proper emphasis on one of the play's most
    significant lines' (*Morning Advertiser*, 6 May 1953).
213–14 **Saucy . . . scald** Cut in the bowdlerising of the text for Phelps's production (promptbook).
217–20a **Antony . . . whore** Cut in the bowdlerising of the text for Phelps's production (promptbook).

Shall be brought drunken forth, and I shall see
Some squeaking Cleopatra boy my greatness
I'th'posture of a whore.
IRAS   O the good gods!   220
CLEOPATRA Nay, that's certain.
IRAS I'll never see't! For I am sure my nails
Are stronger than mine eyes.
CLEOPATRA   Why, that's the way
To fool their preparation and to conquer
Their most absurd intents.

Enter CHARMIAN

Now, Charmian!   225
Show me, my women, like a queen. Go fetch
My best attires. I am again for Cydnus,
To meet Mark Antony. Sirrah Iras, go –
Now, noble Charmian, we'll dispatch indeed –
And when thou hast done this chare I'll give thee leave   230
To play till Doomsday. Bring our crown and all.
                              [*Exit Iras.*] *A noise within*
Wherefore's this noise?

Enter a GUARDSMAN

GUARDSMAN   Here is a rural fellow
That will not be denied your highness' presence.
He brings you figs.
CLEOPATRA Let him come in.
                              Exit Guardsman
What poor an instrument   235
May do a noble deed! He brings me liberty.
My resolution's placed, and I have nothing
Of woman in me. Now from head to foot
I am marble-constant; now the fleeting moon
No planet is of mine.

219   In the first performances of the play, the boy actor speaking these lines could presumably
      be relied upon not to squeak them: see Introduction, pp. 23–6.

222–5a Cut in Phelps's production (promptbook).

225b   Here Charmian *'whispers'* to Cleopatra, presumably about the figs, in Phelps's production
       (promptbook) and in 1866 and 1867 (Calvert's acting edition).

231 SD In Garrick's production, 'Charmian *falls to adjusting* Cleopatra's *Dress'* as Iras goes out to
        fetch her regalia (printed text); in Phelps's, Iras *'goes behind Screen'* at 228 and Charmian
        'passes behind screen for crown' at 232a (promptbook); similarly, in 1866 and 1867 Iras
        'goes behind screen for robes, &c' at 226 (Calvert's acting edition).

Enter GUARDSMAN, *and* CLOWN [*bringing in a basket*]

GUARDSMAN This is the man. 240
CLEOPATRA Avoid, and leave him.

Exit Guardsman

Hast thou the pretty worm of Nilus there,
That kills and pains not?
CLOWN Truly I have him, but I would not be the party that should
desire you to touch him, for his biting is immortal. Those that 245
do die of it do seldom or never recover.
CLEOPATRA Remember'st thou any that have died on't?

239–40a At this point in Phelps's production, Glyn '*goes up to couch back*', where she remained until
her regalia was brought (promptbook). In 1921 Dorothy Green was praised for her 'quiet
intensity' once she decided to devote herself to death (*Morning Post*, 26 April 1921). Michael
Billington thought Helen Mirren managed convincingly the 'transition to marble constancy
after Antony's death: you feel this Cleopatra lives like a woman but dies like a queen'
(*Guardian*, 14 October 1982), and said that Judi Dench 'achiev[es] a kind of fulfilment on
[these lines]. After the boggling inconstancy of her life, Ms Dench goes to her death with
single-minded certainty' (*Guardian*, 11 April 1987). In Caird's production, just before the
Soothsayer/Clown's entrance, Clare Higgins 'rips off her wig and faces death with a close-
cropped head' (*Independent on Sunday*, 31 May 1993), and thereby 'turns instantly from
icon to suffering woman' (Jeremy Kingston, *Times*, 29 May 1993).

240a SD–73 This passage affirms the convention of the Jacobean clown as a rustic given to
malapropisms; Martin Holmes thinks the role was originally doubled with Enobarbus's and
that the Clown is 'after the old Armin fashion, sturdy and independent, and ready to give
gratuitous advice . . . he will not be got rid of until he has delivered himself of everything he
wants to say about asps' (*Shakespeare and Burbage*, p. 192). The episode is also typically
Jacobean in its use of grimly comic suspense to heighten tension. In Kemble's production,
the scene was cut, and in a much abbreviated death-scene Cleopatra called for the basket
(which Charmian fetched) rather than her robe and crown (printed text); in 1833 the
arrangement was similar, but Charmian brought in '*robe, crown, wreath, &c*' and Iras the
basket (promptbook). In Phelps's production, 'with a proper exercise of discretion, the part
of the Clown who brings the asps to Cleopatra was cut down to three or four lines'
(*Examiner*, 27 October 1849). In 1866 Adelaide Calvert's 'stricken gaze upon the clown's
basket was fine, and from this point to the end, Mrs Calvert played with a fervour for which
the earlier scenes had not prepared us' (unidentified newspaper review, pasted into Beck's
copy of the play in the NY Public Library). Archer, writing of Louis Calvert's 1897 production,
thought 'the effect of this scene . . . would be heightened if the Clown who brings the asps
were made a frankly comic personage. Shakespeare knew what he was about in introducing
this grim jester' (*1897*, p. 72). Modern theatrical opinion has largely been otherwise: some

reviewers have been wary of the episode itself, as at odds with modern taste, and directors have tended to emphasise the non-comic aspects of the Clown's rusticity. Trewin says approvingly of George Weir in 1900 that he gave a 'startling performance'; 'for once, ["I wish you joy o'th'worm"] kept the house silent' (*Benson*, p. 95). One critic remarked of John Maclean's countryman in Bridges-Adams's 1921 production, 'what a masterpiece of dramatic daring is this character' (R.C.R., *Birmingham Daily Post*, 25 April 1921), and for the next couple of decades, the standard approach to the role was to highlight its sinister element: in Leigh's 1925 production, Horace Sequeira brought a 'note of terror' to the role (unidentified review, Vic-Wells Association scrapbook, quoted in Lamb, *Antony and Cleopatra*, p. 117); Harcourt Williams played the 'rural fellow' as a sinister figure in his own 1930 production, and Crosse commented, 'a modern audience is too tightly strung to want comic relief at this point' (*Shakespearean Playgoing*, p. 68); Dennis Roberts, in Iden Payne's production, 'held the house all through his difficult little scene' (*Morning Post*, 16 April 1935); and in 1936 George Hayes 'spoke in a sustained eerie whisper' (Sprague and Trewin, *Shakespeare's Plays Today*, p. 69). When Sequeira played the part again in Atkins's 1945 production, he appeared as an old man (Ruth Ellis, *Stratford-upon-Avon Herald*, 24 April 1945), doubtless to underline his function as death-bringer. In 1953 Trewin, who saw Cleopatra's chance to die memorably as handicapped by any 'uneasy laughs during the intensely difficult scene of the clown-with-the-asp', wrote 'Miss Ashcroft had to regain the atmosphere when she spoke [274–5]. It was a superb recovery; but she should not have had to recover' (*Illustrated London News*, 16 May 1953). In the Nunn–Scoffield television version, the Clown is a Somerset rustic who is not over-amusing but whose errand with figs does make the Roman guard smirk uncontrollably. A more insidious threat to discipline was Richard Griffiths, whose Clown in Brook's production was the notable exception to the modern rule. 'Teetering on Cleopatra's symbolic death carpet as he offers her the basket of asps' (Rosemary Say, *Sunday Telegraph*, 15 October 1978), he drew on the modern conventions of the circus clown, 'red nose and all, with even a hint of Harlequin about his costume' (Bernard Levin, *Sunday Times*, 15 October 1978). Griffiths 'ended up with his shoes on his hands as he explained the nature of the asp to the Queen' (Scott, *Antony and Cleopatra*, p. 55), but he also played up, in Jacobean fashion, the false exits written into the passage, to delay Cleopatra's 'grand departure from the world' (Irving Wardle, *Times*, 11 October 1978). Michael Billington 'admired Richard Griffiths's red-nosed relief' (*Guardian*, 11 October 1978), but other critics were not amused. Trewin wrote of his 'needless vaudeville playing' (*Lady*, 26 October 1978), Milton Shulman thought it 'snapped irrevocably the dignity of [Cleopatra's] final end' (*Evening Standard*, 11 October 1978) and Felix Barker agreed, disapproving of Glenda Jackson's responding by beginning 'to smile and laugh as she delivered lines which are normally taken with deadly seriousness' (*Evening News*, 11 October 1978). The next two British productions reverted to pre-Brook modes: Jimmy Gardner's Clown is an old man in the BBC television version, and David Troughton offered a 'self-consciously sinister treatment' in Noble's 1983 revival (Robert Cushman, *Observer*, 14

CLOWN Very many, men and women too. I heard of one of them no
longer than yesterday – a very honest woman, but something
given to lie, as a woman should not do but in the way of honesty   250
– how she died of the biting of it, what pain she felt. Truly, she
makes a very good report o'th'worm. But he that will believe all
that they say shall never be saved by half that they do. But this is
most falliable, the worm's an odd worm.

CLEOPATRA Get thee hence, farewell.   255

CLOWN I wish you all joy of the worm. [*Setting down his basket*]

CLEOPATRA Farewell.

CLOWN You must think this, look you, that the worm will do his
kind.

CLEOPATRA Ay, ay, farewell.   260

CLOWN Look you, the worm is not to be trusted but in the keeping
of wise people, for indeed there is no goodness in the worm.

CLEOPATRA Take thou no care; it shall be heeded.

CLOWN Very good. Give it nothing, I pray you, for it is not worth the
feeding.   265

CLEOPATRA Will it eat me?

CLOWN You must not think I am so simple but I know the devil
himself will not eat a woman. I know that a woman is a dish for
the gods, if the devil dress her not. But truly, these same whore-
son devils do the gods great harm in their women, for in every   270
ten that they make, the devils mar five.

April 1983). In the Robertson–Selbie production, Vanessa Redgrave was 'almost at her best
with Gerald James's Welsh asp-bearer whom she treats with unpatronising affection. She
may not be a definitive Cleopatra, but she is an unusually democratic one' (Michael
Billington, *Guardian*, 28 May 1986). In 1992 Geckle disapproved of Caird's getting the
Soothsayer (Jasper Britton, who also appeared in other places without textual justification;
see the commentary at 4.9.7 and 4.12.47) to double as the Clown, wearing a death-mask:
'the effect of this is lugubrious, and in 5.2 it detracts from the magnificent rhetoric that
surrounds the comic scene in prose and, of course, from the pathos of Cleopatra's death
scene' ('The Power of Desire on Stage', p. 16).

248–71 **I . . . five** Cut in Phelps's production; at 247, '*Charmian takes the Basket from Clown and
places it on Stool at head of Couch*' (promptbook).

264–6   In Helpmann's production, the Clown 'got his laugh on "Give it nothing I pray you, for it is
not worth the feeding", and one could feel the next laugh just waiting to be released by the
following line. Instead, came the audible indrawn breath and a startled hush in which the
packed house was completely held, as with a Mona Lisa smile [Margaret Whiting] slowly
turned her head to look at the man and in a quiet, ordinary tone, with level accent, asked,
"Will it eat me?"' (Byrne, 'The Shakespeare Season', p. 475)

266–71 Cut in Garrick's production (printed text).

CLEOPATRA Well, get thee gone. Farewell.
CLOWN Yes, forsooth. I wish you joy o'th'worm.   *Exit*

[*Enter* IRAS *with royal attire*]

CLEOPATRA Give me my robe. Put on my crown. I have

273 **I . . . o'th'worm**   Cut in Phelps's production (promptbook).
274 At this point in Phelps's production, Glyn rose *'from couch advancing to front of stage*
     centre' and took the crown from Charmian at 276 (promptbook); Calvert's acting edition,
     used in 1866 and 1867, repeated the business. In Tree's production 'the corpse of Antony
     was on the stage throughout the whole of the closing scene, without noticeably influencing
     by its presence the behaviour of the survivors sharing the same room' (*Morning Post*, 26
     April 1921). The nature and deployment of the regal costume here is obviously central to the
     stage picture. Directors and designers may choose to play down or adapt, but can scarcely
     ignore altogether, the queen's call for robe and crown. Cora Brown-Potter in 1889 wore over
     her 'black gauzes studded with gold' a 'mulberry mantle embroidered with peacock
     feathers' (Shattuck, *Shakespeare on the American Stage*, vol. II, p. 122) and in 1898
     Constance Benson 'displayed a good deal of dramatic art when, in the last scene, she
     envelopes herself in her royal robes and crown' (*Stratford-upon-Avon Herald*, 22 April
     1898). One reviewer was disturbed in 1931 'to find Cleopatra and her women in Elizabethan
     garb', but relieved that in her death-scene Massingham 'was allowed the traditional
     headgear and robes of Egypt, so that we could guess how impressive her work would have
     been had she been permitted to wear them throughout the play' (*Stratford-upon-Avon*
     Herald, 8 May 1931). Ruth Ellis, reviewing Atkins's 1945 production, set rather less store by
     costume as an aid to good acting: 'Cleopatra's sumptuously beautiful clothes were much
     admired, but I hope that in future the robing for Cydnus will be simplified so that the
     immortal longings may be heard without distraction. Claire Luce speaks this pure gold too
     well to allow it to be smothered in tinsel' (*Stratford-upon-Avon Herald*, 24 April 1945). In
     1951 Vivien Leigh's 'robe depicted the flames of death, while her coronet displayed over her
     brow a small phallic decoration' (Scott, *Antony and Cleopatra*, p. 43), and Rylands asked
     'Who will forget [her], robed and crowned in the habiliments of an Egyptian goddess, beauty
     on a monument smiling extremity out of act?' ('Festival Shakespeare', p. 141). The splendour
     of Peggy Ashcroft's death-robes was, thought one reviewer, inadequately foreshadowed by
     her earlier costumes, and he regretted that 'until the grandeur of her death scene, the
     designer does not allow her greater luxury or pomp of dress' (P.R., *Western Daily Press*, 30
     April 1953). Helpmann's production signalled the special significance of the majestic death
     costume by giving it a different tenor, an iconic quality that Elizabeth I's subjects would have
     appreciated: 'dead, crowned and enthroned in the final scene, she resembled a holy image
     for a Christian festival' (H.G.M., *Theatre World*, April 1957). Salome Jens, in Kahn's 1972

production, wore a costume with more localised symbolic resonance, featuring a cape of golden feathers and a massive headpiece (Cooper, *American Shakespeare Theater*, p. 168), whilst in Nunn's production, Suzman 'transform[ed] herself from black into gold for her ritual suicide with the light fading on a figure like an icon from a pagan age' (Peter Lewis, unidentified newspaper, SCL Theatre Records, vol. 83, 1972, p. 119); in the Nunn–Scoffield television version, she poses with outstretched arms when she is fully adorned as Isis. In Brook's production, Glenda Jackson's costume for dying was 'plain but regal' (Male, *Shakespeare on Stage*, p. 24); Don Chapman, echoing criticism of Ashcroft's costumes, asked, 'what is the point of that dressing up in the death scene if it is not the last act of a beauty determined to bow out in the same stunning style that she lived?' (*Oxford Mail*, 11 October 1978). Lapotaire, in the BBC television version, emphasises the connection between ritualised dressing and death by holding the asp-basket in front of her as she is robed. For Mirren in Noble's production, make-up was as significant as costume: 'symbolically, she scrubs her face clean of both its customary paint and the mourning dirt with which she daubed it after Antony's death' (*Jewish Chronicle*, 29 October 1982); 'with washed cheeks she resumes her former beauty as, for the first time, we see her invested in the panoply of queenliness' (Stanley Wells, *Times Literary Supplement*, 29 October 1982). As in Jackson's case, some were unmoved by her latter-day regality of dress: Michael Coveney found himself 'contemplat[ing] the unfortunate resemblance of her crown to a frying basket' (*Financial Times*, 14 October 1982). The Robertson–Selbie production emphasised the idea of Cleopatra as performer and her 'dressing even for death as her last performance' (Kathy O'Shaughnessy, *Spectator*, 7 June 1986). Like Jackson's and Mirren's, Vanessa Redgrave's final costuming was 'her first hint of regal ritual'; she dressed 'in stern solemnity, constant marble for the one and only time' (Michael Coveney, *Financial Times*, 27 May 1986), and after Antony's crucifixion-like hauling, Mary Harron saw Redgrave as 'dressed for her suicide in blue, white and gold robes and headdress: in the colours associated with the Virgin Mary' (*Observer*, 1 June 1986). In similar, though less specific, religious mode, 'the robed [Dench] die[d] into an icon ablaze with gold' in Hall's production (Barbara Everett, *Times Literary Supplement*, 24 April 1987). In Stein's, 'the self-consciously regal Cleopatra of Edith Clever' was 'swathed from top-to-toe in a serpentine, cloth-of-gold robe' (Michael Billington, *Guardian Weekly*, 14 August 1994), but in her 1995 production, Vanessa Redgrave's robe and crown were 'a curious Edwardian Ascot outfit of gold lamé, yellow chiffon train and a flat wide-brimmed hat' (Michael Coveney, *Observer*, 4 June 1995); Clive Hirschhorn saw her as 'looking like a human lampshade in a get-up better suited to Emily Pankhurst (or Danny La Rue)' (*Sunday Express*, 4 June 1995). The golds of her costume gave her an iconic post-mortem luminosity, 'lampshade' notwithstanding: 'when she finally greets the Romans, it is as a lacquered death-mask through a golden veil. An imperishable image' (Irving Wardle, *Independent on Sunday*, 4 June 1995).

274–5   **I ... me** Critics expect Cleopatra's delivery of these famous lines to be emotionally charged, and are sometimes disappointed. In Tree's production 'some of the noblest lines in the play

Immortal longings in me. Now no more   275
The juice of Egypt's grape shall moist this lip.
[*The women dress her*]
Yare, yare, good Iras; quick. Methinks I hear
Antony call. I see him rouse himself
To praise my noble act. I hear him mock
The luck of Caesar, which the gods give men   280
To excuse their after wrath. Husband, I come!

were delivered almost colloquially. Th[is] speech . . . quite failed in its effect from this cause'
(*Standard*, 28 December 1906). In 1927 Dorothy Green did not hold enough back for the
grand exit: 'She interpreted Cleopatra as a magnificent flirt and a consummate artist in
emotions. The possible criticism is that there was no crescendo in her acting; she had used
up all her royalest attitudes and most thrilling elocution before the death scene, instead of
keeping something in reserve' (K.M.C., *Birmingham Gazette*, 18 July 1927). By contrast,
Catherine Lacey's 'portrait of the courtesan of genius had an intensely glowing human
fascination, and in the death scene, where grandeur is presented directly, she presented it
with profoundly moving effect' (*Times*, 16 April 1935). Claire Luce was too domestic, with
'the affectionate yearnings of a wife, not the great queen taking heaven by storm' (Ruth Ellis,
Stratford-upon-Avon Herald, 24 April 1945), but Vivien Leigh's 'dignity and power in the
death scene were beyond anything we have hitherto seen from her. And her low-pitched
voice is excellent for the speaking of verse' (W.A. Darlington, *Daily Telegraph*, 12 May 1951);
Olivier said he had advised his wife to 'try and lower [her] voice a whole octave' (Olivier, *On
Acting*, pp. 116–17). Margaret Whiting lacked variety: 'It is true that she reached a moment of
grave splendour in her dying scene with the asp, but since she had been using this tone of
voice all evening we can be forgiven if her death torments came as no particular surprise'
(Milton Shulman, *Evening Standard*, 6 March 1957). Janet Suzman, in the Nunn–Scoffield
television version, does surprise by giving an unusual emphasis to the 'me' after 'immortal
longings'. Glenda Jackson 'seem[ed] only to be playing a game, even in the serene moments
of her suicide' (B. A. Young, *Financial Times*, 12 October 1978), but Helen Mirren created a
very different atmosphere by 'speak[ing] in the deep tones she reserves for her best effects'
(*Daily Telegraph*, 14 October 1982): 'so sexually predatory is her nature that when near the
end she declares with a half-smile "I have immortal longings in me", one fears for the virtue
of the gods' (Christopher Hudson, *Standard*, 14 April 1983). In 1986 as Vanessa Redgrave
'approaches death, her thrilling contralto makes the poet's formidable language seem her
own inevitable speech' (John Barber, *Daily Telegraph*, 24 May 1986); the effect in her 1995
production was one of 'enfolding her doomed companions in a monologue of inimitable
tenderness, every word an ecstatic caress' (Irving Wardle, *Independent on Sunday*, 4 June
1995).

281   **Husband . . . come**   At this point in Garrick's production, Cleopatra '*Goes to a Bed, or*

Sopha, which she ascends; her women compose her on it' (printed edition). She also died on *'a couch'* in 1813 (printed edition) and in 1833 on a raised and curtained couch/bed; at 286 Charmian and Iras *'embrace her, and kneel beside her, as she sits on the bed'* (promptbook). In Phelps's production, Glyn stood at the front of the stage to apply the asp but died on the couch (promptbook). Whether Cleopatra should die on a throne or a bed remains a controversial question. Those who favour a bed-death see Cleopatra as 'lying luxuriously in death, as once she lay in her barge upon the Cydnus when first she went to meet Mark Antony', and regard a throne-death as 'an after-effect of the long supremacy of Dryden's play upon the English stage' (*Times,* 18 June 1953). The Folio text does not make it clear where or in what position Cleopatra dies: whilst Caesar's 'Take up her bed' (350) indicates that Cleopatra's body is to be removed on a 'bed' of some kind serving as a bier (it cannot be very grand and heavy, and is presumably a litter), it does not necessarily imply that she dies on it. Dryden's use of a throne in *All for Love* may reflect his reading of Shakespeare's text, and just possibly knowledge of theatrical tradition before the official closing of the theatres. 'Show me, my women, like a queen' (226) might be thought to imply a throne as well as a robe and crown; certainly the throne property was the most common indicator of the full panoply of majesty on Elizabethan and Jacobean stages. Whether Cleopatra's image of herself as wet-nursing the asp implies a seated position is another matter. For the theatre historian, a throneless death may be attributable to one or more of the following factors: historical consciousness, a particular way of reading the text, and an attempt to de-emphasise, for interpretative reasons, the grandeur of Cleopatra's death.

In Chatterton's production, the setting for Cleopatra's death was changed (under Dryden's influence) to the temple of Isis, and the queen died falling on the altar (Halliday's edition). Mrs Langtry was probably the first actress to die on a throne, and the *Athenaeum* critic enthused: 'the aspect of the queen, motionless and erect in her robes, with her handmaidens prostrate and dying before her, is superb' (22 November 1890). Janet Achurch also used a throne, and made Bernard Shaw think 'I have actually looked on Cleopatra enthroned dead in her regal robes, with her hand on Antony's' (*Plays and Players*, p. 189). Edith Evans died on a sofa, both in 1925 and 1946, but Agate was not impressed. He said of the former production, 'I did definitely object to Cleopatra's refusal to die sitting bolt upright on a throne. This is obviously the proper thing to do. Any objection that the Monument did not contain a throne would be frivolous; neither, probably, did it contain Cleopatra's robe and crown. And I submit that she would certainly not have bothered to put these on if she was going to curl up and die on the sofa like a naughty consumptive in the reign of Dumas *fils*' (*Brief Chronicles*, p. 176). Both Leigh and Ashcroft had memorable throne-deaths, but Suzman dies on a bed in the Nunn–Scoffield television version, and such a death may help avoid a criticism levelled at Brook's production, that 'she applies the asp and remains upright in death – an unlikely occurrence' (P.B., *Worcester Journal*, 19 October 1978); in that production Cleopatra died on the red hanging/carpet and Bernard Levin complained that 'Cleopatra hasn't even a chair, let alone a throne, to die on' (*Sunday Times*, 15 October

Now to that name my courage prove my title!
I am fire and air; my other elements
I give to baser life. So, have you done?
Come, then, and take the last warmth of my lips.   285
Farewell, kind Charmian. Iras, long farewell.
[*She kisses them. Iras falls and dies*]
Have I the aspic in my lips? Dost fall?
If thou and nature can so gently part,
The stroke of death is as a lover's pinch,
Which hurts, and is desired. Dost thou lie still?   290
If thus thou vanishest, thou tell'st the world
It is not worth leave-taking.
CHARMIAN Dissolve, thick cloud, and rain, that I may say
The gods themselves do weep!

1978). The same was true of the Talawa Theatre production, when Jeffrey Wainwright read
Cleopatra's unsupported posture symbolically – 'against every superficial appearance, she
is the play's most steadfast character . . . So when Dona Croll's sinuous Cleopatra dies rigidly
upright in her monumental finery her posture symbolises that she at least knows and is true
to herself and her culture' (*Independent*, 30 April 1991) – though Tony Dunn objected to her
'ridiculously kneeling upright after death while Octavius pronounces her eulogy' (*Tribune*, 31
May 1991).

283   **I . . . air** Dench 'here gave the same elongated treatment to "air" that she had earlier given
to "earth" [at 4.15.65] to underline her transcendence of the physical universe she had so
long personified' (Crowl, *Shakespeare Observed*, p. 100).

284   **I . . . life** William Archer disapproved of Janet Achurch's emphasising the word 'give' 'as
though it were likely that she should sell or lease them' (*1897*, p. 72). When Janet Suzman
'tries to set aside her own wantonness, we aren't quite sure whether this is another self-
deception or whether we are witnessing that most heroic struggle of all, a human being
trying to regain a lost integrity' (John Elsom, *Observer*, 20 August 1972).

285   This is an opportunity for the women to display the warmth of their relationship. Of Bridges-
Adams's 1924 production one critic wrote, 'yet what could be more sympathetic than this
Cleopatra's tender leave-taking of her women at the end' (*Birmingham Mail*, 16 July 1924);
another said of Atkins's 1945 production, 'she is delicately kind with her women in the last
scenes, but Iras and Charmian do not rise to the splendour of their farewell to the "lass
unparalleled"' (Ruth Ellis, *Stratford-upon-Avon Herald*, 24 April 1945). In Brook's
production, the waiting-women had 'an intuitive measure of [Cleopatra's] real inner
feelings', especially poignant at her death (Male, *Shakespeare on Stage*, p. 24). In Caird's
1992 production, 'Iras puts her hand in the jar, gets bitten, and dies; it makes better sense
than Shakespeare's text, which has Iras die of grief, but the dramatic parallelism with
Enobarbus is lost. Charmian, as well as Cleopatra, then dies from the asp' (Geckle, 'The
Power of Desire on Stage', p. 16).

CLEOPATRA   This proves me base.
    If she first meet the curlèd Antony,   295
    He'll make demand of her, and spend that kiss
    Which is my heaven to have. Come, thou mortal wretch,

295   Glyn memorably stressed the romantic element in the image – 'the glory that irradiated her
       countenance at the glad thought that she should meet her "curled Antony" in the shades,
       was strikingly sublime' (Heraud, 'Memoir', n.p.) – which Caird's 1992 production
       reproduced pictorially (see the commentary at 5.2.359–60). In the Robertson–Selbie
       production, Vanessa Redgrave 'can even make a joke of her hasty suicide: if she is not quick,
       her serving-maid will die first and grab dead Antony in the after-life' (John Barber, *Daily
       Telegraph*, 24 May 1986). In her own production of 1995, she presented the notion as 'a
       quick flash of jealous competitiveness' which 'occurs to her, when preparing to apply the asp
       to her bosom' (Alastair Macaulay, *Financial Times*, 5 June 1995).

297   **Come . . . wretch** Cleopatra's putting an asp to her breast is the most dramatic part of the
       stage picture of her death: see Introduction, pp. 22, 25. That Cleopatra's bosom remains
       partly visible after her death is suggested by 342–3. Byron said of Cleopatra, after seeing
       Harriet Faucit on the first night of Kemble's production, that she is 'coquettish to the last, as
       well with the "asp" as with Anthony' (*'Alas! the Love of Women!'*, vol. III, p. 207). Isabella
       Glyn, in Phelps's production, 'allows her face to be kindled by a sort of joyous rapture' whilst
       applying the asp to her bosom (*Times*, 24 October 1849). Cora Brown-Potter on her opening
       night in 1889 'became so rapt that she tore away the concealing silks and literally laid bare
       her breast for the audience to see and the asp to bite' (Shattuck, *Shakespeare on the
       American Stage*, vol. II, p. 123). John Barber said of Vivien Leigh, 'when the moment came –
       when Cleopatra put the asp to her breast – she smiled. It was a childish smile, the upper lip
       pointed. I saw it through tears' (*Daily Express*, 12 May 1951). Peggy Ashcroft was impressive
       here: 'at the end, as she clasped the asp to take her life, she presented a moving picture of
       queenly dignity that added the final masterly touch to a performance of classic perfection'
       (J.A.P., *Warwick Advertiser*, 1 May 1953). Whilst Suzman slips the asp inside her robe and
       keeps her hand over it in the Nunn–Scoffield television version, Kathleen Gaffney took the
       asp bare-breasted in Estelle Parsons's 1979 production. The audience see the asp but only a
       partly bare shoulder in the BBC television version. Cramphorn's 1983 Melbourne production
       used a 'slim four foot infant of a python', for which Lindy Davies 'never quite overcame her
       distaste. She kept the creature at arm's length, holding it by the neck, and then swiftly placed
       its head against a ripe, exposed, autumnal breast. The audience, both thrilled and horrified
       by the realism, paid little attention to Shakespeare's verbal poetry' (Heales and
       Bartholomeusz, 'Shakespeare in Sydney and Melbourne', p. 484). Alan Hulme wrote of
       Vanessa Redgrave in 1986, 'clasping the asp to her bosom with more real affection than she
       showed to Antony, she at last gains something approaching grandeur' (*Review*, 16 May
       1986); Michael Coveney said of Judi Dench 'I have never seen a Cleopatra take so much joy
       in the worm' (*Financial Times*, 10 April 1987).

> [*She applies an asp*]
> With thy sharp teeth this knot intrinsicate
> Of life at once untie. Poor venomous fool,
> Be angry, and dispatch. O, couldst thou speak,   300
> That I might hear thee call great Caesar ass
> Unpolicied!

CHARMIAN   O eastern star!

CLEOPATRA   Peace, peace!
> Dost thou not see my baby at my breast,
> That sucks the nurse asleep?

CHARMIAN   O, break! O, break!

CLEOPATRA As sweet as balm, as soft as air, as gentle –   305
> O Antony! – Nay, I will take thee too.
> [*She applies another asp*]
> What should I stay –   *Dies*

299–300 **Poor . . . angry** In Garrick's production, Mrs Yates encouraged the asp at her breast by
         'stirring it' here (printed text).

302a   Suzman, in the Nunn–Scoffield television version, 'with a little wince between "un" and
         "policied" subtly lets us know the moment of [the asp's] fatal pinch, reminding us of the
         politics as well as the romance . . . of her death' (Crowl, 'A World Elsewhere', p. 155).

302c–3   In speaking these lines in 1898, Constance Benson's 'acting was majestic and dignified, and a
         strong contrast to [her style in] the previous [scene], where she is overwhelmed with rage
         and indignation at the thought of being taken to follow in Caesar's triumph' (*Worcester
         Daily Times*, 16 April 1898). Speaight thought Peggy Ashcroft delivered this speech 'as the
         staunchest lover of this play must have dreamt to hear it spoken' (*Shakespeare on the
         Stage*, p. 250), though one critic did not like her emphasis on 'baby' rather than 'breast':
         'Under the strain of a first night . . . Miss Ashcroft, otherwise perfection, could speak of "my
         baby at my breast"' (*Scotsman*, 30 April 1953).

307   In Phelps's production, Glyn *'As tho' entranced with the thoughts of meeting Antony . . .
         gradually sinks on Couch and dies'*. Calvert's acting edition (used in 1866 and 1867) has
         simply *'falls on a bed, and dies'*, but makes provision for the play to end either with
         Cleopatra's death ('*slow and mournful Music from the application of the second asp*') or
         with a '*Dead March, Tableau*' after Caesar's speech. In the Langtry–Wingfield production,
         the play ended at Cleopatra's death on 'O Antony!' (306). In Helpmann's, Whiting 'moved
         slowly to the throne, where she sat motionless, with Antony's red robe at her feet. She spoke
         more and more slowly as the poison began to work, until Cleopatra died suddenly in the
         middle of a sentence' (Lamb, *Antony and Cleopatra*, p. 159). In Hall's production, 'as
         [Dench] slumped on her throne, which tilted her crown awry . . . the last brilliant sign of
         movement emanating from this presence was that of the second asp still wriggling in the
         clutch of her right hand' (Crowl, *Shakespeare Observed*, p. 100).

CHARMIAN In this wild world? So, fare thee well.
　　Now boast thee, Death, in thy possession lies
　　A lass unparalleled. Downy windows, close; 310
　　And golden Phoebus never be beheld
　　Of eyes again so royal! Your crown's awry;
　　I'll mend it, and then play –

Enter the GUARD *rustling in*

I GUARD Where's the queen?
CHARMIAN 　　　　　　　　Speak softly. Wake her not.
I GUARD Caesar hath sent –
CHARMIAN 　　　　　　　　Too slow a messenger. 315
　　[*She applies an asp*]
　　O, come apace, dispatch! I partly feel thee.
I GUARD Approach, ho! All's not well. Caesar's beguiled.
2 GUARD There's Dolabella sent from Caesar. Call him.
　　　　　　　　　　　　[*Exit a Guardsman*]
I GUARD What work is here, Charmian? Is this well done?
CHARMIAN It is well done, and fitting for a princess 320
　　Descended of so many royal kings.
　　Ah, soldier! 　　　　　　　　*Charmian dies*

Enter DOLABELLA

DOLABELLA How goes it here?
2 GUARD 　　　　　　　　All dead.
DOLABELLA 　　　　　　　　　　Caesar, thy thoughts
　　Touch their effects in this. Thyself art coming
　　To see performed the dreaded act which thou 325
　　So sought'st to hinder.

308–13　It is in the nature of her role that Charmian has the potential to upstage Cleopatra, but it was
　　to resonant voice and general acting ability that Agate referred when he said of Margaret
　　Rawlings's Charmian in Komisarjevsky's production, 'The Queen once dispatched, the tiring-
　　maid let us know in six lines who should have been playing what' (*Brief Chronicles*, p. 184).

315b　Charmian took the asp from Cleopatra at this point in Macready's production
　　(promptbook); she holds an asp to her throat in the Nunn–Scoffield television version.

322　Cut in the BBC television version. In Hack's 1983 production Emma Piper 'invests
　　[Charmian's] role with a lot of flirtatious detail, dying almost on the kiss of a gaoler' (Michael
　　Coveney, *Financial Times*, in *London Theatre Record*, 9–22 April 1983, p. 298).

323b　The *Daily Telegraph* reviewer of Chatterton's production found 'the final act, with its
　　mournful close, comes as a kind of anti-climax having nothing but histrionic art to
　　recommend it. Even by making Cleopatra's death chamber the Temple of Isis, and filling up
　　the stage at the end with flambeau-bearing mourners, the eye, after so much lavish display

Enter CAESAR *and all his train, marching*

ALL A way there, a way for Caesar!
DOLABELLA O sir, you are too sure an augurer:
    That you did fear is done.
CAESAR   Bravest at the last,
    She levelled at our purposes and, being royal,   330
    Took her own way. The manner of their deaths?
    I do not see them bleed.
DOLABELLA   Who was last with them?
1 GUARD A simple countryman, that brought her figs.
    This was his basket.
CAESAR   Poisoned, then.
1 GUARD   O Caesar,
    This Charmian lived but now; she stood and spake.   335
    I found her trimming up the diadem
    On her dead mistress; tremblingly she stood,
    And on the sudden dropped.
CAESAR   O, noble weakness!
    If they had swallowed poison, 'twould appear
    By external swelling; but she looks like sleep,   340
    As she would catch another Antony
    In her strong toil of grace.
DOLABELLA   Here on her breast
    There is a vent of blood, and something blown;

of pomp and pageantry, refuses to be comforted' (22 September 1873). In 1922 Atkins's
'frozen monument of death' was 'impressive in the extreme' (unidentified review, Vic-Wells
Association scrapbook, quoted in Lamb, *Antony and Cleopatra*, p. 108); in 1931 Bridges-
Adams contrived 'a tableau of green and black, where the rich pall of dead Egypt, the
shimmering emerald of her ladies' dresses, and the flickering funeral lights made a picture
that lives in the memory' (*Stratford-upon-Avon Herald*, 8 May 1931). Symmetry was an
important aspect of the presentation of Cleopatra's death in Benthall's production – Vivien
Leigh 'died head erect, eyes closed, blended into the marble of death itself, while at each
foot the soldiers found one of her companions' (Scott, *Antony and Cleopatra*, p. 43) – and in
Brook's: 'After closing the Queen's eyes, Charmian painted the lids and adjusted the crown
before applying the asp to her own bosom. She then fell at right angles downstage-left of
the throne, parallel in death with the body of Iras' (Scott, *Antony and Cleopatra*, p. 55). In
the BBC television version, the focus is on Caesar and we see the dead Cleopatra only from
the back or the side.

331–51 **The . . . monument** Cut in Phelps's production (promptbook), and also, apart from
340–42a, in the Nunn–Scoffield television version, where 'the ending is edited, as the play
is, toward Cleopatra' (Coursen, *Shakespearean Performance*, pp. 193–4).

             The like is on her arm.

1 GUARD   This is an aspic's trail, and these fig-leaves   345
             Have slime upon them, such as th'aspic leaves
             Upon the caves of Nile.

CAESAR   Most probable
             That so she died; for her physician tells me
             She hath pursued conclusions infinite
             Of easy ways to die. Take up her bed,   350
             And bear her women from the monument.
             She shall be buried by her Antony.
             No grave upon the earth shall clip in it
             A pair so famous. High events as these
             Strike those that make them; and their story is   355
             No less in pity than his glory which
             Brought them to be lamented. Our army shall
             In solemn show attend this funeral,
             And then to Rome. Come, Dolabella, see
             High order in this great solemnity.   360

                    Exeunt omnes, [*bearing the dead bodies*]

---

345   **This . . . trail** A real snake was used in Noble's production, as a 'symbol of a new live relationship achieved only in death' (Male, *Shakespeare on Stage*, p. 25); Cramphorn had a problematic four-foot python (see the commentary at 5.2.297); Hall used 'a frisky North American garter snake' and 'a realistic prop' (Lowen, *Peter Hall*, p. 93). In Vanessa Redgrave's multicultural production of 1995 the asp was Indonesian; it wriggled, but was 'a docile little sunbeam serpent that turns out to be as tame as her own Moving Theatre production' (Maureen Paton, *Daily Express*, 5 June 1995). There are two minor staging issues here. If the asp is to be presented realistically, one difficulty is, as Noble discovered in rehearsal, that grass snakes do not leave a trail. The other issue is how the trail comes to the guard's attention (whether or not it is actually there): it is probably simplest for him to kneel, squat or stoop in the spirit of enquiry.

349–50   **She . . . die** Omitted in 1953 (Leech, 'Stratford 1953', p. 464).

350   **Take . . . bed** Wherever Cleopatra dies, it is clear that her body is meant to be removed on a 'bed', as on a bier. Possibly in early performances the same litter was used for Pacorus's body, for the carrying (and even the lifting) of the wounded Antony (and the exit of his corpse), and again here; if the queen is to die on the bed, something grander would seem appropriate, but a rich covering might serve the turn. If Cleopatra dies elsewhere, it is not practical to move her before Caesar's entrance, since Iras has predeceased her; Charmian seems, wisely, to attempt only to 'mend' her crown (313). In Kemble's production 'the bodies of Antony and Cleopatra were brought into the mausoleum'; 'the biers . . . were narrow, gaudy fabrications, like children's cradles' (*Times*, 16 November 1813). In Hall's production

Judi Dench 'is carried out feet first in the show's final procession of all' (Michael Coveney, *Financial Times*, 10 April 1987).

359–60   **Come . . . solemnity** The last line and a half were omitted in Louis Calvert's production (Archer, *1897*, p. 69) and in the Nunn–Scoffield television version, changing the emphasis from funeral solemnity to Roman business. Benedict Nightingale said that David Schofield spoke these lines like 'a salivating necrophiliac' in 1973 (*New Statesman*, 17 August 1973). At the end of Brook's production, Pryce took 'a prolonged backward look at [Cleopatra] before his departure' (Hunt and Reeves, *Peter Brook*, p. 229). In Caird's 1992 production 'the last image . . . is that of Antony and Cleopatra looking outward (with their backs to the audience) towards the Elysian Fields . . . silhouetted against a cerulean background in a spectacular finale to a production notable for its lighting effects' (Geckle, 'The Power of Desire on Stage', p. 16). The 1993 revival omitted 'the absurd apotheosis of the two lovers after their deaths, united above the sands like the posters for a Dietrich/Boyer romance. In its place, we see the pair lying in golden state on the monument, just as Caesar ordered. They need to be seen dead, all passion finally spent' (Jeremy Kingston, *Times*, 29 May 1993). Vanessa Redgrave's 1995 production ended with 'the black Octavia gazing prophetically at the map of Europe' (*Guardian*, 3 June 1995).

BIBLIOGRAPHY

PROMPTBOOKS FOR PRODUCTIONS OF *ANTONY AND CLEOPATRA*

Asche, Oscar (dir.) Theatre Royal, Melbourne and Australian tour, 1912–13. Shakespeare Centre Library.

Atkins, Robert (dir.) Stratford, 1945. Shakespeare Centre Library.

Bridges-Adams, W. (dir.) Stratford, 1931. Shakespeare Centre Library.

Brook, Peter (dir.) Stratford, 1978. Shakespeare Centre Library.

Garrick, David (dir.) Drury Lane, 1759. Folger Shakespeare Library.

Hall, Peter (dir.) National Theatre, 1987. Royal National Theatre archives.

Kemble, J. P. (dir.) Manuscript, *c.* 1800; never performed. Folger Shakespeare Library.

Macready, W. C. (dir.) Drury Lane, 1833. Folger Shakespeare Library.

Noble, Adrian (dir.) Stratford, 1982. Shakespeare Centre Library.

Nunn, Trevor (dir.) Stratford, 1972. Shakespeare Centre Library.

Nunn, Trevor (dir.) Aldwych revival, 1973. Shakespeare Centre Library.

Payne, Ben Iden (dir.) Stratford, 1935. Shakespeare Centre Library.

Phelps, Samuel (dir.) Sadler's Wells, 1849. Folger Shakespeare Library.

Robertson, Toby (dir.) Prospect Theatre, 1977–8. Theatre Museum, London.

Shaw, Glen Byam (dir.) Stratford, 1953. Shakespeare Centre Library.

FILMS AND VIDEOTAPES

Antony and Cleopatra Colour film, dir. Charlton Heston, prod. Peter Snell, Switzerland, Spain and UK, Transac, Izaro and Folio Films: 1972.

Antony and Cleopatra Colour videotape, dir. Trevor Nunn, prod. Jon Scoffield, UK, RSC and Audio-Visual Productions: 1974.

Antony and Cleopatra Colour videotape, dir./prod. Jonathan Miller, UK and USA, BBC and Time-Life TV: 1981.

EDITIONS OF *ANTONY AND CLEOPATRA*

Anthony and Cleopatra, ed. Michael Neill, World's Classics, Oxford and New York, Oxford University Press: 1994.

Anthony and Cleopatra: a historical play, in *Cumberland's British Theatre*, vol. XLIV, no. 357, London, G.H. Davidson: n.d. (*c.* 1850).

Antony and Cleopatra, ed. John F. Andrews, Everyman Library, London
and Vermont, J. M. Dent & Charles E. Tuttle: 1993.

Antony and Cleopatra, ed. David Bevington, New Cambridge Shakespeare,
Cambridge, Cambridge University Press: 1990.

Antony and Cleopatra, ed. John Dover Wilson, New Shakespeare,
Cambridge, Cambridge University Press: 1950.

Antony and Cleopatra, ed. H. H. Furness, New Variorum Edition,
Philadelphia and London, J. B. Lippincott Co.: 1907.

Antony and Cleopatra, ed. Emrys Jones, New Penguin Shakespeare,
Harmondsworth, Penguin: 1977.

Antony and Cleopatra, ed. F. A. Marshall, Henry Irving Edition, London,
Blackie & Son: 1889.

Antony and Cleopatra, ed. M. R. Ridley, Arden Shakespeare, London,
Methuen: 1970 (1954).

Antony and Cleopatra, ed. John Wilders, New Arden Shakespeare, London,
Methuen: 1995.

Antony and Cleopatra 1758 (facsimile of the printed edition of the text used
in Garrick's production), introduction by H. Neville Davies, London,
Cornmarket Press: 1969.

Antony and Cleopatra 1813 (facsimile of the printed edition of the text used
in Kemble's production), introduction by H. Neville Davies, London,
Cornmarket Press: 1970.

Antony and Cleopatra, in *Lacy's Acting Edition of Plays, Drama, Farces,
Extravaganzas* (Calvert's acting edition), vol. LXXV, London, Thomas
Hailes Lacy: n.d. (1867).

Antony and Cleopatra, as arranged for the stage by H. Beerbohm Tree,
London, Warrington & Co.: 1907.

*The Play of Antony and Cleopatra, as performed for the First Time Under Mrs
Langtry's Management, at the Royal Princess's Theatre, London, on
Tuesday, 18th November, 1890*, London, Leadenhall Press: n.d.

*The Tragedy of Antony and Cleopatra. Arranged and adapted for
representation by A. Halliday*, London, Tinsley Brothers: 1873.

*The Tragedy of Antony and Cleopatra: Arranged for Representation in Four
Acts by Charles Calvert, Prince's Theatre, Manchester*, Edinburgh,
Schenk and M'Farlane: n.d. George Beck's copy, with annotations and
a pasted-in review, Theatre Collection, New York Public Library.

OTHER BOOKS AND ARTICLES

Adams, William Davenport. '*Antony and Cleopatra*: its Stage History', *The
Theatre*, NS 16 (1890), 267–71.

A Book of Burlesque: sketches of English stage travestie and parody,
    London, Henry & Co.: 1891.
Agate, James. *Brief Chronicles*, London, Jonathan Cape: 1943.
Allen, Shirley S. *Samuel Phelps and Sadler's Wells Theatre*, Middletown,
    Wesleyan University Press: 1971.
Anderson, James R. *An Actor's Life*, Newcastle, Walter Scott: 1902.
Anon. *A Horrible Creuel and Bloody Murther*, London, 1614.
Anton, Robert. *Philosophers Satyrs*, London, 1616.
Archer, William. *The Theatrical 'World' for 1893*, London, Walter Scott:
    1894.
    The Theatrical 'World' for 1897, London, Walter Scott: 1898.
Armstrong, William A. 'Shakespeare and the Acting of Edward Alleyn',
    Shakespeare Survey, 7 (1954), 82–9.
    'Actors and Theatres', *Shakespeare Survey*, 17 (1964), 191–204.
Asche, Oscar. *Oscar Asche: His Life*, London, Hurst & Blackett: n.d. (1929).
Babula, W. *Shakespeare in Production, 1935–78*, London, Garland: 1981.
Baker, Herschel. *John Philip Kemble: the Actor in His Theatre*, Cambridge,
    Mass., Harvard University Press: 1942.
Baldwin, Thomas W. *The Organization and Personnel of the Shakespearean
    Company*, Princeton, Princeton University Press: 1927.
Banke, Cecile de. *Shakespearean Stage Production Then and Now*, London,
    Hutchinson: 1954.
Barker, Felix. *The Oliviers: a Biography*, London, Hamish Hamilton: 1953.
Barroll, J. Leeds. 'The Chronology of Shakespeare's Jacobean Plays and the
    Dating of *Antony and Cleopatra*', in *Essays on Shakespeare*, ed. Gordon
    Ross Smith, University Park and London, Pennsylvania State
    University Press: 1965, pp. 115–62.
Barroll, J. Leeds, Leggatt, Alexander, Hosley, Richard and Kernan, Alvin.
    The Revels History of Drama in English, vol.III, London, Methuen:
    1975.
Barthelemy, Anthony G. *Black Face Maligned Race*, Baton Rouge and
    London, Louisiana State University Press: 1987.
Benson, Constance. *Mainly Players*, London, Thornton Butterworth:
    1926.
Bentley, Eric. *In Search of Theater*, New York, Vintage Books: 1954.
Bentley, G. E. (ed.). *The Seventeenth Century Stage*, Chicago, University of
    Chicago Press: 1968.
    The Jacobean and Caroline Stage, 7 vols., Oxford, Oxford University
    Press: 1941–68.
Bevan, Ian. *The Story of the Theatre Royal*, Sydney, Currency Press: 1993.

Boaden, James. *Memoirs of the Life of John Philip Kemble, Esq.*, 2 vols., London, Longman: 1825.

Bordman, Gerald. *American Theatre: a Chronicle of Comedy and Drama, 1869–1914*, New York and Oxford, Oxford University Press: 1994.
The Oxford Companion to American Theatre, 2nd edn, New York and Oxford, Oxford University Press: 1992.

Brisbane, Katharine (ed.). *Entertaining Australia: an Illustrated History*, Sydney, Currency Press: 1991.

Brown, John Russell (ed.). *Shakespeare: Antony and Cleopatra*, Casebooks Series, revised edn, London, Macmillan: 1991.

Brown, T. Allston. *A History of the New York Stage: From the First Performance in 1732 to 1901*, 3 vols., New York, B. Blom: 1964 (1903).

Bullough, Geoffrey (ed.). *Narrative and Dramatic Sources of Shakespeare*, vol. v, London, Routlege & Kegan Paul: 1964.

Bulman, J. C. and Coursen, H. R. (eds.). *Shakespeare on Television: an Anthology of Essays and Reviews*, Hanover and London, University Press of New England: 1988.

Burnim, Kalman. *David Garrick, Director*, Pittsburgh, University of Pittsburgh Press: 1961.

Byrne, M.StC. 'The Shakespeare Season', *Shakespeare Quarterly*, 8 (1957), 461–76.

Byron, George Gordon. *'Alas! the Love of Women!' Byron's Letters and Journals*, vol.iii, ed. Leslie A. Marchand, London, John Murray: 1974.

Calvert, Adelaide. *Sixty-Eight Years on the Stage*, London, Mills & Boon: 1911.

Chambers, E. K. *The Elizabethan Stage,* 4 vols., Oxford, Oxford University Press: 1967 (1923).

Clarke, Mary. *Shakespeare at the Old Vic*, London, Hamish Hamilton: 1957.

Collier, Constance. *Harlequinade*, London, John Lane: 1929.

Cook, (Edward) Dutton. *Nights at the Play*, 2 vols., London, Chatto & Windus: 1883.

Cooper, Roberta Krensky. *The American Shakespeare Theater, Stratford, 1955–1988*, Washington, London and Toronto, Folger Books, Associated University Presses: 1986.

Coryat, Thomas. *Coryats Crudities . . .* London, 1611.

Coursen, H. R. *Shakespearean Performance as Interpretation*, Newark, London and Toronto, University of Delaware Press, Associated University Presses: 1992.

Cross, Richard. *Diary*, Folger Manuscript, Folger Shakespeare Library.

Crosse, Gordon. *Shakespearean Playgoing 1890–1952*, London, A. R.
Mowbray & Co.: 1953.

Crowl, Samuel. 'A World Elsewhere: the Roman Plays on Film and
Television', in *Shakespeare and the Moving Image: the Plays on Film
and Television*, ed. Anthony Davies and Stanley Wells, Cambridge,
Cambridge University Press: 1994, pp. 146–62.

Shakespeare Observed: Studies in Performance on Stage and Screen,
Athens, Ohio, Ohio University Press: 1992.

Cunnington, C. W. and P. *Handbook of English Costume in the Seventeenth
Century*, London, Faber: 1972.

Darbyshire, Alfred. *The Art of the Victorian Stage: Notes and Recollections*,
London and Manchester, Sherratt & Hughes: 1907.

Darlington, W. A. *Through the Fourth Wall*, London, Chapman & Hall:
1922.

Davies, H. Neville. 'Jacobean *Antony and Cleopatra*', *Shakespeare Studies*,
17 (1985), 123–58.

Davies, Thomas. *Dramatic Miscellanies*, 3 vols., New York, Benjamin Blom:
1971 (London, 1784).

Memoirs of the Life of David Garrick, Esq., 2 vols., London, 1780.

Davies, W. Robertson. *Shakespeare's Boy Actors*, London, Dent: 1939.

Dawson, R. Mac G. 'But Why Enobarbus?', *Notes and Queries*, NS 34
(1987), 216–17.

Dessen, A. C. 'The Image and the Script: Shakespeare on Stage in 1993',
Shakespeare Bulletin, 12 (1) (1994), 5–8.

Dickens, Charles. *Letters*, ed. Walter Dexter, 3 vols., Bloomsbury,
Nonesuch Press: 1938.

Downer, Alan S. *The Eminent Tragedian: William Charles Macready*,
Cambridge, Mass., Harvard University Press, 1966.

'Prolegomenon to a Study of Elizabethan Acting', *Maske und Kothurn*,
10 (1965), 625–36.

Downes, John. *Roscius Anglicanus*, ed. Montague Summers, London,
Fortune Press: 1928.

Dryden, John. *Works*, gen. ed. Alan Roper, vol. XIII, ed. Maximillian E.
Novak, Berkeley, Los Angeles and London, University of California
Press: 1984.

Dusinberre, Juliet. 'Squeaking Cleopatras: Gender and Performance in
Antony and Cleopatra', in *Shakespeare, Theory, and Performance*, ed.
James C. Bulman, London and New York, Routledge: 1996, pp.
46–67.

Ellis, Ruth. *The Shakespeare Memorial Theatre*, London, Winchester
Publications: 1948.

Elsom, John. *Post-War British Theatre*, London, Routledge & Kegan Paul: 1976.

Farjeon, Herbert. *The Shakespearean Scene*, London, Hutchinson: n.d. (1949).

Fluchère, Henri. 'Shakespeare in France: 1900–1948', *Shakespeare Survey*, 2 (1949), 115–25.

Foucault, Michel. *Discipline and Punish*, trans. A. Sheridan, London, Allen Lane: 1977.

Foulkes, Richard (ed.). *Shakespeare and the Victorian Stage*, Cambridge, Cambridge University Press: 1986.

Garrick, David. *The Letters*, ed. D. M.Little and G. M. Kahrl, Cambridge, Mass., Harvard University Press: 1963.

Geckle, George L. 'The Power of Desire on Stage: Stratford-upon-Avon, Fall 1992', *Shakespeare Bulletin*, 2 (2) (1993), 15–16.

Genest, John. *Some Account of the English Stage from the Restoration in 1660 to 1830*, 10 vols., New York, Burt Franklin: n.d. (Bath, 1832).

Gielgud, John. *Early Stages*, London, Macmillan: 1939.

Gilder, Rosamond. 'Shakespeare in New York: 1947–48', *Shakespeare Survey*, 2 (1949), 130–1.

Granville-Barker, Harley. *Prefaces to Shakespeare: Second Series*, London, Sidgwick & Jackson: 1930.

Greville, Fulke. *The Prose Works*, ed. John Gouws, Oxford, Oxford University Press: 1986.

Gurr, Andrew. *The Shakespearean Stage 1574–1642*, 3rd edn, Cambridge, Cambridge University Press: 1992.

Hamer, Mary. *Signs of Cleopatra: History, Politics, Representation*, London and New York, Routledge: 1993.

Hankey, Julie. 'Body Language, the Idea of the Actress, and Some Nineteenth-Century Actress-Heroines', *New Theatre Quarterly*, 8 (1992), 226–40.

'Helen Faucit and Shakespeare: Womanly Theater', in *Cross-Cultural Performances: Differences in Women's Re-visions of Shakespeare*, ed. Marianne Novy, Urbana and Chicago, University of Illinois Press: 1993, pp. 50–69.

Hart, A. 'The Length of Elizabethan and Jacobean Plays', *RES*, 8 (1932), 139–54.

Hattaway, Michael. *Elizabethan Popular Theatre: Plays in Performance*, London, Boston, Melbourne and Henley, Routledge & Kegan Paul: 1982.

Heales, Robyn and Bartholomeusz, Dennis. 'Shakespeare in Sydney and Melbourne', *Shakespeare Quarterly*, 35 (1984), 479–84.

H(eraud), J. A. 'Memoir of Miss Glyn', prefaced to Webster's *The Duchess of Malfi*, London, 1851.

Hill, John (attrib.) *A letter to the Hon. Author of the New Farce, called The Rout . . . With an Appendix; containing: Some Remarks upon the new-revived Play of Antony and Cleopatra*, London, 1759.

Hobson, Harold. *Theatre 2*, London, New York, Toronto, Longmans Green: 1950.

Hogan, Charles B. *Shakespeare in the Theatre 1701–1800*, Oxford, Clarendon Press: 1957.

Holmes, Martin. 'A Regency Cleopatra', *Theatre Notebook*, 8 (1954), 46–7. *Shakespeare and Burbage*, London and Chichester, Phillimore: 1978.

Howe, Elizabeth. *The First English Actresses: Women and Drama, 1660–1700*, Cambridge, Cambridge University Press: 1992.

Hughes-Hallett, Lucy. *Cleopatra: Histories, Dreams and Distortions*, London, Bloomsbury: 1990.

'The Riddle of the Minx', *Harpers and Queen* (January 1990), 38.

Humbert, Jean-Marcel, Pantazzi, Michael and Ziegler, Christiane. *Egyptomania: Egypt in Western Art, 1730–1930*, Paris and Ottowa, Réunion des Musées Nationaux & National Gallery of Canada: 1994.

Hunt, Albert and Reeves, Geoffrey. *Peter Brook*, Directors in Perspective, Cambridge, Cambridge University Press: 1995.

Irvin, Eric. *Dictionary of Australian Theatre, 1788–1914*, Sydney, Hale & Iremonger: 1985.

Jameson, Anna. *Characteristics of Women*, 2 vols., London, 1858.

Johnson, Samuel. *Prose and Poetry*, ed. Mona Wilson, London, Rupert Hart-Davis: 1963.

Kemp, T. C. and Trewin, J. C. *The Stratford Festival: a History of the Shakespeare Memorial Theatre*, Birmingham, Cornish Brothers: 1953.

Kennedy, Dennis (ed.). *Foreign Shakespeare: Contemporary Performance*, Cambridge, Cambridge University Press: 1993.

Kerr, Walter. *Thirty Plays Hath November: Pain and Pleasure in the Contemporary Theater*, New York, Simon & Schuster: 1969.

Klein, David. 'Did Shakespeare Produce His Own Plays?', *MLR*, 57 (1962), 556–60.

Knight, Joseph. Introduction to *Antony and Cleopatra*, ed. F. A. Marshall, Henry Irving edition, London, Blackie & Son: 1889.

Knutson, Roslyn Lander. *The Repertory of Shakespeare's Company 1594–1613*, Fayetteville, University of Arkansas Press: 1991.

Kott, Jan. *Shakespeare Our Contemporary*, Garden City, NY, Anchor Books: 1964.

Lamb, Margaret. *'Antony and Cleopatra' on the English Stage*, Rutherford,

Madison, Teaneck, London and Toronto, Fairleigh Dickinson
University Press, Associated University Presses: 1980.

Langtry, Lillie. *The Days I Knew*, New York, George H. Doran Co.: 1925.

Leech, Clifford. 'Stratford 1953', *Shakespeare Quarterly*, 4 (1953), 461–6.

Leiter, Samuel L. (editor-in-chief) and Hill, Holly (assoc. ed.). *The
Encyclopedia of the New York Stage, 1920–1930*, 2 vols., Westport,
Conn. and London, Greenwood Press: 1985.

Leiter, Samuel L. *The Encyclopedia of the New York Stage, 1930–1940*, New
York, Westport, Conn. and London, Greenwood Press: 1989.

(ed.). *Shakespeare Around the Globe: a Guide to Notable Postwar Revivals*,
New York, Westport, Conn. and London, Greenwood Press: 1986.

Levi, P. *The Life and Times of William Shakespeare*, London, Macmillan:
1988.

Lowen, Tirzah. *Peter Hall Directs 'Antony and Cleopatra'*, London,
Methuen Drama: 1990.

MacLiammóir, Micheál. 'Three Shakespearian Productions: A
Conversation', *Shakespeare Survey*, 1 (1948), 89–97.

Macready, William Charles. *The Diaries, 1833–1851*, vol. 1, ed. William
Toynbee, New York, Putnam's Sons: 1912.

Male, David A. *Shakespeare on Stage: 'Antony and Cleopatra'*, Cambridge,
Cambridge University Press: 1984.

Mares, F. H. 'Shifting Perspectives in the Sexual Politics of *Antony and
Cleopatra'*, *Studies in Shakespeare 1: the Proceedings of the Australian
and New Zealand Shakespeare Association, 1990*, ed. D. Bartholomeusz,
Clayton, ANZSA: 1991, pp. 57–79.

Marston, John. *The Works*, ed. A. H.Bullen, 3 vols., London, John C.
Nimmo: 1887.

Marston, Westland. *Our Recent Actors*, London, Sampson, Low, Marston:
1890.

Mazer, Cary M. *Shakespeare Refashioned: Elizabethan Plays on Edwardian
Stages*, Ann Arbor, UMI Research Press: 1981.

McGuire, Paul, Arnott, Betty and McGuire, Frances M.*The Australian
Theatre: an Abstract and Brief Chronicle in Twelve Parts*, Melbourne
and London, Oxford University Press: 1948.

Merchant, W. M. *Shakespeare and the Artist*, London and New York,
Oxford University Press: 1959.

Merwe, Pieter van der. 'Roberts and the Theatre', in *David Roberts*, ed.
Helen Guiterman and Briony Llewellyn, London, Phaidon &
Barbican Art Gallery: 1986, pp. 27–44.

Miller, Edward. *That Noble Cabinet: a History of the British Museum*,
London, Andre Deutsch: 1973.

Mullin, Donald (ed.). *Victorian Actors and Actresses in Review*, Westport, Conn. and London, Greenwood Press: 1983.

Neale, J. E. *Queen Elizabeth*, London, Jonathan Cape: 1944 (1934).

Nelsen, Paul. 'Sizing Up the Globe: Proposed Revisions to the ISGC Reconstruction', *Shakespeare Bulletin*, 2 (4) (1993), 11.

Nicoll, J. R. A. '"Passing over the Stage"', *Shakespeare Survey*, 12 (1959), 47–55.

Nungezer, Edwin. *A Dictionary of Actors*, New York, Greenwood Press: 1968 (1929).

Odell, George C. D. *Annals of the New York Stage*, 15 vols., New York, Columbia University Press: 1927–49.

    Shakespeare – From Betterton to Irving, 2 vols., London, Constable: 1963 (1920).

Olivier, Laurence. *On Acting*, London, Weidenfeld & Nicolson: 1986.

Pearson, Hesketh. *Beerbohm Tree: His Life and Laughter*, London, Methuen: 1956.

Phelps, W. May and Robertson, John Forbes. *The Life and Life-Work of Samuel Phelps*, London, Sampson, Low, Marston, Searle & Rivington: 1880.

Pitt, Angela. *Shakespeare's Women*, Newton Abbot and Totowa, NJ, David & Charles and Barnes & Noble: n.d. (1981).

Redgrave, Michael. *Actor*, London, Heinemann: 1956.

Rees, Joan. 'An Elizabethan Eyewitness of *Antony and Cleopatra*?', *Shakespeare Survey*, 6 (1953), 91–3.

Ripa, Cesare. *Iconologia*, Rome, 1603.

Robinson, Alice M., Roberts, Vera Mowry and Barranger, Milly S. *Notable Women in the American Theater: a Biographical Dictionary*, New York, Westport, Conn. and London, Greenwood Press: 1989.

Rosenfeld, Sybil. *A Short History of Scene Design in Great Britain*, Oxford, Basil Blackwell: 1975.

Rutter, Carol C. (ed.). *Documents of the Rose Playhouse*, Revels Plays Companion Library, Manchester, Manchester University Press: 1984.

Rylands, George. 'Elizabethan Drama in the West End', *Shakespeare Survey*, 1 (1948), 103–5.

    'Festival Shakespeare in the West End', *Shakespeare Survey*, 6 (1953), 140–5.

Salgado, Gamini. *Eyewitnesses of Shakespeare: First Hand Accounts of Performances 1590–1890*, London, Chatto and Windus for Sussex University Press: 1975.

Scott, Michael. *Antony and Cleopatra*, Text and Performance, London, Macmillan: 1983.

Shakespeare, William. *Hamlet*, ed. Philip Edwards, New Cambridge Shakespeare, Cambridge, Cambridge University Press: 1985.

King Lear, ed. J. S. Bratton, Plays in Performance, Bristol, Bristol Classical Press: 1987.

King Lear, ed. Jay L. Halio, New Cambridge Shakespeare, Cambridge, Cambridge University Press: 1992.

Othello, ed. Julie Hankey, Plays in Performance, Bristol, Bristol Classical Press: 1987.

Titus Andronicus, ed. Alan Hughes, New Cambridge Shakespeare, Cambridge, Cambridge University Press: 1994.

The Riverside Shakespeare, ed. G. Blakemore Evans et al., Boston, Houghton Mifflin: 1974.

Shattuck, Charles H. *Shakespeare on the American Stage*, 2 vols., Washington, Folger Shakespeare Library: 1976 (vol.I), Washington, London and Toronto, Folger Shakespeare Library & Associated University Presses: 1987 (vol.II).

The Shakespeare Promptbooks: a Descriptive Catalogue, Urbana and London, University of Illinois Press: 1965.

Shaw, George Bernard. *Plays and Players*, ed. A. C. Ward, London, Oxford University Press: 1952.

Three Plays for Puritans, London, Grant Richards: 1901.

Shrimpton, Nicholas. 'Shakespeare Performances in Stratford-upon-Avon and London, 1982–3', *Shakespeare Survey*, 37 (1984), 163–73.

Speaight, Robert. *Shakespeare on the Stage*, London, Collins: 1973.

Sprague, A. C. *Shakespeare and the Actors: the Stage Business in His Plays (1660–1905)*, Cambridge, Mass., Harvard University Press: 1944.

Shakespearian Players and Performances, London, A.&C. Black: 1954.

Sprague, A. C. and Trewin, J. C. *Shakespeare's Plays Today: Some Customs and Conventions of the Stage*, London, Sidgwick and Jackson: 1970.

Sprinchorn, Evert. 'An Intermediate Level in the Elizabethan Theatre', *Theatre Notebook*, 46 (1992), 73–94, and *Theatre Notebook*, 48 (1994), 51–2.

Stephen, Leslie, Lee, Sidney et al. (eds.). *The Dictionary of National Biography*, with Supplements to 1950, 26 vols., London, Oxford University Press: 1912–59.

Steppat, Michael. *The Critical Reception of Shakespeare's 'Antony and Cleopatra' from 1607 to 1905*, Amsterdam, Gruner: 1980.

Stirling, Edward. *Old Drury Lane: Fifty Years' Recollections*, 2 vols., London, Chatto & Windus: 1881.

Stokes, John, Booth, Michael R. and Bassnett, Susan. *Bernhardt, Terry, Duse: the Actress in Her Time*, Cambridge, Cambridge University Press: 1988.

Stone, George W., Jr. 'Garrick's Presentation of *Antony and Cleopatra*', *RES*, 13 (1937), 20–38.

The London Stage, 1660–1800, Part 4 (1747–1776), Carbondale, University of Southern Illinois Press: 1962.

Sturgess, Keith. *Jacobean Private Theatre*, London and New York, Routledge & Kegan Paul: 1987.

Taylor, George. *Players and Performances in the Victorian Theatre*, Manchester, Manchester University Press: 1989.

Thomson, Peter. 'No Rome of Safety: the Royal Shakespeare Season 1972', *Shakespeare Survey*, 26 (1973), 139–50.

Thomson, Leslie. '*Antony and Cleopatra*, Act 4 Scene 16, "A heavy sight"', *Shakespeare Survey*, 41 (1989), 79–90.

Towse, John Ranken. *Sixty Years of the Theater: an Old Critic's Memories*, New York and London, Funk & Wagnalls Co.: 1916.

Trewin, J. C. *Benson and the Bensonians*, London, Barrie & Rockliff: 1960.

Going to Shakespeare, London, Boston and Sydney, George Allen & Unwin: 1978.

Mr Macready: a Nineteenth-century Tragedian and His Theatre, London, George G. Harrap: 1955.

The Night Has Been Unruly, London, Robert Hale: 1957.

A Play To-night, London, Elek: 1952.

Shakespeare on the English Stage, 1900–1964, London, Barrie & Rockliff: 1964.

'Shakespeare in Britain', *Shakespeare Quarterly*, 29 (1978), 212–22.

'Shakespeare in Britain', *Shakespeare Quarterly*, 31 (1980), 153–61.

Tynan, Kenneth. *A View of the English Stage, 1944–63*, London, Davis-Poynter: 1975.

Venezky, Alice. 'Current Shakespearian Productions in England and France', *Shakespeare Quarterly*, 2 (1951), 335–42.

Walkley, Arthur B. *Playhouse Impressions*, London, T. Fisher Unwin: 1892.

Warren, Roger. 'Shakespeare in England, 1982–83', *Shakespeare Quarterly*, 34 (1983), 336–7.

Watson, G. 'The Death of Cleopatra', *Notes and Queries*, NS 25 (1978), 409–14.

Webster, John. *The Duchess of Malfi*, facsimile of 1623 Quarto, Menston, Scolar Press: 1968.

Wiggins, Martin. 'An Early Misinterpretation of *Antony and Cleopatra*', *Notes and Queries*, NS 35 (1988), 483–4.

Wiles, David. *Shakespeare's Clown*, Cambridge, Cambridge University Press: 1987.

Williams, Harcourt. *Old Vic Saga*, London, Winchester Publications: 1949.

Four Years at the Old Vic, 1929–1933, London, Putnam & Co.: 1935.

Williams, Neville. *The Life and Times of Elizabeth I*, London, Sphere Books: 1975.

Winter, William. *Shakespeare on the Stage: Third Series*, New York and London, Benjamin Blom: 1969 (1916).

Wolfit, Donald. *First Interval*, London, Odhams: 1954.

Young, C. B. 'The Stage-History of *Antony and Cleopatra*', in *Antony and Cleopatra*, ed. John Dover Wilson, New Shakespeare, Cambridge, Cambridge University Press: 1950, pp. xxxvii–xlvi.

Young, William C. *Famous Actors and Actresses on the American Stage: Documents of American Theater History*, 2 vols., New York and London, R. R. Bowker Co.: 1975.

INDEX

A-level, 120
Aaron, 3
Abbey, Henry, xiii, 57, 60, 144
Abbot, William, 36
ABC, xiv
Abyssinian, 171
Achurch, Janet, xiii, 70, 71, 96n, 220, 303, 318, 319
Actium, 27, 37, 42n, 56, 58, 59, 65, 82n, 238, 240, 248
Actors Touring Company, xv, 129, 141
Adams, John, 131n
Adams, William Davenport, 44n
Adelaide, 60n, 82n
Afghan, 171
African, 129, 130
Afro hairstyle, 191
Agate, James, 70, 74, 76, 79, 80, 82, 83, 85, 86, 86n, 87, 144, 160, 181, 207, 228, 249, 251, 252, 259, 286, 290, 292, 294, 303, 306, 318, 322
Agrippa, 36, 121, 177, 182, 299
Albert, Ernest, 63
Aldwych, xiv, xv, 109, 111, 213
Alexandria, 9, 27, 29, 59, 66, 79, 99, 110, 201, 223, 260
Alexandrian, 11, 93, 144, 162, 188
Alexas, 27, 28, 78, 81, 85, 141, 195
All for Love, xv, 26, 28, 29, 30, 32n, 33, 34, 35, 36, 49, 80, 90, 111n, 318
Allan Wilkie Shakespearean Company, 74
Allen, Shirley S., 46n, 48
Alleyn, Edward, 21
Alma-Tadema, Lawrence, 64, 80, 126, 224
Almeida Theatre, 120n
Ambassador, 242
Ambassadors, 147
America, 5, 45

American Shakespeare Festival, 101, 104n
American, 14, 44, 55, 55n, 59, 68, 86, 88, 90, 90n, 101, 135, 270
American, North, 324
Amsterdam, 93
Amyot, Jacques, 12
Anderson, James, xii, 55n, 57, 58, 67, 72, 238, 268
Anderson, John, 83
Anderson, Lawrence, 207
Anderson, Paul, 122, 124
Andrews, Harry, 93, 97, 181, 184, 270
Anglicised, 72, 82
Anglo-Egyptian, 59
Anglo-Saxon, 70, 118, 129
Anton, Robert, 17n
Antony (*also* Mark Antony), 3, 4, 7, 8, 9, 10, 13, 13n, 15, 16, 20, 25, 26, 27, 28, 29, 30, 31, 32, 33, 34, 35, 36, 37, 40, 41, 41n, 42, 44n, 45, 46, 47, 50, 51, 52, 53(illus.), 54, 55, 55n, 57, 58, 59, 60, 61, 62(illus.), 65, 66, 67, 68, 68n, 70, 72, 73, 77, 78, 79, 81, 82, 83, 84, 85, 86, 88, 88n, 89, 89n, 90, 91(illus.), 92, 95, 96, 97, 99, 100, 101, 102n, 103, 104, 105(illus.), 106, 107, 108, 108n, 109, 110, 111, 112, 113, 114, 115, 115n, 116, 117, 118, 118(illus.), 119, 120, 121, 122, 127, 128, 130, 131, 132, 133(illus.), 134, 135, 136, 137, 141, 143, 144, 145, 146, 147, 148, 149, 150, 151, 153, 157, 161, 163, 169, 174, 176, 177, 178, 180, 182, 184, 185, 188, 189, 190, 191, 194, 196, 198, 199, 203, 204, 209, 210, 211, 212, 213, 217, 218, 219, 221, 223, 224, 225, 227, 229, 230, 235, 237, 238, 239, 240, 241, 247, 248, 249, 250, 251, 252, 254, 255, 257, 259, 260, 262, 267, 269, 270, 273, 275, 276, 277, 278, 279, 281, 282, 283, 284, 286, 287,

288, 289, 290, 291, 292, 293, 294, 295,
  296, 298, 301, 304, 305, 307, 315, 316,
  318, 320, 321, 324, 325
Antony and Cleopatra (Barber), 101
Antony and Cleopatra (Heston), 116n
Antony and Cleopatra, passim.
ANZSA (Australian and New Zealand
  Shakespeare Association), 121n
Apache, 210
Archer, William, 70, 73, 241, 303, 312, 319,
  325
Arditti, Michael, 131
Armin, Robert, 20, 312
Armstrong, William A., 20, 21n
Artaud, Antonin, 112
Aryan, 254
Asche, Oscar, xiii, 65, 73, 73n, 90n, 144, 147,
  171, 198, 203, 237, 259, 286, 290, 293,
  307
Ascot, 316
Ashcroft, Peggy, xiv, 2, 6, 93, 94(illus.), 95,
  96, 100, 107, 115n, 122, 124, 127, 150,
  161, 168, 190, 191, 193, 196, 197, 219,
  241, 313, 315, 316, 318, 320, 321
Asian, 130
Asiatic, 54
Aspatia, 86n
Atheneum, 127
Athens, 221, 223
Atkins, Robert, xiii, xiv, 74, 75, 77, 78, 79, 80,
  85n, 86, 87n, 147, 259, 269, 278, 290,
  307, 313, 315, 319, 323
Atkinson, Brooks, 83, 83n
ATV, xiv
Auden, W.H., 30n
Augustan, 14n
Augustus Caesar, 14
Augustus, Second, 14
Australia, 73, 73n, 74, 132
Australian Performing Group, 132n
Australian, 55, 59, 65, 73, 90n, 97, 97n, 144,
  147, 171, 198, 203, 237, 259, 286, 287,
  290, 293, 307
Austrians, 84
Ayrton, Randle, 73, 78, 181, 269
Aztec, 119

Bacchanalian, 204
Bacchanals, 211
Bacchus, 46, 56, 147
Bach, Reginald, xiv, 83n, 180
Bacon, Francis (painter), 291
Baker, Herschel, 34, 35
Baldwin Theatre (San Francisco), 61n
Baldwin, Thomas W., 24
Balkan, 135
Balling, Michael, 65
Banke, Cecile de, 16n
Bankhead, Tallulah, xiv, 14, 83, 84
Banks, Miss (singer), 203
Bankside Globe, xv, 109
Bara, Theda, 119n
Barber, John, 96n, 108, 219, 238, 291, 292,
  317, 320
Barber, Samuel, 101
Barbican, xvi, 116, 125, 128
Barker, Felix, 92n, 114, 313
Barkstead, William, 20n
Barnes, Barnabe, 17
Barnes, E.C., 63
Barrault, Jean-Louis, 86, 204, 235
Barroll, J. Leeds, 16
Barry, Ann, 34
Barry, Elizabeth, 29
Barry, Spranger, 34
Barthelemy, Anthony G., 4n
Bartholomeusz, Dennis, *see* Heales, Robyn
  and Bartholomeusz, Dennis
Baryshnikov, 210
Bassnett, Susan, *see* Stokes, John, Booth,
  Michael R. and Bassnett, Susan
Baughan, E.A., 85
Baxter, Keith, xv, 103, 108, 110, 115, 119,
  121, 150, 212, 237, 287
Baylis, Lilian, 74, 89
Bayreuth, 65
BBC series, 97, 116
BBC television version (Miller), 81n, 115,
  128, 146, 153, 157, 162, 167, 182, 189,
  192, 195, 207, 212, 213, 220, 221, 224,
  226, 241, 248, 250, 254, 259, 275, 279,
  283, 290, 292, 298, 299, 306, 308, 313,
  316, 320, 322, 323

BBC/Time-Life, xv
BBC2, xv
Beaumont and Fletcher, 17n
Beaumont, Penelope, 119, 221
Beavers, 144
Beck, George, 55, 57, 240, 245, 303, 304, 312
Beckett, Samuel, 112
Bedouin, 65
Beerbohm, Max, 255
Bell, Marie, 87n
Bellew, Kyrle, xiii, 60, 72
Belzoni, Giovanni Battista, 42, 43, 43n
Belzoni, Sara, 43
Benedict, Claire, 128
Bennett, George, 48, 50, 278
Bennison, Ishia, xvi, 136, 163, 192, 240, 246
Benson, Constance, xiii, 71, 191, 289, 315, 321; *see also* Bensons
Benson, Frank, xiii, 2, 61, 64, 65, 66, 71, 72, 73, 78, 144, 146, 203, 209, 251, 259, 269, 278, 286, 289, 301; *see also* Bensons
Bensons, 90
Benthall, Michael, xiv, 90, 91(illus.), 92, 93, 97, 204, 213, 269, 290, 307, 323
Bentley, Eric, 74, 88
Bentley, G.E., 24n
Berlin, xiii, 57, 128, 132, 134, 291
Berliner Ensemble, 102n, 134
Bernhardt, Sarah, 60, 60n, 71
Berry, Edward, 31, 180
Berry, Ralph, 82
Bertish, Suzanne, 111
Betterton, Thomas, 23n
Bevan, Ian, 147
Beverley, William, 64
Bevington, David, 18n, 32n, 35, 73n, 82n
Biblical, 130
Biddle, Esme, 78, 185
Billington, Michael, 2n, 106, 107, 109, 110, 113n, 114, 115, 117, 118, 119, 121, 122, 123, 124, 125, 126, 127, 128, 131, 134, 135, 137, 141, 150, 168, 169, 170, 177, 182, 192, 193, 194, 196, 198, 205, 206, 208, 210, 213, 220, 228, 230, 238, 240, 241, 246, 250, 252, 254, 255, 257, 260,

261, 262, 263, 279, 286, 304, 305, 308, 312, 313, 314, 316
Birmingham Repertory Theatre, 100n, 131n
Birmingham, 81n
Bishop, Henry, 38, 56
Black, G.F., 73
Black, Pauline, xv, 130
Blackfriars, xii, 1n, 15, 16, 16n, 18, 18n, 24
Blackpool, 118
Blakely, Colin, xv, 116, 157, 248, 275
Blanchard, E.L., 45n
Bland, Harriet, xii, 5, 45
Bland, Humphrey, 45
Blane, Sue, 125
Bloomsbury Theatre, xv, 130
Boaden, James, 3n, 27, 33
Boito, Arrigo, 70
Bonaparte, Napoleon, 35
Bones, Ken, 121, 211
Bonomi, Joseph, 52, 52n
Booth, Agnes, xii, 68
Booth, Michael R., *see* Stokes, John, Booth, Michael R. and Bassnett, Susan
Bordman, Gerald, 60n, 68n, 70n
Borisova, Iuliana, 103
Bosnia, 135
Bosnian, 135
Boutell, Elizabeth, 28
Bowen, Christopher, 177
Bracegirdle, Anne, 29
Bradley, A.C., 7
Bradshaw, John, 51, 254
Bratton, J.S., 19n
Brayton, Lily, xiii, 73, 73n, 90n
Brecht, Bertolt, 112, 132
Brechtian, 132, 137
Brewster, Yvonne, xv, 130, 141, 145, 167, 171, 182, 196, 205, 249, 259, 305, 309
Bridges-Adams, William, xiii, xiv, 74, 75, 75n, 76, 77, 78, 79, 80, 80n, 81, 85n, 112, 130, 148, 159, 162, 181, 185, 195, 204, 209, 269, 278, 290, 291, 294, 313, 319, 323
Brisbane, Katharine, 73n, 74n, 82n
Britain, 5, 59, 100, 128

British Museum, 38, 43, 43n, 52n, 56, 63, 64, 105

British, 35, 39, 59, 102, 122, 129, 130, 135, 141, 313

Britton, Jasper, 127, 141, 270, 314

Britton, Tony, 97

Brixton, 71

Broadsides, *see* Northern Broadsides

Broadway Theatre (New York), xii, 54, 55n, 60

Broadway, off-Off-, 129

Brook, Peter, xv, 12n, 111, 112, 113, 113n, 114, 115, 116, 117, 118, 125, 128, 131, 137, 143, 146, 147, 151, 157, 178, 182, 185, 188, 190, 192, 193, 199, 205, 206, 210, 211, 213, 223, 230, 235, 237, 238, 245, 247, 248, 250, 251, 252, 253, 254, 255, 263, 270, 273, 274, 277, 279, 283, 287, 290, 291, 293, 308, 313, 316, 318, 319, 323, 325

Brooke, Paul, 115

Broun, Heywood, 82

Brown, Ivor, 3, 80, 81, 82, 84, 84n, 85, 89, 92, 96, 106n, 143, 174, 206

Brown, T. Allston, 44n, 55n

Brown-Potter, Cora, xiii, 68, 69, 84n, 228, 291, 315, 320

Browne, Coral, 97n

Brussels, 93

Brutus, 198

Bryant, Michael, 125, 180, 182, 183, 184

Bryden, Ronald, 102n, 103, 294

Buckle, Richard, 96n

Buddhists, 113n

Bullock, William, 35

Bulman, J.C. and Coursen, H.R., 116n

Bunn, Alfred, xii, 39, 40, 42

Burbage, Richard, xii, 20, 21, 24n, 26

Burgtheater (Vienna), 84

Burnand, Francis, 44n, 138n

Burnim, Kalman, 31n

Burton, Richard, 84n, 101, 135

Bussy D'Ambois, 17n

Butler, Paul, xvi, 89n, 135, 136, 156, 157, 261, 284

Butler, Robert, 136, 182, 235, 240, 293

Byford, Roy, 78, 153

Byrne, Muriel StC., 181, 314

Byron, George Gordon, 2, 34, 218, 320

Caesar and Cleopatra (Pascal), 90

Caesar and Cleopatra (Shaw), xiv, 90, 290

Caesar, Octavius, *see* Octavius

Caird, John, xvi, 81n, 86, 101n, 115, 125, 126, 126(illus.), 127, 128, 135, 141, 145, 162, 171, 178, 182, 189, 192, 198, 201, 207, 218, 224, 225, 250, 254, 259, 263, 270, 276, 283, 290, 299, 302, 305, 308, 312, 314, 319, 320, 325

Calatani, Madame, 3n

Caldwell, Zoe, xiv, 101, 102, 103, 277, 294

Caligula, 204

Calvert's acting edition, 146, 159, 161, 162, 165, 171, 185, 188, 191, 193, 195, 203, 205, 209, 215, 221, 223, 232, 233, 240, 242, 247, 249, 250, 253, 257, 259, 261, 266, 267, 268, 272, 273, 274, 282, 285, 287, 294, 295, 297, 302, 311, 315, 321

Calvert, Adelaide, xii, 55, 56, 57, 303, 304, 312; *see also* Calverts

Calvert, Charles, xii, 50, 53, 54, 55, 56, 57; *see also* Calverts

Calvert, Louis, xiii, 60, 65n, 66, 70, 72, 74, 218, 284, 312, 325

Calverts, 90

Cambridge, 88

Campbell, John, 33

Canidius, 141, 146

Capell, Edward, 18n, 30, 31, 33, 295

Caravaggio, 121, 122

Caribbean, 130

Carne, Rosalind, 120, 205, 293, 306

Carr, David, 171

Carter, Howard, 79

Carter, Michael, 208

Case, R.H., 16n, 17n

Cass, Henry, xiv, 82n, 144, 259

Cassius, 198

Castro, Fidel, 109

Central Park (New York), 102n

Cesarion, 224, 302

Chambers, E.K., 17n, 21n

Chapel, Children of the, 18n
Chapman, Don, 113n, 114, 316
Charles, Louise Stafford, 135, 270
Charleson, Ian, 115, 224, 254, 298
Charmian (*also* Charmion), 8, 25, 34, 38, 46,
    56, 74, 78, 81, 83, 86, 111, 116,
    118(illus.), 119, 123(illus.), 128,
    133(illus.), 135, 141, 151, 153, 159, 162,
    167, 170, 189, 193, 195, 197, 238, 247,
    287, 294, 295, 301, 311, 312, 314, 315,
    318, 319, 322, 323, 324
Chatterton, Frederick, xii, 2, 47n, 50, 55n,
    57, 58, 59, 63, 64, 67, 73, 143, 146, 171,
    180, 198, 203, 234, 235, 252, 269, 282,
    286, 306, 318, 322
Chicago, 88
Chichester, xiv, xv, 108, 120, 121, 203, 279,
    288, 290, 308
China, 121n
Chinese, 86n
Chitty, Alison, 122, 194, 205
Christ, 14, 291
Christian, 291, 315
Christian, King of Denmark, 203
Christie, Anna, 95
Christie, Ian, 14
Christmas pantomime, 58n
Churchill, Winston, 203
Cinema (Stratford), xiii, xiv, 76, 81n
Clarimond, A., 87n
Clarke, Mary, 283
Clayton, Lucy, 120
Clements, Frank, xii, 58
Clements, John, xiv, 102, 149
Cleopatra (Mankiewicz), 101
Cleopatra (Mille), 97n
Cleopatra and Antony, xv, 129, 141
Cleopatra's monument, 9, 16, 35, 46, 54, 57,
    61, 63, 64, 65, 66, 87, 90, 93, 99, 104,
    106, 107, 110, 117, 124, 132, 287, 288,
    289, 290, 291, 292, 293, 296, 299, 301,
    302, 315, 318
Cleopatra's Needles, 59, 99
Cleopatra, 3, 4, 5, 6, 7, 8, 9, 10, 11, 12, 13, 14,
    16, 17, 22, 22n, 23, 23n, 24, 25, 25n, 26,
    26n, 27, 28, 29, 30, 32, 33, 35, 36, 37,

37(illus.), 38, 40, 41, 41n, 42, 42n, 43,
    44n, 45, 46, 47, 48, 49, 50, 52, 53(illus.),
    54, 55, 55n, 57, 58, 59, 60, 61, 61n, 65,
    66, 67, 68, 69, 69n, 70, 70n, 71, 71n, 72,
    73, 73n, 74, 76, 77, 78, 79, 80, 81, 82,
    82n, 83, 84, 86, 88, 89, 89n, 90,
    91(illus.), 92, 93, 94(illus.), 95, 96, 96n,
    98(illus.), 99, 100, 101, 101n, 102n, 103,
    105, 105(illus.), 106, 107, 107n, 108,
    109, 110, 111, 112, 113, 113n, 114, 115,
    115n, 116, 117, 118, 118(illus.), 119,
    120, 120n, 121, 122, 123(illus.), 125,
    126(illus.), 127, 128, 129, 130, 131,
    133(illus.), 134, 134(illus.), 135, 136,
    141, 143, 145, 146, 147, 148, 149, 150,
    151, 153, 159, 161, 162, 165, 167, 168,
    170, 174, 180, 181, 182, 185, 188, 189,
    190, 191, 192, 193, 194, 195, 196, 218,
    220, 221, 224, 225, 227, 228, 238, 240,
    241, 247, 249, 250, 251, 252, 260, 261,
    267, 275, 276, 277, 278, 279, 284, 286,
    287, 288, 289, 290, 291, 292, 293, 296,
    301, 302, 304, 305, 306, 307, 308, 309,
    311, 312, 313, 314, 315, 316, 317, 318,
    319, 320, 321, 322, 323, 324, 325; *see also*
    Egyptian Queen
Cleveland, Louisa, xii, 55
Clever, Edith, 128, 220, 262, 316
Clown, 13n, 20, 30, 31, 34, 40, 57, 77, 78, 86,
    111n, 115, 127, 130, 141, 312, 313, 314
Clytemnestra, 95
Coan purple, 204
Cockneyfied, 125
Coe, John, 144
Coghlan, Charles, xiii, 72
Colbert, Claudette, 97n
Cole, Megan, xvi, 125n
Coleman, John, 45n, 46
Coleridgean, 5
Collier, Constance, xiii, 66, 67n, 70, 71, 82n,
    100n, 180, 191, 193, 194, 196, 218, 225
Collins, Wilkie, 51, 254
Colman, George, 34n
Colonna, Robert, 128
Colorado Shakespeare Festival, 101n, 104n
Colosseum, 53

Colvin, Clare, 117, 189, 212
Comédie-Française, 87, 204, 235
Commodus, 204
Commonweal Theatre Company, xv, 131
Consul-General, British, 42
Conway, Harold, 92
Conway, Lydia, 130
Cook, Dutton, 57
Cookman, Anthony, 7, 174, 204
Cooper (actor), 40
Cooper, Frank Kemble, 73
Cooper, Roberta Krensky, 101n, 104n, 145, 210, 316
Cooper, Rosa, xii, 55n
Coppi, Carlo, 204
Corbin, John, 82n
Cordelia, 25n
Corey, Katherine, 28
Corinthian-columned, 90
Coriolanus, 34, 114
Coriolanus, xiv, 12, 101, 104
Cornell, Katharine, xiv, 88, 88n, 90, 92
Cornwell, Judy, 185
Cottonopolis, 54, 57
Couling, Della, 234
Coursen, H.R., 146, 151, 168, 174, 205, 221, 224, 225, 248, 275, 323; *see also* Bulman, J.C. and Coursen, H.R.
Coveney, Michael, 119n, 120, 122, 136, 137, 142, 157, 218, 227, 249, 259, 270, 283, 293, 294, 316, 320, 322, 325
Covent Garden, xii, 32, 34, 35, 37(illus.), 39
Cowl, Jane, xiii, 82
Cox, Alan, 192, 218
Cox, Michael Graham, 110n
Cramphorn, Rex, xv, 132, 320, 324
Crawford, Alice, 74
Cressall, Maud, 185
Creswell (actor), 36
Croft, John, 100n
Croll, Dona, xv, 130, 131, 196, 249, 305, 307, 309, 319
Cross, Richard, 32
Crosse, Gordon, 80, 81, 86, 88, 89, 181, 204, 267, 310, 313
Crouch, J.H., 101n

Crowl, Samuel, 109n, 116n, 146, 149, 150, 151, 180, 182, 183, 184, 216, 268, 280, 281, 291, 292, 294, 319, 321
Crumpton (actor), 36
Cryer, Andrew, 137
Crystal Palace, 52, 52n
Cuddon, J.A., 174, 292
Culliford, James, 191
Cunnington, C.W. and P., 25n
Cupid, 147
Curll, Edmund, 28
Curnow, Susan, xv, 131
Cusack, Sorcha, 118(illus.), 119
Cushman, Robert, 111, 114, 114n, 115, 157, 182, 205, 230, 252, 253, 254, 290, 313
Cydnus, 58, 143, 181, 315, 318

D'Arcy, Eamon, 132
D'Arms, Ted, 111n
Dale (actor), 51
Dalton, Timothy, xv, 121, 122, 147, 257, 283
Daniel, Samuel, 16, 16n, 289
Darbyshire, Alfred, 55n
Dare, Daphne, 120
Darlington, W.A., 76, 77, 85, 86, 88, 89, 92, 159, 317
David, Richard, 116
Davies, H. Neville, 14n, 34n, 203
Davies, Lindy, xv, 132, 320
Davies, Thomas, 31, 32, 33, 39
Davies, W. Robertson, 16n
Dawson, Helen, 103n
Dawson, R. Mac G., 22
Deacon, Brian, 120
Dean Clough, 136
Demetrius, 146, 151
Dench, Judi, xv, 6, 71n, 122, 123(illus.), 124, 127, 149, 150, 151, 168, 169, 170, 193, 194, 220, 294, 303, 304, 312, 316, 319, 320, 321, 325
Denon, Dominique-Vivant, 35
Dent, Alan, 89
Dercetus (*also* Dercetas), 141, 297, 299
Desdemona, 4, 25
Dessen, A.C., 125n, 254, 259, 280, 298, 299, 302

Devil's Charter, The, 17

Dewhurst, Colleen, 90n, 102n

Dews, Peter, xiv, 100, 100n, 102, 103, 104, 149

Dexter, Sally, 227

Dickens, Charles, 51, 52, 68, 254

Dickinson, G.K., 48

Dietrich/Boyer, 325

Diomedes, 141, 191

Dobson, Agnes, 60n, 82n

Dolabella, 27, 28, 35, 137, 151, 305

Dormandy, Simon, 131n

Dorn, Franchelle, xv, 129

Dorset Garden, 26

Double First, 3, 84

Douglass, John, xii, 50, 51, 68, 254

Downer, Alan S., 21n, 39n, 45n

Downes, John, 23n

Dr Faustus, 132n

Drury Lane, xii, 1, 26, 30, 31, 32, 33, 35, 39, 57, 73n

Dryden, John, 5, 26, 27, 28, 29, 30, 31, 34, 35, 40, 40n, 49, 55, 58, 120n, 130, 153, 171, 180, 278, 286, 287, 318

Drydenised text, 36, 45

Dublin Gate Theatre, 90n

Dublin, 90n

Duchess of Malfi, The, 1n, 15, 17n, 106n

Dumas *fils*, 318

Dunlop, Frank, 110n

Dunn, Tony, 130, 131, 182, 249, 259, 319

Durban, xiii

Duse, Eleanora, 70, 241

Dusinberre, Juliet, 3n, 24n, 95n

Dyce, Alexander, 18n

East End (of London), 50

East, 66, 74, 77, 143

Eastern, 44, 71, 77, 81, 84, 224

Eddy, Edward, xii, 30, 54, 55, 55n

Edfou, 56

Edinburgh Festival, xv, 111, 132

Edinburgh, 134, 213, 228, 260

Edmans, John, xii, 24

Edwardes, Jane, 136, 205

Edwardian, 66, 71, 81, 129, 143, 180, 316

Edwards, Malcolm, xv, 129, 130

Egypt, 8, 9, 10, 11, 12, 18, 19, 35, 38, 42, 42n, 43, 55, 58, 59, 67, 81, 86, 87, 88, 90, 93, 99, 103, 104n, 105, 108, 116, 117n, 120, 121, 122, 125, 129, 130, 135, 136, 146, 185, 189, 315, 323

Egyptian Court (Crystal Palace), 52

Egyptian Hall (Piccadilly), 35, 43

Egyptian Queen, 58, 69, 82, 92, 148, 184

Egyptian, 1, 4, 9, 10, 11, 12, 12n, 30, 32, 35, 36, 38, 42, 43, 43n, 44, 46, 48, 49, 52, 52n, 54, 58, 59, 63, 64, 65, 66, 69, 70, 75n, 76, 79, 80, 82, 83, 84, 85, 93, 106, 107n, 109, 109n, 113, 115, 117, 119, 121, 129, 130, 131, 131n, 141, 142, 143, 145, 146, 149, 150, 162, 211, 278, 299, 308, 315

Egyptianness, 106

Egyptians, 90, 90n, 113, 116, 129, 135, 144, 252

Egypto-Hellenic, 82n

Egypto-Roman, 64

Egyptological, 52n

Egyptology, 64

Egyptomania, 8-11, 35, 52, 59, 101, 105

Ek, Anders, 110

Elizabeth I, 13, 17, 24, 88n, 107n, 114, 190, 191, 218, 315

Elizabethan Stage Society, 74n

Elizabethan, 13, 14, 14n, 19n, 20, 21, 21n, 24, 44n, 63, 68, 75, 75n, 78, 79, 80, 81, 85, 87, 102, 132, 135, 162, 315, 318

Ellis, Ruth, 161, 181, 196, 278, 304, 313, 315, 317, 319

Elsom, John, 104, 104n, 105, 107, 108, 112, 114, 115, 145, 157, 205, 210, 213, 319

Elysian Fields, 325

Emerton, Roy, xiv, 84

Emery, John, 83

Emperor, 66

Emsley, Clive, 100n

England, 30, 43, 52, 75, 128, 131

English actresses, 3, 4, 11, 57, 71, 81, 95, 100, 106n

English, 6, 11, 14, 19, 23n, 27, 52, 54, 55, 57, 61, 64n, 70, 71, 72, 74, 77, 80, 84, 84n,

86, 86n, 87, 92, 95, 96, 100, 101, 103,
    106n, 108, 111, 118, 119, 120, 121, 122,
    124, 125, 129, 130, 132, 134, 136, 143,
    241, 318
English-speaking, 73n, 129
Englishmen, 72, 108
Englishness, 6, 71, 77, 84, 86, 95, 100
Englishwoman, 3, 120
Enobarbus, 19, 22, 27, 31, 35, 40, 45, 48, 54,
    58, 59, 62(illus.), 64, 66, 73, 77, 78, 80,
    85, 89, 92, 97, 108, 110, 111, 113, 115,
    116, 119, 120, 121, 125, 127, 136, 137,
    144, 146, 153, 156, 157, 180, 181, 182,
    184, 185, 188, 205, 209, 210, 211, 228,
    235, 248, 255, 263, 269, 270, 271, 312,
    319
Eros, 31, 35, 40, 48, 72, 92, 107, 130, 137,
    141, 259, 260, 278, 279, 280, 281, 282,
    283
Essex, Earl of, 13, 13n, 191
Esslin, Martin, 125, 305
Eunuch, 146, 153, 189, 279
Eunuchs, 144, 277
Euphronius, 141
Europe, 11, 51, 325
European, 128
Europeans, 11
Eustrel, Anthony, xiv, 86
Evans, Arthur, 162
Evans, Edith, xiii, xiv, 79, 80, 82, 83, 87, 88,
    89, 89n, 95, 96, 162, 163, 168, 190, 267,
    306, 318
Everett, Barbara, 71n, 194, 316
Everyman Theatre (Liverpool), xv, 130
Evita, 205
Eytinge, Rose, xii, 59, 65, 68, 180
Ezueb, 56

Fahey, Joseph, 52
Falangist, 174
Farjeon, Herbert, 83, 85, 162, 163
Fascist, 87, 87n
Faucit, Harriet, xii, 5, 34, 36, 37(illus.), 42,
    42n, 70, 83, 320
Faucit, Helen, 5
Felliniesque, 106

Felsenreitschule (Salzburg), 128
Female Eunuch, The, 106
Fenton, F., 49
Fenton, George, 117
Festival of Britain, 90
Festival Theatre (Chichester), xiv, xv, 102
Festival Theatre (Stratford, Conn.), xiv, 101
Festival Theatre (Stratford, Ont.), xiv, xv,
    101, 102
Ffolkes, David, 82n
Field, J.M., 44n
Findlater, Richard, 96, 148, 174, 185, 187,
    238, 239, 241, 275
Fischer, Bobby, 14
Fisher White, J., 144
Fitzgerald, M., 118(illus.)
Flecknoe, Richard, 21, 21n
Fleming, Peter, 2
Fluchère, Henri, 87n, 204, 235
Flynn, Jeremy, 141
Folio, First, 1, 18, 18n, 24, 31, 33, 47, 78, 80,
    116, 146, 206, 234, 254, 259, 287, 288,
    289, 294, 318
Folland, F., 44n
Forbes, Lorna, xiii, 74n
Forbes, Norman, 62(illus.), 207
Foster, Miranda, 123(illus.)
Fotopoulos, Dionissis, 128
Foucault, Michel, 13n
Foulkes, Richard, 82n
France, 59
Frank, Philip, 121
Freemantle, Hugh, 65
French, 29, 64n, 110n
Fulvia, 7, 141, 147, 157, 161, 284
Furse, Roger, 90
Fyfe, H. Hamilton, 61, 207, 221

Gaffney, Kathleen, xv, 129, 320
Gallacher, Frank, xv, 132
Galloway, David, 18n
Gallus, 302
Gambon, Michael, xv, 116, 117, 118(illus.),
    119, 150, 177, 212, 237, 274, 293
Garbo, Greta, 82, 83
Gardner, Jimmy, 313

Garrick, David, xii, 1, 29, 30, 31, 32, 33, 34, 35, 38, 39, 41, 43, 45, 46, 61, 74, 141, 151, 153, 156, 157, 167, 171, 179, 180, 183, 184, 185, 188, 191, 193, 198, 205, 209, 210, 211, 213, 215, 221, 223, 226, 238, 239, 242, 246, 249, 254, 257, 259, 271, 274, 275, 282, 289, 293, 294, 295, 302, 308, 311, 314, 317, 321
Garside, John, 80
Gayley, Charles, 17n
Gazzolo, Nando, 93
Geckle, George L., 125n, 145, 189, 192, 225, 228, 250, 254, 260, 270, 276, 283, 290, 314, 319, 325
Gedda, Mlle A. (dancer), 203
Genest, John, 3, 6, 27, 31n, 36
Georgiadis, Nicholas, 111
German, 58, 64n
Gide, André, 87n
Gielgud, John, xiv, 75n, 80, 81, 85, 99
Gilbert and Sullivan, 293
Gilbert, Kenneth, 111n
Gilbert, Stephen, 205
Gilder, Rosamond, 88n
Gill, Basil, 62(illus.), 73, 225
Glasgow, 85n
Globe, xii, 1n, 15, 16, 17, 18, 18n, 19, 19n, 20, 288
Glover, Julian, xv, 109, 110, 292
Gluckman, Leon, 97
Glyn, Isabella, xii, 30, 42n, 44, 45, 46, 47, 49, 50, 51, 51n, 52, 53, 53(illus.), 54, 57, 58, 67, 71n, 77, 80, 89n, 95, 159, 189, 191, 246, 295, 312, 315, 318, 320, 321
Godfrey, Derek, 97, 181
Goodliffe, Michael, 89, 204
Goodsall, Arthur, 74n
Gordon, Charles George, 59
Gore, Sandy, xvi, 132, 133(illus.)
Goring, Marius, 96, 97, 204, 216
Göring, Hermann, 88
Graham (actor), 48
Grand Shakespeare Festival, 60
Granger (theatrical costumier), 72
Grant, Michael, 137n
Grant, Steve, 124, 218

Granville-Barker, Harley, 31n, 74, 75, 78, 80, 81, 81n, 107, 146, 161, 162, 213, 234
Great Depression, 74
Greco-Roman, 75n, 85
Greece, 43n
Greek fire, 58
Greek, 9, 10, 11, 64, 82n
Green, Dorothy, xiii, xiv, 24, 71, 76, 77, 79, 80, 81, 83, 88, 96, 148, 168, 189, 191, 194, 294, 308, 312, 317
Greenhill Street (Stratford), 76
Greville, Fulke, 13
Grey, Alice, 55n
Grieve, Thomas, 53, 54, 55
Griffiths, Richard, 115, 313
Grimwood, Herbert, 62(illus.)
Guardian, 121
Guérin, Jules, 63
Gulbenkian Studio (Newcastle), xv, 116
Gully, John, 137
Gurr, Andrew, 288
Gypsies Metamorphosed, The, 4

Hack, Keith, xv, 81n, 119, 120, 121, 130, 142, 205, 228, 237, 270, 287, 322
Haigh, Kenneth, xv, 129
Hale, Lionel, 88n
Halifax, 136
Hall, Peter, xv, 81n, 104n, 115, 122, 123(illus.), 124, 125, 126, 127, 141, 148, 151, 157, 162, 178, 180, 182, 184, 190, 203, 205, 208, 211, 216, 227, 228, 234, 268, 275, 284, 290, 291, 292, 294, 298, 299, 309, 316, 321, 324
Hall, W., 65
Halliday's edition, 58, 59, 269, 282, 318
Halliday, Andrew, 58, 59
Hamelin, Clement, 194
Hamlet, 18, 20, 21n, 23n, 24n, 87, 259
Hamlet, 20, 21n, 23n, 24n, 296
Hammond, Aubrey, 84
Hankey, Julie, 4n, 5, 5n, 6n
Hanmer, Thomas, 18n
Harben, Hubert, 85
Harben, Joan, 310
Harding, Lyn, 62(illus.), 73, 144, 180

Harewood, David, 136, 270
Harington, John, 13
Harker, Joseph, 64, 66, 73
Harlequin, 313
Harris, Alfred, 78
Harris, Frank, 185, 204, 207
Harrison, Wayne, xvi, 132, 133(illus.)
Harron, Mary, 121, 220, 291, 316
Harrow (School), 52n
Hart, A., 17n, 18n
Hartington, Lord, 64
Harvey, Brian, 95, 97
Hathor, 75n
Hattaway, Michael, 24n, 26n, 132n
Hauser, Frank, 100n
Hayes, George, 313
Hayne, Julia Dean, 55n
Hayward, Susie Lee, 128
Hazlitt, William, 36, 70
Heales, Robyn and Bartholomeusz, Dennis, 132, 320
Hegarty, Tony, xv, 131
Heister, George, 65
Heliopolis, 59
Hellenic, 96
Hellenistic, 10
Helmsley, W.J., 65
Helpmann, Robert, xiv, 92, 97, 97n, 98(illus.), 99, 100, 102, 102n, 141, 144, 148, 174, 188, 203, 204, 221, 235, 242, 252, 257, 259, 260, 283, 292, 293, 294, 296, 314, 315, 321
Henry VIII, 33
Henry, Susan, 130
Hepburn, Katharine, xiv, 101, 101n
Hepton, Bernard, 100n, 147
Her Majesty's Opera House (Melbourne), xiii, 60
Heraud, J.A., 320
Herculean, 163
Hercules, 9, 137, 137n, 229, 259
Heston, Charlton, 116n
Hewison, Robert, 126, 127, 201
Hicks, Zoe, 111
Hield, William, xii, 45
Higgins, Clare, xvi, 101n, 125, 126(illus.),

127, 148, 189, 192, 193, 194, 195, 196, 228, 246, 250, 260, 312
Higgins, Michael, 102n
Higlett, Simon, 121
Hiley, Jim, 161, 257
Hill, Dave, 137, 182
Hill, Holly, *see* Leiter, Samuel and Hill, Holly
Hill, John, 33, 34
Hilton, 201
Hiroshima, 113
Hirschhorn, Clive, 124, 135, 316
His Majesty's Theatre, xiii, 57, 62(illus.), 66
Hispanic, 129
Hitler, Adolf, 97
Hobart, 74n
Hobson, Harold, 89, 92, 151, 181, 206, 292
Hogan, Charles B., 26n
Holder, Nick, 189
Holding, Frederick, 55
Holland, Charles, 180
Holloway, Baliol, xiii, 73, 77, 82, 148, 181, 249, 251, 269
Hollywood Egyptian, 125
Hollywood, 97, 101, 116n, 129, 134
Holmes, Martin, 31n, 38n, 141, 312
Hope, Thomas, 35, 38
Hope-Wallace, Philip, 219, 278, 280
Hopkins, Anthony (actor), xv, 122, 124, 127, 149, 150, 151, 157, 211, 248, 252, 257, 276, 280, 281, 284, 291
Hopkins, Antony (composer), 93
Horrible, Creuel and Bloody Murther, A, 17n
Horus, 22
Howard, Alan, xv, 113, 114, 147, 149, 150, 151, 155, 157, 178, 230, 237, 238, 245, 251, 252, 263, 274, 287, 293
Howe, Elizabeth, 4n
Hoyle, Martin, 122, 131, 141, 167, 211, 307
Huddle, Elizabeth, 111n
Hudson, Christopher, 317
Hughes-Hallett, Lucy, 83n, 91n, 101n
Hugo, Jean, 87n
Hulme, Alan, 320
Humbert, Jean-Marcel, 8, 11n
Hunt, Albert and Reeves, Geoffrey, 112, 155, 163, 188, 211, 223, 237, 273, 277, 325

Hunter-Watts, Frediswyde, xiii, 74n, 90n
Hurren, Kenneth, 106, 107, 124
Hutt, William, 184
Hyde, Jonathan, 119, 298

Iago, 45n
Ibert, Jacques, 87n
Iceland, 87
Independent Theatre (Adelaide), 82n
Indonesian, 324
Ingham, C.W., 99
Ingham, Richard, 248
Insatiate Countess, The, 20n
Interart Theatre (New York), xv, 129
International Shakespeare Globe Centre,
    15n
Iras, 40, 74, 78, 86, 111, 116, 118(illus.), 128,
    133(illus.), 135, 151, 159, 167, 189, 195,
    197, 238, 294, 295, 301, 310, 311, 312,
    318, 319, 323
Irvin, Eric, 55n
Irving, Ellis, 306
Isabella, 20n
Isham, Gyles, xiv, 81
Isis, 9, 22, 58, 243, 316, 322
Israel in Egypt (Poynter), 144
Italian, 141
Italy, 70n

Jackson, Frank, 99
Jackson, Glenda, xv, 6, 100n, 111n, 113, 114,
    115n, 118, 121, 147, 149, 150, 151, 163,
    168, 192, 194, 195, 196, 197, 240, 251,
    252, 292, 305, 306, 308, 313, 316, 317
Jackson, Henry, 4, 25
Jacob, Gordon, 235
Jacobean, 3, 4, 11, 14, 18, 19n, 20, 21, 23, 25,
    26, 30, 32, 68, 75, 80, 113, 115, 121, 135,
    141, 146, 150, 161, 167, 190, 194, 205,
    206, 224, 234, 247, 259, 275, 288, 289,
    290, 293, 299, 301, 302, 312, 313, 318
Jacobeans, 13, 181
Jacobi, Derek, 111
Jacobs, Sally, 112, 113, 213
James I, 4, 13, 14, 14n, 26, 203
James, Emrys, 116, 157, 182, 212

James, Gerald, 314
James, Henry, 6n
Jameson, J.H., 38
Japanese, 113, 279
Jefford, Barbara, 100n, 111n
Jenkins, Peter, 113n, 114
Jens, Salome, 315
Jesson, Paul, 127, 182
Jesuit, 13
Johnson, Edith, 78
Johnson, Richard, xiv, xvi, 89n, 105(illus.),
    108, 108n, 109, 125, 127, 148, 150, 157,
    177, 198, 201, 207, 237, 239, 250, 263
Johnson, Samuel, 2
Jones, Emrys, 7n, 14n, 15
Jones, Owen, 52
Jones, Rick, 130, 131, 145
Jongh, Nicholas de, 89n, 109, 110, 126, 127,
    135, 136, 148, 174, 270, 305
Jordan, Louise, xiii, 68
Joseph, B.L., 21n
Judas, 22
Julius Caesar, xiv, 64, 101, 104, 104n

Kabuki, 279, 283
Kahn, Michael, xv, 104n, 129, 145, 210, 315
Kean, Charles, 52, 53, 56
Keene, Thomas, xii
Kellaway, Kate, 128, 182, 192, 207
Kemble, Charles, 46, 51, 51n
Kemble, Fanny, 51n
Kemble, John Philip, xii, 5, 30, 34, 34n, 35,
    36, 37, 37(illus.), 38, 39, 40, 41n, 42, 43,
    44, 45, 46, 47, 49, 51, 53, 56, 171, 177,
    180, 185, 190, 191, 198, 203, 218, 234,
    238, 259, 263, 265, 269, 278, 287, 305,
    312, 320, 324
Kemp, Peter, 124, 125, 227, 276
Kemp, T.C. and Trewin, J.C., 78, 81, 85n
Kempe, Will, 20
Kempson, Rachel, 95, 185, 216
Keneally, Laura, 133(illus.)
Kennedy, Dennis, 103n
Kent, Jonathan, 120n
Kerr, Walter, 160, 174, 184, 277
Key, Janet, 116

Khartoum, 59
King (actor), 40, 41
King Lear, 18, 19n, 22, 24, 25n, 26, 132n
King Lear, 20, 25n
King's Company, 26
King's Men, 1n, 15, 16, 17, 18, 18n, 24, 25, 289
King's Theatre (Edinburgh), 132, 134(illus.)
King's Theatre (Hammersmith), xiii, 77n
King, Dave, 110, 270
King, Francis, 124, 291, 293
Kingsley, Ben, 247
Kingston, Jeremy, 101n, 126, 127, 130, 141, 171, 178, 190, 193, 223, 224, 263, 268, 312, 325
Kismet, 73, 73n
Kissoon, Jeffery, xv, 130, 131, 249, 263
Klein, David, 23n
Knight, Esmond, 207
Knight, G. Wilson, 12n
Knight, Joseph, 2n
Knight, Richard Payne, 38
Knossos, 162
Knutson, Roslyn, 14
Koenig, Rhoda, 156, 157, 162, 284, 304
Komisarjevsky, Theodore, xiv, 12n, 76, 85, 86, 87, 109, 144, 181, 207, 251, 252, 259, 290, 292, 293, 322
Koreya, Senda, 128, 130n
Kott, Jan, 102n

L'Estrange, Julian, 62(illus.), 207
La Rue, Danny, 316
Lacey, Catherine, xiv, 68n, 84, 95, 106n, 115n, 168, 194, 306, 317
Lacy's acting edition, 54, 57; *see also* Calvert's acting edition
Lamb, Margaret, 12n, 17, 30, 31, 32n, 35, 38n, 54, 61, 73, 78n, 82n, 95, 100, 102n, 104n, 110n, 150, 170, 191, 197, 289, 290, 313, 321, 323
Lambert, J.W., 111, 204
Lamprius, 141
Landau, Jack, xiv, 101, 101n
Langham, Michael, xiv, 97, 101, 102, 103, 107, 160, 174, 184, 277, 294

Langtry, Lillie, xiii, 59, 60, 61, 63, 64, 65, 66, 67, 69, 69n, 70, 80, 165, 193, 318; *see also* Langtry-Wingfield
Langtry-Wingfield, 60, 66, 72, 73, 143, 146, 287, 321
Lapotaire, Jane, xv, 116, 167, 189, 192, 195, 241, 292, 316
Last Supper, The, 205
Latin, 11
Laurie, John, 78n, 195
Lawrence of Arabia, 134
Lawson, Wilfrid, xiv, 83, 84
LCC (London County Council), 144
Le Blanc Grainger, 56
Le Maistre, M., 65
Lea, Kathleen, 88n
Leech, Clifford, 307, 324
Leggatt, Alexander, 21n, 23n
Leibovici, Leo, 117
Leigh, Andrew, xiii, 76, 77, 79, 80, 85n, 181, 286, 313
Leigh, Vivien, xiv, 90, 91, 91(illus.), 92, 95, 100, 230, 315, 317, 318, 320, 323; *see also* Oliviers
Leighton, Margaret, xiv, 102, 103, 149
Leiter, Samuel and Hill, Holly, 82
Leiter, Samuel L., 83, 101n, 102n, 104n, 110n, 128n, 180, 290
Leontovich, Eugenie, xiv, 85, 86, 160, 228, 294
Lepidus, 38, 62(illus.), 66, 77, 97, 115, 135, 205, 206, 207, 209
Lepsius, Karl Richard, 52, 64n
Levey, W.C., 203
Levi, P., 24
Levin, Bernard, 112, 113, 150, 213, 235, 245, 251, 263, 274, 279, 283, 313, 318
Levith, Murray, 121n
Lewis, Norah, 113n
Lewis, Peter, 316
Lewsen, Charles, 105, 108, 145, 181, 189, 251, 307
Livesey, Julie, 163
Lloyd Evans, Gareth, 118
Lloyds, Frederick, 53
Lockhart, Calvin, 243

London, 26, 44, 44n, 52, 54, 55, 57, 59, 60n,
  65n, 69, 70, 73n, 93, 95, 100n, 101, 120,
  131, 144, 252, 254; *see also* East End,
  Oxford Street, South Bank, West End
London, John, 134, 291
Loper, Robert, 111n
Loraine, Henry, xii, 52, 53(illus.), 54
Lord Chamberlain's Men, 17
Lord Chamberlain's records, 15, 16
Love's Labour's Lost, 26n
Lowen, Tirzah, 124, 148, 203, 205, 208, 211,
  324
Luce, Claire, xiv, 86, 88, 194, 196, 304, 306,
  315, 317
Ludwig I of Bavaria, 69n
Lyceum Theatre (New York), xiii, 82n
Lyceum Theatre, xiii, 61
Lyndon, Neil, 109, 110
Lyric Studio (Hammersmith), xv, 130

Macaulay, Alastair, 131, 131n, 132, 145, 170,
  305, 309, 320
Macbeth, 21n
Macbeth, Lady, 82n
Machiavel, 131, 255
Maclean, John, 78, 313
MacLiammóir, Micheál, 90n
Macquoid, Percy, 64
Macready, William Charles, xii, 34, 39, 40,
  41, 41n, 42, 43, 44, 45, 45n, 46, 47, 48,
  57, 58, 143, 150, 160, 167, 168, 169, 171,
  174, 191, 203, 218, 237, 238, 247, 259,
  278, 305, 322
Maecenas, 36, 121, 177, 182
Magni, Eva, 93
Maid's Tragedy, The, 86n
Makaryk, Irena R., 103n
Malarsalen (Stockholm), 110
Male, David A., 104n, 108, 181, 182, 248,
  316, 319, 324
Manchester, 55, 60
Mankiewicz, Joseph, 101
Mannerist, 122
Mansfield Theatre (New York), xiv, 83n
Mantegna, Andrea, 122
Marcell, Joe, 282

Mardian, 23, 58, 78, 118(illus.), 122, 145,
  148, 149, 153, 167, 189, 191, 195, 279,
  280, 293
Mares, F.H., 13, 88n
Marie Antoinette, Queen, 228
Markham, Miss, 56
Marlowe Society, 88
Marlowe, Julia, xiii, 60n, 70, 70n, 71, 90n, 191
Marrakesh, 109
Mars and Venus Bound by Cupid, 122
Mars, 107, 119
Marston, Henry, xii, 50, 51
Marston, John, 20n, 24
Marston, Westland, 48
Martin Beck Theatre (New York), xiv, 88
Martin, Theodore, 5
Mary, Queen of Scots, 218
Masham, Dominic, 305
Massingham, Dorothy, xiv, 81, 315
Massino, 20n
Mathews, Charles, 51
Mattes, Eva, 134(illus.), 135, 228
Maxon, Eric, 78
Mazer, Cary, 56, 64
McAfee, Annalena, 130, 131
McAndrew, Deborah, 137, 163
McClintic, Guthrie, xiv, 12n, 88, 109, 167
McCowen, Alec, xv, 111
McCoy, Sylvester, 171
McCulloch, Ian, 117n
McDonald, Andrew, xv, 131
McFarlane, Cassie, 116
McGarry, Peter, 114, 119, 189
McGuire, Paul, 55n
Mediterranean, 10, 41, 104, 145
Melbourne, 60, 68, 73n, 101, 132, 132n, 320
Memorial acting edition, 61
Memorial Library, 64n
Memorial Theatre (Stratford), xiv, xv, xvi,
  84, 94(illus.)
Memorial Theatre Company, 100
Menas, 17n, 62(illus.), 85, 141, 207, 208, 209,
  297
Mendelssohn, Felix, 56
Merchant, W.M., 30
Merseyside, 130

Merwe, Pieter van der, 42n

Messenger, 3, 12, 13n, 24, 30, 33, 35, 40, 47, 54, 58-9, 60, 67, 72, 77, 80, 124, 126(illus.), 141, 190, 191, 192, 193, 194, 195, 196, 218, 220; *see also* Mardian

Metropolitan Opera House (New York), 101

Meyerbeer, Giacomo, 56

Michell, Keith, xiv, 92, 97, 99, 101, 148, 174, 204, 283

Midsummer Night's Dream, A, 111, 114

Mikami, Isao, 128

Milan, 70n

Mille, Cecil B. de, 97, 97n, 113n

Miller, Edward, 43n

Miller, Jonathan, xv, 81n, 115, 116, 116n, 128, 153, 162, 298; *see also* BBC television version

Miln, George C., xiii, 60

Milne, Kirsty, 125n

Minks, Wilfried, 134

Mirren, Helen, xv, 100n, 116, 117, 118, 118(illus.), 121, 163, 169, 193, 194, 196, 218, 247, 292, 294, 305, 306, 308, 309, 312, 316, 317

Modjeska, Helena, 61n

Moiseiwitsch, Tania, 102

Mold, 121

Mona Lisa, 314

Montez, Lola, 44n, 69

Montfaucon, Bernard de, 38, 38n

Montgomery, Walter, xii, 55, 55n

Moore, Meriel, 90n

Moreau, Emile, 60

Morgan, Charles, 86, 294

Morley, Christopher, 105

Morley, Sheridan, 113, 114, 145, 171, 302

Morris, Mary, 101

Moscow, 103

Mossop, Henry, 31

Motley, 87, 93, 102

Moving Theatre, 324

Mullin, Donald, 180

Murray, John, 34n

Napoleon, *see* Bonaparte

Napoleonic, 131n

Nashe, Thomas, 25n

Nasser, Gamal Abdel, 100

Nathan, David, 194

National Theatre (Tokyo), 128

National Theatre, 100, 122, 123(illus.)

National Youth Theatre, 100n

Nazis, 88

Neale, J.E., 13, 218

Neeson, Liam, 108n

Neill, Michael, 107, 108n, 113n, 129, 130

Nelsen, Paul, 15n

Nemean, 229

Nesbitt, Cathleen, 75n

Nettles, John, 127, 178, 254

New Orleans, xii, 45

New Theatre (New York), xiii, 60, 63, 70n

New Theatre, xiv, 85

New York Shakespeare Festival, 102n

New York, 5, 44, 44n, 51n, 52, 55, 57, 59, 60, 61n, 65, 68, 70, 72, 82, 82n, 83, 83n, 88, 92, 129, 144

New Yorkers, 45

Newcastle, 41, 46

Newcombe, Mary, xiv, 82, 83, 84, 96, 106n, 303

Niblo's Garden Theatre (New York), xii, 59, 65, 68

Nicoll, J.R.A., 234

Nightingale, Benedict, 103, 106, 107, 113, 114, 118, 135, 136, 137, 145, 147, 149, 161, 163, 185, 192, 193, 194, 195, 205, 270, 291, 292, 293, 325

Nightingale, John, 100n

Nile, 52, 53, 55, 56, 65, 84, 143

Nile, Battle of the, 35

Nile, Queen of the, 147

Noble, Adrian, xv, 12n, 15, 111, 115, 116, 117n, 118, 118(illus.), 120, 147, 174, 182, 189, 190, 206, 208, 210, 211, 213, 218, 221, 239, 248, 259, 270, 290, 298, 304, 306, 313, 316, 324

Nobody and Somebody, 17n

Norden, Frederick L., 38, 38n

Norman, Jessye, 167

North, Thomas, 12

Northern Broadsides, 136, 137n

Northern English, 141
Northern Irish, 108n
Nottingham Playhouse, 117n
Novak, E., 29, 29n
Nungezer, Edwin, 21n
Nunn, Trevor, xiv, 3, 14, 103, 104, 104n, 105,
    105(illus.), 106, 108, 109, 115, 117,
    117n, 119, 130, 135, 145, 146, 149, 176,
    181, 189, 190, 193, 204, 213, 223, 228,
    237, 238, 239, 243, 251, 268, 281, 293,
    298, 306, 316; *see also* Nunn-Scoffield
Nunn-Scoffield, 116, 146, 148, 149, 150, 157,
    159, 161, 162, 167, 168, 171, 174, 182,
    185, 189, 190, 191, 198, 203, 204, 210,
    217, 218, 221, 224, 225, 226, 237, 246,
    247, 248, 249, 250, 251, 270, 275, 277,
    279, 282, 283, 290, 292, 294, 295, 299,
    303, 306, 308, 313, 316, 317, 318, 320,
    321, 322, 323, 325
Nurse, Keith, 117, 118, 292

O'Mahoney, Robert, 121, 182
O'Mara, Kate, 117n
O'Shaughnessy, Kathy, 121, 147, 316
Oberon, 114
Octavia, 10, 13, 27, 28, 29, 32, 54, 58, 59, 60,
    78, 95, 97, 103, 108, 111, 119, 130, 137,
    141, 142, 177, 182, 185, 190, 191, 194,
    203, 216, 218, 220, 221, 223, 227, 298,
    325
Octavius, 10, 12, 13n, 14, 27, 35, 36, 38, 40,
    48, 51, 54, 56, 59, 62(illus.), 66, 68, 68n,
    73, 78, 84, 86, 88, 89, 92, 96, 97, 103,
    104, 104n, 106, 108, 109, 110, 111, 115,
    116, 119, 120, 121, 125, 126, 127, 128,
    130, 131, 131n, 135, 136, 137, 142, 144,
    174, 177, 178, 184, 185, 204, 205, 209,
    210, 211, 212, 216, 217, 221, 224, 225,
    237, 243, 245, 246, 247, 248, 251, 254,
    255, 257, 273, 281, 299, 302, 305, 306,
    307, 308, 309, 318, 319, 321, 323, 324,
    325
Odell, George, 35, 43, 44n, 45, 45n, 51n, 55,
    55n
Old Prices riots, 36
Old Vic, xiii, xiv, xv, 74, 76, 77, 78, 79, 80, 82,
    85, 89, 97, 98(illus.), 99, 100, 102, 111,
    144, 162, 260
Oldfield, Anne, 26
Olivier Theatre, xv, 122, 149, 194, 292
Olivier, Laurence, xiv, 91, 91(illus.), 92, 95,
    99, 174, 204, 230, 237, 248, 280, 281,
    283, 317; *see also* Oliviers
Oliviers, 88, 90, 92, 93
Olympic Theatre, xiii, 60
Ontario, 117n, 119, 120
Oregon Shakespeare Festival, 111n, 125n
Oregon, xvi
Orientalism, 143
Orientalist, 52
Osborne, Charles, 141, 228, 284, 294
Ostler, William, xii, 24
Othello, 4n, 25
Othello, 20, 45n
Other Place (Stratford), xv, 116, 117, 117n
OUDS (Oxford University Dramatic
    Society), 75n, 290
Owen, Michael, 239, 294
Oxford Playhouse, 100n
Oxford Street (London), 52
Oxford, 25, 75, 111n, 190
Ozu, Yasujiro, 113n

Pacorus, 31, 112, 213, 324
Paddington Station, 108
Palmer's Theatre (New York), xiii, 60, 68, 72
Pankhurst, Emily, 316
Papp, Joseph, 102n
Pardo, Etela, 135
Parfitt, Judy, xv, 119, 150, 170, 228, 306
Paris, 56, 60, 72, 93, 111
Park Theatre (New York), xii, 45
Parks, J. Gower, 86
Parsons, Estelle, xv, 129, 135, 320
Parsons, Gordon, 150, 182
Parsons, Philip, xvi, 132, 133(illus.)
Parthia, 112
Parthian, 213
Pascal, Gabriel, 90
Pasternak, Boris, 103
Patarot, Helene, 135
Paton, Maureen, 125, 136, 324

Payne, Ben Iden, xiv, 68n, 76, 84, 85, 96n, 143, 144, 159, 181, 204, 206, 235, 313
PBS, xv
Peacham, Henry, 18
Pearson, Hesketh, 180
Peaslee, Richard, 113, 205
Peck, Bob, 119, 182, 270
Peel, David, 278
Perth, 121n
Peter, John, 120, 121, 122, 124, 125, 177, 309
Peters, Rollo, xiii
Phelps, Samuel, xii, 45, 45n, 46, 48, 49, 50, 51, 54, 55, 57, 58, 95, 146, 149, 151, 153, 157, 159, 165, 167, 183, 184, 188, 193, 194, 197, 199, 201, 203, 205, 206, 209, 210, 211, 212, 215, 218, 221, 223, 225, 226, 228, 232, 233, 237, 238, 239, 242, 245, 246, 247, 248, 250, 251, 257, 259, 261, 266, 267, 268, 271, 275, 278, 279, 282, 283, 284, 287, 288, 292, 294, 295, 297, 298, 302, 304, 307, 310, 311, 312, 314, 315, 318, 320, 321, 323
Phelps, W. May and Robertson, John Forbes, 48, 49
Philadelphia, 44n
Phillips, Louisa Anne, xii, 6, 39, 41, 42, 42n, 48, 49, 71n, 143
Phillips, Robin, xv, 110, 117n, 119, 120, 121, 130, 130n, 203, 279, 288, 290, 308
Philo, 3, 19, 22, 109, 113, 141, 143, 144, 145, 146, 151, 190, 224
Phoebus, 4, 168
Piccadilly Theatre, xiv, 87
Pigott-Smith, Tim, 125, 178, 211, 227, 298, 308
Piper, Emma, 141, 322
Pit (Barbican), xv, 116
Pitt, Angela, 108, 294
Playbox (Melbourne), xv, 132
Playbox Theatre Company, 132
Pleasence, Donald, 97, 206
Plessen, Elisabeth, 134
Plummer, Christopher, xiv, 101, 102, 103, 160, 174
Plutarch, 12, 25, 64, 130, 289

Poel, William, 74n, 75, 78
Pollock, Jackson, 112
Pomeroy, Louise, xiii, 68
Pompey's galley, 30, 34, 40, 46, 48, 53, 54, 58, 60, 65, 66, 85, 85n, 87, 93, 99, 103, 104, 109, 112, 115, 117, 119, 120, 122, 131, 134, 198, 203, 204, 205, 207, 210, 213
Pompey, 17n, 30, 34, 40, 48, 51, 58, 59, 62(illus.), 65, 66, 85n, 88, 97, 109, 115, 128, 130, 135, 137, 171, 198, 199, 203, 205, 207, 208, 209, 211, 212, 213, 237
Ponisi, Elizabeth, xii, 55
Pooley, Olaf, 153
Pope, Alexander, 18n, 150
Porter, Neil, 80n, 181, 194
Potter, Cora, 68n; *see* Brown-Potter, Cora
Potter, Stephen, 89, 153, 174, 204
Potter-Brown, Cora, 68n; *see* Brown-Potter, Cora
Powell, William, 33
Poynter, Edward, 144
Prado, Francisco, xv, 129
Pram Factory Back Theatre (Melbourne), 132n
Pre-Raphaelite, 119n
Press, Fiona, 133(illus.)
Prince of Wales Theatre (Birmingham), xiv, 81n
Prince of Wales Theatre (Sydney), xii, 55n
Prince of Wales, 14, 32, 69
Prince's Theatre (Manchester), xii, 55
Prince's Theatre, xiv, 93
Princess's Theatre, xii, xiii, 52, 53, 53(illus.), 60
Prisse d'Avennes, 64n
Proculeius, 302
Prospect Theatre, xv, 111
Proteus, 21n
Prozac, 136
Prussian, 52n
Pryce, Jonathan, 115, 185, 254, 325
Ptolemaic, 38, 41, 96, 106, 107, 113, 116
Ptolemy, 13n
Punch, 138n
Puritan, 4, 25, 182
Puritans, 146

Quartermaine, Charles, 194, 196
Quartermaine, Leon, 85, 181
Quayle, Anthony, 89
Queen's Revels, Children of the, 16n, 18n, 20n
Queen's Theatre (Manchester), xiii, 60
Quilley, Denis, xv, 120
Quong, Rose, 86n

Radin, Victoria, 117, 118, 119, 147, 182, 193, 221, 239, 290
Raleigh, Walter, 13
Rameses II, 43
Randall, Tony, 168
Ratcliffe, Michael, 124, 178, 303
Rawlings, Margaret, 86, 322
Rawson, Tristan, 181, 269
Ray, Robin, 124
Read, David, 86
Redgrave, Corin, 14, 108, 109, 115, 225, 298
Redgrave, Michael, xiv, 2, 84n, 88, 93, 95, 96, 96n, 97, 99, 122, 148, 150, 174, 185, 187, 238, 239, 241, 248, 274, 275, 278, 279, 280
Redgrave, Vanessa, xv, xvi, 89n, 109, 110, 121, 122, 135, 136, 137, 145, 148, 156, 157, 161, 162, 170, 174, 194, 195, 205, 218, 219, 220, 261, 270, 284, 291, 304, 305, 314, 316, 317, 320, 324, 325
Rees, Joan, 16n, 289
Rees, Leslie, 82, 82n
Reeves, Geoffrey, *see* Hunt, Albert and Reeves, Geoffrey
Rehberg, Hans Michael, 128
Reicher, Frank, xiii, 82n
Reid, Helen, 113n
Reinhardt, Mattie, xii, 55
Renaissance Theatre, 86n
Renaissance, 10, 14, 19, 24, 80, 81, 81n, 111, 122, 205
Restoration, 2, 5, 23n, 26, 28, 29, 111n
Rhenamus, Johannes, 23n
Rhode Island Shakespeare Theatre, 128
Rhodes, Percy, 78
Ricci, Renzo, 93
Richard III, 185
Richardson, Frank, 144

Richardson, Ralph, 80, 181
Richardson, Tony, xv, 12n, 109, 110, 151, 194, 270, 292
Ridley, M.R., 16n, 17n
Rigg, Diana, xv, 120, 120n, 121
Riley, Molly, 101n
Ripa, Cesare, 22n
Riverside Studio 1, xvi, 135
Roberts, David, 53, 53n
Roberts, Dennis, 313
Robertson, John Forbes, *see* Phelps, W. May and Robertson, John Forbes
Robertson, Toby, xv, 81n, 111, 121, 247, 288, 292; *see also* Robertson-Selbie
Robertson-Selbie, xv, 68n, 121, 147, 171, 177, 182, 211, 218, 240, 257, 283, 291, 302, 314, 316, 320
Rodway, Norman, 120
Roman history plays, 15, 19, 104
Roman, 1, 8, 9, 10, 11, 12, 12n, 14, 21n, 32, 49, 54, 58, 63, 64, 65, 66, 72, 80, 81, 92, 99, 102n, 104, 104n, 109n, 113, 116, 117, 121n, 122, 128, 130, 131, 131n, 134, 135, 142, 145, 146, 147, 149, 174, 182, 190, 207, 213, 225, 228, 234, 270, 302, 313, 325
Romanness, 10
Romans, 4, 7, 9, 10, 11, 12, 13, 32, 64, 79, 90, 90n, 105, 117, 129, 135, 252, 316
Rome, 10, 11, 12, 18, 19, 35, 43n, 54, 55, 79, 86, 87, 88, 90, 93, 97, 99, 103, 104, 104n, 105, 108, 110, 116, 117n, 120, 121, 122, 125, 129, 130, 135, 136, 145, 146, 149, 174, 177, 188, 203, 211, 223, 224, 281
Romeo and Juliet, 87
Romeo, 45n, 88
Rooth, Miriam, 6n
Rose, 20
Rosenfeld, Sybil, 75n
Rossettian, 70
Rossi, Alfred, 104n
Rossiter, Philip, 21n
Rowe, Nicholas, 1, 18n, 294
Royal Academy, 43n
Royal Dramatic Theatre, 110
Royal Olympic Theatre (Launceston), 44n

Royal Shakespeare Company, 100, 105(illus.), 111, 116, 118(illus.), 125, 126(illus.)

Royal Victoria Theatre (Sydney), 44n

Roze, Raymond, 65

RSC, *see* Royal Shakespeare Company

Rugby Club, 276

Russian, 86, 103n

Rutherford, Malcolm, 127

Rutter, Barrie, xvi, 12n, 136, 137, 137n, 145, 163, 182, 192, 205, 229, 235, 240, 246, 259, 293

Rutter, Carol, 23n, 24n

Ryan, Robert, xiv, 101

Ryan, T.E., 64, 66

Ryder, John, 73, 180

Rylands, George, 87, 88, 89, 90, 91, 213, 308, 315

Saddler, Howard, 136

Sadler's Wells Theatre, xii, 45, 46n, 49, 58

Sainthill, Loudon, 97, 99

Salt, Henry, 42, 43n

Salzburg Festival, 128

San Francisco, xii, 61n

Santa Claus, 136

Sapte, W., Jr, 44n

Sardou, Victorien, 60, 60n

SAS, 302

Saturnine, 119

Saturninus, 13n

Say, Rosemary, 313

Sayers, Michael, 82n

Scarus, 141, 266, 267, 273

Schirach, Baldur von, 88

Schofield, David, 110, 325

Schoolmaster, 141

Schubert, Veit, 135

Scoffield, Jon, xiv, 108; ; *see also* Nunn-Scoffield

Scott, George C., 90n, 102n

Scott, Michael, 92, 149, 151, 153, 163, 167, 176, 191, 192, 193, 195, 196, 197, 228, 237, 238, 239, 247, 248, 250, 251, 252, 275, 281, 283, 293, 298, 308, 313, 315, 323

Scottish and Newcastle Breweries, 205

Scottish, 141

Seaton, Ray, 105

Sedley, Charles, 5, 26, 27, 31n

Selbie, Christopher, 121; *see* Robertson-Selbie

Selby, Charles, 44n

Selector, The, 130

Seleucus, 33, 46, 86, 125, 307, 308

Sequeira, Horace, 81, 313

Seti I, 43

Setna, Renu, 182

Seyrig, Delphine, 110n

Shadow of the Swastika, The, 97

Shakespeare Jubilee, 32, 32n

Shakespeare Theatre (Washington), xv, 129

Shakespeare, William, *passim.*; as director, xii, 23

Shattuck, Charles H., 45n, 60n, 61n, 69, 228, 292, 315, 320

Shaw Theatre, xv, 131

Shaw, George Bernard, 6n, 7, 70, 72, 90, 92, 220, 284, 318

Shaw, Glen Byam, xiv, 68n, 81n, 87, 88, 89, 93, 94(illus.), 102, 143, 144, 150, 153, 170, 174, 184, 204, 206, 216, 235, 252, 259, 266, 270, 274, 275, 278, 290, 292, 306, 307, 310

Sheridan, Thomas, 33

Sheringham, Peter, 6n

Sherwood, Benson, xii, 59, 65

Sherwood, Lydia, 78

Shoreditch, 50

Shorter, Eric, 287

Shrimpton, Nicholas, 118, 309

Shulman, Milton, 100, 109, 110, 114, 149, 168, 194, 313, 317

Siddons, Sarah, 3, 3n, 6, 27, 33, 34, 35, 36, 46, 51, 219

Simon, Josette, 118(illus.), 119

Simonov, Evgenii, 103, 104n

Simpson, Edmund, xii, 45

Simpson, Wallis, 14

Sjöberg, Alf, 110, 290

Sjöblom, Ulla, 110

Ska, 130

Skillan, George, 181
Skoglund, Rolf, 110
Sly, William, 16n
Smith, Kent, 92
Smith, Maggie, xv, 110
Smyth, Paul, 80
Soane Museum, 52n
Soane, John, 43, 43n
Soho Square (London), 38
Somerset, 313
Soothsayer, 34, 40, 86, 127, 141, 144, 153,
   242, 270, 276, 312, 314
Sothern, E.H., xiii, 60n, 72, 90n
Souper, Kay, 206
South Africa, 6
South African, 107
South Bank (London), 100
Soviet, 103
Spanish, 129
Speaight, Robert, 75n, 80, 80n, 148, 321
Spencer, Charles, 119, 125, 127, 134, 135,
   270, 302
Sphinx, 61, 61n, 90
Sprague, A.C. and Trewin, J.C., 313
Sprague, A.C., 193
Spread of the Eagle, The, 100, 104
Spriggs, Elizabeth, 100n
Sprinchorn, Evert, 234, 288
St James's Theatre, xiv, 90, 91(illus.)
Stalin, Joseph, 203
Standard Theatre, xii, 50, 51, 53
Stanfield, Clarkson, 40, 42, 43, 64
Stanton, Barry, 120, 270
Stanton, John, xvi, 132, 133(illus.)
Starlight, 147
Stationers' Register, 16
Steedman, Tony, 100n
Steele, J.B., xiii
Steevens, George, 32, 174
Stein, Peter, 104, 128, 134, 220, 262, 316
Steinway Hall (New York), 52
Stephens, Toby, 128, 171
Steppat, Michael, 17n
Stewart, Ian, 113, 182, 218, 240
Stewart, Patrick, 108, 109, 115, 157, 181,
   182, 188, 253, 270

Stockholm, 110, 290
Stoic, 270
Stokes, John, Booth, Michael R. and
   Bassnett, Susan, 70n
Stone, George W., 30n, 31n
Stone, Marcus, 144
Stratford Festival, 61, 65, 75, 86, 93
Stratford Festival, Canada, 110
Stratford Summer Festival, xiv, 77
Stratford, 61, 65, 74, 76, 78, 81n, 85, 95, 100,
   104, 111, 116, 125, 127, 144, 146
Stratford, Conn., xiv
Stratford, Ont., xiv, xv, 103, 110
Strindbergian, 110
Strunk, William Jr, 83n, 180
Stuart-Jones, Prof., 234
Sturgess, Keith, 16n, 18n, 19n
Stuyvesant Institute (New York), 51n
Suchet, David, 115, 199
Sudan, 59
Suez Canal, 52, 97, 100
Sulivan, Miss (actor), 41n
Suzman, Janet, xiv, 6, 105(illus.), 106, 106n,
   107, 108, 109, 114, 121, 127, 129, 148,
   161, 162, 163, 167, 191, 194, 228, 238,
   239, 246, 251, 260, 292, 293, 294, 295,
   303, 307, 316, 317, 318, 319, 320, 321
Swedish, 110
Swete, Lyall, 64, 73, 269
Sydney Theatre Company, 132
Sydney, 44, 55n, 60, 68, 69
Symons, Arthur, 71
Syms, Sylvia, 131n
Syria, 213

Talawa Theatre, xv, 130, 131, 141, 241, 255,
   263, 286, 307, 319
Talma, François Joseph, 72
Tarzan, 82
Taylor, Elizabeth, 84n, 101, 101n, 135
Taylor, John, 33
Taylor, Paul, 126, 127, 218, 225
Tearle, Conway, xiv, 84
Tearle, Godfrey, xiv, 87, 88, 88n, 89, 92, 248,
   252
Teatro Eliseo (Rome), 93

Tempest, The, 204
Ter-Arutunian, Rouben, 101
Thatcher, Margaret, 114
Theatr Clwyd (Mold), xv, 121, 122
Theatre Royal (Drury Lane), *see* Drury Lane
Theatre Royal (Haymarket), xv, 121
Theatre Royal (Hobart), xiii
Theatre Royal (Melbourne), xii, xv, 55, 73n, 147
Theatre Royal (Sydney), xiii, 60, 147
Thebes, 43
Theobald, Lewis, 31
Thersites, 119
Theseus, 114
Thidias, 27, 31, 31n, 53(illus.), 116, 141, 243, 247, 248, 250, 254; *see also* Thyreus
Thomas, Ben, 131, 205, 255
Thomson, Leslie, 289
Thomson, Peter, 177
Thyreus, 31, 31n, 151, 180, 247
Tieck, Dorothea, 128
Tierney, Malcolm, 131n
Tinker, Jack, 100n, 115, 119n, 120, 122, 147, 228, 291
Titus Andronicus, 21, 21n
Titus Andronicus, xiv, 4, 13n, 19, 21, 22, 104
Tokyo, 128
Toms, Carl, 102
Towers, Charles, xvi, 125n, 259, 279, 299
Towse, John Ranken, 72
Tragedy of Cleopatra, The, 16
Tree, Ellen, xii, 45
Tree, Herbert Beerbohm, xiii, 57, 61, 62(illus.), 63, 64, 64n, 65, 66, 67, 69n, 72, 73, 74, 78, 82n, 126, 141, 143, 144, 146, 150, 162, 165, 180, 185, 187, 191, 193, 195, 196, 203, 204, 207, 209, 218, 221, 224, 225, 237, 239, 247, 286, 289, 293, 306, 315, 316
Trewin, J.C., 3, 41n, 73, 75n, 80n, 84, 86, 87, 90, 92, 96, 99, 101, 104, 106n, 110n, 111n, 114, 115, 143, 144, 146, 147, 150, 162, 168, 182, 188, 234, 235, 242, 259, 260, 266, 269, 278, 279, 280, 281, 292, 294, 307, 313; *see also* Kemp, T.C. and

Trewin, J.C. *and* Sprague, A.C. and Trewin, J.C.
Tristan, 293
Triumvirate, 174
Troughton, David, 313
Tudor interlude, 19n
Turk, 121
Turner, Helen, 130
Turner, John, 100n, 111n
Tutankhamun, 79, 103, 105, 106, 112
Tutankhamunism, 106
Tutin, Dorothy, xv, 111
Two Gentlemen of Verona, 26n
Tynan, Kenneth, 95, 95n, 153, 190, 191, 221, 257

Ul'ianov, Mikhail, 103
Ullman, Tracey, 136
Urquhart, Cora, 68n; *see* Brown-Potter, Cora
US, 113n

Vakhtangov Theatre (Moscow), 103
Valentino, Rudolph, 122
Vandenhoff, George, xii, 45, 51n
Venezky, Alice, 90, 92, 204, 230, 270
Ventidius, 27, 35, 40, 78, 112, 146, 180, 278
Venus, 147
Verdi, Giuseppe, 70
Veronese, Paolo, 11, 14, 80, 81, 81n, 83, 85, 87, 116, 122, 125, 162
Viaduct (Halifax), xvi
Victoria, Queen, 88n
Victorian, 5, 6, 11, 44, 45n, 47, 49, 50, 51, 56, 57, 58, 65, 69, 71, 74, 81, 87, 112, 138n, 143, 144, 180
Vienna, 84, 132
Vietnam, 104, 113
Vietnamese, 113n, 135
Vining, George, xii, 52, 53, 53(illus.), 54
Virgin Mary, 316
Voss, Gert, 135, 260
Voytek, 119

Wagner Festival, 65
Wainwright, Jeffrey, 131n, 136, 137, 137n, 141, 145, 163, 229, 246, 259, 319

Waldron, G.B., 180

Walkley, Arthur B., 69, 72

Wallis, Ellen, xii, 58, 60, 67, 71n

Walter, Wilfrid, xiii, 77, 157, 278, 290

Warburton, William, 150

Warde, Frederick, xii

Wardle, Irving, 103n, 114, 115, 117, 118, 119, 120, 121, 136, 178, 182, 194, 199, 237, 287, 290, 293, 298, 308, 313, 316, 317

Wardour Street (London), 81

Ware, William Henry, 38n

Warren, Henry, 52

Wars of the Roses, The, 104n

Washington, 129

Waterhouse, Esther, xiii, 79, 80

Waters, Harry, 116

Watson, G., 25n

Webber, David, 167

Webster, John, 1n, 15, 22n, 106n

Weir, George, 313

Wells, Stanley, 117, 182, 190, 206, 211, 259, 305, 306, 309, 316

Welsh, 314

West End (of London), 49, 52, 87, 88, 89, 121

West Indian, 147

West, Timothy, 111, 111n

Wharf Theatre (Sydney), xvi, 132

Wheaton, Andrew, 177

Wheelock, Joseph Sr, xii

Wheen, Francis, 121

Whipple, Sidney B., 84

White Devil, The, 22n

Whitefriars, 20n

Whiting, Margaret, xiv, 68n, 97, 98(illus.), 99, 100, 106n, 148, 162, 191, 197, 314, 317, 321

Wicksteed, Kenneth, 78, 81

Wiener Festwochen, 134

Wiggins, Martin, 17n

Wilde, Patrick, xv, 130, 141

Wilders, John, 16n

Wiles, David, 25n

Wilkie, Allan, xiii, 74, 74n, 90n, 286, 287, 307

Wilkinson, John Gardner, 43, 52, 52n

Willard, Edmund, xiii, 77

Williams, Harcourt, xiv, 14, 74, 75, 75n, 80, 81, 81n, 162, 259, 313

Williams, Neville, 13n

Williams, Stephen, 266

Wilson, Cecil, 95

Wilson, John Dover, 18n, 92

Windsor, 14

Wingfield, Lewis, xiii; *see also* Langtry-Wingfield

Winter, William, 2n, 27, 31, 32, 33, 41n, 46, 51n, 57, 58, 63, 68, 69, 72, 73, 180, 191

Wiseman, Joseph, 167

Woddis, Carole, 122, 131, 171

Woffington, Peg, 26, 33

Wolfit, Donald, xiv, 85

Woman Hater, The, 17n

Wood, Clive, 211, 212

Wooland, Norman, 92, 93, 181, 269

Woolfenden, Guy, 105

World War I, 75, 134

World's Folly, This, 25n

Woronicz, Henry, xvi, 125n

Worsley, T.C., 90, 93, 95, 96, 143, 147, 181, 237, 248, 280

Wraight, Robert, 99

Yalta, 203

Yates, Mary Ann, xii, 26, 32n, 33, 42n, 47, 48, 246, 308, 321

Yorkshire, 136

Young Vic, xv, 110n, 119, 212

Young, B.A., 107n, 114, 204, 243, 279, 317

Young, C.B., 44n

Young, Charles M., xii, 34, 36

Young, William C., 60n, 69n

Zadek, Peter, 12n, 115, 128, 132, 134, 134(illus.), 135, 137, 213, 228, 260, 291

Zara, 65

Zeffirelli, Franco, 101

Ziegfield Theatre (New York), xiv

Ziegler, Christiane, 9, 9n, 10, 11n